法藏知津

四編：佛教歷史與文獻研究專輯

杜 潔 祥 主編

第2冊

鳩摩羅什《妙法蓮華經・序品第一》「信譯」之研究（中）

賴 信 川 著

花木蘭文化出版社

國家圖書館出版品預行編目資料

鳩摩羅什《妙法蓮華經・序品第一》「信譯」之研究（中）／賴信川 著 — 初版 — 新北市：花木蘭文化出版社，2015〔民104〕

目 4+302 面；19×26 公分

（法藏知津四編：佛教歷史與文獻研究專輯　第 2 冊）

ISBN：978-986-254-295-8（精裝）

1. 佛經　2. 翻譯　3. 法華部

224.57　　99016384

ISBN-978-986-254-295-8

9789862542958

法藏知津四編：佛教歷史與文獻研究專輯

第 二 冊　　ISBN：978-986-254-295-8

鳩摩羅什《妙法蓮華經・序品第一》「信譯」之研究（中）

作　　者　賴信川

主　　編　杜潔祥

副總編輯　楊嘉樂

編　　輯　許郁翎

出　　版　花木蘭文化出版社

社　　長　高小娟

聯絡地址　235 新北市中和區中安街七二號十三樓

電話：02-2923-1455／傳眞：02-2923-1452

網　　址　http://www.huamulan.tw 信箱 hml 810518@gmail.com

印　　刷　普羅文化出版廣告事業

初　　版　2015 年 5 月

定　　價　四編 15 冊（精裝）新台幣 25,000 元　

鳩摩羅什《妙法蓮華經・序品第一》「信譯」之研究（中）

賴信川　著

目次

【第九段】

अथ खलु मैत्रेयो बोधिसत्त्वो महासत्त्वो मञ्जुश्रियं कुमारभूतमाभिर्गाथाभिरध्यभाषत–

【羅馬譯音】

Atha khalu maitreyo bodhisattvo mahāsattvo mañjuśriyaṁ kumārabhūtamābhirgāthābhiradhyabhāṣata–

【第一句】

Atha khalu Maitreyo bodhisattvo mahāsattvo Mañjuśriyaṁ kumāra-bhūtam ābhir gāthābhir adhyabhāṣata

【辭彙研究】

1. आभिर् ābhir 副詞　到這裡

 1.1 【詞尾變化】ābhir 根據連音規則是從 ābhiḥ 變化過來，而 ābhiḥ 則是 ābhi 的單數主格形。而 ābhi 根據連音規則是由 ā-abhi 所構成，而 abhi 資料前面已有說明，所以字典要查 ā。

 1.2 【摩威梵英,p126】As an adv. after words expressing a number or degree fully , really , indeed.

 1.3 【梵漢辭典,p1】（副詞）〔構成副詞和形容詞的接頭〕到達～；至～。

2. गाथाभिर् gāthābhir 名詞　詩句

 2.1 【詞尾變化】gāthābhir 根據連音規則是從 gāthābhiḥ 變化過來，而 gāthābhiḥ 則是 gāthā 的複數工具格形。所以字典查 gāthā。

 2.2 【摩威梵英,p352】

  2.2.1 m. a song RV. ;

  2.2.2（gāthā）f. id. RV. ; a verse , stanza（especially one which is neither Ṛg , nor Sāman , nor Yajus , a verse not belonging to the Vedas , but to the epic poetry of legends or Ākhyānas , such as the Śunaḥṣepa-Ākhyāna or the Suparṇ.）AV.; the metrical part of a Sūtra Buddh. ; N. of the Āryā metre ; any metre not enumerated in the regular treatises on prosody.

2.3 【梵漢辭典,p452】（陰性名詞）讚歌，詩句，頌文；（佛教經典）詩句的部份；（經文）句，頌，諷頌，攝，記句經。

3. अध्यभाषत adhyabhāṣata 動詞 向～說話

3.1 【詞尾變化】adhyabhāṣata 是由 adhy-abhāṣata 所構成。又根據連音規則，adhy-abhāṣata 是由 adhi-√bhāṣ 變化而來。而 abhāṣata 是√bhāṣ 的過去式，√bhāṣ 資料前面已有說明，所以字典查 adhi。

3.2 【摩威梵英,p20, adhi】

3.2.1 m. anxiety ,

3.2.2（*is*）f. a woman in her courses, as a prefix to verbs and nouns , expresses above , over and above , besides. As a separable adverb or preposition ; over ; from above , from ; from the presence of ; after; for ; instead of RV.,（with loc.）over ; on ; at ; in comparision with ;（with acc.）over , upon , concerning.

3.3 【梵漢辭典,p259, adhi-√bhāṣ】（動詞）向～說話，講述～，背誦；（經文）宣。

【筆者試譯】：於是，到這裡，彌勒大菩薩用詩歌的方式，向文殊師利法王子菩薩說：

【什公漢譯】：於是彌勒菩薩，欲重宣此義，以偈問曰：

【英 譯 本】：Then it was that Maitreya, the Bodhisattva Mahâsattva, addressed Mañgusrî, the prince royal, in the following stanzas:

【信譯研究】：信譯。

【第一頌】

किं कारणं मञ्जुशिरी इयं हि
रश्मिः प्रमुक्ता नरनायकेन।
प्रभासयन्ती भ्रमुकान्तरातु
ऊर्णाय कोशादियमेकरश्मिः॥ १॥

【羅馬譯音】

kiṁ kāraṇaṁ Mañjuśirī iyaṁ hi
raśmiḥ pramuktā naranāyakena|
prabhāsayantī bhramukāntarātu
ūrṇāya kośādiyamekaraśmiḥ||1||

【句義解析】

kiṁ kāraṇaṁ Mañjuśirī iyaṁ hi
raśmiḥ pramuktā nara-nāyakena|
prabhāsayantī bhramukāntarātu
ūrṇāya kośād iyam eka-raśmiḥ||1||

【辭彙研究】

1. कारणं kāraṇaṁ　名詞　原因
   1.1 【詞尾變化】kāraṇaṁ 根據連音規則是由 kāraṇam 變化而來，kāraṇam 是 kāraṇa 的對格單數形，所以字典查 kāraṇa。
   1.2 資料前面已有說明。
2. इयं iyaṁ 代名詞　這個
   2.1 【詞尾變化】iyaṁ 根據連音規則是由 iyam 變化而來，所以字典查 iyam。
   2.2 【摩威梵英,p168】f. nom. sg. of the demonstrative pronoun idam.
   2.3 【梵漢辭典,p513】（代名詞）是 idam 的陰性主格單數，這個；（經文）此。
3. हि hi　不變格　由於
   3.1 【詞尾變化】沒有詞尾變化，爲不變格。
   3.2 【摩威梵英,p1297】ind.（used as a particle and usually denoting）for , because , on account of（never standing first in a sentence , but generally after the first word and used enclitically , sometimes after pronouns）RV. ; just , pray , do; indeed , assuredly , surely , of course , certainly.
   3.3 【梵漢辭典,p491】（該字永不放在句子之前，通常出現於第一字之後；或在其他位置中則出現於強調語（代名詞）之後；文章中的動詞常帶有重音。）由於，爲～之故；正好，只是，請（經文）故。

4. रश्मि: raśmiḥ 名詞　光輝；光明

4.1 【詞尾變化】raśmiḥ 是 raśmi 的陽性單數主格形，所以字典查 raśmi。

4.2 資料前面已有說明。

5. प्रमुक्ता pramuktā 動詞　放射

5.1 【詞尾變化】pramuktā 是 pra-√muc 的過去被動分詞陰性主格變化，故字典查 pra-√muc。

5.2 【摩威梵英,p686】

5.2.1 P. A1., to set free , let go , liberate , release from RV. MBh. ; to loosen , loose , untie , unbind , undo RV. ; to rid one's self of（gen.）, escape R. ;

5.2.2（ind. p. *-mucya* , having liberated one's self from）; to drive away , banish , shake off RV. MBh. ; to give up , resign , renounce MBh.; to discharge , emit , throw out , shed AV. MBh.; to hurl , fling , throw , shoot MBh.; to utter ; to throw or put on（as a garland &c.）; to lend , bestow MBh.: Pass. *-mucyate* , to free one's self from（abl. or instr.）MBh. BhP; to be loosened , become loose or detached , fall off（as fruits）MBh. ; to leave off , cease , to liberate from MBh. ; to loosen , untie, to be about to give up or resign MBh.

5.3 【梵漢辭典,p742】（動詞）放射，發射，射出，解放；（經文）放，出，散，住。

6. नर nara 名詞　丈夫；男人

6.1 【詞尾變化】沒有詞尾變化。

6.2 【摩威梵英,p529】

6.2.1 m. a man , a male , a person（pl. men , people）; husband; hero ; a man or piece at chess or draughts; the pin or gnomon of a sun-dial; person , personal termination; the primeval Man or eternal Spirit pervading the universe MBh.;（pl.）a class of myth. beings allied to the Gandharvas and Kiṁ-naras MBh. ; N. of a son of Manu Ta1masa BhP. ; of a sñson of Viśvāmitra; of a sñson of Gaya and father of Virāñ; of a sñson of Su-dhṛiti and fñfather of Kevala ; of a sñson of Bhavan-manyu（Manyu）and fñfather of Saṁkṛiti; of Bhāradvāña ; of 2 kings of Kaśmīra Rājat. ; of one of the 10 horses of the Moon ;

6.2.2（*ī*）f. a woman（=*nārī*）；

6.2.3 n. a kind of fragrant grass.

6.3 【梵漢辭典,p767】（陽性名詞）人，男人，人物，丈夫，勇士，原人（經文）人，男。

7. नायकेन nāyakena 名詞　嚮導，導師

7.1 【詞尾變化】nāyakena 是 nāyaka 的單數工具格形，所以字典查 nāyaka。

7.2 【摩威梵英,p536】

7.2.1 m. a guide , leader , chief , lord , principal MBh.; a husband BhP. ;（in dram.）the lover or hero ; the central gem of a necklace（implying also ` a genera''' cf. *nāyakāya* and *mahā-nāyaka*）; a paradigm or example（in gram.）;

7.2.2 N. of Gautama Buddha Buddh. ; of a Brāhman; of an author（also *bhaṭṭa-n-*）;

7.2.3 m. or n. a kind of musk;

7.2.4（*ikā*）f. see *nāyikā* ;

7.2.5 *-tva* n. leadership.

7.3 【梵漢辭典,p774】（陽性名詞）嚮導，領導者，首長，主人，丈夫（經文）佛，世尊，導師，導，大導師，智者，船筏，爲導者，諸佛，大將。

8. प्रभासयन्ती prabhāsayantī 形容詞　發光；閃耀

8.1 【詞尾變化】prabhāsayantī 是 prabhāsayat 的複數主格形，而 prabhāsayat 是√bhās 的使役動詞，所以字典查 pra-√bhās。

8.2 【摩威梵英,p684】to shine , glitter , be brilliant MBh. ; to appear like（iva）MBh.: Caus. -bhāsayati , to irradiate , illuminate , enlighten MBh.

8.3 【梵漢辭典,p260】（分詞）（形容詞）發光，閃耀（經文）照。

9. भ्रमुकान्तरअतु bhramukāntarātu 名詞　眉間

9.1 【詞尾變化】bhramukāntarātu 是 bhra-mukhāntara 的異讀，由於這個字是佛教混合梵文緣故。〔註 29〕

9.2 【摩威梵英】無此資料。

〔註 29〕這個說法請見江島惠教等編《梵藏漢法華經原典總索引》，東京：靈友會，1988 年出版。頁 785。

9.3 【梵漢辭典,p274】（中性名詞）（正確爲～mukha）（=bhrū-mukhantâra）（經文）眉間。

【筆者試譯】：文殊師利，是什麼原因？
導師要放出
發光閃耀的眉間
從旋毛裡蘊藏的那一道光明？

【什公漢譯】：文殊師利，導師何故，眉間白毫，大光普照？

【英 譯 本】：Why, Mañgusrî, does this ray darted by the
guide of men shine forth from between his brows?
this single ray issuing from the circle of hair?

【信譯研究】：信譯。

【第二頌】

मान्दारवाणां च महन्त वर्षं
पुष्पाणि मुञ्चन्ति सुराः सुहृष्टाः।
मञ्जूषकांश्चन्दनचूर्णमिश्रान् दिव्यान्
सुगन्धांश्च मनोरमांश्च॥२॥

【羅馬譯音】

māndāravāṇāṁ ca mahanta varṣaṁ
puṣpāṇi muñcanti surāḥ suhṛṣṭāḥ|
mañjūṣakāṁścandanacūrṇamiśrān
divyān sugandhāṁśca manoramāṁśca||2||

【句義解析】

māndāravāṇāṁ ca mahanta-varṣaṁ
puṣpāṇi muñcanti surāḥ suhṛṣṭāḥ|
mañjūṣakāṁś candana-cūrṇa-miśrān
divyān sugandhāṁś ca mano-ramāṁś ca||2||

【辭彙研究】

1. मुञ्चन्ति muñcanti 動詞 釋放；投擲

1.1 【詞尾變化】muñcanti 是√muc（第六類動詞）的第三人稱複數形，所以字典查√muc。

1.2 【摩威梵英,p820】cl. 6. to loose , let loose , free , let go , slacken , release , liberate from; RV. ; to spare , let live ; to set free , allow to depart , dismiss , despatch to ,MBh. ; to relinquish , abandon , leave , quit , give up , set aside , depose; to yield , grant , bestow; to send forth , shed , emit , utter , discharge , throw , cast , hurl , shoot at MBh.; to put on, to be loosed , to be set free or released RV.; to deliver one's self from , to get rid of , escape MBh. ; to abstain from; to be deprived or destitute of MBh, to cause to loose or let go or give up or discharge or shed（with two acc.）; to unloose , unyoke , unharness（horses）MBh.; to set free , liberate , absolve from MBh.; to redeem（a pledge）; to open（a road）; to give away , spend , bestow; to gladden , delight , yield enjoyment, to wish to deliver, to wish or be about to set free; to be about to give up or relinquish（life）; to wish or intend to cast or hurl ; to wish to free one's self; to desire final liberation or beatitude RV.

1.3 【梵漢辭典,p741】（第六類動詞）分離，放開，釋放或解放，准許，放鬆分散，放任，離棄，終止，投，擲，丟。（經文）解，解脫，得解脫，脫，開，放，捨，捨棄，除，擲下。

2. सुराः surāḥ 名詞 天眾

2.1 【詞尾變化】surāḥ 是 sura 的複數主格形，所以字典查 sura。

2.2 【摩威梵英,p1234】

2.2.1 m. a god , divinity , deity MBh.; the image of a god , an idol; a symbolical N. for the number `thirty-three'（from the 33 gods ; see *deva*）; a sage , learned man ; the sun ;（said to be）= kṣura MBh. ;

2.2.2（*ī*）f. a goddess;

2.2.3（*am*）n. see *surā*.

2.3 【梵漢辭典,p1238】（陽性名詞）神；（經文）天，天眾。

3. सहृष्टाः suhṛṣṭāḥ 形容詞 非常歡喜的

3.1 【詞尾變化】suhṛṣṭāḥ 是由 su-hṛṣṭāḥ 所構成，也就是 su-hṛṣṭa 的複數主格形，所以字典查 su-hṛṣṭa。

3.2 【摩威梵英,p1303, hṛṣṭa】 mfn. thrilling with rapture , rejoiced , pleased , glad , merry MBh.; bristling , erect , standing on end（said of the hairs of the body）MBh. ; rigid , stiff; blunted; surprised , astonished.

3.3 【摩威梵英,p1219,su】ind. good , excellent , right , virtuous , beautiful , easy , well , rightly , much , greatly , very , any , easily , willingly , quickly RV.

3.4 【梵漢辭典,p498, hṛṣṭa】（過去被動分詞）（形容詞）（體毛）倒豎，驚悸，打哆嗦；硬直的，豎起的，可喜的，愉快的，快活的；（經文）舉身毛豎，歡喜。

3.5 【梵漢辭典,p1216, su】（副詞）好，巧妙，確實地，正確地，非常地，充分地；（經文）善，妙，可。

3.6 所以兩個字合起來，就是「非常歡喜的」。

4. मञ्जूषकांश्चन्दन mañjūṣakāṁś candana 名詞　曼殊沙花（與）白旃檀香

4.1 【詞尾變化】mañjūṣakāṁś candana 根據連音規則是從 mañjūṣakān-candana 變化過來，而 mañjūṣakān 是 mañjūṣaka 的複數對格形，資料前面已有說明。字典查 candana。

4.2 【摩威梵英,p386】

4.2.1 m. n. sandal（Sirium myrtifolium , either the tree , wood , or the unctuous preparation of the wood held in high estimation as perfumes ; hence a term for anything which is the most excellent of its kind MBh.）;

4.2.2 m. N. of a divine being; of a prince ; = -*naka*; N. of an ape;

4.2.3 n. the grass Bhadra-kālī ;

4.2.4（*ā*）f. a kind of creeper ; N. of a river .

4.3 【梵漢辭典,p310】（陽性與中性名詞）白檀樹材，粉末或油膏；（經文）白檀，白旃檀，檀香，旃檀妙香。

5. चूर्ण cūrṇa 名詞　粉末

5.1 【詞尾變化】沒有詞尾變化。

5.2 【摩威梵英,p401】

5.2.1 mfn.（*carv*）minute;

5.2.2 m. 〔MBh.〕 n. powder flour , aromatic powder , pounded sandal , MBh. ;

5.2.3 m. chalk , lime ; N. of a man ;

5.2.4 n. rice mixed with sesam; a kind of easy prose ; dividing a word by separating double consonant for obtaining a different sense.

5.3 【梵漢辭典,p337】(過去被動分詞)始變成粉的，微小，瑣細；(陽性／中性名詞)粉末，穀粉，芳香的或藥用的粉末；(經文)粉，末，碎末，散，香末，抹香，末香，細末香。

6. मिश्रान् miśrān 形容詞　結合

6.1 【詞尾變化】miśrān 是 miśra 的複數對格形，所以字典查 miśra。

6.2 【摩威梵英,p818】

6.2.1 mf（ā）n. mixed , mingled , blended , combined RV; manifold , diverse , various ; mixed or connected or furnished with , accompanied by ;

6.2.2 pl. mixing , adulterating ;

6.2.3 m. a kind of elephant ;（in music）a kind of measure Saṁgīt. ; N. of various authors and other men（also abbreviation for some names ending in miśra）;

6.2.4 n. principal and interest; a species of radish.

6.3 【梵漢辭典,p730】(形容詞)混合的，混堯的，摻雜的，結合的，各種的，多樣的，不同的，交纏的，糾葛的；(經文)雜，合。

7. सुगन्धांश्च sugandhāṁś ca 形容詞　芳香的

7.1 【詞尾變化】sugandhāṁś ca 根據連音規則是從 sugandhān ca 變化過來，而 sugandhān 是 sugandha 的複數對格形，所以字典查 sugandha。

7.2 【摩威梵英,p1222】

7.2.1 m. a fragrant smell , fragrance ; a perfume;

7.2.2 mf（ā）n. fragrant MBh.;

7.2.3 m. sulphur ; the chick-pea ib. ; Andropogon Schoenanthus ib. ; marjoram ib. ; a red-blossomed Moringa ib. ; = tumburu ; a fragrant ointment（made of various substances）; N. of a mountain ; a trader , dealer MW. ;

7.2.4（ā）f. the ichneumon plant ; Curcuma Zedoaria ; a fragrant grass ; a sort of lime ; sacred basil ; N. of various other plants and trees; a form of Dākshāyaṇi ; N. of ais Apsaras MBh.; of a Tirtha Vishṇ. MBh. ; of a woman;

7.2.5（*ī*）f. the small Banana L. ; N. of a female servant of Vasu-deva ;

7.2.6 n. small cumin seed ; the blue lotus; sandal ;civet ; N. of a Tirtha MBh. ;

7.2.7 -*tā* f. fragrance , perfume MW. ;

7.2.8 -*taila-niryāsa* n.（?）civet ; a partic. perfume made from roses MW. ;

7.2.9 -*pattrā* f. a kind of plant;

7.2.10 -*bhūtṛṇa* n. a kind of fragrant grass ;

7.2.11 -*mukha* m. N. of a Bodhi-sattva ;

7.2.12 -*mūlā* f. Averrhoa Acida ; Hibiscus Mutabilis ib. ;

7.2.13 -*yukti* f. preparation of perfumes（one of the 64 arts）BhP;

7.2.14 -*vat* mfn. fragrant MBh. ;

7.2.15 -*vanamāhātmya* n. N. of wk. ;

7.2.16 -*dhāḍhya* mfn. rich in fragrance ;

7.2.17 *ā* f. Jasminum Sambac ;

7.2.18 -*dhāditya* m. N. of a man ;

7.2.19 -*dhāmalaka* m. a kind of mixture of various herbs ;

7.2.20 -dheśa m. N. of a temple erected by Su-gandhā ; an image of the tutelary deity of Su-gñgandhā.

7.3 【梵漢辭典,p1225】（陽性名詞）芳香，香料，（形容詞）芳香的（經文）香，好香，香味。

8. मनोरमांश्च mano-ramāṁś ca 形容詞　令人愉快的

8.1 【詞尾變化】mano-ramāṁś ca 根據連音規則是從 mano-ramān ca 變化過來，而 ramān 是 rama 的複數對格形。至於 ca 資料前面已有說明，所以字典查 mano-rama。

8.2 【摩威梵英,p785】

8.2.1 mf（*ā*）n. gratifying the mind , attractive , pleasant , charming , beautiful MBh. ;

8.2.2 m. N. of a Nāga ; of a mountain ;

8.2.3（*ā*）f. see next ;

8.2.4 n. a kind of house ; N. of a pleasure-garden.

8.3 【梵漢辭典,p708】（形容詞）令人欣喜，吸引人的，令人愉快的，迷人的，可愛的，美麗的；（經文）可意，悅意，得意，適意，意樂，悅可心，可愛，微妙，端嚴。

【筆者試譯】：如落雨般的眾多曼陀羅花
落花繽紛，令天眾非常歡喜！
曼殊沙花，交織著白旃檀香木的粉香，
芬芳的氣氛，令天人們身心愉快！

【什公漢譯】：雨曼陀羅，曼殊沙華，栴檀香風，悅可眾心。

【英 譯 本】：And why this abundant rain of Mandâravas?
The gods, overjoyed, let drop Mañgûshakas
And sandal powder, divine, fragrant, and delicious.

【信譯研究】：信譯。

【第三頌】

येही मही शोभतियं समन्तात्
पर्षाश्च चत्वार सुलब्धहर्षाः।
सर्वं च क्षेत्रं इमु संप्रकम्पितं
षड्भिर्विकारेहि सुभीष्मरूपम्॥ ३॥

【羅馬譯音】

yehī mahī śobhatiyaṁ samantāt
parṣāśca catvāra sulabdhaharṣāḥ|
sarvaṁ ca kṣetraṁ imu saṁprakampitaṁ
ṣaḍbhirvikārehi subhīṣmarūpam||3||

【句義解析】

yehī mahī śobhati yaṁ samantāt
parṣāś ca catvāra sulabdha-harṣāḥ|
sarvaṁ ca kṣetraṁ imu saṁprakampitaṁ
ṣaḍbhir vikārehi subhīṣma-rūpam||3||

【辭彙研究】

1. येही yehī 關係代名詞+感歎詞　關於啊！

1.1 【詞尾變化】yehī 爲 ye-hī 所組成。Ye 爲 ya 的複數主格形，而前面已有資料說明。所以字典查 hī。

1.2 【摩威梵英,p1300】ind.（an exclamation of surprise or astonishment or horror or sorrow or hilarity or satisfaction , usually translatable by）ah! oh! alas ;（also said to be so used in giving a reason or cause , and translatable by）therefore , so , because , for.

1.3 【梵漢辭典,p491】（感歎詞）表驚訝與恐懼，歡喜與滿足。

2. मही mahī 名詞　大地

2.1 【詞尾變化】沒有詞尾變化。

2.2 【摩威梵英,p803】

2.2.1 f. , the great world, the earth RV. ; earth（as a substance）; the base of a triangle or other plane figure; space RV ; a host , army ; a cow RV. ; du. heaven and earth RV;

2.2.2 pl. waters , streams RV; Hingtsha Repens ; a kind of metre; N. of a divine being; of a river MBh; of the number `one'.

2.3 【梵漢辭典,p689】（陰性名詞）大地，地面，土地，陸地，國家，王國，土壤，底邊，空間。（經文）地，大地。

3. शोभति śobhati 動詞　莊嚴

3.1 【詞尾變化】śobhati 是 śubh 的第三人稱單數形，所以字典查 śubh。

3.2 【摩威梵英,p1083】cl. 1. to beautify , embellish , adorn , beautify one's self. look beautiful or handsome , shine , be bright or splendid RV ; to prepare , make fit or ready ,prepare one's self. RV. AV. ; to flash or flit i.e. glide rapidly past or along RV.; wrongly for AV.; to harm , injure, to cause to shine beautify , ornament , decorate AV. ; to ornament , decorate , decorate one's self. RV.;to fly rapidly along RV. to wish to prepare or make ready, to shine brightly or in tensely , be very splendid or beautiful MBh.

3.3 【梵漢辭典,p1217】（第一類動詞）裝飾，美化，始生色（經文）妙，好，端嚴，莊嚴，照耀，爲妙。

4. समन्तात् samantāt 形容詞　週遍

4.1 【詞尾變化】samantāt 是 samanta 的單數從格變化，所以字典查 samanta。

4.2 【摩威梵英,p1155】

4.2.1 mf(*ā*)n. ` having the ends together' , contiguous , neighbouring , adjacent RV. AV. ; `being on every side' , universal , whole , entire , all AV. ;

4.2.2（*ā*）f.（pl.）neighbour. hood; N. of a grammar ;

4.2.3 n. N. of various Samans ;

4.2.4 n. or m.（?）N. of a country Buddh.

4.3 【梵漢辭典,p1076】（形容詞）連續的，鄰接的，完結的，完整的，完全，完全地；（經文）普，週，遍，普遍，週遍。

5. पर्शाश्च parṣāś 名詞　會

5.1 【詞尾變化】parṣāś 後面跟隨的是 ca，根據連音規則是從 parṣāḥ 變化而來。而 parṣāḥ 則是 parṣā 的複數主格形，所以字典查 parṣā。

5.2 資料前面已有說明

6. चत्वार catvāra 名詞　四衢道

6.1 【詞尾變化】沒有詞尾變化，這個字也等於 catvara，所以字典查 catvara。

6.2 【摩威梵英,p386】n. rarely m. a quadrangular place , place in which many ways meet , cross-way MBh. ; a levelled spot of ground prepared for a sacrifice.

6.3 【梵漢辭典,p320】（陽性名詞）四角形，中庭，十字路，市街的區劃；（經文）衢，四衢，四衢道。

7. सुलब्ध sulabdha 形容詞　得大利益

7.1 【詞尾變化】沒有詞尾變化。

7.2 【摩威梵英】沒有。）

7.3 【梵漢辭典,p1231】（形容詞）（經文）善得，善利，大利，大善利，得大利益。

8. हर्शाः harṣāḥ 形容詞　歡喜的

8.1 【詞尾變化】harṣāḥ 是 harṣa 的複數主格形，所以字典查 harṣa。

8.2 【摩威梵英,p1292】

8.2.1 m. bristling , erection（esp. of the hair in a thrill of rapture or delight）

MBh. ; joy , pleasure , happiness（also personified as a son of Dharma）MBh. ; erection of the sexual organ , sexual excitement , lustfulness ; ardent desire MBh. ; N. of an Asura Kathās. ; of a son of Kṛishṇa BhP. ; of various authors, %{mizra} ;

8.2.2 mfn. happy , delighted.

8.3 【梵漢辭典,p485】（陽性形容詞）（毛髮）豎起的，站立，歡喜，快樂，幸福，喜悅；（經文）喜，歡，歡喜。

9. इमु imu 代名詞　如此

9.1 【詞尾變化】事實上 imu 這個字是不在梵文辭典當中，但日本學者江島惠教認爲 imu 就是 imam，也就是 idam 的單數對格形。）

9.2 有關 idam 的資料前面已有說明。

10. संप्रकम्पितं saṁprakampitaṁ 分詞／形容詞　普遍震動

10.1 【詞尾變化】saṁprakampitaṁ 根據連音規則是從 saṁ-prakampitam 變化而來。而 saṁ-prakampitam 則是 saṁ-prakampita 的單數對格形，但因 saṁ 此處是等於 sam，所以字典查 sam-prakampita。

10.2 【摩威梵英,p1152, sam】ind. with , together with , along with , together , altogether RV.

10.3 【摩威梵英,p652, prakampita】

10.3.1 mfn. trembling , quaking; made to tremble , shaken ;

10.3.2 n. trembling or violent motion.

10.4 【梵漢辭典,p1105, saṁprakampita】（過去被動分詞）（形容詞）普動，普遍動。

11. षड्भिर् ṣaḍbhir 數詞　六

11.1 【詞尾變化】ṣaḍbhir 是 ṣaṣ 的工具格。

11.2 資料前面已有說明。

12. विकारेहि vikārehi 片語 因爲變動的原因

12.1 【詞尾變化】vikārehi 是由 vikāre-hi 兩個字構成。其中 vikāre 是 vikāra 的單數於格變化，所以字典查 vikāra-hi。

12.2 【摩威梵英,p954, vikāra】

12.2.1 m. change of form or nature , alteration or deviation from any natural state , transformation , modification , change（esp. for the worse）of bodily or mental condition , disease , sickness , hurt , injury ,（or）perturbation , emotion , agitation , passion MBh. ; an apparition , spectre ; extravagance; a product ;（in Sāṁkhya）a production or derivative from Prakṛti; the derivative of a word; contortion of the face , grimace; change of sentiment , hostility , defection MBh.;

12.2.2 -*tas* ind. from or through change ;

12.2.3 -*tva* n. the state of change , transformation Vedāntas. ;

12.2.4 -*maya* mf（*ī*）n. consisting of derivatives（from Prakṛti）;

12.2.5 -*vat* mfn. undergoing changes;

12.2.6 -*hetu* m. `cause of perturbation' , temptation , seduction.

12.3 【梵漢辭典,p1297, hi】ind.（used as a particle〔cf. *ha* and *gha*〕and usually denoting）for , because , on account of（never standing first in a sentence , but generally after the first word and used enclitically , sometimes after pronouns）RV.; just , pray , do; indeed , assuredly , surely , of course , certainly.

12.4 【梵漢辭典,p1428, vikāra】（陽性形容詞）變換，變更，變化，變形，不同，變樣或異常狀態；（經文）變，異，轉，變異，變易，變異無常，轉變，反，返。

12.5 【梵漢辭典,p491, hi】（不變格）由於，因爲～之故，正好，只是，請；（經文）故，即，唯，定，謂（該字永不放在句首，常見於第一字之後）。

13. सुभीष्म subhīṣma 形容詞 非常可怖的

13.1 【詞尾變化】subhīṣma 是由 su-bhīṣma 所構成。而 su 的部份已於前面有所說明。所以字典查 bhīṣma。

13.2 【摩威梵英,p758】

13.2.1 mfn. terrible , dreadful ;

13.2.2 m. death; N. of Śiva ; a Rākshasa ; N. of a son of Sāṁtanu and Gaṇgā（in the great war of the Bharatas he took the side of the sons of Dhṛitarāṣṭra against the sons of Pāṇḍu , and was renowned for his continence , wisdom , bravery , and fidelity to his word MBh. ;

13.2.3 pl. the race or followers of Bhīṣma MBh. ;

13.2.4 n. horror , horribleness.

13.3 【梵漢辭典,p271】(形容詞) 恐怖的，可怕的；(經文) 怖，可怖，威，大威猛。

【筆者試譯】：因爲這樣，讓大地變得美麗，這般地遍及於（一切）！
讓來這裡參加集會的(眾生)都得到了大利益！感到很歡喜！
所有的佛國淨土都震動了！〔註 30〕
這六種震動是令人畏懼的景象！

【什公漢譯】：以是因緣，地皆嚴淨，而此世界，六種震動，
時四部眾，咸皆歡喜，身意快然，得未曾有。

【英 譯 本】：This earth is, on every side, replete with splendour,
and all the four classes of the assembly are
filled with delight, while the whole field shakes in
six different ways, frightfully.

【信譯研究】：信譯。不過特別的是，鳩摩羅什是用八句頌來譯寫四句梵頌。

〔註 30〕 案《佛光大辭典》的說法：「六種震動」指大地震動之六種相。又作六變震動、六反震動。略稱六震、六動。《大品般若經》卷一《序品》，依地動之方向，舉出東涌西沒、西涌東沒、南涌北沒、北涌南沒、邊涌中沒、中涌邊沒等六相。《新華嚴經》卷十六、《廣博嚴淨不退轉輪經》卷一等則舉出動、起、涌、震、吼、擊（搖）等六相，各相復分小、中、大等三種，故計有動、遍動、等遍動、起、遍起、等遍起、涌、遍涌、等遍涌、震、遍震、等遍震、吼、遍吼、等遍吼、擊、遍擊、等遍擊等十八相。《大方廣大莊嚴經》卷二則舉出搖動、極搖動、遍搖動、扣擊、極扣擊、遍扣擊、移轉、極移轉、遍移轉、涌覆、極涌覆、遍涌覆、出聲、極出聲、遍出聲、邊涌中沒中涌邊沒、東涌西沒西涌東沒、南涌北沒北涌南沒等十八相。《長阿含經》卷二《遊行經》載有地動之八種因緣：(一) 地在水上，水止於風，風止於空，空中大風自起則大水擾，大水擾則普地震動。(二) 得道之比丘、比丘尼及大神尊天，觀水性多，觀地性少，欲知試力則普地震動。(三) 若菩薩由兜率天降神母胎，專念不亂，普地大動。(四) 菩薩始出母胎，從右脅生，專念不亂，則普地震動。(五) 菩薩初成無上正覺，地大震動。(六) 佛初成道轉無上法輪，則普地震動。(七) 佛之說教將畢，欲捨性命，則普地震動。(八) 如來於無餘涅槃界般涅槃時，地大震動。同經卷二亦載有大地震動之六時：(一) 佛入胎時，(二) 出胎時，(三) 成道時，(四) 轉法輪時，(五) 由天魔勸請將捨性命時，(六) 入涅槃時。請見《佛光大辭典》，台北市：佛光圖書出版公司，1983 年出版。頁 1307。

【第四頌】

सा चैव रश्मी पुरिमादिशाय

अष्टादशक्षेत्रसहस्र पूर्णाः।

अवभासयी एकक्षणेन सर्वे

सुवर्णवर्णा इव भोन्ति क्षेत्राः॥४॥

【羅馬譯音】

sā caiva raśmī purimādiśāya

aṣṭādaśakṣetrasahasra pūrṇāḥ|

avabhāsayī ekakṣaṇena sarve

suvarṇavarṇā iva bhonti kṣetrāḥ||4||

【句義解析】

sā caiva raśmī purimā-diśāya

aṣṭādaśa-kṣetra-sahasra pūrṇāḥ|

avabhāsayī eka-kṣaṇena sarve

suvarṇa-varṇā iva bhonti kṣetrāḥ||4||

【辭彙研究】

1. दिशाय diśā　名詞　方向

1.1 【詞尾變化】沒有詞尾變化。

1.2 【摩威梵英,p227】f. direction , region , quarter or point of the compass MBh. ; N. of the wife of Rudra.

1.3 【梵漢辭典,p393】（陰性名詞）方角；方向。

2. अवभासयी avabhāsayī　動詞　發光，普照

2.1 【詞尾變化】這個單字並未見收於《摩威梵英》，《梵漢辭典》與《艾格混梵》等三部辭典當中，江島惠教認爲該字根爲 ava-√bhās），筆者疑爲轉寫問題。所以字典查 ava-√bhās。

2.2 【摩威梵英,p101】-bhasate , to shine forth , be brilliant MBh. BhP. ; to become manifest , appear as（instr.），to illuminate MBh.; to make manifest.

2.3 【梵漢辭典,p260】（動詞）發光，如～一樣清楚的，看得見，如～一般的；（經文）普照，片照，傍照，晃耀，舒光，曉悟。

3. क्षणेन kṣaṇena 名詞　剎那，瞬間

3.1 【詞尾變化】kṣaṇena 是 kṣaṇa 的單數工具格形，所以字典查 kṣaṇa。

3.2 【摩威梵英,p101】-bhasate , to shine forth , be brilliant MBh. BhP. ; to become manifest , appear as（instr.）, to illuminate MBh.; to make manifest.

3.3 【梵漢辭典,p621】（陽性名詞）瞬間，機會，空閒（時間），愉快，片刻，節日（經文）時，節，暇，有暇，須臾，須臾間，念，念念，剎那。

4. सुवर्ण suvarṇa 形容詞　有美麗色彩的

4.1 【詞尾變化】沒有詞尾變化。

4.2 【摩威梵英,p1236】

4.2.1 mf（*ā*）n. of a good or beautiful colour , brilliant in hue , bright , golden , yellow RV ; gold , made of gold; of a good tribe or caste MBh.;

4.2.2 m. a good colour MW. ; a good tribe or class; a kind of bdellium; the thorn-apple; a kind of metre;

4.2.3 m. N. of a Deva-gandharva MBh. ; of an ascetic; of a minister of Daśa-ratha; of a son of Antari1ksha; of a king of Kāśmīra; of a poet ;

4.2.4 m.（rarely n.）a partic. weight of gold（= 1 Karsha , = 16 Ma1shas , = 80 Raktika1s , = about 175 grains troy）MBh.; a gold coin Mṛicch. ; a kind of bulbous plant ; a kind of aloe; a kind of sacrifice;

4.2.5（*ā*）f. turmeric ; Sida Rhomboidea or Cordifolia; another plant; a bitter gourd , colocynth; N. of one of the seven tongues of fire; of a daughter of īkshvāku（the wife of Su-hotra）MBh. ;

4.2.6（*ī*）f. the plant Salvinia Cucullata;

4.2.7（*am*）n. gold（of which 57 synonyms are given）AV.; money , wealth , property , riches; a sort of yellow sandal-wood; the flower of Mesua Roxburghii ; a kind of vegetable; red ochre; the right pronunciation of sounds; N. of a Tīrtha MBh. ; of a partic. world.

4.3 【梵漢辭典,p1247】（形容詞）有美麗色彩的，燦爛的，金光閃閃的，金碧輝煌的；金造的。（經文）金，好，美，金色，黃金，眞金，好色，妙色，色好，鮮色。

5. वर्णा varṇā 名詞　色身

5.1 【詞尾變化】varṇā 是 varṇa 的單數工具格，所以字典查 varṇa。

5.2 【摩威梵英,p924】

5.2.1 m. a covering , cloak , mantle ; a cover; outward appearance , exterior , form , figure , shape , colour RV. ; colour of the face ,（esp.）good colour or complexion , lustre , beauty MBh.; colour , tint , dye , pigment（for painting or writing）MBh.; colour = race , species , kind , sort , character , nature , quality , property（applied to persons and things）RV. ; class of men , tribe , order , caste; a letter , sound , vowel , syllable , word; a musical sound or note（also applied to the voice of animals）MBh.; the order or arrangement of a song or poem; praise , commendation , renown , glory ;（in alg.）an unknown magnitude or quantity ;（in arithm.）the figure , ` one ' ;（accord. to some）a co-efficient ; a kind of measure ; gold ; a religious observance ; one who wards off , expeller RV. ;

5.2.2（*ā*）f. Cajanus Indicus ;

5.2.3 n. saffron.

5.3 【梵漢辭典,p1392】（陽性名詞）遮覆，蓋，外觀，外貌，顏色，（好的）面色；人種，種，種類，性格，性質，特質，形狀，種性，文字，聲音；名聲，著名。（經文）色，顯，誦，音，讚，性，姓，譽，顯色，讚歎，讚美，稱揚，稱讚，稱名，讚念，色身，色像，色形，形色，色類，光色，色相，妙色，德號，族姓，功德。

6. भोन्ति bhonti 形容詞　出現，產生

6.1 【詞尾變化】bhonti 根據艾格頓的說法，是從 bhavanti 變化過來，[註31] 而 bhavanti 是√bhū 的現在式主動分詞做形容詞單數呼格形，所以字典查√bhū。

6.2 資料前面已有說明。

【筆者試譯】：這樣的光明照耀了東方，

[註31] bhonti 當中的 o，梵文寫法是用來代替 ava，所以 bhonti=bhavanti，請見 Franklin Edgerton 編《Buddhist Hybrid Sanskrit Grammar And Dictionary》，Reprint：1993，By Motilal Banarsidass Publishers Pvt.Ltd., Dehli,India,p.412。

照亮了一萬八千個佛國淨土！
瞬間就照亮了一切，
（各個）國土顯出現了金碧輝煌的人種色身！

【什公漢譯】：眉間光明，照于東方，萬八千土，皆如金色。

【英 譯 本】：And that ray in the eastern quarter illuminates
The whole of eighteen thousand Buddha-fields,
Simultaneously, so that those fields appear as gold coloured.

【信譯研究】：信譯。

【第五頌】

यावानवीची परमं भवाग्रं
क्षेत्रेषु यावन्ति च तेषु सत्त्वाः।
षट्सू गतीषू तहि विद्यमाना
च्यवन्ति ये चाप्युपपद्यि तत्र॥५॥

【羅馬譯音】

yāvānavīcī paramaṁ bhavāgraṁ
kṣetreṣu yāvanti ca teṣu sattvāḥ|
ṣaṭsū gatīṣū tahi vidyamānā
cyavanti ye cāpyupapadyi tatra||5||

【句義解析】

yāvān avīcī paramaṁ bhavāgraṁ
kṣetreṣu yāvanti ca teṣu sattvāḥ|
ṣaṭsū gatīṣū）〔註 32〕tahi vidyamānā
cyavanti ye cāpy upapadyi tatra||5||

〔註 32〕這個字並非正規梵文，說明請見江島惠教等編《梵藏漢法華經原典總索引》，東京：靈友會，1988 年出版。頁 322。

【辭彙研究】

1. अवन्ति avanti 動詞 支配

1.1 【詞尾變化】avanti 是√av 的現在主動分詞第三人稱單數形，所以字典查√av。

1.2 【摩威梵英,p96】cl. I .to drive , impel , animate（as a car or horse）RV. ; Ved. to promote , favour ,（chiefly Ved.）to satisfy , refresh ; to offer（as a hymn to the gods）RV.; to lead or bring to, to be pleased with , like , accept favourably（as sacrifices , prayers or hymns）RV. ,（chiefly said of kings or princes）to guard , defend , protect , govern BhP.; to consume , devour RV. AV.

1.3 【梵漢辭典,p205】（動詞）急促，疾馳，照顧，幫助，消除疲勞，

2. विद्यमाना vidyamānā 動詞 知道了

2.1 【詞尾變化】vidyamānā 等同 vidyamāna，也就是√vid 的現在分詞形，所以字典查 vid。

2.2 資料前面已有說明。

3. च्यवन्ति cyavanti 分詞，形容詞 搖動

3.1 【詞尾變化】cyavanti 是√cyu 的現在主動分詞作形容詞第三人稱複數變化形，所以字典查√cyu。

3.2 【摩威梵英,p403】cl. I. to move to and fro , shake about RV; to stir , move from one's place , go away , retire from（abl.）, turn off BhP ; to deviate from, abandon MBh. ; to come forth from , come out of. drop from , trickle , stream forth from; to fall down , fall , slide from; to fall from any divine existence（so as to be re-born as a man）Jain. ; to die Buddh. ; `to fall from' , be deprived of , lose（with abl.）; to fall away , fade away , disappear , vanish , perish MBh. BhP; to fail MBh; to sink down , sink（lit. and fig.）;（in the series of re-births）; to decrease（with instr.）MBh.; to bring about , create , make RV; to cause to go away , make forget ; to cause to move , shake , agitate RV. to be moved or shaken RV.; to loosen; to remove from a place , drive away from（abl.）MBh. ; to cause to fall; to deprive any one（acc.）of（acc.）; Intens. to shake RV.

3.3 【梵漢辭典,p338】（動詞）搖動，移動離開，逃離，奪取，讓師，消失，

滅亡，死，不足，墮落，使毀滅（經文）死，歿，命終，命盡，退，墮，下，下生。

4. चाप्य् cāpy 連接詞+介係詞　同樣，也

4.1 【詞尾變化】cāpy 是由 ca-apy 組成，另根據連音規則，可視爲 ca-api 所組成。所以字典查 ca-api。

4.2 資料前面已有說明。

5. उपपद्यि upapadyi 動詞　來到

5.1 【詞尾變化】upapadyi 是由 upa-padyi 所構成。根據學者江島惠教的看法，認爲這個字就是 upa-√pad 所構成)，所以字典查 upa-√pad。

5.2 【摩威梵英,p201】1 -padyate , -ti , to go towards or against , attack AV. ; to approach , come to , arrive at , enter MBh. ; to approach or come to a teacher（as a pupil）MBh. ; to approach for succour or protection ; to approach or join with in speech; to reach , obtain , partake of ; to enter into any state MBh.; to take place , come forth , be produced , appear , occur , happen ; to be present , exist; to be possible , be fit for or adequate to（with loc.）MBh.; to be regular or according to rules ; to become , be suitable MBh. , to bring to any state（with two acc.）; to cause anything（acc.）to arrive at（loc. or dat.）, cause to come into the possession of , offer , present MBh. ; to cause to come forth or exist ; to accomplish , effect , cause , produce MBh. ; to get ready , prepare , make fit or adequate for , make conformable to MBh.; to furnish or provide or endow with MBh.; to make anything out of Prab. ; to examine ; to find out , ascertain; to prove , justify; to attend on a patient , physic.

5.3 【梵漢辭典,p823】（動詞）來到；前往～處，進入，到達，開始，發起，發生，產生，出現，存在，出來，有可能，對～適合或適當的，值得～（經文）生，往生，受生，生，下生入，發，興發，得。

6. तत्र tatra 副詞　在那裡

6.1 【詞尾變化】沒有詞尾變化。

6.2 【摩威梵英,p433】ind. used for the loc.（sg. du. and pl.）of tād RV. AV. ; in that place , thereRV. ; thither , to that place; in that , therein , in that case , on that occasion , under those circumstances , then , therefore.

6.3 【梵漢辭典,p1248】（副詞）在那裡，向其處，在這裡，在此機會，因爲

彼的，在其時，在那時，（經文）其，此中，於中，於彼，於此中，此處，彼處。

【筆者試譯】：照亮了大阿鼻地獄，同樣地也照亮了最高的阿迦尼吒天，
滿足了（照亮了）許多淨土與這些有情眾生們！
（也）明白了有六道（存在），
而在那裡也有（明白了）生死（輪迴的道理）。

【什公漢譯】：從阿鼻獄，上至有頂，諸世界中，六道眾生，
生死所趣，

【英 譯 本】：（The universe）as far as the（hell）Avîki（and）
the extreme limit of existence, with all beings
of those fields living in any of the six states of
existence, those who are leaving one state to be born in another;

【信譯研究】：信譯。但是鳩摩羅什是用五句偈來翻譯梵頌四句偈。

【第六頌】

कर्माणि चित्रा विविधानि तेषां
गतीषु दृश्यन्ति सुखा दुखा च।
हीना प्रणीता तथ मध्यमा च
इह स्थितो अद्दशि सर्वमेतत्॥६॥

【羅馬譯音】

karmāṇi citrā vividhāni teṣāṁ
gatīṣu dṛśyanti sukhā dukhā ca|
hīnā praṇītā tatha madhyamā ca
iha sthito addaśi sarvametat||6||

【句義解析】

karmāṇi citrā vividhāni teṣāṁ
gatīṣu dṛśyanti sukhā dukhā ca|

hīnā praṇītā tatha madhyamā ca
iha sthito addaśi sarvam etat||6||

【辭彙研究】

1. कर्माणि karmāṇi 名詞 業

1.1 【詞尾變化】karmāṇi 是 karman 的複數主格形，所以字典查 karman。

1.2 【摩威梵英,p258】a n.（ā m.）, act , action , performance , business RV. AV. MBh. ; office , special duty , occupation , obligation; any religious act or rite RV. AV. ; work , labour , activity; physicking , medical attendance; action consisting in motion ; calculation ; product , result , effect ; organ of sense; the object ; former act as leading to inevitable results , fate（as the certain consequence of acts in a previous life）Buddh.; the tenth lunar mansion.

1.3 【梵漢辭典,p571】（中性名詞）行爲，作業，作用，職業，儀式，結果，行爲的直接目的，命運（經文）業，行，作，作業，業用，行業，所作，所作業，因業，業因，作法，事，辦事，相，轉變事。

2. चित्रा citrā 形容詞 明顯的

2.1 【詞尾變化】citrā 根據學者江島惠教認爲，等於 citra)，因此字典查 citra。

2.2 【摩威梵英,p396】

2.2.1 mf（*ā*）n. conspicuous , excellent , distinguished RV. ; bright , clear , bright-coloured RV. ; clear（a sound）RV. ; variegated , spotted , speckled（with instr. or in comp.）; agitated; various , different , manifold MBh. ;（execution）having different varieties（of tortures）; strange , wonderful; containing the word;

2.2.2（*ām*）ind. so as to be bright RV ;in different ways ;（to execute）with different tortures ;

2.2.3（*ās*）m. variety of colour; Plumbago zeylanica ; Ricinus communis ; Jonesia Aśoka ; a form of Yama Tithyād. ; N. of a king RV.; of a Jābāla-gṛihapati（with the patr. Gauṣrāyaṇi）; of a king（with the patr. Gāṇgyāyani）; of a son of Dhritarāṣṭra MBh ; of a Draviḍa king; of a Gandharva ;

2.2.4（*ā*）f. Spica virginis , the 12th（in later reckoning the 14th）lunar mansion AV; a kind of snake ; N. of a plant ; a metre of 4 X 16 syllabic instants ; another of 4 x 15 syllables ; another of 4 x 16 syllables ; a kind of stringed instrument ; a kind of Mūrchanā（in music）; illusion , unreality ; `born under the asterism Citrā, N. of Arjuna's wife; of a daughter of Gada; of an Apsaras ; of a river;

2.2.5 f. pl. the asterism ;

2.2.6（*ām*）n. anything bright or coloured which strikes the eyes RV; a brilliant ornament , ornament RV; a bright or extraordinary appearance , wonder ; strange , curious; strange; the ether , sky; a spot MBh. ; a sectarial mark on the forehead ; a picture , sketch , delineation MBh. of variegated appearance; various modes of writing or arranging verses in the shape of mathematical or other fanciful figures（syllables which occur repeatedly being left out or words being represented in a shortened form）; punning in the form of question and answer , facetious conversation , riddle.

2.3 【梵漢辭典,p331】（形容詞）明顯的，易見的，顯著的，明白的，發亮的，清楚的，可聽到的（聲音），雜色的，有斑點的，斑駁的，各種的，多樣的，奇異的，令人驚訝的；（經文）種種，種種不同，雜類，雜飾，雜色，妙色，有殊，稀奇。

3. विविधानि vividhāni 形容詞　形形色色的，各種的

3.1 【詞尾變化】vividhāni 是 vividha 的主格複數形，所以字典查 vividha。

3.2 資料前面已有說明。

4. तेषां teṣāṁ 代名詞　他們

4.1 【詞尾變化】teṣāṁ 根據連音規則，是從 teṣām 變化過來，而 teṣām 屬於 tad 的屬格複數形，所以字典查 tad。

4.2 資料前面已有說明。

5. सखा sukhā 形容詞　快樂

5.1 【詞尾變化】sukhā 可看作 sukha，情況本頌同第 2 個單字。）所以字典查 sukha。

5.2 【摩威梵英,p1221】

5.2.1 mfn. running swiftly or easily（only applied to cars or chariots , superl. , easy RV. ; pleasant (rarely with this meaning in Veda), agreeable , gentle , mild; comfortable , happy , prosperous ; virtuous , pious;

5.2.2 m. N. of a man g. a kind of military array Ka1m.

5.2.3 (*ā*) f. (in phil.) the effort to win future beatitude , piety , virtue; (in music) a partic. ; N. of the city of Varuṇa; of one of the 9 Śaktis of Śiva ;

5.2.4 (*am*) n. ease , easiness , comfort , prosperity , pleasure , happiness (in m. personified as a child of Dharma and Siddhi Mārk.) , joy , delight in, the sky , heaven , atmosphere ; water; N. of the fourth astrol. house; the drug or medicinal root called Vṛiddhi ;

5.2.5 (*ām*) ind. easily , comfortably , pleasantly , joyfully , willingly VS.

5.3 【梵漢辭典,p1227】(形容詞)輕快奔馳的;舒適的,愉快的,溫厚的,悅耳的,氣氛宜人的,因~愉快的;快樂,安慰,快樂,享樂,幸福,歡喜。(經文)樂,安,快,安樂,安穩,悅樂,請快,快樂,怡樂。

6. दुखा dukhā 形容詞 痛苦;困難

6.1 【詞尾變化】dukhā 可看作 duḥkha,情況本頌同第 2 個單字。)所以字典查 duḥkha。

6.2 【摩威梵英,p483】

6.2.1 mfn. (according to grammarians properly written *duṣ-kha* and said to be from *dus* and *kha* 〔cf. *su-khā*〕 ; but more probably a Prākritized form for *duḥ-stha*) uneasy , uncomfortable , unpleasant , difficult (compar. -*tara* MBh.) ;

6.2.2 n. (ifc. f. *ā*) uneasiness , pain , sorrow , trouble , difficulty MBh. (personified as the son of Naraka and Vedanā) ;

6.2.3 (*am*) ind. with difficulty , scarcely , hardly (also *at* and *ena*) MBh.; impers. it is difficult to or to be;

6.2.4 *duḥkham - as* , to be sad or uneasy ; - *kṛ*, to cause or feel pain MBh.

6.3 【梵漢辭典,p405】(形容詞)不愉快的,艱難的,可憐的(經文)苦,難,一切行苦。

7. हिना hīnā 形容詞/過去被動分詞 不足,缺乏

7.1 【詞尾變化】hīnā 可看作 hīna,情況本頌同第 2 個單字。)所以字典查 hīna。

7.2 【摩威梵英,p1296】

7.2.1 mfn. left , abandoned , for saken RV. ; left behind , excluded or shut out from , lower or weaker than , inferior to MBh. ; left out , wanting , omitted MBh. ; defeated or worsted（in a lawsuit）; deficient , defective , faulty , insufficient , short , incomplete , poor , little , low , vile , bad , base , mean S3Br. &c. &c. ; bereft or deprived of , free from , devoid or destitute of , without MBh. ; lost or strayed from（a caravan）; brought low , broken down in circumstances;

7.2.2 m. a faulty or defective witness; subtraction ; Mesua Ferrea ;

7.2.3（*ā*）f. a female mouse;

7.2.4（*am*）n. deficiency , want , absence.

7.3 【梵漢辭典,p492】（過去被動分詞）（形容詞）不足，缺乏。

8. प्रणीता praṇītā 形容詞　最好的

8.1 【詞尾變化】praṇītā 可看作 praṇīta，情況本頌同第 2 個單字。）所以字典查 praṇīta。

8.2 【摩威梵英,p660】

8.2.1（*prā-*）mfn. led forwards , advanced , brought , offered , conveyed RV.; brought into , reduced to; directed towards（loc.）; hurled , cast , shot MBh. ; led towards i.e. delivered , given MBh.; performed , executed , finished , made , done , prepard MBh. ; inflicted , sentenced , awarded MBh. ; established , instituted , taught , said , written MBh. ;

8.2.2（*-tva* n.）wished , desired; good（as food）; entered , approached ;

8.2.3 m. fire consecrated by prayers or mystical formulas ;

8.2.4（*ā*）f. a partic. vessel used at sacrifices , a sort of cup ; N. of a river ;

8.2.5 pl. water fetched on the morning of a festival for sacrificial uses , holy water;

8.2.6 n. anything cooked or dressed（such as a condiment）;

8.2.7 *-tavijñāpana* n. begging for dainties L. ;

8.2.8 *-tā-caru* m. the vessel for the holy water ;

8.2.9 *-tā-praṇāyana* n. the vessel in which holy water is fetched.

8.3 【梵漢辭典,p926】（形容詞）（過去被動分詞）有特徵的，傑出的，優秀的（經文）妙，最妙，微妙，上妙，美妙，珍妙，勝，最勝，每，多美，上，好，上好，勝好，好善，精，芳，富貴，廣大，淨利。

9. तथ tatha 副詞　如此

9.1 【詞尾變化】tatha 可看作 tathā，情況本頌同第 2 個單字。）所以字典查 tathā。

9.2 【摩威梵英,p433】ind.（tā-thā , correlative of yā-thā）in that manner , so , thus RV; yes , so be it , so it shall be（particle of assent , agreement , or promise ; generally followed by iti）AV.; so also , in like manner MBh.

9.3 【梵漢辭典,p1281】（副詞）如此，這樣，那樣，彼如是，彼然，好的，是的，如實地，用香四的方法，也，同樣地；（經文）如，此如，如是，如實，亦，亦爾，似。

10. मध्यमा madhyamā 形容詞　正中的

10.1 【詞尾變化】madhyamā 可看作 madhyama，情況本頌同第 2 個單字。）所以字典查 madhyama。

10.2 【摩威梵英,p782】

10.2.1 mf（*ā*）n. middle MBh. ; being or placed in the middle , middlemost , intermediate , central RV. ; middle-born（neither youngest nor oldest）; of a middle kind or size or quality , middling , moderate; standing between two persons or parties , impartial , neutral MBh.;（in astron.）mean ; relating to the meridian ib. ;

10.2.2 m. the middlemost prince（whose territory lies between that of a king seeking conquest and that of his foe）; the middle character in plays; the midland country ;（in music）the 4th or 5th note ; the middlemost of the 3 scales ; a partic. ;（in gram.）the 2nd person ; the governor of a province ; a kind of antelope ; N. of the 18th Kalpa. ;

10.2.3 pl. a class of gods;（with Buddhists）N. of a partic. Buddh. sect;

10.2.4 m. n. the middle of the body , waist MBh. ;

10.2.5（*ā*）f. the womb ; the middle finger; midnight ; a girl arrived at puberty ; the pericarp of a lotus ; a central blossom ; a kind of metre ;（in music）a partic.;

10.2.6 n. the middle ; mediocrity , defectiveness ,; N. of the 12th（14th）Kāṇḍa of the ŚBr. ;（in astron.）the meridian ecliptic point.

10.3 【梵漢辭典,p673】(形容詞最高級)最中央的，正中的，位居中間的，在中央，中央的，中等種類或力量的；中型的，中等的，平凡的，適度的，中立的(經文)中，處中，中道。

11. इह iha 副詞　在此刻

11.1 【詞尾變化】沒有詞尾變化。

11.2 【摩威梵英,p170】ind.(fr. Pronom.), in this place , here ; to this place ; in this world ; in this book or system ; in this case ; now , at this time RV. ;

11.3 【梵漢辭典,p503】(副詞)在此處，到這裡，在人間，於此世，在此書中，以下，現在，既然如此，此時，在此刻(通常=idam)；(經文)此，於此，此處，此上，世，今世，今生，於此身，於是身，今，此間，復次，謂。

12. स्थितो sthito 形容詞／過去被動分詞　站著的，站立的

12.1 【詞尾變化】sthito 根據連音規則，是從 sthitāḥ 變化過來，也就是 sthita 的複數主格形，所以字典查 sthita。

12.2 資料前面已有說明。

13. अद्दशि addaśi 動詞　注目，看

13.1 【詞尾變化】addaśi 並非標準梵文，而是俗語，意思與√dṛś 相當。

13.2 【摩威梵英,401】有關√dṛś 資料已有說明。但無 addaśi 的資料。

13.3 【梵漢辭典,p28】(動詞)(經文)見。

【筆者試譯】:(佛國淨土裡面)顯示出眾生們各種的業報
顯示出了他們所作與所受的一切苦樂
如此也有中間的(果報)，(但)缺少最好的
在此刻(會場內全體)站著眾生們目睹了這一切！

【什公漢譯】:善惡業緣，受報好醜，於此悉見。

【英 譯 本】:Their various and different actions in those
states have become visible; whether they are in
a happy, unhappy, low, eminent, or intermediate
position, all that I see from this place.

【信譯研究】:信譯。不過特別的是用三句頌來翻譯梵詩四句偈。

【第七頌】

बुद्धांश्च पश्यामि नरेन्द्रसिंहान्
प्रकाशयन्तो विवरन्ति धर्मम्।
प्रशासमानान् बहुसत्त्वकोटीः
उदाहरन्तो मधुरस्वरां गिरम्॥७॥

【羅馬譯音】

buddhāṁśca paśyāmi narendrasiṁhān
prakāśayanto vivaranti dharmam|
praśāsamānān bahusattvakoṭīḥ
udāharanto madhurasvarāṁ giram||7||

【句義解析】

buddhāṁś ca paśyāmi narendra-siṁhān
prakāśayanto vivaranti dharmam|
praśāsamānān bahu-sattva-koṭīḥ
udāharanto madhura-svarāṁ giram||7||

【辭彙研究】

1. बुद्धांश्च buddhāṁś（ca）動詞　覺悟

1.1 【詞尾變化】buddhāṁś ca 根據連音規則是從 buddhān ca 變化過來。Ca 的意思前面已有資料說明，而 buddhān 則是從√budh 的複數對格過去被動分詞的變化，所以字典查√budh。

1.2 【摩威梵英,p733】

1.2.1 cl. 4. to wake , wake up , be awake RV.; to recover consciousness（after a swoon）; to observe , heed , attend to（with acc. or gen.）RV. ; to perceive , notice , learn , understand , become or be aware of or acquainted with RV. ; to think of i.e. present a person（` with' instr.）RV.; to know to be , recognize as（with two acc.）MBh.; to deem , consider or regard as（with two acc.）, to be awakened or restored to consciousness ; see above, to wake up , arouse , restore to life or consciousness RV. ; to revive the scent（of a perfume）; to cause（a flower）to expand; to cause to observe or attend , admonish , advise RV.; to make a person acquainted with , remind or inform of. impart or communicate anything to（with two acc.）MBh., to wish to observe , desire to become acquainted with Nyāyas. BhP, to have an insight into , understand thoroughly（with acc.）

1.3 【梵漢辭典,p301】（動詞）覺醒，義是的恢復，睡醒的，未眠的，發掘，注意，對～留意的，發覺，親近而知的，注意的，留意的，醒悟，使覺醒；（經文）覺，能知，了知，成，成佛。

2. पश्यामि paśyāmi 動詞　看見

2.1 【詞尾變化】paśyāmi 是√paś 的第一人稱單數現在式，故字典查√paś。

2.2 【摩威梵英,p611】P. A1. pāśyati , -te, to see（with na `to be blind'）, behold , look at , observe , perceive , notice RV.; to be a spectator , look on; to see a person（either `visit' or `receive as a visitor'）MBh.; to live to see , experience , partake of. undergo , incur MBh.; to learn , find out ; to regard or consider as , take for ; to see with the spiritual eye , compose , invent（hymns , rites &c.）RV. ;（also with sādhu）to have insight or discernment MBh.; to consider , think over , examine ; to foresee.

2.3 【梵漢辭典,p874】（動詞）看，看見，眺望，觀看，觀察，注意，注視，旁觀，與人會面，早訪，露面，引進，考察，思量；（經文）見，觀見，睹，觀察，瞻觀，省。

3. नरेन्द्र narendra 名詞　人中尊

3.1 【詞尾變化】沒有詞尾變化。

3.2 【摩威梵英,p529】

3.2.1 m. `mñman-lord' , king , prince , MBh. ; a physician , master of charms or antidote; N. of a poet; of another man; a kind of metre ;

3.2.2 -*kanyā* f. a princess;

3.2.3 -tā f.（Priy.）, -*tva* n.（Rājat.）kingship , royalty ;

3.2.4 -*deva* m. N. of a king;

3.2.5 -*druma* m. Cathartocarpus Fistūa;

3.2.6 -nagarī（?）m. N. of a grammarian;

3.2.7 -*putra* m. a prince ;

3.2.8 -*mārga* m. `king's road' , high street ;

3.2.9 -*svāmin* m. N. of a temple built by Narendrāditya , Rājat. ;

3.2.10 drācārya m. N. of a grammarian;

3.2.11 -*drāditya* m. N. of 2 kings of Kaśmīra;

3.2.12 -*drāhva* n. Agallochum.

3.3 【梵漢辭典,p769】(陽性名詞)人類的首長,國王,親王,醫生,精通皺術或解毒劑,魔術師;(經文)聖主,人中之尊,人中尊,是尊,如來,佛。

4. प्रकाशयन्तो prakāśayanto 動詞　出現;照耀

4.1 【詞尾變化】prakāśayanto 根據連音規則是 prakāśayantaḥ,由於並非規則梵文變化,根據學者江島惠教的看法,這個字的字根是 pra-√kāś。〔註 33〕故字典查 pra-√kāś。

4.2 【摩威梵英,p653】-kāśate, to become visible , appear , shine , become evident or manifest MBh.: Caus. -kāśayati (rarely -te), to make visible , cause to appear or shine , illumine , irradiate , show , display , manifest , reveal , impart , proclaim: Intens. (only pr.p. -cākaśat) to illumine (and) to survey RV.

4.3 【梵漢辭典,p577】(動詞)(被動)能明。

5. विवरन्ति vivaranti 動詞　開示演說

5.1 【詞尾變化】vivaranti 是 vi-√vṛ 的第三人稱複數現在式變化,所以字典查 vi-√vṛ。

5.2 【摩威梵英,p988】 to uncover , spread out , open , display , show , reveal , manifest RV.; to illumine (darkness) RV. ; to unsheath (a sword) ; to part , comb (hair) ; to explain , describe , comment upon MBh.; to cover , cover up , stop up MBh. ;

5.3 【梵漢辭典,p1471】(動詞)去掉遮蓋,打開,開劍鞘,分開,梳理,照明,顯示,表明,表示,說明,註解;(經文)開,張,捨,止,離,開示,舉發,能捨,遠離。

〔註 33〕請見江島惠教等編《梵藏漢法華經原典總索引》,東京:靈友會出版,1988 年出版。頁 651。

6. प्रशासमानान् praśāsamānān 動詞／分詞／形容詞　教導

6.1 【詞尾變化】這個單字在兩本字典都找不到，疑似爲佛教混合梵文，與 praśāsyamānān 相近，praśāsyamānān 爲 pra-√śās 的過去被動分詞之陽性複數對格形，故字典查 pra-√śās。

6.2 【摩威梵英,p695】P. -śāsti , to teach , instruct , direct RV. ; to give instructions to , order , command（acc.）MBh.; to chastise , punish MBh.; to govern , rule , reign , be lord of MBh. ; to decide upon MBh.

6.3 【梵漢辭典,p1146】（動詞）（現在主動分詞）（形容詞）指示，教授，給予指示，管理，成爲～的主人；（經文）教。

7. उदाहरन्तो udāharanto 動詞　宣說

7.1 【詞尾變化】udāharanto 根據連音規則是 udāharantaḥ 變化而來，而 udāharantaḥ 則是 udā-√hṛ 的現在主動分詞之複數主格變化，所以字典查 udā-√hṛ。

7.2 【摩威梵英,p185】P. -ā-harati , to set up , put up; to relate , declare , announce ; to quote , cite , illustrate ; to name , call. MBh. , to be set up or put up.

7.3 【梵漢辭典,p496】（動詞：現在主動分詞）置於頂上，對～（人）或～（事）列拒，引用，發言，背誦，詳細說明或敘述，舉出名字，取名爲～，稱呼，做爲實例引用；（經文）說，宣說，談說。

8. स्वरां svarāṁ 名詞　樂音

8.1 【詞尾變化】svarāṁ 根據連音規則是從 svarām 變化過來，但 svarām 並非標準梵文，兩字典均無此字，疑似佛教混合梵文，接近 svarān，即 svara 的複數對格。故字典查 svara。

8.2 【摩威梵英,p1285】

8.2.1 m. sound , noise RV. ; voice MBh. ; tone in recitation（either high or low）, accent（of which there are three kinds , *udātta* , *anudātta* , and *svarita*）, a note of the musical scale（of which seven 〔rarely six or eight〕 are enumerated , 1. *niṣāda* ; 2. *ṛṣabha* ; 3. *gāndhāra* ; 4. *ṣaḍja* ; 5. *madhyama*; 6. *dhaivata* ; 7. *pañcama* 〔described as resembling respectively the notes of an elephant , bull , goat , peacock , curlew or heron , horse , and Koil; and designated by their initial letters or syllables thus , *ni* ; *ṛ* ; *ga* ; *ṣa* ; *ma* ; *dha* ; *pa*〕 , but the order is sometimes changed , *ṣadja* being placed first , and *niṣāda* last）MBh.; a symbolical expression for the number ` seven' ; a vowel（either *dīrgha* , `long' ; or *hrasva* , `short' ; or *pluta* , `prolated'）MBh. ; air breathed through the nostrils ; N. of Vishṇu ;

8.2.2（*ā*）f. N. of the chief wife of Brahmā ;

8.2.3（*am*）n. a musical note RV. ; N. of various Sāmans.

8.3 【梵漢辭典,p1256】（陽性名詞）音，聲響，噪音，聲，音調（隨讀誦時的抑揚頓挫而別）；重音，樂音（七個音階），母音；（經文）音，聲，言，語，音聲。

9. गिरम् giram 名詞　稱讚

9.1 【詞尾變化】giram 是 gir 的單數對格形，所以字典查 gir。

9.2 【摩威梵英,p355】

9.2.1 mfn. addressing , invoking , praising RV. ;

9.2.2（*īr*）f. invocation , addressing with praise , praise , verse , song RV. AV. ; speech , speaking , language , voice , words , MBh. , fame , celebrity ; a kind of mystical syllable.

9.3 【梵漢辭典,p466】（陰性名詞）呼叫聲，語，聲，語言，言詞，稱讚，讚歌。

【筆者試譯】：（在場會眾們又）看見了佛陀們，這些人中獅子們，
顯示了他們開示解說佛法（的情景）。
他們曾經教導過了無數量的有情眾生，
用優美樂音來讚頌宣說（佛法）。

【什公漢譯】：又覩諸佛，聖主師子，演說經典，微妙第一，
其聲清淨，出柔軟音，教諸菩薩，無數億萬。

【英 譯 本】：I see also the Buddhas, those lions of kings,
revealing and showing the essence of the law,
comforting many kotis of creatures and emitting sweet
sounding voices.

【信譯研究】：信譯。不過卻是用八句偈來翻譯梵詩四句偈。

【第八頌】

गम्भीरनिर्घोषमुदारमद्भुतं
मुञ्चन्ति क्षेत्रेषु स्वकस्वकेषु।
दृष्टान्तहेतूनयुतान कोटिभिः
प्रकाशयन्तो इमु बुद्धधर्मम्॥८॥

【羅馬譯音】

gambhīranirghoṣamudāramadbhutaṁ
muñcanti kṣetreṣu svakasvakeṣu |
dṛṣṭāntahetūnayutāna koṭibhiḥ
prakāśayanto imu buddhadharmam||8||

【句義解析】

Gambhīra-nirghoṣam udāram adbhutaṁ
muñcanti kṣetreṣu svaka-svakeṣu |
dṛṣṭānta-hetū-nayutāna koṭibhiḥ
prakāśayanto imu buddha-dharmam||8||

【辭彙研究】

1. गम्भीर gambhīra 形容詞 甚深

1.1 【詞尾變化】沒有詞尾變化。

1.2 【摩威梵英,p346】

1.2.1 m. the lemon tree ; a lotus ; a Mantra of the RV.;

1.2.2 (=*gabh-*) N. of a son of Bhautya VP. ;

1.2.3 (*ā*) f. a hiccup , violent singultus ; N. of a river ;

1.2.4 (*am*) n. `depth' , with jamad-agneḥ N. of a Sāman.

1.3 【梵漢辭典,p444】(形容詞)(經文)深,甚深,深遠,深妙,極甚深,深寬廣,深奧,幽,濬。

2. निघोषम् nirghoṣam 名詞 音聲

2.1 【詞尾變化】nirghoṣam 是 nirghoṣa 單數對格形,所以字典查 nirghoṣa。

2.2 【摩威梵英,p541】

2.2.1 mf（*ā*）n. soundless , noiseless MBh. ;

2.2.2 -śākśara-vimukta m. N. of a Samādhi.

2.2.3 m.（f. *ā*）sound , noise , rattling , tramping MBh.;

2.3 【梵漢辭典,p794】（陽性名詞）音，音響，噪音；（經文）音，聲，音聲，妙音，響。

3. उदारम् udāram　形容詞　美好的

3.1 【詞尾變化】udāram 是 udāra 的單數對格形，所以字典查 udāra。

3.2 【摩威梵英,p185】

3.2.1 mf(*ā* and *ī*)n.（*ṛ*), high , lofty , exalted ; great , best ; noble , illustrious , generous ; upright , honest MBh. ; liberal , gentle , munificent ; sincere , proper , right ; eloquent ; unperplexed ; exciting , effecting RV. ; active , energetic Sarvad. ;

3.2.2 m. rising fog or vapour（in some cases personified as spirits or deities）AV.; a sort of grain with long stalks ; a figure in rhetoric（attributing nobleness to an inanimate object）.

3.3 【梵漢辭典,p1317】（形容詞）鼓舞，高揚，高大的，多量的，著名的卓越的，名門的，有威嚴的，高聲的，愉快的，巨大的；（經文）上，最上，妙，上妙，殊妙，微妙，勝，妙勝，最勝，勝者，大乘，廣，廣大，大，高大，勝廣大，有多，深，甚深，良，好，珍，尊貴，豪貴，微妙（甚可樂）。

4. मञ्चन्ति muñcanti 形容詞　放射；放送；演說

4.1 【詞尾變化】muñcanti 是√muc 的現在式第三人稱複數形，所以字典查√muc。

4.2 資料前面已有說明。

5. स्वकस्वकेषु svaka-svakeṣu 形容詞　在各自

5.1 【詞尾變化】svakeṣu 是 svaka 的於格複數形，所以字典查 svaka。

5.2 【摩威梵英,p1278】

5.2.1 mf（*akā* or *ikā*）n. = *sva* , one's own , my own MBh. ;

5.2.2 m. one of one's own people , a relation , kinsman , friend ;

5.2.3 pl. one's own people , friends;

5.2.4 n. one's own goods property , wealth , riches MBh.

5.3 【梵漢辭典,p1253】（形容詞）自己的；（經文）自，己。（陽性）自己部族的人，親戚，朋友。（複數）自己的人民，朋友們；（中性）自己的物品，財產；（經文）自事。

【筆者試譯】：（佛陀們）用非常美好的聲音，
在各自國土當中宣說著，
用百千萬億（很多無可計數）的譬喻，
來展現（解說）覺悟的教法。

【什公漢譯】：梵音深妙，令人樂聞，各於世界，講說正法，
種種因緣，以無量喻，照明佛法，開悟眾生。

【英 譯 本】：They let go forth, each in his own field, a
Deep, sublime, wonderful voice, while proclaiming
The Buddha-laws by means of myriads of kotis of
Illustrations and proofs.

【信譯研究】：信譯。和上一首一樣用八句詩來對譯梵詩四句偈。

【第九頌】

दुःखेन संपीडित ये च सत्त्वा
जातीजराखिन्नमना अजानकाः।
तेषां प्रकाशेन्ति प्रशान्तनिर्वृतिं
दुःखस्य अन्तो अयु भिक्षवे ति॥९॥

【羅馬譯音】

duḥkhena saṁpīḍita ye ca sattvā
jātījarākhinnamanā ajānakāḥ|
teṣāṁ prakāśenti praśāntanirvṛtiṁ
duḥkhasya anto ayu bhikṣave ti||9||

【句義解析】

duḥkhena saṁpīḍita ye ca sattvā
jātī-jarā-khinna-manā ajānakāḥ|
teṣāṁ prakāśenti praśānta-nirvṛtiṁ
duḥkhasya anto ayu bhikṣave ti||9||

【辭彙研究】

1. संपीडित saṁpīḍita 形容詞／過去被動分詞　所逼迫

1.1 【詞尾變化】沒有詞尾變化。

1.2 【摩威梵英,p1173】to compress , press or squeeze together , torment , harass , force（ind. p. -pīḍya = ` by pressure or force ' , ` forcibly '）MBh.; to reckon up , calculate together Su1ryas. Kull. ;（in astron.）to obscure , eclipse.

1.3 【梵漢辭典,p1104】（過去被動分詞）（形容詞）壓榨，壓擠；使痛苦，使困惑；一起壓擠（經文）遭苦，所逼迫。

2. जाती jātī 陰性形容詞　生

2.1 【詞尾變化】沒有詞尾變化。

2.2 【摩威梵英,p418】

2.2.1 f. = -ti;

2.2.2 f. birth , production, MBh. ; re-birth ; the form of existence（as man , animal）fixed by birth ;position assigned by birth , rank , caste , family , race , lineage MBh. ; kind , genus（opposed to species）, species（opposed to individual）, class; the generic properties（opposed to the specific ones）; natural disposition to; the character of a species , genuine or true state of anything MBh ; reduction of fractions to a common denominator ; a self-confuting reply（founded merely on similarity or dissimilarity）;（in rhet.）a particular figure of speech ; a class of metres ; a manner of singing ; a fire-place ;（=-tī）mace , nutmeg; Jasminum grandiflorum;

2.3 【梵漢辭典,p527】（陰性形容詞）（經文）生。

3. जरा jarā 形容詞　年老的

3.1 【詞尾變化】沒有詞尾變化。

3.2 【摩威梵英,p414】f. old age.

3.3 【梵漢辭典,p525】（陰性形容詞）消耗的，年老的，老邁；（經文）老，衰老，耆年。

4. खिन्न khinna 形容詞　疲累

4.1 【詞尾變化】沒有詞尾變化。

4.2 【摩威梵英,p340】mfn. depressed , distressed , suffering pain or uneasiness MBh. ; wearied , exhausted.

4.3 【梵漢辭典,p595】（過去被動分詞）（形容詞）（經文）厭，卷，厭倦，帶厭倦，疲倦，皮必，勞卷，皮驗，退，懈退，沮壞，頓乏。

5. मना manā 形容詞　慾望

5.1 【詞尾變化】沒有詞尾變化。

5.2 【摩威梵英,p784】f. devotion , attachment , zeal , eagerness RV. ; envy , jealousy.

5.3 【梵漢辭典,p697】（陰性形容詞）慾望，熱心，專注，忌妒。

6. अजानकाः ajānakāḥ 形容詞　無知

6.1 【詞尾變化】ajānakāḥ 是 ajānaka 的複數主格形，梵英辭典找不到，梵漢辭典找得到，疑似佛教混合梵文，由於 a 表示相反的意思，所以字典查 jānaka。

6.2 【摩威梵英,p, jānaka】

6.2.1 m.（fr. *janakā*）patr. of Kratu-vid; of āyasthūṇa（also -*ki*）;

6.2.2（*ī*）f. patr. of Sitā MBh.; a metre of 4 X 24 syllables.

6.2.3 m.（*j□ā*）knower（a Buddha）Divyāv.;

6.2.4 pl. the Buddhists Sūtrakṛit.（Prākṛit）.

6.3 【梵漢辭典,p53, a-jānaka】（形容詞）（經文）不知，無知，無知者，無智愚人，不生，無生。

7. प्रशान्त praśānta 形容詞／過去被動分詞　寂靜

7.1 【詞尾變化】沒有詞尾變化。

7.2 【摩威梵英,p695】

7.2.1 mfn. tranquillized , calm , quiet , composed , indifferent MBh.;（in augury） auspicious , boni ominis; extinguished , ceased , allayed , removed , destroyed , dead MBh.;

7.2.2 -kāma mfn. one whose desires are calmed , content BhP. ;

7.2.3 -cāritramati m. N. of a Bodhi-sattva;

7.2.4 -cārin m. pl. `walking tranquilly' ,（prob.）N. of a class of deities.;

7.2.5 -citta mfn. `tranquil-minded' , calm ;

7.2.6 -ceṣṭa mfn. one whose efforts have ceased , resting;

7.2.7 -tā f. tranquillity of mind MBh. ;

7.2.8 -dhī mfn. = -citta BhP. ;

7.2.9 -bādha mfn. one who has all calamities or hindrances quelled; -bhūmipāla mfn. `having the kings extinguished' , without a king（said of the earth）;

7.2.10 -mūrti mfn. of tranquil appearance. ;

7.2.11 -rāga m. N. of a man. ;

7.2.12 -viniścaya-pratihārya-nirdeśa m. N. of a Buddh. ;

7.2.13 -vinīteśvara m. N. of a divine being;

7.2.14 -tātman mfn. `tranquil-souled' , composed in mind , peaceful , calm. BhP. ;

7.2.15 -tārāti mfn. one whose enemies have been pacified or destroyed

7.2.16 -tārja mfn. one whose strength has ceased , weakened , prostrated ;

7.2.17 -tolmuka mfn. extinguished ;

7.3 【梵漢辭典,p932】(過去被動分詞)(形容詞)(經文)寂，極寂，勝寂，寂靜，邊寂靜，最極寂靜，至極寂靜，寂滅，寂定，寂然，銷滅，除滅，滅盡，盡，息，休息，靜默，極柔善。

8. निर्वृतिं nirvṛtiṁ 形容詞　涅槃

8.1 【詞尾變化】nirvṛtiṁ 根據連音規則是 nirvṛtim 變化而來，而 nirvṛtim 是 nirvṛti 的單數對格形，所以字典查 nirvṛti。

8.2 【摩威梵英,p558】

8.2.1 f. complete satisfaction or happiness , bliss , pleasure , delight MBh. ; emancipation , final beatitude（= nir-vāṇa）Bhām.; attainment of rest ;

extinction（of a lamp）; destruction , death ;

8.2.2 m. N. of a man; of a son of Vṛishṇi Pur. ;

8.2.3 -*cakśus* m. N. of a Ṛiśi;

8.2.4 -*mat* mfn. quite satisfied , happy Mālatīm. ;

8.2.5 -*śatru* w.r. for *ni-vṛtta-ś-* ;

8.2.6 -*sthāna* n. place of eternal bliss.

8.3 【梵漢辭典,p803】（陰性名詞）內心的寂靜，滿足，喜悅，愉快，幸福，慶福；（燈火的）熄滅；（經文）滅渡，及滅，寂靜，解脫，出罹，磨滅，涅槃。

9. अन्तो anto 形容詞　邊際；結束

9.1 【詞尾變化】anto 根據連音規則是 antaḥ 變化而來，而 antaḥ 爲 anta 的單數主格形。所以字典查 anta。

9.2 【摩威梵英,p42】

9.2.1 m. end , limit , boundary , term ; end of a texture ; end , conclusion ; end of life , death , destruction（in these latter senses some times neut.）; a final syllable , termination ; last word of a compound ; pause , settlement , definite ascertainment , certainty ; whole amount ; border , outskirt; nearness , proximity , presence ; inner part , inside ; condition , nature ;

9.2.2（e）loc. c. in the end , at last ; in the inside ;

9.2.3（am）ind. as far as ;

9.2.4（mfn.）, near , handsome , agreeable.

9.3 【梵漢辭典,p103】（陽性）（中性）（名詞）端，邊緣，界線，接近，結局，死；末端的文字，最終語；（經文）至，末，終，盡，際，邊，邊際，後，後際，近，面。

10. अयु ayu 形容詞／名詞　生命

10.1 【詞尾變化】兩辭典均無見收此字，疑爲 āyu 的轉寫。所以字典查 āyu。

10.2 【摩威梵英,p148】

10.2.1 mfn. living , movable RV. VS. ;

10.2.2 us m. a living being , man ; living beings collectively , mankind RV. ; son , descendant , offspring ; family , lineage RV. ; a divine personification presiding over life RV; N. of fire（as the son of Purūravas and Urvaśī）MBh. ; N. of a man persecuted by Indra RV. ; N. of several other men MBh. ; N. of a king of frogs MBh. ;

10.2.3（u）n. 〔and（us）m. L.〕 life , duration of life RV.

10.3 【梵漢辭典,p230】（形容詞）活動的，活的；（陽性名詞）生物，人類，子，子孫，血統，門第；（中性名詞）生命，壽命。

11. भिक्षवेति bhikṣave 名詞　由比丘；由出家

11.1 【詞尾變化】bhikṣave 是 bhikṣu 的單數爲格形，所以字典查 bhikṣu。

11.2 資料前面已有說明。

12. ति ti 副詞　如上所說

12.1 【詞尾變化】ti 是 iti 的省略寫法，字典查 iti。

12.2 【摩威梵英,p446,ti】for iti（after kā）.

12.3 【摩威梵英,p165,iti】ind.（fr. pronominal base 3. i）, in this manner , thus（in its original signification iti refers to something that has been said or thought , or lays stress on what precedes ; in the Brāhmaṇas it is often equivalent to `as you know' , reminding the hearer or reader of certain customs , conditions. supposed to be known to him）. In quotations of every kind iti means that the preceding words are the very words which some person has or might have spoken , and placed thus at the end of a speech it serves the purpose of inverted commas. It may often have reference merely to what is passing in the mind iti is sometimes followed by evam , iva , or a demonstrative pronoun pleonastically. iti may form an adverbial compound with the name of an author. It may also express the act of calling attention. It may have some other significations e.g. something additional, order , arrangement specific or distinctive , and identity. It is used by native commentators after quoting a rule to express `according to such a rule'.（In the Śatapatha-brāhmaṇa ti occurs for iti ; cf. Prākṛit ti and tti.）

12.4 【梵漢辭典,p512】（副詞）如上（所述）〔用於語言或思想的引用，此如同引用符號，普通在接近句子前後使用，屬間接之代言性質，另外亦用於列舉，附有 ca 字時表示不然之意〕；（經文）然，如是，此事，如此，言，前說，相。

【筆者試譯】：有情眾生們讓痛苦所逼迫，
生存，年老，疲累，慾望，無知
他們（佛陀們）宣告用涅槃寂靜，
（來）結束生命的痛苦。

【什公漢譯】：若人遭苦，厭老病死，爲說涅槃，盡諸苦際。

【英 譯 本】：And to the ignorant creatures who are
oppressed with toils and distressed in mind by birth
and old age, they announce the bliss of Rest, saying:
This is the end of trouble, O monks.

【信譯研究】：信譯。

【第十頌】

उदारस्थामाधिगताश्च ये नराः
पुण्यैरुपेतास्तथ बुद्धदर्शनैः।
प्रत्येकयानं च वदन्ति तेषां
संवर्णयन्तो इम धर्मनेत्रीम्॥१०॥

【羅馬譯音】

udārasthāmādhigatāśca ye narāḥ
puṇyairupetāstatha buddhadarśanaiḥ|
pratyekayānaṁ ca vadanti teṣāṁ
saṁvarṇayanto ima dharmanetrīm||10||

【句義解析】

udāra-sthāmādhigatāś ca ye narāḥ
puṇyair upetās tatha buddha-darśanaiḥ|
Pratyeka-yānaṁ ca vadanti teṣāṁ
saṁvarṇayanto ima dharma-netrīm||10||

【辭彙研究】

1. स्थामाधिगताश्च sthāmādhigatāśca 形容詞　獲得果位

1.1 【詞尾變化】sthāmādhigatāśca 根據連音規則，是 sthāma-adhigatāḥ ca 變化過來，而 sthāma，根據學者江島惠教的看法，就是 sthāman）。而 adhigatāḥ 則是 adhigata 的複數主格形，所以字典查 sthāman-adhigata。

1.2 【摩威梵英,p1264, sthāman】n. station , seat , place AV. ; strength , power SaddhP. ; the neighing of a horse MBh.

1.3 【摩威梵英,p20, adhigata】mfn. found , obtained , acquired ; gone over , studied , learnt.

1.4 【梵漢辭典,p1210, sthāman】（中性名詞）位置，座位，地點，力，勢力；（經文）力，勢，身力，威神，勇銳，威德勢。

1.5 【梵漢辭典,p31, adhigata】（過去被動分詞）（經文）得，證，證得，通達，知，所知，獲，橫取。

2. पुण्यैर् puṇyair 形容詞　功德，福德

2.1 【詞尾變化】puṇyair 根據連音規則是從 puṇyaiḥ 變化過來，而 puṇyaiḥ 是 puṇya 的工具格複數，所以字典查 puṇya。

2.2 【摩威梵英,p632】

2.2.1 mf（*ā*）n. auspicious , propitious , fair , pleasant , good , right , virtuous , meritorious , pure , holy , sacred RV. ; ni. N. of a poet ; of another man Buddh. ;

2.2.2 m. or n. N. of a lake MBh. ;

2.2.3 （*ā*）f. holy basil ; Physalis Flexuosa ; N. of a daughter of Kratu and Saṃnati ;

2.2.4 n.（f. *ā*）the good or right , virtue , purity , good work , meritorious act , moral or religious merit MBh.; a religious ceremony（esp. one performed by a wife in order to retain her husband's affections and to obtain a son ; also -*ka*）MBh. Hariv. ; a brick trough for watering cattle.

2.3 【梵漢辭典,p987】（形容詞）吉祥的，吉利的，幸運的，相符的，美麗的舒適的，芳香的，善良的，有德的，正確的，有價值的，純粹的，清淨的，神聖的；（經文）勝，福，善，福德，福，福行，福利，福慶，福祚，福業，功德，善根，善輪。

3. उपेतास् upetās 形容詞　成就

3.1 【詞尾變化】upetās 根據學者江島惠教的看法，意思等同 upeta)，所以字典查 upeta。

3.2 【摩威梵英,p215】

3.2.1 mfn. one who has come near or approached , one who has betaken himself to , approached（for protection）, arrived at , abiding in MBh. ; one who has obtained or entered into any state or condition , one who has undertaken（e.g. a vow）MBh.; come to , fallen to the share of ;（a pupil）who has approached（a teacher）, initiated; accompanied by , endowed with , furnished with , having , possessing MBh.; one who has approached（a woman sexually）.

3.3 【梵漢辭典,p1349】（過去被動分詞）（經文）具足，具，具足，具修，有，成，成就，圓滿。

4. दर्शनैः darśanaiḥ 形容詞　凝視；看見

4.1 【詞尾變化】darśanaiḥ 是 darśana 的複數工具格形，所字典查 darśana。

4.2 【摩威梵英,p471】

4.2.1 mf（ī）n. showing. seeing , looking at ; knowing ; exhibiting , teaching MBh. ;

4.2.2 n. seeing , observing , looking , noticing , observation , perception RV. MBh. ; ocular perception ; the eye-sight; inspection , examination; visiting ; audience , meeting; instr. with or without *saha*; in comp; experiencing BhP. ; foreseeing ; contemplating ; apprehension , judgment , discernment , understanding , intellect; opinion ; intention; view , doctrine , philosophical system MBh.; the eye ; the becoming visible or known , presence MBh.; appearance（before the judge）; the being mentioned（in any authoritative text）MBh. ; a vision , dream; appearance , aspect , semblance MBh.; colour ; showing, a mirror ; a sacrifice ;

4.3 【梵漢辭典,p350】（形容詞）凝視，會意的，展示，教授的；（經文）看，關，睹，見，見照，望，如。

5. यानं yānaṁ 形容詞／名詞　乘

5.1 【詞尾變化】yānaṁ 根據連音規則是從 yānam 變化過來，而 yānam 則是 yāna 的單數對格，所以字典查 yāna。

5.2 【摩威梵英,p849】

5.2.1 mfn. leading , conducting ;

5.2.2 f. a path , course;

5.2.3 n. a journey , travel ; going , moving , riding , marching. to（loc. or comp.）or upon（instr. or comp.）or against（acc. with *prati*）MBh. ; a vehicle of any kind , carriage , waggon , vessel , ship , litter , palanquin RV. ;（with Buddhists）the vehicle or method of arriving at knowledge , the means of release from repeated births（there are either 3 systems , the *śrāvaka-yāna* , the *pratyeka-buddha-y-* or *pratyeka-y-* , and the *mahā-y-* ; or more generally only 2 , the *mahā-yāna* or `Great method ' and the *hina-y-* or ` Lesser method ' ; sometimes there is only ` One Vehicle' , the eka-yāna , or ` one way to beatitude'）SaddhP. Dharmas.

5.3 【梵漢辭典,p1504】（形容詞）引導，帶路，帶領，行進，行走，騎行，前往，通路，路線，運輸工具，馬車或戰車，運載工具，（經文）乘，車乘，車輿，輿，騎乘，車，大車。

6. संवर्णयन्तो saṁvarṇayanto 動詞　讚歎

6.1 【詞尾變化】saṁvarṇayanto 根據連音規則是 saṁvarṇayantaḥ 變化而來，saṁvarṇayantaḥ 是 saṁ-√varṇ 現在主動分詞的主格複數形，所以字典查 saṁ-√varṇ。

6.2 【摩威梵英,p1114】P. -varṇayati , to communicate , narrate , tell MBh. ; to praise commend , approve , sanction MBh. SaddhP.

6.3 【梵漢辭典,p1119】（經文）讚嘆，讚，稱讚，稱探，讚說。

7. नेत्रीम् netrīm 形容詞　法眼；佛法

7.1 【詞尾變化】netrīm 是 netrī 的對格單數形，所以字典查 netrī。

7.2 【摩威梵英】沒有資料。說明這個字並非標準梵文。

7.3 【艾格混梵,p311】

7.3.1（=Pali netti）1.adj. leading, conducive;

7.3.2 Way, method, rule, usage;

7.3.3 The way, of the law, of Buddha, *rarely* alone.

7.4 【梵漢辭典,p775】（陰性名詞）（經文）眼，（法）眼，正法，法流，法輪，我法，所說法論。

【筆者試譯】：那些人獲得成果（修成正果），
成就了功德，能夠看到如來佛祖，
他們（爲他人）演說緣覺乘（獨覺乘）佛法，
讚歎這個佛法（的好處）。

【什公漢譯】：若人有福，曾供養佛，志求勝法，爲說緣覺。

【英 譯 本】：And those who are possessed of strength
and vigour and who have acquired merit by virtue
or earnest belief in the Buddhas, they show the
vehicle of the Pratyekabuddhas, by observing this rule of the law.

【信譯研究】：信譯。不過，英譯本把「darśanaiḥ」（看見）翻成「信仰」。鳩摩羅什則翻譯成「供養」，就等於把原文的意思更加延伸，即不論看到眞的佛陀，或是塑像佛陀，只要有供養，將供品上呈佛陀，都算看到了佛陀。

【第十一頌】

ये चापि अन्ये सुगतस्य पुत्रा
अनुत्तरं ज्ञान गवेषमाणाः।
विविधां क्रियां कुर्विषु सर्वकालं
तेषां पि बोधाय वदन्ति वर्णम्॥११॥

【羅馬譯音】

ye cāpi anye sugatasya putrā
anuttaraṁ jñāna gaveṣamāṇāḥ|
vividhāṁ kriyāṁ kurviṣu sarvakālaṁ
teṣāṁ pi bodhāya vadanti varṇam||11||

【句義解析】

ye cāpi anye sugatasya putrā
anuttaraṁ jñāna gaveṣamāṇāḥ|
vividhāṁ kriyāṁ kurviṣu sarva-kālaṁ
teṣāṁ pi bodhāya vadanti varṇam||11||

【辭彙研究】

1. गवषमाणाः gaveṣamāṇāḥ 過去中間分詞／形容詞　尋求

1.1 【詞尾變化】gaveṣamāṇāḥ 是√gaveṣ 的過去中間分詞的主格複數形，所字典查√gaveṣ。

1.2 【摩威梵英,p351】cl. 1. -ṣate , to seek , search or inquire for（acc.）SaddhP. -ṣayati , -te MBh.

1.3 【梵漢辭典,p454】（過去中間分詞）（形容詞）尋求，探求；（經文）求，推求，窺求。

2. क्रियां kriyāṁ 形容詞　從事

2.1 【詞尾變化】kriyāṁ 根據連音規則是從 kriyām 變化過來，而 kriyām 則是 kriyā 的單數對格，所以字典查 kriyā。

2.2 【摩威梵英,p320】f. , doing , performing , performance , occupation with（in comp.）, business , act , action , undertaking , activity , work , labour.; bodily action , exercise of the limbs ;（in Gr.）action（as the general idea expressed by any verb）, verb.（according to later grammarians a verb is of two kinds , sakarma-kriyā , ` active' , and akarma-k- , `intransitive '）; a noun of action ; a literary work; medical treatment or practice , applying a remedy , cure（see sama-kriya-tva and viṣama-k-）Sus3r. ; a religious rite or ceremony , sacrificial act , sacrifice MBh. ; with caramā , `the last ceremony' , rites performed immediately after death , obsequies , purificatory rites（as ablution）MBh. ; religious action , worship BhP. ; Religious Action（personified as a daughter of Dakśa and wife of Dharma MBh.; or as a daughter of Kardama and wife of Kratu BhP.）; judicial investigation（by human means , as by witnesses , documents , &c. , or by superhuman means , as by various ordeals）Comm. on; atonement ; disquisition ; study ; means , expedient.

2.3 【梵漢辭典,p611】（陰性名詞／形容詞）製作，構成，實行，工作，業務，處理，行動，行爲，勞務，操心，努力（經文）作，能作，所做，動作，造，造作，行，果，業，業用，事業，事，做事，所做事，用，力用，作用。

3. कुर्विषु kurviṣu　動詞／分詞／形容詞　實行，做

3.1 【詞尾變化】kurviṣu 是 kurvi 的複數於格形，但根據學者江島惠教的看法，〔註 34〕kurvi 的字根是√kṛ，所以字典查√kṛ。

3.2 【摩威梵英,p】

3.2.1 to do , make , perform , accomplish , cause , effect , prepare , undertake RV.; to do anything for the advantage or injury of another（gen. or loc.）MBh.; to execute , carry out（as an order or command）; to manufacture , prepare , work at , elaborate , build ib. ; to form or construct one thing out of another（abl. or instr.）; to employ , use , make use of（instr.）MBh.; to compose , describe; to cultivate; to accomplish any period , bring to completion , spend; to place , put , lay , bring , lead , take hold of; *haste* or *pāṇau-kṛ* , to take by the hand , marry ; *hṛdayena-kṛ* , to place in one's heart , love Mṛcch. ; *hṛdi-kṛ* , to take to heart , mind , think over , consider ; manasi-kṛ; to determine , purpose ; *vaśe-kṛ* , to place in subjection , become master of; to direct the thoughts , mind ,towards any object , turn the attention to , resolve upon , determine on ;to think of（acc.）R. i , 21 , 14 ; to make , render RV.; to procure for another , bestow , grant（with gen. or loc.）RV.; Ā. to procure for one's self , appropriate , assume; to give aid , help any one to get anything（dat.）RV. VS. ; to make liable to（dat.）RV. ; to injure , violate ; to appoint , institute ; to give an order , commission ; to cause to get rid of , free from; to proceed , act , put in practice ; to worship , sacrifice RV. ; to make a sound（svaram or śabdam）MBh. , utter , pronounce, pronounce any formula ; to divide , separate or break up into parts ; to make like or similar ,

〔註 34〕請見江島惠教等編《梵藏漢法華經原典總索引》，東京：靈友會出版，1988 年出版。頁 285。

consider equivalent; to reduce anything to , cause to become , make subject. The above senses of *kṛ* may be variously modified or almost infinitely extended according to the noun with which this root is connected , as in the following examples: , to contract friendship with ; to honour ; to reign ; to show affection ;, to perform any one's command or wish or request; to do one's duty Mn.; to offer a libation of Water to the dead ; to perform ablutions ; to practise the use of weapons MBh. ;, to breathe the flute; to inflict punishment; %{kAlaM-kR} , to bring one's time to an end i.e. to die ; to be long in doing anything , delay ; to place in one's mind , think of , meditate MBh. ; to place on one's the head ; to place on one's head , obey , honour. Very rarely in Veda , but commonly in the auxiliarily used to form the periphrastical perfect of verbs , especially of causatives ; in Veda some other forms of *kṛ* are used in a similar way;

3.2.2 3. pl. according to ,to cause to act or do , cause another to perform , have anything made or done by another; to cause to place or put , have anything placed , put upon , Sometimes the Caus. of *kṛ* is used for the simple verb or without a causal signification; to wish to make or do , intend to do , design , intend , begin , strive after AV.; to wish to sacrifice or worship AV. to do repeatedly RV. ;

3.3 【梵漢辭典,p605】（動詞）（分詞／形容詞）作，為，形成，構成，實行，履行，生長，施行，成就，結交，顯示，表示，實施，準備，調理，組織，耕作，因～而做，以～為；（經文）起，作，起作，修作，施作，為，能修，發，能成辨，奉行。

4. कालं kālaṁ　名詞／形容詞　一個時間點

4.1 【詞尾變化】kālaṁ 根據連音規則是從 kālam 變化過來，而 kālam 是 kāla 的單數對格。

4.2 【摩威梵英,p278】

4.2.1 m. a fixed or right point of time , a space of time , time（in general）AV; the proper time or season for MBh.; occasion , circumstance MBh. ; season ; meal-time; hour; a period of time , time of the world; a section , part ; the end; death by age; time, destiny , fate MBh.; time(as destroying all things）, death , time of death;

4.2.2（*am*）acc. ind. for a certain time ,in the course of time MBh.; with. ; during a long time MBh. ; after a long time;

4.2.3（āt）abl. ind. in the course of time ;

4.3 【梵漢辭典,p548】（陽性名詞／形容詞）適當的季節，時；機會；季節；半日，時間，齡；時代；韻律，時陳，命運，死，死神。（經文）時，時節，十分，時限；世。

【筆者試譯】：而同樣地，也有佛陀的孩子們（佛子們），
尋求無上（正等正覺）的門徑（知識），
在所有的世間從事各種（修）行，
佛陀們也爲他們說獲證菩提的道理。

【什公漢譯】：若有佛子，修種種行，求無上慧，爲說淨道。

【英 譯 本】：And the other sons of the Sugata who, striving
after superior knowledge, have constantly accomplished
their varous tasks, them also they admonish
to enlightenment.

【信譯研究】：信譯。

【第十二頌】

शृणोमि पश्यामि च मञ्जुघोष
इह स्थितो ईदृशकानि तत्र।
अन्या विशेषाण सहस्रकोट्यः
प्रदेशमात्रं ततु वर्णयिष्ये॥१२॥

【羅馬譯音】

śṛṇomi paśyāmi ca mañjughoṣa
iha sthito īdṛśakāni tatra|
anyā viśeṣāṇa sahasrakoṭyaḥ
pradeśamātraṁ tatu varṇayiṣye||12||

【句義解析】

śṛṇomi paśyāmi ca mañjughoṣa
iha sthito īdṛśakāni tatra|
anyā viśeṣāṇa sahasra-koṭyaḥ
pradeśa-mātraṁ tatu varṇayiṣye||12||

【辭彙研究】

1. शृणोमि śṛṇomi 形容詞　聽到，聽說

1.1 【詞尾變化】śṛṇomi 是√śru 的第一人稱現在式形，所以字典查√śru。

1.2 【摩威梵英,p1101】cl. 5., to hear , listen or attend to anything（acc.）, give ear to any one（acc. or gen.）, hear or learn anything about（acc.）or from , or that anything is（two acc.）RV. ; to hear（from a teacher）, study , learn MBh. ; to be attentive , be obedient , obey MBh. ; and in RV. with pass. meaning ; to be heard or perceived or learnt about（acc.）or from RV. ; to be celebrated or renowned , be known as , pass for , be called（nom.）RV. ; to be heard or learnt（from a teacher）; to be taught or stated（in a book）; to be heard i.e. pronounced or employed（as a sound or word）, to cause to be heard or learnt , announce , proclaim , declare RV.; to cause to hear , inform , instruct , communicate , relate , tell MBh., to be informed of（acc.）MBh., to wish or like to hear（acc.）, desire to attend or listen to（dat.）RV.; to attend upon , serve , obey（acc. , rarely gen.）MBh, to wait upon , be at the service of（acc.）.

1.3 【梵漢辭典,p1203】（動詞）聽聞，關於，聽到，學習，研究；（經文）聞，聽，聽聞，聽受，樂聞，諦聽。

2. मञ्जुघोष mañjughoṣa 形容詞　文殊師利菩薩

2.1 【詞尾變化】沒有詞尾變化。

2.2 【摩威梵英,p774】

2.2.1 mfn. uttering a sweet sound BhP. ;

2.2.2 m. a dove ; = *-śrī* SaddhP. ;

2.2.3（*ā*）f. N. of an Apsaras ; of a Suraṅgana Siṇhās.

2.3 【梵漢辭典,p706】（形容詞）發出甜美聲音的；（經文）和雅音，音深妙。（陽性）（經文）文殊師利。

3. ईदृशकानि īdṛśakāni 形容詞　如此的

3.1 【詞尾變化】īdṛśakāni 是 īdṛśaka 的複數對格形，所以字典查 īdṛśaka。

3.2 【摩威梵英,p170】mf（ikā）n. endowed with such qualities , such; 〔with the final syllables dṛś and dṛśa of these words.

3.3 【梵漢辭典,p503】（形容詞）（經文）若斯。

4. वशेषाण viśeṣāṇa 形容詞　個別的

4.1 【詞尾變化】viśeṣāṇa 疑似 viśeṣaṇa，由於該字並未見收於兩本字典，且 viśeṣa 之八格並未有 viśeṣāṇa 的變化，故引用之。

4.2 【摩威梵英,p991】

4.2.1 mfn. distinguishing , discriminative , specifying , qualifying ; distinctive（as a property）;

4.2.2 n. the act of distinguishing , distinction , discrimination , particularization BhP. ; a distinguishing mark or attribute MBh. ;（in gram.）`differencer' , a word which particularizes or defines（another word which is called *vi-śeṣya*）, attribute , adjective , adverb , apposition , predicate ; a species , kind MBh. ; surpassing , excelling ;（in rhet.）= viśeṣokti;

4.2.3 -*khaṇḍana* n. -*jñāna-vādārtha* m. N. of wks. ;

4.2.4 -*tā* f. the state of a distinguisher or of distinguishing; individuality ;

4.2.5 -*traya-vaiyarthya n.* N. of wk. ;

4.2.6 -*tva* n. -*tā* . ; adjectival nature ;

4.2.7 -*dvaya-vaiyarthya* n. N. of wk. ;

4.2.8 -*pada* n. a title of honour ;

4.2.9 -*mātraprayoga* m. the use of an adjective for a substantive;

4.2.10 -*viśeṣya-tā* f. -*viśeṣyabhāva* m. the relation of predicate and subject;

4.2.11 -*vat* mfn. endowed with discrimination ; having a distinguishing attribute;

4.2.12 -*varga* m. N. of a ch. of the Śabda-ratnāvali lexicon.

4.3 【梵漢辭典,p1458】（形容詞）有區別的，特殊化的（中性形容詞）有差別的，特殊的品種，種類，傑出的；（經文）差別，能別，檢別，分別。

5. प्रदेश pradeśa 名詞　地點

5.1 【詞尾變化】沒有詞尾變化。

5.2 【摩威梵英,p680】

5.2.1 m.（f. *ā*）pointing out , showing , indication , direction , decision , determination ; appeal to a precedent ; an example（in grammar , law）MBh.; a spot , region , place , country , district MBh. ; a short while（see comp. below）; a wall ; a short span（measured from the tip of the thumb to that of the forefinger）;（with Jainas）one of the obstacles to liberation ;

5.2.2 -*kārin* m. N. of a kind of ascetic ;

5.2.3 -*bhāj* mfn. of short duration;

5.2.4 -*vat* mfn. possessing or occupying a place;

5.2.5 -*vartin* mfn. = -bhāj（-*ti-tvā* f.）;

5.2.6 -*śāstra* n. a book containing examples MBh. ;

5.2.7 -*stha* mfn. = -bhāj; being or situated in a district.

5.3 【梵漢辭典,p904】（陽性）稱呼，言及，決定，明示，提出前例；案例，地點；廠所，部位，暫時；（經文）言，分，一分，少分，處，所，處所，方處，域，邊，國，地，陸地，高地，處，相，此處，如是處。

6. मात्रं mātraṁ 名詞 數量

6.1 【詞尾變化】mātraṁ 根據連音規則是從 mātram 變化過來，而 mātram 是 mātra 的單數對格形，所以字典查 mātra。

6.2 【摩威梵英,p804】

6.2.1 m. a Brāhman of the lowest order i.e. only by birth;

6.2.2（*ā*）f. see s.v. ;

6.2.3 n. an element , elementary matter BhP. ;（ifc.）measure , quantity , sum , size , duration , measure of any kind（whether of height , depth , breadth , length , distance , time or number, a finger's breadth; *artha-mātram* , a certain sum of money; *krośa. mātre* , at the distance of a; *māsa-mātre* , in a month; *śata-mātram* , a hundred in number）; the full or simple measure of anything , the whole or totality , the one thing and no more , often = nothing but , entirely , only;

6.2.4 mf（*ā* and *ī*）n.（ifc.）having the measure of i.e. as large or high or long or broad or deep or far or much or many; Possessing（only）as much as or no more than; amounting (only) to (pleonastically after numerals) ; being nothing but , simply or merely.

6.3 【梵漢辭典,p720】（中性）要素，大小，高度，深度，長度，寬度，距離，分亮，總額，持續，間隔；（經文）量，如，唯，但有，分齊，但，但是，少，微。

7. ततु tatu 副詞　從那裡，因此

7.1 【詞尾變化】根據江島惠教的看法，tatu 等同 tatas），故字典查 tatas。

7.2 【摩威梵英,p432】ind.（ta-tas , correlative of ya-tas）used for the abl.（sg. du. and pl.) of tad RV. AV. ; from that place , thence RV. AV. ; in that place , there MBh. ; thither; thereupon , then , after that , afterwards（sometimes corresponding to preceding particles like agre , puras , purvam , prathamam , prāk; corresponding to prathama RV.; also correlative of yad, yatra, yadā, yadi, ced; often superfluous after an ind. p. or after tadā or atha）; from that , in consequence of that , for that reason , consequently MBh.

7.3 【梵漢辭典,p1281】（副詞）在那裡，從那裡，向那邊，在那邊，在其上，因此，那時，當時（經文）然後，從彼處，爾時，又，是故。

8. वर्णयिष्ये varṇayiṣye 動詞　解說

8.1 【詞尾變化】varṇayiṣye 是√varṇ 的未來式第一人稱單數形，所以字典查√varṇ。

8.2 資料前面已有說明。

【筆者試譯】：文殊師利菩薩，我聽了、看了，
此刻他們站著，向那裡，
其他的數量眾多的
地點（佛國淨土）因爲那裡（發生的事情）而解說。

【什公漢譯】：文殊師利，我住於此，見聞若斯，及千億事，
如是眾多，今當略說。

【英 譯 本】：From this place, O Mañgughosha, I see and hear such things and thousands of kotis of other particulars besides; I will only describe some of them.

【信譯研究】：信譯。特別用六句偈來翻譯梵詩四句頌。

【第十三頌】

पश्यामि क्षेत्रेषु बहूषु चापि

ये बोधिसत्त्वा यथ गङ्गवालिकाः।

कोटीसहस्राणि अनल्पकानि

विविधेन वीर्येण जनेन्ति बोधिम्॥१३॥

【羅馬譯音】

paśyāmi kṣetreṣu bahūṣu cāpi

ye bodhisattvā yatha gaṅgavālikāḥ|

koṭīsahasrāṇi analpakāni

vividhena vīryeṇa janenti bodhim||13||

【句義解析】

paśyāmi kṣetreṣu bahūṣu cāpi

ye bodhisattvā yatha Gaṅga-vālikāḥ|

koṭī-sahasrāṇi analpakāni

vividhena vīryeṇa janenti bodhim||13||

【辭彙研究】

1. गण्ग gaṅga 名詞 恆河

1.1 【詞尾變化】gaṅga 等於 gaṅgā（摩威梵英,p341），故字典查 gaṅgā。

1.2 【摩威梵英,p341】f.（√gam）` swift-goer' , the river Ganges（personified and considered as the eldest daughter of Himavat and Mena ; as the wife of Śāntanu and mother of Bhīśma MBh.; or as one of the wives of Dharma; there is also a Gaṅgā in the sky and one below the earth; Bhagī-ratha is said to have conducted the heavenly Gaṅgā down to the earth ; N. of the wife of Nīla-kaṇṭha and mother of Śaṁkara ;

1.3 【梵漢辭典,p448】（陰性名詞）Ganges 河（經文）天堂來，恆河，殑伽；強伽，恆伽。

2. वालिकाः vālikāḥ 名詞 沙

2.1 【詞尾變化】vālikāḥ 是 vālikā 的複數主格形，所以字典查 vālikā。

2.2 【摩威梵英】無此字，疑爲非梵文。

2.3 【艾格混梵,p478】

2.3.1（text Bāl）, n of a Licchavi woman; and Vālikāchavī（tex Bāl, with 1 ms. Bālika-, v.l. Pārikalecchavī, which suggests that the second member was a form of the tribal name !）

2.3.2 n. of a place donated by her to the Buddha and the order（identified by Senart with Pāli Vālikārāma, v.l. Vālukā; Pāli seems to know no Vālikā; *the v. l. suggests the word for sand.*）

2.4 【梵漢辭典,p1382】（陰性名詞）沙。（經文）沙。

3. अनल्पकानि analpakāni 形容詞 很多

3.1 【詞尾變化】analpakāni 是從 an-alpaka 變化出來的形容詞，an 爲否定的意思，故字典查 alpaka。

3.2 【摩威梵英,p96,alpaka】

3.2.1 mf（ikā）n. small , minute , trifling ;

3.2.2（*am*）ind. little Naigh. ;

3.2.3（*at*）abl. ind. shortly after;

3.2.4 m. the plants Hedysarum Alhagi and Premna Herbacea.

3.3 【梵漢辭典,p85,analpaka】（形容詞）（經文）眾。

4. वार्यण vīryeṇa 形容詞 精進

4.1 【詞尾變化】vīryeṇa 爲 vīrya 的單數工具格形，所以字典查 vīrya。

4.2 【摩威梵英,p1006】

4.2.1 n.（ifc. f. *ā*）manliness , valour , strength , power , energy RV.; heroism , heroic deed; manly vigour , virility , semen virile MBh.; efficacy（of medicine）; poison BhP. ; splendour , lustre ; dignity , consequence ib. ;

4.2.2（*ā*）f. vigour , energy , virility ; N. of a serpent-maid.

4.3 【梵漢辭典,p1451】（中性名詞／形容詞）男子氣概，勇氣，力，能力，效力，英雄的行爲，男性的精力，精液；（經文）力，勤，進，精進，正勤，精勤，勇健，勇猛，威猛，強健，秦永，進策，勤精進。

5. जनेन्ति janenti 動詞　了解

5.1 【詞尾變化】janenti 據學者江島惠教看法，是從 jānanti 的異寫）。jānanti 是√jñā 的第三人稱複數形。所以字典查√jñā。

5.2 【摩威梵英,p425】cl. 9. to know , have knowledge , become acquainted with（acc. ; rarely gen. MBh.）, perceive , apprehend , understand, experience , recognise , ascertain , investigate RV.; to know as , know or perceive that , regard or consider as ; to acknowledge , approve , allow; to recognise as one's own , take possession of SaddhP. ; to visit as a friend; to remember（with gen.）MBh. ; to engage in ; to teach any one（acc.）; to make known , announce , teach anything MBh.; to inform any one（gen.）that（double acc.）MBh. ; to request , ask MBh. to wish to know or become acquainted with or learn , investigate , examine MBh.; to wish for information about（acc.）; to conjecture AV, to wish to make known or inform ;

5.3 【梵漢辭典,p535】（動詞）了解，察知，有～知識，從～認識，領悟，覺悟，經驗，查明，檢查，確認，以～了解，認爲～，假設，推測～。（經文）知，能之，解，測，證，能識，明達，能明瞭，普明了，了，了知，能了知，了達，思惟，籌量。

【筆者試譯】：我看在很多的佛國淨土也有，
菩薩多得像恆河沙那樣，
百千萬億那麼多，
由各自努力（願力）追求覺悟（菩提）。

【什公漢譯】：我見彼土，恒沙菩薩，種種因緣，而求佛道。

【英 譯 本】：I see in many fields Bodhisattvas by many thousands of kotis, like sands of the Ganges, who are producing enlightenment according to the different degree of their power.

【信譯研究】：信譯。梵本「vīryeṇa」是「願力、努力」，但鳩摩羅什翻譯成「因緣」，此爲意譯。

【第十四頌】

ददन्ति दानानि तथैव केचिद्
धनं हिरण्यं रजतं सुवर्णम्।
मुक्तामणिं शङ्खशिलाप्रवालं
दासांश्च दासी रथअश्वएडकान्॥१४॥

【羅馬譯音】

dadanti dānāni tathaiva kecid
dhanaṁ hiraṇyaṁ rajataṁ suvarṇam|
muktāmaṇiṁ śaṅkhaśilāpravālaṁ
dāsāṁśca dāsī rathaaśvaeḍakān||14||

【句義解析】

dadanti dānāni tathaiva kecid
dhanaṁ hiraṇyaṁ rajataṁ suvarṇam|
muktā-maṇiṁ śaṅkha-śilā-pravālaṁ
dāsāṁś ca dāsī ratha-aśva-eḍakān||14||

【辭彙研究】

1. ददन्ति dadanti 動詞　布施

1.1 【詞尾變化】dadanti 是√dā 的現在式第三人稱複數的變化形，所以字典查√dā。

1.2 【摩威梵英,p474】

1.2.1 cl. 3. dadāti（pl. *-dante*）, to give , bestow , grant , yield , impart , present , offer to（dat. , in later language also gen. or loc.）RV.; to give（a daughter）in marriage MBh. ; to hand over ;（with *haste*）;to give back , MBh. ; to pay（*daṇḍam* , ` a fine '; ṛṇam , a debt）; to give up , cede（*āsanam* , ` one's seat'）;（*panthānam* or *mārgam* , `to give up the road , allow to pass'）; to sell（with instr. of the price）; to sacrifice（*ātmānam* , `one's self.'; *āt- khedāya* , to give one's self up to grief）; to offer（an oblation）; to communicate , teach , utter（blessings , *āśiṣas*）, give（answer , *prati-vacas, -canam* , *praty-uttaram*）, speak（*satyaṃ vacas* , the truth; *vacam* , to address a speech to）; to permit , allow（with inf.）MBh. ; to permit sexual intercourse; to place , put , apply（in med.）MBh. ; to add; with *varam* , to grant a boon MBh. ; *śoham* , to cause grief; avakāśam , to give room or space , allow to enter ; *prāṇān* or *jīvitam* , ` to spare any one's life' MBh.; *talam* or *-lān* , to slap with the palms of the hands MBh. ; *-la-prahāram* , to strike with the palm *tālam* , to beat time with the hands MBh. ; *saṃjñām* , to make a sign ; *saṃketakam* , to make an appointment *samayam* , to propose an agreement; *upamām* , to compare with〔gen.〕; *paṭaham* , to proclaim with the drum; *śabdam* , to make a noise , call out; *śāpam* , to utter a curse MBh.; *gāīh., anuyātram* , to accompany; *āliṅganane* , *parirambhaṇam* , to embrace; *jhampam* , to jump ; *śrāddham* , to perform a *Srāddha* MBh. ; *vratakam* , to accomplish a vow; *yuddham* , *niy-* , *saṃgrāmam* , to give battle , fight with MBh.; *ājñām, ādeśam* , to give an order , command; *saṃdeśam* , to give information; *prayogam* , to give a dramatic representation *vṛtim* , to fence ; *darśanam* , to show one's self; *dṛṣṭim dṛśam akṣi caksus* , to fix the eyes on（loc.）; *karṇam* , to give ear , listen; *manas* , to direct the mind to（loc.）MBh.; *kars kapolam* , to rest the cheek on the hand; *nigaḍāni* to put on or apply fetters *pāvakam* , to set on fire ; *agnīn* to consume by fire ; *śāram* , to move a chess-man ; *argalam* , to draw a bolt , bar ; *jānu* , to kneel upon（gen.）MBh.; *padam* , to tread upon〔loc.〕; to direct the steps; *viṣam* , to poison（with acc.!）; *garam*（with gen.）;

1.2.2 to carry , hold , keep , preserve RV. AV. ; to show; to cause to give or be given , cause to bestow or present or give up , oblige to pay , make restore; to demand from（abl.）; to cause to utter or speak *ghoṣaṇām* , to cause to be made known ; to cause to place or advance; to cause to perform to cause to be put on（loc.）MBh. to wish to give , be ready to bestow RV. ; to wish to give in marriage MBh.

1.3 【梵漢辭典,p339】(動詞)把~(對格/屬格)給予~(對格/屬格/於格);贈與,交付,交出;出售,支付,讓出,恢復,奉獻,告知,教導,宣告,言表(幸福);講(眞理),發(言),向~說話;(經文)與,賜與,賞與,施予,施捨,給施,布施,奉施,奉,奉獻,奉上,授,賜,貢,付,惠,能捨。

2. दानानि dānāni 名詞 佈施品

2.1 【詞尾變化】dānāni 是 dāna 的複數對格形,所以字典查 dāna。

2.2 【摩威梵英,p474】m.(√dad) gift , donation MBh;

2.3 【梵漢辭典,p340】(陽性名詞)布施品,捐贈品。

3. तथैव tathaiva 片語 如是

3.1 【詞尾變化】tathaiva 根據連音規則即 tathā-eva 的變化而來,所以字典查 tathā-eva。

3.2 資料前面已有說明。

4. केचिद् kecid 短詞,片語 誰都~

4.1 【詞尾變化】kecid 爲 ka-cid 變化而來。ke 是 ka 的主格複數形,所以字典查 ka-cid。

4.2 【摩威梵英,p204,ka】kas , kā , kim , interrog. pron.(see kim and kad , and cf. the following words in which the interrogative base ka appears , katama , katara , kati , katham , kadā , karhi , kā), who? which? what? In its declension ka follows the pronoun tad except in nom. acc. sing. neut. , where kim has taken the place of kad or kat in classical Sanskṛit ; but the old form kad is found in the Veda; The interrogative sentence introduced by ka is often terminated by iti, but iti may be omitted and the sentence lose its direct interrogative character. ka with or without as may express `how is it possible that? ' `what power have I , you , they? ka is sometimes repeated, and the repetition is often due to a kind of attraction, which book is to be read by whom. When kim is connected with the inst. c. of a noun or with the indecl. participle it may express ` what is gained by doing so ? '(=ko'rthas); ka is often followed by the particles iva , u , nāma , nu , vā , svid , some of which serve merely to generalize the interrogation, what can this be? ka is occasionally used alone as an indefinite pronoun , especially in negative sentences. Generally , however , ka is only made indefinite when connected with the particles ca , cana , cid , vā , and api , in which case ka may sometimes be preceded by the relative ya. The particle cana , being composed of ca and na , properly gives a negative force to the pronoun, but the negative sense is generally dropped, and a relative is sometimes connected with it. Examples of cid with the interrogative are common ; vā and api are not so common , but the latter is often found in classical Sanskṛit. ka may sometimes be used , like kad , at the beginning of a compound.

4.3 【摩威梵英,p397,cid】ind. even , indeed , also（often merely laying stress on a preceding word ; requiring a preceding simple verb to be accentuated as well as a verb following , if cid is preceded by an interrogative pron.; in Class. only used after interrogative pronouns and adverbs to render them indefinite , and after jātu）RV.; like（added to the stem of a subst. e.g. agni- , rāja-）; cid-cid or cid-ca or cid-u , as well as , both , and RV.

4.4 【梵漢辭典,p544,ka】（疑問代名詞）誰，什麼，哪一個。Kaś-cit, kva-cit（經文）一切處。

4.5 【梵漢辭典,p324,cid】（附屬）（質詞）〔原爲疑問詞中性，在吠陀中用來加強先行詞，但在翻譯中經常以強勢表現。〕連～，剛好，非常，至少，各個，總的，一體，曾經，全部，連～也不～。

5. धनं dhanaṁ 名詞　財產

5.1 【詞尾變化】dhanaṁ 根據連音規則是從 dhanam 變化過來，dhanam 則是 dhana 的單數對格形，所以字典查 dhana。

5.2 【摩威梵英,p508】

5.2.1 n. the prize of a contest or the contest itself（lit. a running match , race , or the thing raced for）RV. ; booty , prey RV. AV. ; any valued object ,（esp.）wealth , riches ,（movable）property , money , treasure , gift RV. ; capital; = *go-dhana*;（arithm.）the affirmative quantity or plus; N. of the 2nd mansion Var. ;

5.2.2 m. N. of a merchant.

5.3 【梵漢辭典,p365】(中性名詞)給予勝利者的獎賞，獎品，俘獲物，戰利品，賭金，或賭博所贏來的金錢；競爭；動產，貨物，財產，富，財寶，貨幣，報酬，賑濟品；(經文)財，財物，財寶，珍寶，錢財，珍財，物，道物。

6. हिरण्यं hiraṇyaṁ 名詞 黃金

6.1【詞尾變化】hiraṇyaṁ 根據連音規則是從 hiraṇyam 變化過來，而 hiraṇyam 則是 hiraṇya 的單數對格，故字典查 hiraṇya。

6.2 【摩威梵英,p1299】

6.2.1 n.(f. *ā*; prob. connected with *hari* , *harit* , *hiri*) gold(orig. `uncoined gold or other precious metal `; in later language ` coined gold ' -or `money') RV.; any vessel or ornament made of gold (as `a golden spoon') RV. AV.; a gold piece or coin (generally with *suvarṇa* as opp. to base metal) Br. ; a cowry ; semen virile ; substance , imperishable matter ; a partic. measure ; the Datura or thorn apple; N. of a Varsha (= *hiraṇ-maya*) ;

6.2.2 m. a kind of bdellium ; N. of a , Daitya; of a son of Agnidhra (= *hiraṇ-maya*) ; of a king of Kaśmīra ;

6.2.3 (*ā*) f. one of the seven tongues of fire ;

6.2.4 mfn. golden , made of gold MBh.

6.3 【梵漢辭典,p493】(中性名詞)金塊，黃金，貴金屬，黃金的器具或飾品，金片，或金幣；(經文)金，七珍，珍寶，寶貝，金錢。

7. रजतं rajataṁ 形容詞 銀飾品

7.1 【詞尾變化】rajataṁ 根據連音規則是從 rajatam 變化過來，而 rajatam 則是 rajata 的單數對格，故字典查 rajata。

7.2 【摩威梵英,p863】

7.2.1 mfn. whitish , silver-coloured , silvery RV. TS. ; silver , made of silver ;

7.2.2 n.(m. g. ardharcodi) silver AV. ;(only L.) gold ; a pearl ornament ; ivory ; blood ; an asterism ; N. of a mountain and of a lake.

7.3 【梵漢辭典,p1010】(形容詞)銀色的，帶白色的；銀製的；(中性名詞)銀；(經文)可染，銀，白銀。

8. सुवर्णं suvarṇam 形容詞 金碧輝煌；金色的東西

8.1 【詞尾變化】suvarṇam 是 suvarṇa 的單數對格形，所以字典查 suvarṇa。

8.2 資料前面已有說明。

9. मुक्ता muktā 名詞 珍珠

9.1 【詞尾變化】沒有詞尾變化。

9.2 【摩威梵英,p821,muktā】f. of mukta , in comp.

9.3 【摩威梵英,p820,mukta】

9.3.1 mfn. loosened , let loose , set free , relaxed , slackened , opened , open MBh. ; liberated , delivered , emancipated（esp. from sin or worldly existence）MBh.（with instr. or ifc. = released from , deprived or destitute of）; fallen or dropped down（as fruit）; abandoned , relinquished , quitted , given up , laid aside , deposed MBh. ; sent forth , emitted , discharged , poured out , hurled , thrown ib. ; left free（as a road）; uttered（as sound）MBh. ; shed（as tears）; let fly , applied（as a kick）; gone , vanished , disappeared;

9.3.2 m. N. of one of the 7 sages under Manu Bhautya MBh. ; of a cook;

9.3.3（*ā*）f.（with or scil. *dis*）the quarter or cardinal point just quitted by the sun ; *a pearl (as loosened from the pearl-oyster shell)*MBh. ; an unchaste woman ; a species of plant（=rāsnā）; N. of a river ;

9.3.4 n. the spirit released from corporeal existence ;

9.3.5（*e*）ind , beside（with instr.）.

9.4 【梵漢辭典,p746】（陰性）（形容詞）（名詞）珍珠。（經文）眞珠。

10. मणिं maṇiṁ 名詞 摩尼珠；珍珠

10.1 【詞尾變化】maṇiṁ 根據連音規則是從 maṇim 變化過來，而 maṇim 則是 maṇi 的單數對格，故字典查 maṇi。

10.2 【摩威梵英,p774】m.（*i* f. only ; *ī* f. ; *maṇīva* = *maṇī ,iva*）a jewel , gem , pearl（also fig.）, any ornament or amulet , globule , crystal RV.; a magnet , loadstone ; glans penis; N. of the jewel-lotus prayer; clitoris; the hump（of a camel）MBh. ; the dependent fleshy excrescences on a goat's neck; thyroid cartilage; the wrist（= *mñmaṇi-bandha*）; a large water-jar ; N. of a Nāga MBh. ; of a companion of Skanda（associated with Su-*maṇi*）ib. ; of a sage ib. ; of a son of Yuyudhāna; of a king of the Kim-ṇaras; of various wks. and a collection of magical formulas（also abridged for Tattva-cintāmaṇi and Siddhanta-śiromaṇi）.

10.3 【梵漢辭典,p704】（陽性名詞）珍珠，珠玉，寶石，小球，磁鐵；（經文）珠，意珠，寶珠，如意寶珠，明珠，珠寶，寶，摩尼珠，摩尼寶，摩尼寶珠。

11. शण्ख śaṅkha 名詞 法螺

11.1 【詞尾變化】沒有詞尾變化。

11.2 【摩威梵英,p535】m. n. conch-shell（used to blow upon or as ornament）; m. the temporal bone, temple, one of the treasures of Kubera, N. of an Asura, etc.

11.3 【梵漢辭典,p1126】（陽性／中性名詞）海螺殼，法螺（管樂器的一種，Viṣṇu 神的象徵；固定在象的前腳或耳朵的一種裝飾）（陽性名詞）太陽穴；（經文）貝，螺，珂，蠡，蠡貝，珂貝，螺貝，螺文，螺鼓，珂鼓，海螺，內肥，硨磲渠。

12. शिला śilā 名詞 玉石

12.1 【詞尾變化】沒有詞尾變化。

12.2 【摩威梵英,p1073】f.（perhaps connected with √śi）a stone , rock , crag AV.; red arsenic ; camphor ; the lower mill-stone ; the lower timber of a door ; the top of the pillar supporting a house ; a vein , tendon（for śira）; N. of a river R. ; of a woman.

12.3 【梵漢辭典,p1171】（陰性名詞）石，岩，嚴；（經文）石，砥，玉石，美玉，瓦石，碧玉，玻璃，璧玉。

13. प्रवालं pravālaṁ 名詞 珊瑚

13.1 【詞尾變化】pravālaṁ 根據連音規則是從 pravālam 變化過來，而 pravālam 則是 pravāla 的複數對格，故字典查 pravāla。

13.2 【摩威梵英,p691】

13.2.1 m. n.（prob. fr. √*val* , but also written *pra-bāla* ; ifc. f. *ā*）a young shoot , sprout , new leaf or branch（to which feet and lips are often compared）MBh. ; coral MBh.（in this sense also written *pra-vāḍa*）; the neck of the Indian lute; m. an animal ; a pupil;

13.2.2 mfn. having shoots or sprouts; having long or beautiful hair

（=*prakṛṣṭa-keśa yukta*）.

13.3 【梵漢辭典,p967】（陽性／中性名詞）芽，嫩芽〔通常爲足或唇的比喻〕；珊瑚；（經文）珊瑚。

14. दासांश्च dāsāṁś ca 名詞　奴僕

14.1 【詞尾變化】dāsāṁś ca 根據連音規則是從 dāsān ca 變化過來，而 dāsān 則是 dāsa 的複數對格，故字典查 dāsa。

14.2 【摩威梵英,p477】

14.2.1 m. fiend , demon ; N. of certain evil beings conquered by Indra（e.g. Namuci , Pipru , Śambara , Varcin）RV. ; savage , barbarian , infidel（also *dāsa* , opp. to *ārya*）; slave , servant RV. AV.; a Sūdra ; one to whom gifts may be made ; a fisherman（v.l. for *dāśa*）; of names , esp. of Śūdras and Kāya-sthas ;

14.2.2（*ī*）f. a female servant or slave AV. MBh.; harlot ; N. of a plant; an altar ; N. of a river ;

14.2.3（*dāsa*）mf（*ī*）n. fiendish , demoniacal , barbarous , impious RV.

14.3 【梵漢辭典,p351】（陽性名詞）敵人，惡魔，布信教者，奴隸，僕役；（經文）奴，僕，奴僕，僮僕，從僕，僕使。

15. दासी dāsī 名詞　女奴婢

15.1 【詞尾變化】沒有詞尾變化。

15.2 【摩威梵英,p477】（also -*sīka* ifc.）f. of dāsa（q.v.）.

15.3 【梵漢辭典,p354】（陰性名詞）女僕役；女奴隸；（經文）婢，使女。

16. अश्व aśva 名詞　馬

16.1 【詞尾變化】沒有詞尾變化。

16.2 【摩威梵英,p114】

16.2.1 m. f. ā , a horse , stallion RV. ; the , horse（in the game of chess）; the number `seven'（that being the number of the horses of the sun）; the archer（in the zodiac）; a particular kind of lover（horse-like in strength）; N. of a teacher（with the patron. Sāmudri）; of a son of Citraka; of a Dānava MBh.;

16.2.2（*ā*）f.（g. *ajādi* q.v.）a mare RV.

16.3 【梵漢辭典,p185】（陽性名詞）馬；（經文）馬；所乘。

17. एडकान् eḍakān 名詞　羊

17.1 【詞尾變化】eḍakān 是 eḍaka 的對格複數形，所以查 eḍaka。

17.2 【摩威梵英,p231】

17.2.1 m. a kind of sheep , ram , wild goat MBh.; a kind of medicinal plant ;

17.2.2（*ā* g. *ajādi* and *ikā*）f. the female of the above sheep , a ewe.

17.3 【梵漢辭典,p428】（經文）羊。

【筆者試譯】：不論是誰，都如此布施了東西，
財產，黃金，白銀，金色的飾品，
珍珠，摩尼寶珠，法螺，玉石，珊瑚，
男僕和婢女，寶物與馬羊。

【什公漢譯】：或有行施，金銀珊瑚，眞珠摩尼，車磲馬腦。
金剛諸珍，奴婢車乘。

【英 譯 本】：There are some who charitably bestow wealth,
gold, silver, gold money, pearls, jewels, conch shells,
stones, coral, male and female slaves, horses, and
sheep;

【信譯研究】：非信譯。原因是鳩譯的第四句有一個「馬腦」，案《大正新修大藏經》第九冊在《妙法蓮華經》經文「車磲馬腦」在下面有註解說：「車璖馬腦=硨磲碼碯」，〔註 35〕或許就前後文提及諸項珍寶，「馬腦」被看作是「碼碯」似爲理所當然。不過，瑪瑙的梵文是：अश्मगर्भ aśma-garbha【梵漢辭典,p176】，與梵本內的 अश्वेडकान् aśva-eḍakān 是不一樣的兩件事物。但很巧的是，鳩摩羅什翻譯成「馬腦」，馬的部份爲正確，但是後面的 एडकान् eḍakān 並非爲「腦」（梵文的「腦」常用字是 मस्तिष्क mastiṣka【梵漢辭典,p718】），是指羊群。而另外，日本學者土田勝彌所校訂的《梵本法華經》裡面的梵文也是 एडकान् eḍakān，〔註 36〕並且日本學者，南條文雄與

〔註 35〕請見《大正新修大藏經》，台北市：新文豐圖書出版公司，1983 年出版。頁 3。

〔註 36〕請見 Prof. U. Wongihara and C. Tsuchida（土田勝彌）《改訂梵文法華經，SADDHARMPUṆḌRĪKA-SŪTRAM Romanized and Revised Text fo The BiBliotheca Buddhica Publication by consulting A Skt. MS. & Tibetan and Chinese Translations》，日本東京：山喜房佛教書店出版，1994 年出版。頁 8。

泉芳璟共譯的《梵漢對照新譯法華經》在本頌此句譯為「奴婢馬羊をも與へけり」當中也是翻譯成「羊」。〔註 37〕所以推論若非版本差異，即爲誤譯。但今日解經者大多視爲「碼碯」。

【第十五頌】

शिबिकास्तथा रत्नविभूषिताश्च
दतन्ति दानानि प्रहृष्टमानसाः।
परिणामयन्तो इह अग्रबोधौ
वयं हि यानस्य भवेम लाभिनः॥१५॥

【羅馬譯音】

śibikāstathā ratnavibhūṣitāśca
dadanti dānāni prahṛṣṭamānasāḥ|
pariṇāmayanto iha agrabodhau
vayaṁ hi yānasya bhavema lābhinaḥ||15||

【句義解析】

śibikās tathā ratna-vibhūṣitāś ca
dadanti dānāni prahṛṣṭa-mānasāḥ|
pariṇāmayanto iha agra-bodhau
vayaṁ hi yānasya bhavema lābhinaḥ||15||

【辭彙研究】

1. शिबिकास् śibikās 名詞 擔架；肩輿

1.1 【詞尾變化】śibikās 根據連音規則是從 śibikāḥ 變化過來，而 śibikāḥ 是 śibikā 複數主格形，所以字典查 śibikā。

1.2 【摩威梵英,p1072】f.（also written śivikā）a palanquin , palkee , litter , bier MBh.; a partic. weapon of Kubera（god of wealth）; a stage or platform erected for exhibitions; a proper.

〔註 37〕請見南條文雄、泉芳璟共譯《梵漢對照新譯法華經》，日本京都：平樂寺書店出版，昭和 48 年第六刷。頁 17。

1.3 【梵漢辭典,p1168】（陰性名詞）擔架，（二人抬的）肩輿；Kubera 神的武器；靈柩車。

2. विभूषिताश्च vibhūṣitāś ca 形容詞　裝飾的

2.1 【詞尾變化】vibhūṣitāś ca 根據連音規則是從 vibhūṣitāḥ ca 變化過來，而 vibhūṣitāḥ 是 vibhūṣita 複數主格形，所以字典查 vibhūṣita。

2.2 【摩威梵英,p979】

2.2.1 mfn. adorned , decorated MBh.;

2.2.2 n. an ornament , decoration;

2.2.3 -*tāṇga* mfn. decorated about the body ;

2.2.4 -*tālaṃkārā* f. N. of a Gandharvī and of a Kiṃ-narī Kāraṇḍ.

2.3 【梵漢辭典,p1411】（過去被動分詞）（形容詞）（經文）飾，嚴，嚴飾，莊嚴，嚴儀。

3. प्रहृष्ट prahṛṣṭa 形容詞　非常高興的；踴躍的

3.1 【詞尾變化】沒有詞尾變化。

3.2 【摩威梵英,p701】

3.2.1 mfn. erect , bristling（as the hair of the body）MBh. BhP. ; thrilled with delight. exceedingly pleased , delighted ib.;

3.2.2 citta mfn. delighted at heart at heart , exceedingly glad.;

3.2.3 -*manas* mfn. id. MBh. ;

3.2.4 -*mukha* mfn. having a cheerful face , looking pleased（*a-pr-*）.;

3.2.5 -*mudita* mfn. exceedingly pleased and cheerful ;

3.2.6 -*rūpa* mfn. of pleasing form MBh. ; erect in form;

3.2.7 -*roman* mfn. one who has erected hair ;

3.2.8 m. N. of an Asura Katha1s. ;

3.2.9 -*vadana* mfn. = -*mukha* ;

3.2.10 -*ṭātman*. mfn. = -*ṭa-citta*. MBh.

3.3 【梵漢辭典,p910】（過去動分詞）（形容詞）非常高興的，歡喜的；（經文）喜，歡喜，樂，踴躍。

4. मानसाः mānasāḥ 形容詞　心靈的

4.1 【詞尾變化】mānasāḥ 是 mānasa 的複數主格形，所以字典查 mānasa。

4.2 【摩威梵英,p810】

4.2.1 mf（*ī*, once *ā*）n.（fr. *manas*）belonging to the mind or spirit , mental , spiritual ; expressed only in the mind , performed in thought i.e. silent , tacit（as a hymn or prayer）MBh. ; conceived or present in the mind , conceivable , imaginable; relating to or dwelling on the lake Mānasa（see n. below）BhP. ;

4.2.2 m. a form of Viśṇu ; N. of a serpent-demon MBh. ; of a son of Vapush-mat;

4.2.3 pl. a partic. class of deceased ancestors（regarded as sons of Vasiśṭha）; a class of ascetics; N. of the Vaiśyas in Śkadvīpa MBh. ; of the worlds of the Soma-pa ;

4.2.4（*ī*）f.（with *pūja*）mental or spiritual devotion ; N. of a Kiṃ-narī Kāraṇḍ. ; of a Vidyā-devī ;

4.2.5 n.（ifc. f. *ā*）the mental powers , mind , spirit , heart , soul（=*manas* g. *prajñādi*）MBh. ;（in law）tacit or implied consent ; a kind of salt ; the 25th mansion from that under which one is born; N. of a sacred like and place of pilgrimage on mount Kailāsa（the native place of the wild geese , which migrate to it every year at the breeding season）MBh.; N. of wk. on Śīpa or art.

4.3 【梵漢辭典,p699】（形容詞）關於心或由心生的，心靈的，精神上的，在內心陳述的（祈禱），內心默想的，可被想像的，住在或與 Mānasa 湖有關的；（經文）心，意，依意根，心依止，（中性名詞）心裏的作用，心，心臟。

5. परिणामयन्तो pariṇāmayanto 動詞　迴向

5.1 【詞尾變化】pariṇāmayanto 根據連音規則是從 pariṇāmayantaḥ 變化過來，而 pariṇāmayantaḥ 是 pariṇāmayant 複數主格形，而 pariṇāmayant 是 pari-√nam 的使役動詞之現在主動分詞，所以字典查 pari-√nam。

5.2 【摩威梵英,p594】（√nam）P. Ā. -ṇamati , -te, to bend or turn aside AV. ; to bend down , stoop; to change or be transformed into（instr.）Vedantas. ; to develop , become ripe or mature; to become old; to be digested MBh. ; to be fulfilled（as a word）: Caus. -ṇāmayati, to make ripe , ripen , mature ; to bring to an end , pass（as a night）; to bend aside or down , stoop MBh.

5.3 【梵漢辭典,p763】(動詞)(使役動詞之現在主動分詞)側彎，朝向旁邊，變成～（工具格），轉向～，向～（工具格）發達，成熟，老的，被消化的，到達眞義；(經文)變現，轉變，迴向。

6. अगर agra 形容詞　最高的

6.1 【詞尾變化】沒有詞尾變化。

6.2 【摩威梵英,p6】

6.2.1 mfn.（fr. √aṅg）, foremost , anterior , first , prominent , projecting , chief , best L. ; supernumerary ;

6.2.2（*ā*）f. measure of amplitude（i.e. the distance from the extremity of the gnomon-shadow to the line of the equinoctial shadow）;

6.2.3（*am*）n. foremost point or part ; tip ; front ; uppermost part , top , summit , surface ; point ; and hence , figuratively , sharpness ; the nearest end , the beginning ; the climax or best part ; goal , aim ; multitude ; a weight , equal to a pala ; a measure of food given as alms ;（in astron.）the sun's amplitude ;

6.2.4（*am*）ind. in front , before , ahead of ;

6.2.5（*agreṇa*）ind. in front , before（without or with acc.）;

6.2.6（*agre*）ind. in front , ahead of , in the beginning , first ; further on , subsequently , below（in a book）; from - up to（*ā*）.

6.3 【梵漢辭典,p46】(中性形容詞)前部，開始，點，尖端，頂點，主要者；(經文)前，始，端，末；頂，極，高，重，上，勝，尊，過，最，最上，最勝，最極，上妙，吾等，第一，最第一，上妙，妙，增上。

7. बोधौ bodhau 名詞　菩提

7.1 【詞尾變化】bodhau 是 bodhi 的於格單數，所以字典查 bodhi。

7.2 【摩威梵英,p734】

7.2.1 mf.（with Buddhists or Jainas）perfect knowledge or wisdom（by which a man becomes a Buddha or Jina）, the illuminated or enlightened intellect（of a Buddha or JñJina）;

7.2.2 m. the tree of wisdom under which perfect wisdom is attained or under which a man becomes a Buddha , the sacred fig-tree; `wakener ' , a cock ;

N. of a man（= Buddha in a former birth）Jātakam. ; of a mythical elephant ; of a place ;

7.2.3 pl. N. of a people ;

7.2.4 mfn. learned , wise.

7.3 【梵漢辭典,p288】（陰性／陽性名詞）（完全）開悟（如此徹悟得成 Buddha 或 Jina）；（經文）覺，道，得道，菩提。

8. वयं vayaṁ 代名詞（複數主格）我們

8.1 【詞尾變化】vayaṁ 根據連音規則是從 vayam 變化過來，所以字典查 vayam。

8.2 資料前面已有說明。

9. यानस्य yānasya 名詞 乘

9.1 【詞尾變化】yānasya 是 yāna 的單數屬格，所以字典查 yāna。

9.2 資料前面已有說明。

10. भवेम bhavema 動詞 願成爲

10.1 【詞尾變化】bhavema 是√bhū 的願望法第三人稱複數形，所以字典查√bhū。

10.2 資料前面已有說明。

11. लाभिनः lābhinaḥ 形容詞 獲得了～

11.1 【詞尾變化】lābhinaḥ 是 lābhin 的主格複數形，所以字典查 lābhin。

11.2 【摩威梵英,p897】mfn.（ifc.）obtaining , meeting with , finding;

11.3 【梵漢辭典,p647】（形容詞）獲得～，發現～；（經文）得，得者，獲得，已得，具，受。

【筆者試譯】：用如此寶物來裝飾的肩輿，
心靈上歡喜布施了東西，
用來迴向（轉求）這一世的最高的菩提正覺，
是爲了我們願意獲得（成就）這一乘（佛法）的緣故！

【什公漢譯】：寶飾輦輿，歡喜布施。迴向佛道，願得是乘。

【英 譯 本】：As well as litters adorned with jewels. They
are spending gifts with glad hearts, developing themselves

for superior enlightenment, in the hope of
gaining the vehicle.

【信譯研究】：信譯。

【第十六頌】

त्रैधातुके श्रेष्ठविशिष्टयानं
यद्बुद्धयानं सुगतेहि वर्णितम्।
अहं पि तस्यो भवि क्षिप्र लाभी
ददन्ति दानानि इमीदृशानि॥१६॥

【羅馬譯音】

traidhātuke śreṣṭhaviśiṣṭayānaṁ
yadbuddhayānaṁ sugatehi varṇitam|
ahaṁ pi tasyo bhavi kṣipra lābhī
dadanti dānāni imīdṛśāni||16||

【句義解析】

traidhātuke śreṣṭha-viśiṣṭa-yānaṁ
yad buddha-yānaṁ sugatehi varṇitam|
ahaṁ pi tasyo bhavi kṣipra lābhī
dadanti dānāni im īdṛśāni||16||

【辭彙研究】

1. त्रैधातुके traidhātuke 形容詞 於三界
   1.1 【詞尾變化】traidhātuke 是 traidhātuka 的單數於格形，所以字典找 traidhātuka。
   1.2 【摩威梵英,p462】n. the 3 worlds SaddhP.
   1.3 【梵漢辭典,p1294】(形容詞)(經文)三界，三有。
2. श्रेष्ठ śreṣṭha 形容詞 最殊勝
   2.1 【詞尾變化】沒有詞尾變化。

2.2 【摩威梵英,p1102】

2.2.1 mf（*ā*）n. most splendid or beautiful , most beautiful of or among（with gen.）RV. AV; most excellent , best , first , chief（n. `the best or chief thing'）, best of or among or in respect of or in（with gen. loc. , or comp.）RV.; better , more , distinguished , superior , better than（abl. or gen.）MBh. ; most auspicious or salutary; oldest , senior ;

2.2.2 m. a king ; a Brāhman; N. of Viśṇu or Kubera; N. of a king ;

2.2.3（*ā*）f. an excellent woman ; Hibiscus Mutabilis L.（prob. w.r. for *lakṣmī-śr-*）; a kind of root resembling ginger ;

2.2.4 n. cow's milk ; copper.

2.3 【梵漢辭典,p1198】（形容詞最高級）中最美麗的（屬格），（屬格／位格）中最好的，最傑出的，最優等的，主要的；比（從格，屬格）購優越的，善的，好的，卓越的；（經文）上，妙，勝，殊妙，殊勝，最，最上，最勝，最妙，無勝，最極，無，上，最尊，最尊勝。

3. विशिष्ट viśiṣṭa 形容詞　卓越的

3.1 【詞尾變化】沒有詞尾變化。

3.2 【摩威梵英,p990】

3.2.1 mfn. distinguished , distinct , particular , peculiar MBh.; characterized by（instr. or comp.）; pre-eminent , excellent , excelling in or distinguished by（loc. , instr. adv. in *tas* , or comp.）, chief or best among（gen.）, better or worse than（abl. or comp.）MBh.;

3.2.2 m. N. of Vishn2u MBh. ;

3.2.3（*ī*）f. N. of the mother of Saṃkaraicārya ;

3.2.4 *–kula* mfn. descended from an excellent race;

3.2.5 -*cāritra* or -*cārin* m. N. of a Bodhi-sattva SaddhP. ;

3.2.6 -*tama* and -*tara* mfn. distinguished , chief. best , better than（abl.）MBh.;

3.2.7 -*tā* f.（Hit.）, -*tva* n. difference , speciality , peculiarity , distinction , excellence , superiority ;

3.2.8 -*buddhi* f. differenced or distinguishing knowledge;

3.2.9 -*liṅga* mfn. different in gender;

3.2.10 -*varṇa* mfn. having a distinguished colour MBh. ; -*vaiśiśrhtya* , ` what is different' and `difference' ;

3.2.11（-jñāna-vādārtha m. -bodha m. -bodha-rahasya n. -bodha-vicāra m. -bodha-vicāra-rahasya n. ;

3.2.12 -tyāvagāhi-vādārtha m. N. of wks. ;

3.2.13 -*ṭādvaita* n. see below ;

3.2.14 -*ṭopamā* f. a partic. comparison MW. ;

3.2.15 -*yukta* n.（scil. *rūpaka*）a metaphor which contains a partic. comparison（said to be a variety of the general Rūpaka）.

3.3 【梵漢辭典,p1458】（過去被動分詞）被區別的，被特殊化的，有個性的，不同的，特殊的，傑出的，卓越的；（經文）別，異，差別；勝，最勝，殊勝，最舒勝，最勝無比，最尊，第一，勝妙，無等，上。

4. सुगतेहि sugatehi 片語 因爲佛的緣故

4.1 【詞尾變化】sugatehi 即 sugate-hi 變化過來。hi 的部份前面已有資料說明，而 sugate 爲 sugata 的單數於格，所以字典查 sugata。

4.2 【摩威梵英,p1222】

4.2.1 mfn. going well; one who has fared well; well-bestowed;

4.2.2 m. a Buddha（-*tva* n.）, Introd. ; a Buddhist , Buddhist teacher;

4.2.3 -*cetanā* f. N. of a Buddhist nun Buddh. ;

4.2.4 -*mitra* m. N. of a man ib. ;

4.2.5 -*śāsana* n. the BudñBuddhist doctrine;

4.2.6 -*tāyatana* n. a BudñBuddhist temple or monastery ;

4.2.7 -*tālaya* m. id. L. ;

4.2.8 -*tāvadāna* n. N. of a Buddhist Sūtra.

4.3 【梵漢辭典,p1225】（形容詞）圓滿離去的；進展順利的，快樂的；（陽性名詞）某佛陀，佛教徒，佛教之師；（經文）佛，善逝，善趣，如來，，諸佛如來。

5. वर्णितम् varṇitam 過去被動分詞／形容詞　讚歎

5.1 【詞尾變化】varṇitam 爲 varṇita 的單數對格形，故字典查 varṇita。

5.2 【摩威梵英,p925】mfn. painted , delineated , described , explained MBh. ; praised , eulogized , extolled ; spread MBh.

5.3 【梵漢辭典,p1393】（過去被動分詞）（形容詞）（經文）讚，讚嘆，所嘆，說，所說，所演說，稱揚，所稱嘆，所讚美。

6. अहं ahaṁ 代名詞　我

6.1【詞尾變化】ahaṁ 根據連音規則是從 aham 變化過來。所以字典查 aham。

6.2 【摩威梵英,p124】nom. sg. , ` I ' RV.;

6.3 【梵漢辭典,p48】（代名詞）（單數主格）我；（經文）我，吾。

7. पि pi 副詞　也，亦

7.1 【詞尾變化】pi 就是 api 的意思，所以字典查 api。

7.2 前面資料已有說明。

8. तस्यो tasyo 代名詞　如此地

8.1 【詞尾變化】tasyo 根據連音規則爲 tasyaḥ 變化過來，tasya 爲 tad 的單數屬格形。故字典查 tad。

8.2 資料前面已有說明。

9. भवि bhavi 動詞　成爲

9.1 【詞尾變化】bhavi 爲 bhave 的異寫），bhave 爲√bhū 的現在式第一人稱形，故字典查√bhū。

9.2 資料前面已有說明。

10. कषिप्र kṣipra 形容詞　快速的；立即的

10.1 【詞尾變化】沒有詞尾變化。

10.2 【摩威梵英,p329】

10.2.1 mf（*ā*）n. springing , flying back with a spring , elastic（as a bow）RV. ; quick , speedy , swift ;（said of certain lunar mansions）;

10.2.2 m. N. of a son of Kṛiśṇa;

10.2.3（*am*）ind. quickly , immediately , directly AV. MBh. ;

10.2.4（*am*）n. a measure of time（= 1/15 Muhu1rta or 15 Etarhis）; the part of the hand between the thumb and forefinger and the corresponding part of the foot Sus3r. ;

10.2.5（*a*）ind.（Ved. acc. pl. n.）with a shot RV.;

10.2.6（*āt*）abl. ind. directly , immediately ;

10.3 【梵漢辭典,p627】（形容詞）有彈性的（弓），敏捷的，快的，迅速的，快捷的；（經文）速，急，疾。

11. लाभी lābhī 形容詞　獲得的

11.1 【詞尾變化】lābhī 是 lābhin 的主格單數形，所以字典查 lābhin。

11.2 【摩威梵英,p897】mfn.（ifc.）obtaining , meeting with , finding ;

11.3 【梵漢辭典,p647】（形容詞）獲得，發現；（經文）得，德者，獲得，已得，具，受。

12. इम् im 代名詞　這個

12.1 【詞尾變化】im 的是從 idam 變化過來）。所以字典查 idam。

12.2 資料前面已有說明。

13. ईदृशानि īdṛśāni 形容詞　如是

13.1 【詞尾變化】īdṛśāni 是 īdṛśa 的中性主格單數形，所以字典查 īdṛśa。

13.2 【摩威梵英,p170】mf（ī）n. or endowed with such qualities , such.

13.3 【梵漢辭典,p503】（形容詞）（經文）如是，等無有異。

【筆者試譯】：三界最殊勝的，好的一乘，
即爲佛乘，爲佛陀世尊所讚嘆，
如此我也很快地，
照樣地布施物品。

【什公漢譯】：三界第一，諸佛所歎。

【英 譯 本】：（Thus they think）:’ the best and most excellent
vehicle in the whole of the threefold world
is the Buddha-vehicle magnified by the Sugatas.
May I, forsooth, soon gain it after my spending such gifts.’

【信譯研究】：非信譯。僅譯出兩頌。梵本此頌後面兩句什公缺譯。

【第十七頌】

चतुर्हयैर्युक्तरथांश्च केचित्
सवेदिकान् पुष्पध्वजैरलंकृतान्।
सवैजयन्तान् रतनामयानि
ददन्ति दानानि तथैव केचित्॥१७॥

【羅馬譯音】

caturhayairyuktarathāṁśca kecit

savedikān puṣpadhvajairalaṁkṛtān|

savaijayantān ratanāmayāni

dadanti dānāni tathaiva kecit||17||

【句義解析】

catur-hayair yukta-rathāṁś ca kecit

savedikān puṣpa-dhvajair alaṁkṛtān|

savaijayantān ratanā-mayāni

dadanti dānāni tathaiva ke-cit||17||

【辭彙研究】

1. हयैर् hayair 名詞 馬

1.1 【詞尾變化】hayair 根據連音規則是從 hayaiḥ 變化過來，而 hayaiḥ 是 haya 複數工具格形，所以字典查 haya。

1.2 【摩威梵英,p1288】

1.2.1 m.（ifc. f. *ā*; fr. √*hi*）a horse RV; a symbolical expression for the number `seven'（on account of the 7 horses of the Sun）; the zodiacal sign Sagittarius ;（in prosody）a foot of four short syllables , proceleusmaticus ; a man of a partic. class ; the Yak or Bos Grunniens; N. of Indra ; of one of the horses of the Moon ; of a son of Sahasra-da ; of a son of Śatā-jit;

1.2.2 pl. the family of Haya;

1.2.3（*ā* , or *ī*）f. a female horse , mare; Physalis Flexuosa ;

1.2.4 mfn. urging on , driving（see aśva-haya）.

1.3 【梵漢辭典,p489】（陽性名詞）軍馬，馬；（經文）馬。

2. युक्त yukta 過去被動分詞／形容詞 扼住

2.1 【詞尾變化】沒有詞尾變化。

2.2 【摩威梵英,p853】

2.2.1 mfn. yoked or joined or fastened or attached or harnessed to（loc. or instr.）RV.；set to work，made use of，employed，occupied with，engaged in，intent upon（instr. loc. or comp.）；ready to，prepared for（dat.）MBh.；absorbed in abstract meditation，concentrated，attentive RV.；skilful，clever，experienced in，familiar with（loc.）MBh.; joined，united，connected，combined，following in regular succession RV. BhP.（*am* ind. in troops）; furnished or endowed or filled or supplied or provided with，accompanied by，possessed of（instr. or comp.）MBh.；come in contact with（instr.）；（in astron.）being in conjunction with（instr.）；added to，increased by；（ifc.）connected with，concerning;（ifc.）subject to，dependent on MBh.；fitted，adapted，conforming or adapting one's self to，making use of；fit，suitable，appropriate，proper，right，established，proved，just，due，becoming to or suitable for（gen. loc. or comp.，e.g. *āyati-yukta*，suitable for the future；or ibc. see below；*yuktam* with *yad* or an inf. = it is fit or suitable that or to；*na yuktam bhavatā*，it is not seemly for you）MBh.；auspicious，favourable（as fate，time）；prosperous，thriving;（with *tathā*）faring or acting thus MBh.；（in gram.）primitive（as opp. to `derivative'）；

2.2.2 m. N. of a son of Manu Raivata; of a Ṛiśi under Manu Bhautya;

2.2.3（*ā*）f. N. of a plant.；

2.2.4 n. a team，yoke; junction，connection; fitness，suitableness，propriety（*am* ind. fitly，suitably，justly，properly，rightly；*ena*，properly，suitably RV.；*buddhi-yuktena*，conformably to reason.）

2.3 【梵漢辭典,p1523】（過去被動分詞）扼住，套在，以～扼住的；應用或專用於，從事～的，埋首於～的，所適用的；爲～預備的，所準備的，位～忙碌的，專心致至於～的；對～熱中的；集中精神的，無雜念的，謹愼的，對～非常用心的，對～熟練的，，有經驗的，接合的，結合的，組合的，有規則連續的，賦予或共給，帶有或擁有，利用，到達或聯絡上的，（經文）應，相應，應爾，應有，與～相應，應理，應正理，理，如理，正理，稱理，道理，如法，契，具，具足，俱，豐具，豐足；合，成，相和，成就，攝，所集，有，應有。

3. रथांश्च rathāṁś ca 形容詞　馬車

3.1 【詞尾變化】rathāṁś ca 根據連音規則是從 rathān ca 變化過來，而 rathān 是 ratha 複數對格形，所以字典查 ratha。

3.2 【摩威梵英,p865】

3.2.1 m.(√4. ṛ)` goer' , a chariot , car , esp. a two-wheeled war-chariot（lighter and swifter than the *anas* q.v.）, any vehicle or equipage or carriage（applied also to the vehicles of the gods）, waggon , cart RV.（ifc. f. *ā*）; a warrior , hero , champion MBh.; the body ; a limb , member , part ; Calamus Rotang ; Dalbergia Ougeinensis; = *pauruṣa*;

3.2.2（*ī*）f. a small carriage or waggon , cart.

3.3 【梵漢辭典,p1020】（陽性名詞）車，（兩輪的）戰車；交通工具；戰士，勇士；（經文）車，能便車，馬車。

4. केचित् kecit 不定詞片語　有些

4.1 【詞尾變化】kecit 爲 ke-cit，ke 爲 ka 的複數主格，所以字典查 ka-cit。

4.2 【摩威梵英,p240】kas, kā , kim , interrog. pron. , who? which? what? In its declension ka follows the pronoun tad except in nom. acc. sing. neut. , where kim has taken the place of kad or kat in classical Sanskṛit ; but the old form kad is found in the Veda; The interrogative sentence introduced by ka is often terminated by iti , but iti may be omitted and the sentence lose its direct interrogative character ka with or without 1. as may express `how is it possible that? ' `what power have I , you , they? ' ka is often connected with a demonstrative pron. or with the potential ka is sometimes repeated, and the repetition is often due to a kind of attraction. When kim is connected with the inst. c. of a noun or with the indecl. participle it may express `what is gained by doing so? '（=ko'rthas）;ka is often followed by the particles iva , u , nāma , nu , vā , svid , some of which serve merely to generalize the interrogation. ka is occasionally used alone as an indefinite pronoun , especially in negative sentences. Generally , however , ka is only made indefinite when connected with the particles ca , cana , cid , vā , and api , in which case ka may sometimes be preceded by the relative ya . The particle cana , being composed of ca and na , properly gives a negative force to the pronoun, but the negative sense is generally dropped, and a relative is sometimes connected with it. Examples of cid with the interrogative are common ; vā and api are not so common , but the latter is often found in classical Sanskṛit.（e.g. kaścid , any one ; kecid , some ; na kaścid , no one ; na kiṃcid api , nothing whatsoever ; yaḥ kaścid , any one whatsoever ; kecit - kecit , some - others ; yasmin kasmin vā deśe , in any country whatsoever ; na ko 'pi , no one ; na kimapi , nothing whatever）. ka may sometimes be used , like 2. kad , at the beginning of a compound.

4.3 【梵漢辭典,p545】（疑問代名詞）誰，什麼，哪一個；〔與 iva, u, nāme 連用〕其實是誰；無論是誰，哪一個或什麼東西皆等同於無；kaiṣa, kathā 那不成問題；kaś-cit kva-cit；（經文）一切處；ko'padeśaḥ（經文）何指示，如何指示；ko hetuḥ kaḥ pratyayaḥ（經文）何因何緣；（不定詞）〔與 cana, cid 或 api 連用〕若干，多少，絲毫，某。

5. सवेदिकान् savedikān 形容詞　其欄杆

5.1 【詞尾變化】savedikān 爲 sa-vedikān 所組成，其中 sa 資料前面已有說明。vedikān 爲 vedika 複數對格形，所以字典查 vedika。

5.2 【摩威梵英,p1017】

5.2.1 m. a seat , bench ;

5.2.2（*ā*）f.（cf. *vedaka* and *vedi*）id. MBh.; a sacrificial ground , altar ; a balcony , pavilion（=*vitardi*）Naish. Vās.

5.3 【梵漢辭典,p1406】（陽性）（陰性=vedikā）壇；長凳子，（經文）欄楯，軒檻，軒陛，欄杆，邊框，台，火供竈邊。

6. ध्वजैर् dhvajair 名詞　幢幡

6.1 【詞尾變化】dhvajair 根據連音規則是從 dhvajaiḥ 變化過來，而 dhvajaiḥ 是 dhvaja 複數工具格形，所以字典查 dhvaja。

6.2 【摩威梵英,p522】

6.2.1 m.（n. only and g. *ardharcādi* ; fr. dhvaj）a banner , flag , standard（ifc. f. *ā*）RV. ; a flag-staff ; mark , emblem , ensign , characteristic , sign MBh.; attribute of a deity; the sign of any trade（esp. of a distillery or tavern）and the business there carried on ; a distiller or vendor of spirituous liquors L. ;

6.2.2（ifc.）the ornament of ; the organ of generation（of any animal , male or female）; a skull carried on a staff（as a penance for the murder of a Brāhman; as a mark of ascetics and Yogīs）; a place prepared in a peculiar way for building（in pros.）an iambic ;（in Gr.）a partic. kind of Krama-pāṭha:（in astrol.）N. of a Yoga ; pride , arrogance , hypocrisy ; N. of a Grāma.

6.3 【梵漢辭典,p385】（陽性名詞）幢，旗，旌旗，記號，標幟，象徵；（神格的）屬性，酒館或造酒者的招牌；（經文）幢，幢幡，幡，寶幢，幢相，表相，相，幢麾，旗。

7. अलंकृतान् alaṁkṛtān 形容詞　被裝飾的

7.1【詞尾變化】alaṁkṛtān 是 alaṁkṛta 的對格複數形，所以字典查 alaṁkṛta。

7.2【摩威梵英,p94】（ataṃ）mfn. adorned , decorated（cf. araṃ-kṛta s.v. aram）

7.3 【梵漢辭典,p68】（過被動分詞）（形容詞）裝扮的，被裝飾的；（經文）嚴，嚴飾，瑩飾。

8. सवैजयन्तान् savaijayantān 名詞　其勝幡

8.1 【詞尾變化】savaijayantān 是由 sa-vaijayantān 所組成，而 vaijayantān 爲 vaijayanta 的複數對格形，所以字典查 vaijayanta。

8.2 【摩威梵英,p1021】

8.2.1 m.（fr. *vi-jayat* , or *-yanta*）the banner of Indra MBh. ; a banner , flag ; the palace of Indra Buddh. ; a house; N. of Skanda ; of a mountain MBh.;

8.2.2 pl.（with Jainas）N. of a class of deities ;

8.2.3（*ī*）f. a flag , banner MBh.; an ensign ; a kind of garland prognosticating victory MBh. ; the necklace of Viśṇu ; N. of the 8th night of the civil month ; Premna Spinosa; Sesbania Aegyptiaca ; N. of a lexicon by Yādavaprakāśa ; of a Comm. to Viśṇu's Dharmaśāstra; of various other wks. ; of a town or a river AV. Pariś. ;

8.2.4 n. N. of a gate in Ayodhya1 ; of a town（=*vana-vāsī*）.

8.3 【梵漢辭典,p1372】（陽性名詞）〔屬於征服者 vijayat〕Indra 神旗；旗幟，軍旗，Indra 神宮；〔某山名〕（中性名詞）某市鎮名；（經文）勝幡，勝殿，天宮，帝釋宮，殊勝殿，殊勝宮殿，最勝法堂。

9. मयानि mayāni 形容詞　所形成；由～構成

9.1 【詞尾變化】mayāni 是 maya 的複數主格形，所以字典查 maya。

9.2 資料前面已有說明。

10. तथैव tathaiva 副詞片語 如是

10.1 【詞尾變化】tathaiva 根據連音規則是由 tathā-eva 所組成，所以字典查 tathā-eva。

10.2 資料前面已有說明。

【筆者試譯】：有些以四匹馬拖拉的馬車，
它的欄杆被飾以花，旗子，
用華美的勝幡，寶物來構成，
像這樣的一些（寶車）也布施！

【什公漢譯】：或有菩薩，駟馬寶車，欄楯華蓋，軒飾布施。

【英 譯 本】：Some give carriages yoked with four horses
and furnished with benches, flowers, banners, and
flags; others give objects made of precious
substances.

【信譯研究】：信譯。

【第十八頌】

ददन्ति पुत्रांश्च तथैव पुत्रीः
प्रियाणि मांसानि ददन्ति केचित्।
हस्तांश्च पादांश्च ददन्ति याचिताः
पर्येषमाणा इममग्रबोधिम्॥ १८॥

【羅馬譯音】

dadanti putrāṁśca tathaiva putrīḥ
priyāṇi māṁsāni dadanti kecit|
hastāṁśca pādāṁśca dadanti yācitāḥ
paryeṣamāṇā imamagrabodhim||18||

【句義解析】

dadanti putrāṁś ca tathaiva putrīḥ
priyāṇi māṁsāni dadanti ke-cit|
hastāṁś ca pādāṁś ca dadanti yācitāḥ
paryeṣamāṇā imam agra-bodhim||18||

【辭彙研究】

1. पुत्रांश्च putrāṁś ca 名詞　兒子

1.1 【詞尾變化】putrāṁś ca 根據連音規則是由 putrān ca 所組成，而 putrān 是 putra 的複數對格形，所以字典查 putra。

1.2 資料前面已有說明。

2. पुत्रीः putrīḥ 名詞　女兒

2.1 【詞尾變化】putrīḥ 是 putrī 的複數對格形，而 putrī 是 putra 的陰性形，所以是女兒。

3. प्रियाणि priyāṇi 形容詞　親愛的

3.1 【詞尾變化】priyāṇi 是 priya 的對格複數形，所以字典查 priya。

3.2 【摩威梵英,p710】

3.2.1 mf（*ā*）n. beloved , dear to（gen. loc. dat. or comp.）, liked , favourite , wanted , own RV. ; dear , expensive , high in price; fond of attached or devoted to（loc.）RV. ;

3.2.2 m. a friend; a lover , husband MBh.; a son-in-law; a kind of deer ; N. of 2 medicinal plants ;

3.2.3（*ā*）f. a mistress , wife MBh. ; the female of an animal; news ; small cardamoms ; Arabian jasmine ; spirituous liquor ; N. of a daughter of Daksha ; of various metres ;

3.2.4 n. love , kindness , favour , pleasure MBh. ;

3.2.5（*am*）ind. agreeably , kindly , in a pleasant way ;

3.3 【梵漢辭典,p977】（形容詞）與～親近的，被～所愛的，受寵愛的，和藹的，令人欣喜的，愉快的，親密的，偏好，專心於，更親愛的；（經文）愛，所愛，可愛，所可愛，所重愛，愛者，慈愛，淨愛，愛念，所愛念，愛樂，樂，軟，惜者，敬伏，喜，欣悅，善，染。

4. मांसानि māṁsāni 名詞　肉

4.1 【詞尾變化】māṁsāni 是 māṁsa 的複數對格形，所以字典查 māṁsa。

4.2 【摩威梵英,p805】

4.2.1 n. sg. and pl. flesh , meat RV.（also said of the fleshy part or pulp of fruit）;

4.2.2 m. N. of a mixed caste MBh.（=*māṃsa-vikretṛ*）; a worm ; time;

4.2.3（*ī*）f. Nardostachys Jatamansi ; = *kakkoī* , f. ; = *māṃsa-cchadā.*

4.3 【梵漢辭典,p696】（中性名詞）肉，獸肉（魚蟹及果實之肉）;漿狀食物；（經文）肉，身肉，（皮）肉。

5. हस्तांश्च hastāṁś ca 名詞　手

5.1【詞尾變化】hastāṁś ca 根據連音規則是由 hastān ca 所變化過來，而 hastān 是 hasta 的複數對格，所以字典查 hasta。

5.2 【摩威梵英,p1294】

5.2.1 m.（ifc. f. *ā* , of unknown derivation）the hand（ifc. = `holding in or by the hand ' ; *haste kṛ* 〔as two words〕 , `to take into the hand' , `get possession of ' ; *haste- kṛ* 〔as a comp.〕 , `to take by the hand , marry' ; *śatru-hastaṃ gam* , `to fall into the hand of the enemy '）RV.; an elephant's trunk（ifc. = `holding with the trunk'）MBh.; the fore-arm（a measure of length from the elbow to the tip of the middle finger , = 24 Aṅgulas or about 18 inches）; the position of the hand（=*hasta-vinyāsa*）; hand-writing; the 11th（13th）lunar asterism（represented by a hand and containing five stars , identified by some with part of the constellation Corvus）AV. ; a species of tree;（in prosody）an anapest; quantity , abundance , mass（ifc. after words signifying `hair'）; N. of a guardian of the Soma; of a son of Vasudeva BhP. ; of another man ;

5.2.2（*hastā*）f. the hand AV; the Nakshatra Hasta ;

5.2.3（*am*）n. a pair of leather bellows ;

5.2.4 mfn. born under the Nakshatra Hasta.

5.3 【梵漢辭典,p486】（陽性名詞）手，（象）鼻；筆跡，豐富；（經文）手，肘；（形容詞）拿在手中的；（經文）持，執，手持，守擊。

6. पादांश्च pādāṁś ca 名詞　腳

6.1【詞尾變化】pādāṁś ca 根據連音規則是由 pādān ca 所變化過來，而 pādān 是 pāda 的複數對格，所以字典查 pāda。

6.2 【摩威梵英,p617】m.（ifc. f. ā , rarely ī）the foot（of men and animals）RV. ; the foot or leg of an inanimate object , column , pillar AV. MBh.; a wheel; a foot as a measure（= 12 Aṇgulas）; the foot or root of a tree ; the foot or a hill at the fñfoot of a mountain MBh.; the bottom MBh.; a ray or beam of light（considered as the fñfoot of a heavenly body）; a quarter , a fourth Part（the fourth of a quadruped being one out of 4）MBh.（pl. the 4 parts i. e. all things required for 〔gen.〕）; the quadrant（of a circle）; a verse or line（as the fourth part of a regular stanza）; the caesura of a verse , the chapter of a book（orig. only of a book or section of a bñbook consisting of 4 parts , as the Adhyāyas of Pāṇini's grammar）.

6.3 【梵漢辭典,p823】（陽性名詞）（人，動物的）腳；（無生物的）足或腳，支柱；（運水皮袋的）底部；車輪；（樹）根；（山的）突出部；山麓的小丘；光線；光；（經文）足，腳。

7. याचिताः yācitāḥ 形容詞／過去被動分詞　豐滿的

7.1 【詞尾變化】yācitāḥ 爲 yā-citāḥ 所組成，其中 yā 爲 ya 的陰性。而 citāḥ 爲 cita 的複數主格形，由於 ya 的資料前面已有說明，故字典查 cita。

7.2 【摩威梵英,p394】

7.2.1 mfn. piled up , heaped RV. AV.; placed in a line RV.; collected , gained ; forming a mass（hair）Buddh. ; covered , inlaid , set with MBh. ;

7.2.2 n. `a building' see *pakveṣṭaka-* ;

7.2.3（*ā*）f. a layer , pile of wood , funeral pile MBh. ; a heap , multitude.

7.3 【梵漢辭典,p330】（過去被動分詞）（經文）饒，豐滿，稠密，充實，所增長；（經文）聚色，微聚。

8. पर्येषमाणा paryeṣamāṇā 形容詞／分詞　求〔註 38〕

【筆者試譯】：也是這樣布施出兒女

〔註 38〕paryeṣamāṇā 於兩本梵文字典均無所獲，疑似非梵文，但亦未見收於艾格混梵字典，據日本學者江島惠教經對照經文後指出，這個字的意思應該是「求」的意思。請見江島惠教等編《梵藏漢法華經原典總索引》，東京：靈友會出版，1988 年出版。頁 617。

也布施一些身（體上的）肉
也捐出了生長良好的手和腳
（來）求得那無上菩提！

【什公漢譯】：復見菩薩，身肉手足，及妻子施，求無上道，

【英 譯 本】：Some, again, give their children and wives;
others their own flesh;（or）offer, when bidden,
their hands and feet, striving to gain supreme
enlightenment.

【信譯研究】：非信譯。這一頌裡面梵文裡面並未看到有關妻子的敘述，不知道爲什麼鳩摩羅什與英譯者不約而同都提到「妻子」，也許這裡面有典故吧？還有待查證。

【第十九頌】

शिरांसि केचिन्नयनानि केचिद्
ददन्ति केचित्प्रवरात्मभावान्।
दत्वा च दानानि प्रसन्नचित्ताः
प्रार्थेन्ति ज्ञानं हि तथागतानाम्॥१९॥

【羅馬譯音】

śirāṁsi kecinnayanāni kecid
dadanti kecitpravarātmabhāvān|
datvā ca dānāni prasannacittāḥ
prārthenti jñānaṁ hi tathāgatānām||19||

【句義解析】

śirāṁsi ke-cin nayanāni ke-cid
dadanti ke-cit pravarātmabhāvān|
datvā ca dānāni prasanna-cittāḥ
prārthenti jñānaṁ hi tathāgatānām||19||

【辭彙研究】

1. शिरांसि śirāṁsi 名詞　頭

1.1 【詞尾變化】śirāṁsi 是 śiras 的複數對格形，所以字典查 śiras。

1.2 【摩威梵英,p1072】n.（prob. originally śaras = karas ; and connected with karaṅka q.v.）the head , skull（acc. with dā , `to give up one's head i.e. life ' ; with dhṛ , or vah , `to hold up one's head , be proud' ; with Caus. of vṛt or with upa-sthā , `to hold out the head ' , ` acknowledge one's self guilty' ; instr. with grah , dhā , dhṛ , vi-dhṛ , bhṛ , vah , or kṛ , `to hold or carry or place on the head , receive deferentially' ; instr. with gam , abhi-gam , pra-grah , yā , pra-ṇam 〔 nam〕 , ni-pat , pra-ṇi-pat , `to touch with the head , bow or fall down before ' ; loc. with kṛ or ni-dhā, `to place on one's head' ; loc. with sthā , `to be on or stand over a person's head , stand far above〔gen.〕)' RV.; the upper end or highest part of anything , top , peak , summit , pinnacle , acme MBh.; the forepart or van（of an army）; the beginning（of a verse）;（ifc.）the head , leader , chief , foremost , first（of a class）; N. of the verse āpo jyotir āpo 'mṛtam Baudh.; of a Sāman（also with indrasya）; of a mountain Buddh.

1.3 【梵漢辭典,p1175】（中性名詞）頭，頂上，峰，前端，前部，（軍隊的）先鋒，首領，首長，（等級上）第一的；（經文）頭，首，髮；頂，頂上。

2. केचिन् ke-cin 不定詞片語　有些

2.1 【詞尾變化】ke-cin 根據連音規則即 ke-cid。

2.2 資料前面已有說明。

3. नयनानि nayanāni 名詞　眼睛

3.1 【詞尾變化】nayanāni 是 nayana 的複數對格，字典查 nayana。

3.2 【摩威梵英,p528】

3.2.1 m. N. of a man;（*ā* or *ī*）f. the pupil of the eye ;

3.2.2 n. leading , directing , managing , conducting ; carrying , bringing ;

3.2.3（*kālasya*）fixing MBh. ; drawing , moving（a man or piece in a game）;

3.2.4（pl.）prudent , conduct , polity BhP.; `the leading organ , the eye（ifc. f. *ā* or *ī*）MBh.

3.3 【梵漢辭典,p774】（中性形容詞／名詞）帶來，施行，楚理，管理，眼睛；（經文）眼，目，將導，至。

4. प्रवरात्मभावान् pravarātmabhāvān 複合名詞　最好的身體

4.1 【詞尾變化】pravarātmabhāvān 根據連音規則即 pravara-ātma-bhāvān 的組合，其中 bhāvān 是 bhāva 的複數對格，所以字典查 pravara-ātma-bhāva。

4.2 【摩威梵英,p690, pravara】

4.2.1 mf（*ā*）n.（fr. *pra* + *vara* or fr. *pra* √2. *vṛ*）most excellent , chief , principal , best MBh. ; eldest（son）MBh. ; better than（abl.）BhP. ; greater; （ifc.）eminent , distinguished by ;

4.2.2 m. a black variety of Phaseolus Mungo ; N. of a messenger of the gods and friend of Indra ;

4.2.3（*ā*）f. N. of a river（which falls into the Godāvarī and is celebrated for the sweetness of its water）MBh. ;

4.2.4 n. aloe wood; a partic. high number Buddh.

4.3 【摩威梵英,p135, ātma- bhāva】m. existence of the soul; the self , proper or peculiar nature Buddh. ; the body.

4.4 【梵漢辭典,p967, pravara】（形容詞）卓越的，高貴的，中首要的，最善的，最優秀的，最年長的（兒子）；比～（從格）更好的；（經文）勝，最勝，殊勝，妙，最妙，微妙，第一，最第一，最上，極，尊，雄猛。

4.5 【梵漢辭典,p196, ātma- bhāva】（陽性名詞）恆久存在的我；自我之存在，個性，身體；（經文）身，自身，己身，身體，內身，本身，身（量），身（命），身分，所依身，形，身形，字體，自性，我相，依內。

5. दत्वाच datvā ca 動名詞　付出；交出

5.1 【詞尾變化】datvā 爲√dā 的動名詞異寫，故字典查√dā。

5.2 資料前面已有說明。

6. प्रसन्न prasanna 形容詞　歡喜

6.1 【詞尾變化】沒有詞尾變化。

6.2 【摩威梵英,p696】

6.2.1 mfn. clear , bright , pure（lit. and fig.）MBh. ; distinct , perspicuous MBh. ; true , right , plain , correct , just; placid , tranquil ; soothed , pleased ; gracious , kind , kindly disposed towards（with loc. gen. , or acc. aod *prati*), favourable（as stars）; gracious , showing favour（as a speech）MBh. ;

6.2.2 m. N. of a prince Hemac. ;（*ā*）f. propitiating , pleasing; spirituous liquor made of rice ;

6.2.3 -*kalpa* mfn. almost quiet , tolerably calm;

6.2.4 -*gātr-tā*. f. having tranquil limbs（one of the 80 minor marks of a Buddha）;

6.2.5 -*caṇḍikā* f. N. of a drama ;

6.2.6 -*candra* m. N. of a prince ;

6.2.7 -*jala* mfn. containing clear water ;

6.2.8 -*tarka* mfn. conjecturing right ;

6.2.9 -*tā* f. brightness , clearness , purity; clearness of expression , perspicuity; complacence , good humour;

6.2.10 -*tva* n. clearness , purity MBh. ;

6.2.11 -*pāda* m. or n.（?）N. of wk. by Dharma-kirti ;

6.2.12 -*prāya* mfn. rather plain or correct , Ma1latim. ;

6.2.13 -*mukha* mfn. `placid-countenanced' , looking pleased , smiling W. ;

6.2.14 -*rasa* mfn. clear-juiced Kpr. ;

6.2.15 -*rāghava* n. N. of a drama by Jaya-deva ;

6.2.16 -*veṅkaṭeśva-māhāmya* n. N. of a legend in the Bhavishyottara-Purāṇa ;

6.2.17 -*sāila* mfn. -*jala* MBh. ;

6.2.18 -*sannātman* mfn. gracious-minded , propitious ;

6.2.19 -*sannerā* f. spirituous liquor made of rice.

6.3 【梵漢辭典,p932】（過去被動分詞）（形容詞）（經文）淨，清淨，善淨，純淨，明淨，澄淨（無穢）；淨信，淨信者，已淨信者，清淨信，歡喜，欣樂，喜明，安，安靜。

7. प्रार्थेन्ति prārthenti 動詞　渴望

7.1 【詞尾變化】根據學者江島惠教研究，prārthenti 與 pra-√arth 第三人稱複數有關，所以字典查 pra-√arth。〔註 39〕

〔註 39〕prārthenti 這個字與 prārthayanti 近似，疑似轉寫的問題，故被看作是與 pra-√arth 有關。請見江島惠教等編《梵藏漢法華經原典總索引》，東京：靈友會出版，1988 年出版。頁 697。

7.2【摩威梵英,p708】(pra-√arth)Ā. prārthayate(ep. also P. -ti and pr. p. -yāna), to wish or long for , desire（acc.）MBh. ; to ask a person（acc.）for（acc. or loc.)or ask anything(acc.)from(abl.)MBh. ; to wish to or ask a person to(inf.)ib. ; to demand in marriage , woo; to look for , search Bhat2t2. ; to have recourse to（acc.）; to seize or fall upon , attack , assail.

7.3 【梵漢辭典】無資料。

8. ज्ञानं jñānaṁ 名詞　知識

8.1【詞尾變化】jñānaṁ 根據連音規則是 jñānam 變化過來，而 jñānam 是 jñāna 的單數對格，所以字典查 jñāna。

8.2　資料前面已有說明。

9. तथागतानाम् tathāgatānām 形容詞　如來的

9.1 【詞尾變化】tathāgatānām 是 tathāgata 的屬格複數形，所以字典查 tathāgata。

9.2 【摩威梵英,p433】

9.2.1 mfn. being in such a state or condition , of such a quality or nature MBh. ; `he who comes and goes in the same way〔as the Buddhas who preceded him〕', Gautama Buddha Buddh; a Buddhist ;

9.2.2 -*kośa-paripālitā* f. N. of a Kiṃnara virgin ;

9.2.3 -*garbha* m. N. of a Bodhi-sattva Buddh. ;

9.2.4 -guṇa-jñānācintya-viṣajyāvatāranirdeśa m. `direction how to attain to the inconceivable subject of the Tathā-gata's qualities and knowledge' N. of a Buddh. Su1tra ;

9.2.5 -*gukyaka* n. `Tathāgata-mystery '　N. of a Buddh. work（highly revered in Nepa1l）;

9.2.6 -*bhadra* m. N. of a pupil of Nāgārjuna.

9.3 【梵漢辭典,p1281】（形容詞）這樣的舉止，在如此狀態，這樣的性質或本性的，如這樣的。（陽性名詞）佛陀，佛教徒；（經文）如來，如去，如來至眞，得如者，得眞如誠如來者；佛，世尊。

【筆者試譯】：有些（是）頭，有些（是）眼睛，
有些人捐出了最好的身體，

他們用歡喜的心布施了，
爲了渴求如來佛祖的智慧。

【什公漢譯】：又見菩薩，頭目身體，欣樂施與，求佛智慧。

【英 譯 本】：Some give their heads, others their eyes,

others their dear own body, and after cheerfully bestowing their gifts they aspire to the knowledge of the Tathâgatas.

【信譯研究】：信譯。

【第廿頌】

पश्याम्यहं मञ्जुशिरी कहिंचित्
स्फीतानि राज्यानि विवर्जयित्वा।
अन्तःपुरान् द्वीप तथैव सर्वान्
अमात्यज्ञातींश्च विहाय सर्वान्॥२०॥

【羅馬譯音】

paśyāmyahaṁ mañjuśirī kahiṁcit
sphītāni rājyāni vivarjayitvā|
antaḥpurān dvīpa tathaiva sarvān
amātyajñātīṁśca vihāya sarvān||20||

【句義解析】

Paśyāmy ahaṁ Mañjuśirī kahiṁ-cit
sphītāni rājyāni vivarjayitvā|
antaḥpurān dvīpa tathaiva sarvān
amātya-jñātīṁś ca vihāya sarvān||20||

【辭彙研究】

1. पश्याम्य paśyāmy 動詞 我看

1.1 【詞尾變化】根據連音規則 paśyāmy 是從 paśyāmi 變化過來，而 paśyāmi 是√paś 的第一人稱單數形，所以字典查√paś。

1.2 資料前面已有說明。

2. कहिंचित् kahiṁ-cit 片語 有多少的～啊！

2.1 【詞尾變化】kahiṁ-cit 根據連音則是從 ka-him-cit 變化過來，而 ka 與 cit 前面已經有資料說明，字典查 him。

2.2 【摩威梵英,p1298】ind. an exclamation（interchangeable with hiṅ, see q.v.）

2.3 【摩威梵英,p1298, hiṅ】ind. the lowing sound or cry made by a cow seeking her calf RV.

2.4 【梵漢辭典,p491】（感歎詞）= hiṅ。

2.5 【梵漢辭典,p491,hiṅ】（感歎詞）(+Kṛ)，牛鳴聲，發出如牛之聲。

3. स्फीतानि sphītāni 過去被動分詞 繁榮

3.1 【詞尾變化】sphītāni 是 sphīta 的複數對格形，而 sphīta 是√sphāy 的過去被動分詞形，所以字典查√sphāy。

3.2 【摩威梵英,p1270】cl. 1. to grow fat , become bulky , swell , increase , expand; to resound, to become fat, to fatten , swell , strengthen , increase , augment.

3.3 【梵漢辭典,p1191】（第一類動詞）長肥，膨脹，增大，回響，發展，繁榮，興盛，旺盛，富裕（國，家等），在順境，富裕，豐饒；豐富的，潤澤的，充滿的或富有的，多量的，填滿的；（經文）豐，盛，興，豐樂，安樂，豐滿，多饒。

4. राज्यानि rājyāni 形容詞 皇家的

4.1 【詞尾變化】rājyāni 是 rājya 的複數對格形，所以字典查 rājya。

4.2 【摩威梵英,p875】

4.2.1 mfn. kingly , princely , royal ;

4.2.2 n.（also *rājya* or *rājyā*）royalty , kingship , sovereignty , empire（`over' loc. or comp. ; `of' gen. or comp. ; acc. with *kṛ* or Caus. of *kṛ* or with *upa-ās* or *vi-dhā* , to exercise government , rule , govern）AV.; kingdom , country , realm（= *rāṣṭra*）.

4.3 【梵漢辭典,p1011】（形容詞）皇家的，王室的；（中性）對～的主權，統治權；王國，領土。（經文）王，帝王，王位，國王位，國位，增上位，國，國城，國土，皇國。

5. विवर्जयित्वा vivarjayitvā 動詞　放棄

5.1 【詞尾變化】vivarjayitvā 是由 vi-varjayitvā 構成，也就是 vi-√vṛj 的不變格使役動詞之分詞形，因此字典查 vi-√vṛj。

5.2 【摩威梵英,p988】Caus. -varjayati , to exclude , avoid , shun , abandon , leave MBh.; to distribute , give.

5.3 【梵漢辭典,p1475】（使役）迴避，避開，放棄；（經文）離，捨，除，反，遠離，捨離，棄捨，退散。

6. अन्तःपुरान् antaḥpurān 名詞　宮殿眷屬

6.1 【詞尾變化】antaḥpurān 是 antaḥpura 的複數對格形，所以字典查 antaḥpura。

6.2 【摩威梵英,p43】n. the king's palace , the female apartments , gynaeceum ; those who live in the female apartments ; a queen.

6.3 【梵漢辭典,p103】（名詞）（內城），王城，後供，婦女之房間，（單，複數）國王的后妃；（經文）家，宮，王宮，宮殿，中宮，後宮，宮人，妃后宮人，內人，妾，中宮婇女，后眷屬，宮殿眷屬，婇女眷屬。

7. अमात्य amātya 名詞　王臣

7.1 【詞尾變化】沒有詞尾變化。

7.2 【摩威梵英,p81】（4）m.（fr. amā）inmate of the same house , belonging to the same house or family RV.; `a companion（of a king）' , minister MBh.

7.3 【梵漢辭典,p75】（名詞）家人，親戚，大臣（經文）臣，大臣，輔臣，王臣，臣佐，官，宰官，達官，輔相，僚庶。

8. ज्ञातींश् jñātīṁś 名詞　親戚

8.1 【詞尾變化】jñātīṁś 根據連音規則是由 jñātīn 變化過來，而 jñātīn 則是 jñāti 複數對格形，所以字典查 jñāti。

8.2 【摩威梵英,p425】m. `intimately acquainted', a near relation（`paternal relation'）, kinsman RV.

8.3 【梵漢辭典,p539】（陽性）近親；親戚；（經文）親，親族，親屬，親戚，親友，宗親，鄉親，眷屬，眷族；親里；恩愛。

9. विहाय vihāya 動名詞　放棄

9.1 【詞尾變化】沒有詞尾變化。

9.2 【摩威梵英,p1003】ind. leaving behind i.e. at a distance from（acc.）; disregarding , overlooking , setting aside = more than（acc.）; in spite of , notwithstanding（acc.）; excepting , with the exception of（acc.）.

9.3 【梵漢辭典,p1424】（動名詞）（經文）滅，棄捨。

10. सर्वान् sarvān 形容詞　一切的

10.1 【詞尾變化】sarvān 是 sarva 的複數對格形，所以字典查 sarva。

10.2 資料前面已有說明。

【筆者試譯】：文殊師利菩薩，我看有多少（人）啊！
放棄了繁榮的國家王位，
也（放棄了）一切的宮殿眷屬，領土，
放下了一切的王臣，與親戚！

【什公漢譯】：文殊師利，我見諸王，往詣佛所，問無上道。

【英 譯 本】：Here and there, O Mañgusrî, I behold beings
who have abandoned their flourishing kingdoms,
harems, and continents, left all their counsellors and
kinsmen,

【信譯研究】：信譯。與下一頌交錯翻譯。

【第廿一頌】

उपसंक्रमी लोकविनायकेषु
पृच्छन्ति धर्मं प्रवरं शिवाय।
काषायवस्त्राणि च प्रावरन्ति
केशांश्च श्मश्रूण्यवतारयन्ति॥२१॥

【羅馬譯音】

upasaṁkramī lokavināyakeṣu
pṛcchanti dharmaṁ pravaraṁ śivāya|
kāṣāyavastrāṇi ca prāvaranti

keśāṁśca śmaśrūṇyavatārayanti||21||

【句義解析】

upasaṁkramī loka-vināyakeṣu
pṛcchanti dharmaṁ pravaraṁ śivāya|
kāṣāya-vastrāṇi ca prāvaranti
keśāṁś ca śmaśrūṇy avatārayanti||21||

【辭彙研究】

1. उपसंक्रमी upasaṁkramī 動詞　到另外一邊

1.1 【詞尾變化】upasaṁkramī 是從 upasaṁ-√kram 變化過來，〔註 40〕所以字典查 upasaṁ-√kram。

1.2 【摩威梵英,p209】-krāmati , -kramate , to step or go to the other side（or other world）: Caus. -kramayati , to cause to go to the other side.

1.3 【梵漢辭典,p608】（動詞）（經文）往彼所。

2. विनायकेषु vināyakeṣu 名詞　引導者

2.1【詞尾變化】vināyakeṣu 是 vināyaka 的複數於格形，所以字典查 vināyaka。

2.2 【摩威梵英,p972】

2.2.1 mf（*ikā*）n. taking away , removing;

2.2.2 m. `Remover（of obstacles）'N. of Gaṇeśa; a leader , guide MBh.; a Guru or spiritual preceptor; a Buddha; N. of Garuḍa; an obstacle , impediment ; = *anātha*（?）L. ; N. of various authors;

2.2.3 pl. a partic. class of demons MBh.; N. of partic. formulas recited over weapons;

2.2.4（*ikā*）f. the wife of Gaṇeśa or Garuḍa;

2.2.5 -*caturthī* f. the fourth day of the festival in honour of Gaṇea;（-*thī-vrata* n. N. of wk.）;

2.2.6 -*carita* n. N. of the 73rd ch. of the Krīḍā-khaṇḍa or 2nd part of the Gaṇeśa-Purāṇa. ;

〔註 40〕請見江島惠教等編《梵藏漢法華經原典總索引》，東京：靈友會出版，1988 年出版。頁 208。

2.2.7 -*dvādaśa-nāma-stotra* n. N. of wk. ;

2.2.8 -*paṇḍita* m. N. of a poet; = *nanda-paṇḍ-* Cat. ;

2.2.9 -*purāṇa* n. -*pūjā-vidhi* m. N. of wks. ;

2.2.10 -*bhaṭṭa* m. N. of various authors Cat. ;

2.3 【梵漢辭典,p1438】（陽性名詞）領導者，嚮導；（障礙的）去除者，（經文）將，導師，善導，如來，廣說者。

3. पृच्छन्ति pṛcchanti 動詞　達成（由他人）

3.1 【詞尾變化】pṛcchanti 是√praś 的現在式第三人稱複數形，所以字典查√praś。但是這個單字不見錄於這兩本辭典中，疑爲非標準梵文。

3.2 【艾格混梵,p353】

3.2.1 requests, asks, something to be done by another.

3.2.2 In mg. of Skt, says goodby.

4. धर्मं dharmaṁ 名詞　法

4.1【詞尾變化】dharmaṁ 根據連音規則是從 dharmam 變化過來，而 dharmam 是 dharma 的單數對格形，所以字典查 dharma。

4.2 資料前面已有。

5. प्रवरं pravaraṁ 形容詞　卓越的；優秀的

5.1【詞尾變化】pravaraṁ 根據連音規則是從 pravaram 變化過來，而 pravaram 是 pravara 的單數對格形，所以字典查 pravara。

5.2 資料前面已有說明。

6. शिवअय śivāya 形容詞　親切的

6.1 【詞尾變化】śivāya 是 śiva 的爲格單數形，所以字典查 śiva。

6.2 【摩威梵英,p1074】

6.2.1 mf（*ā*）n.（fr. √śī , `in whom all things lie' ; perhaps connected with *śvi*）auspicious , propitious , gracious , favourable , benign , kind , benevolent , friendly , dear（*am* ind. kindly , tenderly）RV. ; happy , fortunate BhP. ;

6.2.2 m. happiness , welfare（cf. n.）; liberation , final emancipation; `The Auspicious one 'N. of the disintegrating or destroying and reproducing deity（who constitutes the third god of the Hindu Trimūrti or Triad , the other two being Brahmā '' the creator' and Vishṇu `the preserver' ; in the

Veda the only N. of the destroying deity wss Rudra `the terrible god' , but in later times it became usual to give that god the euphemistic N. Śiva ` the auspicious' , and to assign him the office of creation and reproduction as well as dissolution ; in fact the preferential worship of Śiva as developed in the Purāṇas and Epic poems led to his being identified with the Supreme Being by his exclusive worshippers 〔called Śaivas〕 ; in his character of destroyer he is sometimes called Kāla ` black' , and is then also identified with Time ' , although his active destroying function is then oftener assigned to his wife under her name Kālī , whose formidable character makes her a general object of propitiation by sacrifices ; as presiding over reproduction consequent on destruction Śiva's symbol is the Liṇga or Phallus , under which form he is worshipped all over India at the present day ; again one of his representations is as Ardha-nārī , `half-female' , the other half being male to symbolize the unity of the generative principle; he has three eyes , one of which is in his forehead , and which are thought to denote his view of the three divisions of time , past , present , and future , while a moon's crescent , above the central eye , marks the measure of time by months , a serpent round his neck the measure by years , and a second necklace of skulls with other serpents about his person , the perpetual revolution of ages , and the successive extinction and generation of the races of mankind: his hair is thickly matted together , and gathered above his forehead into a coil ; on the top of it he bears the Ganges , the rush of which in its descent from heaven he intercepted by his head that the earth might not be crushed by the weight of the falling stream ; his throat is dark-blue from the stain of the deadly poison which would have destroyed the world had it not been swallowed by him on its production at the churning of the ocean by the gods for the nectar of immortality ; he holds a *tri-śūla* , or three-pronged trident 〔also called Pināka〕 in his hand to denote , as some think , his combination of the three attributes of Creator , Destroyer , and Regenerator ; he also carries a kind of drum , shaped like an hour-glass , called Ḍamaru: his attendants or servants are called Pramatha; they are regarded as demons or supernatural beings of different kinds , and form various hosts or troops called Gaṇas ; his wife Durgā is the chief object of worship with the Śāktas and Tāntrikas , and in this connection he is fond of dancing and wine-drinking; he is also worshipped as a great ascetic and is said to have scorched the god of love （Kāma-deva） to ashes by a glance from his central eye , that deity having attempted to inflame him with passion for Pa1rvati1 whilst he was engaged in severe penance ; in the exercise of his function of Universal Destroyer he is fabled to have burnt up the Universe and all the gods , including Brahma1 and Vishṇu , by a similar scorching glance , and to have rubbed the resulting ashes upon his body , whence the use of ashes in his worship , while the use of the Rudra7ksha berries originated , it is said , from the legend that Śiva , on his way to destroy the three cities , called Tri-pura , let fall some tears of rage which became converted into these beads: his residence or heaven is Kaila1sa , one of the loftiest northern peaks of the Hima7laya ; he has strictly no incarnations like those of Vishṇu , though Vīra-bhadra and the eight Bhairavas and Khaṇḍo-bā are sometimes regarded as forms of him ; he is especially worshipped at Benares and has even more names than Vishn2u , one thousand and eight being specified in the 69th chapter of the Śiva-Purāṇa and in the 17th chapter of the Anuśāsana-parvan of the Maha-bhārata , some of the most common being Mahā-deva , Śambhu , Śaṃkara , Īśa , Īśvara , Maheśvara , Hara ; his sons are Gaṇeśa and Kārttikeya） MBh. ; a kind of second Siva（with Śaivas）, a person who has attained a partic. stage of perfection or emancipation MBh. ; any god ; a euphemistic N. of a jackal; sacred writings ;（in astron.）N. of the sixth month ; a post for cows（to which they are tied or for them to rub against）; bdellium ; the fragrant bark of Feronia Elephantum ; Marsilia Dentata ; a kind of thorn-apple or = *puṇḍarīka*（the tree）; quicksilver; a partic. auspicious constellation ; a demon who inflicts diseases ;

6.2.3 = *śukra* m. *kāla* m. *vasu* m. ; the swift antelope L. ; rum , spirit distilled from molasses; buttermilk ; a ruby ; a peg ; time ; N. of a son of Medhatithi ; of a son of Īdhma-jihva BhP. ; of a prince and various authors（also with *dīkśita* , *bhaṭṭa* , *paṇḍita* , *yajvan* , *sūri*）; of a fraudulent person ;（du.）the god Śiva and his wife;

6.2.4 pl. N. of a class of gods in the third Manvantara ; of a class of Brāhmans who have attained a partic. degree of perfection like that of Śiva MBh. ;

6.2.5（*ā*）f. Śiva's wife（also *śivī*）;

6.2.6（*am*）n. welfare , prosperity , bliss RV. ; final emancipation ; water ; rock-salt ; sea-salt ; a kind of borax ; iron ; myrobolan ; Tabernaemontana Coronaria ; sandal ; N. of a Pura1n2a（=*śiva-purāṇa* or *śaiva*）; of the house in which the Pāṇḍavas were to be burnt; of a Varsha in Plaksha-dvīpa and in Jambu-dvīpa.

6.3 【梵漢辭典,p1180】（形容詞）親切的，好意的，仁慈的，愉快的，吉祥的，繁榮的，幸福的（經文）精，柔善，寂靜，清涼，淨，清淨，安，樂，常樂，安隱，妙，福壽，吉祥之事，涅槃。

7. काशाय kāṣāya 名詞　臉頰

7.1 【詞尾變化】kāṣāya 是 kāṣa 的爲格單數形，所以字典查 kāṣa。

7.2 【摩威梵英,p281】see kapola-k-.

7.3 【摩威梵英,p251, kapola】

7.3.1 m.（ifc. f. *ā*）, the cheek（of men or elephants）;

7.3.2（*ās*）m. pl. N. of a school belonging to the white Yajur-veda ;

7.3.3（*ī*）f. the fore-part of the knee , knee-cap or pan.

7.4 【梵漢辭典,p578】（陽性）摩擦，=kapola。

7.5 【梵漢辭典,p566, kapola】（陽性）臉頰；（經文）頰，頤，腮。

8. वस्त्राणि vastrāṇi 名詞　衣服

8.1 【詞尾變化】vastrāṇi 是 vastra 的複數對格形，所以字典查 vastra。

8.2 【摩威梵英,p932】

8.2.1 n.（or m. g. *ardharcādi*）cloth , clothes , garment , raiment , dress , cover RV.;

8.2.2（*ā*）f. N. of a river ;

8.2.3 n. a leaf of the cinnamon tree.

8.3 【梵漢辭典,p1399】（中性名詞）服裝，衣服；布；（經文）衣，衣服，衣物，上服，布，繒綵，疊。

9. प्रावरन्ति prāvaranti 動詞　覆蓋；穿戴

9.1 【詞尾變化】prāvaranti 是 prā-√vṛ 的現在式第三人稱複數形，所以字典查 prā-√vṛ。

9.2 【摩威梵英,p709】（prā prob. for pra ; cf. apā-vṛ}）to cover , veil , conceal AV.; to put on , dress one's self in（acc. , rarely instr.）MBh. ; to fill MBh.

9.3 【梵漢辭典,p1471】（動詞）覆蓋，隱藏，穿戴（衣服）；纏上～（工具格）；（經文）被，著。

10. केशांश्च keśāṁś ca 名詞　頭髮

10.1 【詞尾變化】keśāṁś ca 根據連音規則是從 keśān ca 變化過來，而 keśān 是從 keśa 的對格複數形，所以字典查 keśa。

10.2 【摩威梵英,p310】

10.2.1 m.（√*kliś*）the hair of the head AV. VS.; the mane（of a horse or lion）MBh.; a kind of perfume（*hrīvera*）; N. of a mineral; N. of Varuṇa; of Vishṇu ; of a Daitya ; of a locality Romakas. ;

10.2.2（pl.）the tail（of the Bos grunniens）.（v. l. *vāla*）;

10.2.3（*ī*）f. a lock of hair on the crown of the head; the Indigo plant; Carpopogon pruriens; another plant（bhūta-keśī）; N. of Durgā.

10.3 【梵漢辭典,p588】（陽性名詞）髮，尾；（經文）毛，髮，髮毛，頭髮，鬢髮，玄髮，紺髮，毫，頭髻，螺髻。

11. शमश्रूण्य् śmaśrūṇy 名詞　鬍鬚

11.1【詞尾變化】śmaśrūṇy 根據連音規則是從 śmaśrūṇi 變化過來，śmaśrūṇi 是 śmaśru 的複數對格形，所以字典查 śmaśru。

11.2【摩威梵英,p1094】n.（of unknown derivation , but cf. śman）; the beard ,（esp.）moustache , the hairs of the beard（pl.）RV.

11.3 【梵漢辭典,p1184】（名詞）鬍鬚，嘴上的鬍子；（複數）鬚毛；（經文）鬚，髭髮。

12. अवतारयन्ति avatārayanti 動詞　自～下來

12.1 【詞尾變化】avatārayanti 是 ava-√tṝ 的使役動詞現在式第三人稱複數形變化，所以字典查 ava-√tṝ。

12.2 【摩威梵英,p99】

12.2.1 cl. 1. *-tarati*（perf. *-tatāra* , 3. pl. *-teruḥ* ; Inf. *-taritum* or *-tartum* ;

12.2.2 ind. p. *-tīrya*）to descend into（loc. or acc.）, alight from , alight（abl.）; to descend（as a deity）in becoming incarnate MBh. ; to betake one's self to（acc.）, arrive at MBh. ; to make one's appearance , arrive; to be in the right place , to fit; to undertake.

12.2.3 cl. 6.（Imper. 2. sg. *-tira* ; impf. *-atirat* , 2. sg. *-atiras* , 2. du. *-atiratam* ; aor. 2. sg. *-tārīs*） to overcome , overpower RV. AV.

12.2.4 cl. 4.（p. fem. *-tīyatī*） to sink AV.

12.2.5 Caus. *-tārayati*（ind. p. *-tārya*） to make or let one descend , bring or fetch down （acc. or loc.） from （abl.） MBh.; to take down , take off , remove , turn away from ; `to set a-going , render current' see *ava-tārita* below ; to descend （?） AV.

12.3 【梵漢辭典,p1293】（動詞）下至～（對格，位格）；自～（從格）下來；降臨（地上），化現，顯現，示現自己，越過，恢復（疾病）；前往，赴，抵達；在正當的地點，適應；克服；（經文）下，下來，入，能入，深入，趣入，悟入，趣向，能詣，遊止，親近，過度，攝，知，通達，悟解。

【筆者試譯】：他們到世尊的地方，
（為了）（修）證（佛）法上很好的境地，
穿著的（華美）衣服（換）下來，
臉頰上的髫鬚和頭髮也都（剃）下來。

【什公漢譯】：便捨樂土，宮殿臣妾，剃除鬚髮，而被法服。

【英 譯 本】：And betaken themselves to the guides of the world to ask for the most excellent law, for the sake of bliss; they put on reddish-yellow robes, and shave hair and beard.

【信譯研究】：信譯。與上一頌交錯翻譯。

【第廿二頌】

कांश्चिच्च पश्याम्यहु बोधिसत्त्वान्
भिक्षू समानाः पवने वसन्ति।
शून्यान्यरण्यानि निषेवमाणान्
उद्देशस्वाध्यायरतांश्च कांश्चित्॥२२॥

【羅馬譯音】

kāṁścicca paśyāmyahu bodhisattvān
bhikṣū samānāḥ pavane vasanti|
śūnyānyaraṇyāni niṣevamāṇān
uddeśasvādhyāyaratāṁśca kāṁścit||22||

【句義解析】

kāṁś-cic ca paśyāmy ahu bodhisattvān
bhikṣū samānāḥ pavane vasanti|
śūnyāny araṇyāni niṣevamāṇān
uddeśa-svādhyāya-ratāṁś ca kāṁś-cit||22||

【辭彙研究】

1. कांश्चिच् kāṁś-cic ca 形容詞　有些

1.1 【詞尾變化】kāṁś-cic ca 根據連音規則，是從 kān-cit ca 變化過來，而 kān 是 ka 的複數對格形，cit 爲 cid 的主格。所以字典查 ka-cid。

1.2 資料前面已有說明。

2. अहु ahu 代名詞　我

2.1 【詞尾變化】沒有詞尾變化。

2.2 【摩威梵英,p125】mfn. only in paro-'hu q.v.

2.3 【梵漢辭典,p51】（代名詞）（俗語）=ahaṃ；（經文）我，吾。

3. बोधिसत्त्वान् bodhisattvān 名詞　菩薩們

3.1 【詞尾變化】bodhisattvān 是 bodhisattva 的複數對格形，字典查 bodhisattva。

3.2 資料前面已有說明。

4. समानाः samānāḥ 形容詞　同樣地

4.1 【詞尾變化】samānāḥ 是 samāna 的複數主格形，所以字典查 samāna。

4.2 【摩威梵英,p1160】

4.2.1 mf(ī, or ā)n.(connected with 1. and 2. *sama* ; in RV.)RV.; alike , similar , equal（in size , age , rank , sense or meaning &c.）, equal or like to（with instr. gen. , or comp.）; having the same place or organ of utterance , honogeneous（as a sound or letter）; holding the middle between two extremes , middling moderate BhP. ; common , general , universal all RV. BhP. ; whole（as a number opp to `a fraction '）; being（=*sat* , after an adj.）; virtuous , good ; *-varṇa-bhid* ;

4.2.2（*am*）ind. like , equally with（instr.）;

4.2.3 m.an equal. friend BhP. ;

4.2.4（ī）f. a kind of metre ;

4.2.5（prob.）n. N. of wk..

4.3 【梵漢辭典,p1075】（形容詞）完全相同的，同一的，與～（具格）同類的貨相等的；同種的（文字）；共通的，結合的全部的。同樣地，一樣的，（經文）同，等，如，齊，平等，同類，同一，相似，等義。

5. पवने pavane 名詞　風；清淨的

5.1 【詞尾變化】pavane 是 pavana 的於格單數形，所以字典查 pavana。

5.2 【摩威梵英,p610】

5.2.1 m. `purifier ' , wind or the god of wind , breeze , air MBh. ; vital air , breath; the regent of the Nakśatra Svāti and the north-west region; N. of the number 5(from the 5 vital airs); a householder's sacred fire; a species of grass ; N. of a son of Manu Uttama BhP. ; of a mountain; of a country in Bharata-kshetra;

5.2.2（ī）f. a broom ; the wild citron-tree（v.l. *pacanī*）; N. of a river ;

5.2.3 n. or m. purification , winnowing of corn ; a potter's kiln;

5.2.4 n. an instrument for purifying grain, sieve , strainer AV. ; blowing ; water ;

5.2.5 mfn. clean , pure.

5.3 【梵漢辭典,p884】（陽性名詞）（靜晝者，清潔者）風，微風，空氣，風神，生氣，息，家庭的（聖）火；（經文）風；（中性）淨化用的器具：畚箕；撣子；篩子，濾水器，陶工的窯。

6. वसन्ति vasanti 動詞　住在

6.1 【詞尾變化】vasanti 是√vas 的現在式第三人稱複數形，所以字典查√vas。

6.2 【摩威梵英,p932】

6.2.1 cl. 1 to dwell , live , stop（at a place）, stay（esp. `overnight' , with or without *rātrim* or *rātrīs*）RV. ; to remain , abide with or in（with loc. of pers. ; loc. or acc. of place , esp. with *vāsam* or *vasatim*）; to remain or keep on or continue in any condition; to have sexual intercourse with（loc.）; to rest upon（loc.）; to charge or entrust with（instr.）;

6.2.2 cl. 10. P. *vasayati* , to cause to halt or stay（overnight）, lodge , receive hospitably or as a guest MBh.; to cause to have sexual intercourse with（loc.）; to let anything stand overnight; to cause to wait , keep in suspense RV. ; to delay , retard; to cause to exist , preserve; to cause to be inhabited , populate（a country）; to put in , place upon（loc.）MBh.; to produce, to remain , be in , be engaged in.

6.3 【梵漢辭典,p1395】（動詞）停留，留宿，休止，停止，倒流，住，生活，存在，位於，停留在，決定住處，守護，離開的，愉快或舒適生活的；（經文）住，宿，止住，止宿，居，依住，住在。

7. शून्यान्य् śūnyāny 形容詞　空的

7.1 【詞尾變化】śūnyāny 根據連音規則是從 śūnyāni 變化過來，śūnyāni 則是 śūnya 的複數對格形，所以字典查 śūnya。

7.2 【摩威梵英,p1085】

7.2.1 mf（*ā*）n. empty , void（with *vājin* = `a riderless horse' ; with *rājya* = `a kingless kingdom'）, hollow , barren , desolate , deserted; empty i.e. vacant（as a look or stare）, absent , absentminded , having no certain object or aim , distracted MBh.; empty i.e. possessing nothing , wholly destitute MBh. ; wholly alone or solitary , having no friends or companions BhP. ; void of , free from , destitute of（instr. or comp.）, wanting , lacking, non-existent , absent , missing; vain , idle , unreal , nonsensical; void of results , ineffectual（*a-śūnyaṃ-kṛ* , `to effect' , accomplish）; free from sensitiveness or sensation（said of the skin）, insensible; bare , naked; guileless , innocent ib. ; indifferent ib. ;

7.2.2（*ā*）f. a hollow reed ; a barren woman ; Cactus Indicus = malī（for *nalī*）;

7.2.3 n. a void , vacuum , empty or deserted place , desert（*śūnye* , in a lonely place）MBh. ;（in phil.）vacuity , nonentity , absolute non-existence（esp. with Buddhists）; N. of Brahma ;（in arithm.）nought , a cypher ; space , heaven , atmosphere ; a partic. phenomenon in the sky. ; an earring（see next）.

7.3 【梵漢辭典,p1235】（形容詞）空的，空虛的，吾人居住的，荒蕪的，無騎者的（馬）；發呆的（注視）；茫然的，迷亂的，貧困的，奪走～（具格）的，欠缺的，獲得自由的，不足的，沒有，不存在，空虛的，空的，怠情的，（中性）空虛的，被遺棄的（荒廢的）廠所，孤獨，空虛，中空，不存在，非存在，絕對空的；（經文）空，空無，空虛，空義，空曠，空閑，空寂，曠遠。

8. अरण्यानि araṇyāni 形容詞　空曠野外

8.1 【詞尾變化】araṇyāni 是 araṇya 的複數對格形，所以字典查 araṇya。

8.2 【摩威梵英,p86】

8.2.1 n. a foreign or distant land RV. ; a wilderness , desert , forest AV.;

8.2.2 m. the tree also called Kaṭphala ; N. of a son of the Manu Raivata; of a Sādhya; of a teacher（disciple of Pṛithvidhara）.

8.3 【梵漢辭典,p150】（中性形容詞）遠方，外國，荒野，林；（經文）遠離，山林，林野，山澤，空野，曠野；空閑；閑寂，空寂，空林中無人之處，最閑處，空閑處，空閑地，無聲。

9. निषेवमाणान् niṣevamāṇān 形容詞　處於的

9.1 【詞尾變化】niṣevamāṇān 爲 niṣevamāṇa 的複數對格形，所以字典查 niṣevamāṇa。

9.2 【摩威梵英,p562】mfn. being or situated or flowing near（as a river）.

9.3 【梵漢辭典】無此單字資料。

10. उद्देश uddeśa 形容詞　指出；解說

10.1 【詞尾變化】沒有詞尾變化。

10.2 【摩威梵英,p188】

10.2.1 m. the act of pointing to or at , direction ; ascertainment ; brief statement ; exemplification , illustration , explanation ; mentioning a thing by name MBh. ; assignment , prescription ; stipulation , bargain MBh. ; quarter , spot , region , place ; an object , a motive ; upper region , high situation MBh.;（in Nyāya phil.）enunciation of a topic（that is to be further discussed and elucidated）;

10.2.2（*ena* and *āt*）ind.（ifc.）relative to , aiming at.

10.3 【梵漢辭典,p1319】（陽性名詞）參照；陳述，解說，概說，簡單的說明，地方，部分，場處；（經文）標，略標，標說，略，略說，解說，宣說，講說，言談。

11. स्वाध्याय svādhyāya 形容詞　獨自唸誦

11.1 【詞尾變化】沒有詞尾變化。

11.2 【摩威梵英,p1277】

11.2.1 m. reciting or repeating or rehearsing to one's self , repetition or recitation of the Veda in a low voice to one's self; repeating the Veda aloud（acc. with caus. of √śru , `to cause the Veda to be repeated aloud'）; recitation or perusal of any sacred texts ; the Veda ; a day on which sacred recitation is resumed after its suspension; N. of wk. ;

11.2.2 mfn. studying the Veda（*-tama* , perhaps w.r. for *svādhyāyi-t-*）;

11.2.3 *-dhṛk* mfn. one who repeats or recites the Veda;

11.2.4 *-brāhmaṇa* n. N. of ch. in the Taittiriyaraṇyaka ;

11.2.5 *-vat* mfn.（=*-dhṛk*）MBh. ;

11.2.6 m. a repeater or student of the Veda ;

11.2.7 *-yāyārthin* m. one who seeks a maintenance for himself during his studentship.

11.3 【梵漢辭典,p1252】（陽性形容詞）獨自習誦，（吠陀經的）學習；高聲朗誦（吠陀經）；（經文）誦，讀誦；諷誦；誦念，習誦。

12. रतांश्च ratāṁś ca 形容詞／過去被動分詞　執著

12.1 【詞尾變化】ratāṁś ca 根據連音規則是從 ratān ca 變化過來，而 ratān

是 rata 的對格複數形，所以字典查 rata。

12.2 【摩威梵英,p867】

12.2.1 mfn. pleased , amused , gratified BhP. ; delighting in , intent upon , fond or enamoured of , devoted or attached or addicted or disposed to（loc. instr. or comp.）;（ifc.）having sexual intercourse with BhP. ; loved , beloved MW. ;

12.2.2（*ā*）f. N. of the mother of Day MBh. ;

12.2.3 n. pleasure , enjoyment ,（esp.）enjoyment of love , sexual union , copulation ; the private parts.

12.3 【梵漢辭典,p1020】（過去被動分詞）歡喜，滿足，高興，喜歡～（具格／位格），獻身於～，沉迷於～；（經文）樂，可樂，欣樂，娛樂，樂著，著，執著，愛。

【筆者試譯】：我看有些菩薩們，
當了清淨的比丘，住在一起，
有些則置身於空茫茫的野外，
喜歡獨自誦經，宣說佛法。

【什公漢譯】：或見菩薩，而作比丘，獨處閑靜，樂誦經典。

【英 譯 本】：I see also many Bodhisattvas like monks,
living in the forest,
and others inhabiting the empty
wilderness, engaged in reciting and reading.

【信譯研究】：信譯。

【第廿三頌】

कांश्चिच्च पश्याम्यहु बोधिसत्त्वान्
गिरिकन्दरेषु प्रविशन्ति धीराः।
विभावयन्तो इमु बुद्धज्ञानं
परिचिन्तयन्तो ह्युपलक्षयन्ति॥२३॥

【羅馬譯音】

kāṁścicca paśyāmyahu bodhisattvān
girikandareṣu praviśanti dhīrāḥ|
vibhāvayanto imu buddhajñānaṁ
paricintayanto hyupalakṣayanti||23||

【句義解析】

kāṁś-cic ca paśyāmy ahu bodhisattvān
giri-kandareṣu praviśanti dhīrāḥ|
vibhāvayanto imu buddha-jñānaṁ
paricintayanto hy upalakṣayanti||23||

【辭彙研究】

1. गिरि giri 名詞　山巖

1.1 【詞尾變化】沒有詞尾變化。

1.2 【摩威梵英,p355】

1.2.1 m.（for *gari* , *gairi*）a mountain , hill , rock , elevation , rising-ground（often connected with *parvata* , `a mountain having many parts ' RV. AV.）RV. ; the number `eight'（there being 8 mountains which surround mount Meru）; a cloud; a particular disease of the eyes ; = -*guḍa*; a peculiar defect in mercury; = *gairīyaka*; a honorific N. given to one of the ten orders of the Daś-nāmi1 Gosains（founded by ten pupils of Śaṃkarācārya ; the word *giri* is added to the name of each member ; N. of a son of Śvaphāka;

1.2.2 f.（=*girikā*）a mouse ; mfn. coming from the mountains RV;venerable ;

1.3 【梵漢辭典,p460】（陽性名詞）（重物）山；岳；岩；（經文）山，岳，山岳；巖。

2. कन्दरेषु kandareṣu 名詞　洞穴；峽谷

2.1 【詞尾變化】kandareṣu 是 kandara 的複數於格形，所以字典查 kandara。

2.2 【摩威梵英,p249】

2.2.1 *ā* , *am* fn.（*as* m.）,（*kand*; *kaṃ* , *jalena dīryate*）, `great cliff' , an artificial or natural cave , glen , defile , valley;

2.2.2 m. a hook for driving an elephant;

2.2.3（*ā*）f. the lute of the Caṇḍālas ; N. of a mother in the retinue of Skanda MBh. BhP. ;

2.2.4（*am*）n. ginger.

2.3 【梵漢辭典,p561】（中性名詞）洞穴；峽谷；趕象用的木杖；（經文）澤，谷，險谷。

3. प्रविशन्ति pravisanti 動詞　進入

3.1 【詞尾變化】pravisanti 是 pra-√viś 的第三人稱複數形現在式變化，所以字典查 pra-√viś。

3.2 【摩威梵英,p692】-viśati , -te , to entor , go into , resort to（acc. or loc.）RV.; to reach , attain; to have sexual intercourse with（acc. , applied to both sexes）MBh.; to enter upon , undertake , commence , begin , devote one's self to（acc. , rarely loc.）MBh.（with piṇḍīm or tarpaṇam , `to accept or enjoy an oblation'）; to enter into i.e. be absorbed or thrown into the shade by（acc.）. `to shrink , shrivel': Caus. -veśayati , -te , to cause or allow to enter , bring or lead or introduce to , usher into（acc. or loc.）AV.; to lead home as a wife i.e. marry MBh. ; to lay or store up , deposit in , put or throw into（loc. or acc.）MBh. ; to enter i.e. commit to paper , write down ; to initiate into（acc.）; to instil into（loc.）= teach , impart; to spend（money）; to enter , come or be brought into（acc.）: -vivikṣati , to wish to enter into（acc.）MBh.

3.3 【梵漢辭典,p1452】（動詞）進入；登上，佔據；進入，出場，到達；展開；著手，獻身於；接受；享用；（經文）入，遍入，悟入，隨悟入，生，住，來至，得入。

4. धीराः dhīrāḥ 形容詞　心意堅定的

4.1 【詞尾變化】dhīrāḥ 是 dhīra 的複數主格形，所以字典查 dhīra。

4.2 【摩威梵英,p517】

4.2.1 mf（*ā*）n.（√dhṛ or dhā）steady , constant , firm , resolute , brave , energetic , courageous , self-possessed , composed , calm , grave ; deep , low , dull（as sound）; gentle , soft; well-conducted , well-bred;

4.2.2（*am*）ind. steadily , firmly;

4.2.3 m. the ocean , sea（as an image of constancy?）; N. of Bali; of other men;

4.2.4 f. N. of sev. medic. plants（kākoī , *kśīra-kāk-*} , *mahā-jyotiśmatī* , *medā* , *śveta-vacā*）; an intoxicating beverage; a woman who keeps down all expression of resentment or jealousy; N. of a woman;

4.2.5 n. saffron（not always , esp. in comp. , separable from 1. *dhīra*）.

4.3 【梵漢辭典,p380】（形容詞）持續的；安定；不變的；堅固的；心意堅定的；有用啓的；莊重的；平靜的；認眞的；不動的；有重（音）；固守；（經文）勇健；勇猛，勇力，堅固，心決定。

5. विभावयन्तो vibhāvayanto 動詞　令思維

5.1 【詞尾變化】vibhāvayanto 根據連音規則是從 vibhāvayantaḥ 變化過來，而 vibhāvayantaḥ 是 vi-√bhū 的使役法之現在主動分詞形，所以字典查 vi-√bhū。

5.2【摩威梵英,p978】-bhavati , to arise , be developed or manifested , expand , appear RV. ; to suffice , be adequate or equal to or a match for（dat. or acc.）; to pervade , fill; to be able to or capable of（inf.）; to exist（in a-vibhavat , `not existing'）: Caus. -bhāvayati , to cause to arise or appear , develop , manifest , reveal , show forth , display MBh.; to pretend , feign; to divide , separate BhP. ; to perceive distinctly , find out , discover , ascertain , know , acknowledge , recognise as(acc.)MBh; to regard or consider as , take for（two acc.）; to suppose , fancy , imagine BhP. ; to think , reflect; to suppose anything of or about（loc.）BhP. ; to make clear , establish , prove , decide; to convict , convince: Pass. of Caus. -bhāvyate , to be considered or regarded as , appear , seem（nom.）MBh.

5.3 【梵漢辭典,p278】（動詞）明白，發生，出現，相比；（使役動詞）令出現，明示，開示，呈現外觀，裝扮，知覺，發現，探知，看出，想像，考慮，深思，作證，確定，斷定有罪，使確信；（經文）現，知，了知，能知，曉了，分別；見，觀，想，觀想，觀察，思維，思維觀察。

6. परिचिन्तयन्तो paricintayanto 動詞　思惟

6.1 【詞尾變化】paricintayanto 根據連音規則是從 paricintayantaḥ 變化過來，

而 paricintayantaḥ 是 pari-√cint 現在式主動分詞的主格，所以字典查 pari-√cint。

6.2【摩威梵英,p594】P. -cintayati（ind. p. -cintya）, to think about , meditate on , reflect , consider MBh.; to call to mind , remember; to devise , invent.

6.3 【梵漢辭典,p328】（動詞）考慮，正當的思考，熟慮，思考，想辦法。

7. ह्य hy 不變格 由於

7.1 【詞尾變化】hy 根據連音規則是從 hi 變化過來。

7.2 資料前面已有說明。

8. उपलकषयन्ति upalakṣayanti 動詞 看出來

8.1 【詞尾變化】upalakṣayanti 是 upa-√lakṣ 的現在式第三人稱複數形，所以字典查 upa-√lakṣ。

8.2 【摩威梵英,p205】-lakṣayati , -te , to look at , observe , behold , perceive MBh.; to pay attention to , regard MBh. ; to regard or value as MBh.; to distinguish , mark ; to distinguish by a secondary or unessential mark ; to imply in addition , designate implicitly Sa1y.: Pass. -lakṣyate , to be observed; to be implied BhP.

8.3 【梵漢辭典,p1330,ups】（動詞的接頭）在上，在此處，旁邊，附近，尚且，何況，朝向，在～附近，在～以下。

8.4 【梵漢辭典,p649,lakṣ】（動詞）觀察，看出，理解，留意。

【筆者試譯】：我又看到有些菩薩們。
進入了山巖洞穴裡，心意堅定的，
（打坐）思惟佛道，
爲了修證而做的。

【什公漢譯】：又見菩薩，勇猛精進，入於深山，思惟佛道。

【英 譯 本】：And some Bodhisattvas I see, who, full of
wisdom（or constancy）, betake themselves to
mountain caves, where by cultivating and meditating the
Buddha-knowledge they arrive at its perception.

【信譯研究】：信譯。

【第廿四頌】

उत्सृज्य कामांश्च अशेषतोऽन्ये

परिभावितात्मान विशुद्धगोचराः।

अभिज्ञ पञ्चेह च स्पर्शयित्वा

वसन्त्यरण्ये सुगतस्य पुत्राः॥२४॥

【羅馬譯音】

utsṛjya kāmāṁśca aśeṣato'nye

paribhāvitātmāna viśuddhagocarāḥ|

abhijña pañceha ca sparśayitvā

vasantyaraṇye sugatasya putrāḥ||24||

【句義解析】

utsṛjya kāmāṁś ca aśeṣato 'nye

paribhāvitātmāna viśuddha-gocarāḥ|

abhijña pañceha ca sparśayitvā

vasanty araṇye sugatasya putrāḥ||24||

【辭彙研究】

1. उत्सृज्य utsṛjya 動詞　放棄

1.1 【詞尾變化】utsṛjya 學者認爲是從 ut-√sṛj 變化過來，〔註 41〕所以字典查 ut-√sṛj。

1.2 【摩威梵英,p182】(ud-√sṛj), to let loose , let off or go; to set free ; to open RV. MBh.; to pour out , emit , send forth MBh.; to sling , throw , cast forth or away ; to lay aside MBh. ; to quit , leave , abandon , avoid , eschew MBh. ; to discontinue , suspend , cease , leave off; to send away , dismiss , discharge MBh. ; to drive out or away; to hand out , deliver , grant , give AV. BhP.; to bring forth , produce , create AV., to intend to let loose; to intend to leave BhP.

〔註 41〕請見江島惠教等編《梵藏漢法華經原典總索引》，東京：靈友會出版，1988 年出版。頁 193。

1.3 【梵漢辭典,p1201】（動詞）解放，使徘徊（牲獸）；打開（牛舍）；字～分離的；投擲（飛鏢），發射，灌注，使降下（雨），流（淚），吐出（毒液），排泄（糞便），發（音），放在一邊，扔下，去掉，撒（種子），擴展，使（旗）飄揚，驅逐，放逐，捨棄，儀器；漏看；拋棄，放棄，廢止，通過，省略，流下，剩餘，使（火）熄滅，投遞；（經文）吐，起，失，捨，投，放，湧，棄。

2. कामअंश्च kāmāṁś ca 名詞　慾望

2.1 【詞尾變化】kāmāṁś ca 根據連音規則，是從 kāmān ca 變化過來，而 kāmān 是 kāma 的對格複數，字典查 kāma。

2.2 【摩威梵英,p271】

2.2.1 m.（fr. √kam ; once kāma）, wish , desire , longing, desire for , longing after（gen. dat. , or loc.）, love , affection , object of desire or of love or of pleasure RV. MBh. ; pleasure , enjoyment ; love , especially sexual love or sensuality ; Love or Desire personified AV.; N. of the god of love AV. MBh.; N. of Agni; of Viśṇu; of Baladeva; a stake in gambling; a species of mango tree（=mahā-rāja-cūta）; N. of a metre consisting of four lines of two long syllables each ; a kind of bean; a particular form of temple; N. of several men ;

2.2.2（ā）f. `wish , desire'（only instr. kāmayā）; N. of a daughter of Pṛithuśravas and wife of Ayuta-nāyin MBh.;

2.2.3（*am*）n. object of desire; semen virile; N. of a Ti1rtha MBh.;

2.2.4（*am*）ind. see s.v. ;

2.2.5（*ena*）ind. out of affection or love for ;

2.2.6（*āya* , or *e*）ind. according to desire , agreeably to the wishes of , out of love for（gen. or dat.）RV. AV. ;

2.2.7（*āt*）ind. for one's own pleasure , of one's own free will , of one's own accord , willingly , intentionally;

2.2.8（*kāma*）mfn. wishing , desiring RV. ;（ifc.）desirous of , desiring , having a desire or intention.

2.3 【梵漢辭典,p555】（陽性名詞）對～（對格／屬格／位格）的願望，慾望；愛，愛著；意圖；快樂；心願的，利益；（性）愛，愛神；（經文）

欲，所欲，貪欲，婬欲，欲塵，樂，樂欲，育樂；愛，愛樂，攤樂，快樂。

3. अशषतऽन्ये aśeṣato 'nye 形容詞　不剩下；無有餘

3.1 【詞尾變化】aśeṣato 'nye 根據連音規則，是從 aśeṣataḥ anye 變化過來，而 aśeṣataḥ 是 aśeṣatas 的單數呼格，anye 是 anya 的複數主格。所以字典查 aśeṣatas-anya。

3.2 資料前面已有說明。

4. परिभावितात्मान paribhāvitātmāna 動詞　超越

4.1 【詞尾變化】paribhāvitātmāna 是從 pari-√bhū 變化過來，所以字典查 pari-√bhū。

4.2 【摩威梵英,p598】to be round anything , surround , enclose , contain RV. AV.; to go or fly round , accompany , attend to , take care of , guide , govern RV. AV. ; to be superior , excel , surpass , subdue , conquer RV.; to pass round or over , not heed , slight , despise , insult MBh.; to disgrace MBh. ; to disappear , be lost, to spread around , divulge , make known Uttarar. ; to surpass , exceed BhP. ; to soak , saturate , sprinkle ; to contain , include BhP. ; to conceive , think , consider , know , recognise as（acc.）.

4.3 【梵漢辭典,p278】（動詞）在周圍，包含，含有；包圍，陪伴；領導，勝過，優於，卓越，克服，征服，不顧，蔑視，加以侮辱，使感到屈辱，嘲諷；（經文）輕，蔑，輕蔑，輕陵，輕慢，起輕心，起輕想。

5. विशुद्ध viśuddha 形容詞／過去被動分詞　完全清淨

5.1 【詞尾變化】沒有詞尾變化。

5.2 【摩威梵英,p991】

5.2.1 mfn. completely cleansed or purified（also in a ritual sense）, clean , clear , pure（lit.and fig.）MBh.; free from vice , virtuous , honest MBh.; brilliantly white（as teeth）; thoroughly settled or established or fixed or determined or ascertained ib. ;

5.2.2（ifc.）one who has gone through or thoroughly completed; cleared i .e. exhausted , empty（as a treasury）;（in alg.）subtracted Gol. ;

5.2.3 n. a kind of mystical circle in the body ;

5.2.4 -*cāritra* m. \`of virtuous conduct' N. of a Bodhi-sattva SaddhP. ;

5.2.5 *-tā*, f. , *-tva* n. purity ;

5.2.6 *-dhiṣaṇa* mfn. having the mind purified BhP. ;

5.2.7 -dhīra mfn. pure and grave;

5.2.8 *-netra-tā* f. having the eyes bright（one of the minor marks of a Buddha）;

5.2.9 *-pārṣṇi* mfn. having the rear or back protected or covered;

5.2.10 *-prakṛti* mfn. of pure or virtuous disposition ;

5.2.11 *-bhāva*, *-manas* mfn. pure-minded ;

5.2.12 *-mugdha* mfn. pñpure and innocent;

5.2.13 *-vaṃśya* mfn. of a pñpure or virtuous family;

5.2.14 *-sattva* mfn. of a pure character;

5.2.15 *-sattva-pradhāna* mfn. chiefly characterized by pure goodness ;

5.2.16 *-sattva-vijñāna* mfn. of pure character and understanding;

5.2.17 *-siṃha* m. N. of a man Buddh. ;

5.2.18 *svara-nirghośā* f. a partic. Dha1ran2i1 Buddh. ;

5.2.19 *-ddhātman* mfn. of a pñpure nature or character MBh.;

5.2.20 *-ddheśvara-tantra* n. N. of a Tantra.

5.3 【梵漢辭典,p1462】（過去被動分詞）完全清淨或淨化的；（經文）淨，清淨，極清淨，究竟清淨，寂靜，明顯，皓，皓然，挺特。

6. गोचराः gocarāḥ 名詞　境界

6.1 【詞尾變化】gocarāḥ 是 gocara 的複數主格形，所以字典查 gocara。

6.2 【摩威梵英,p364】

6.2.1 m. pasture ground for cattle ; range , field for action , abode , dwelling-place , district MBh.; the range of the organs of sense , object of sense , anything perceptible by the senses , esp. the range of the eye MBh. ; the distance of the planets from the Lagna and from each other;

6.2.2 mf（*ā*）n. being within the range of , attainable for（gen.）BhP.; perceptible（esp. to the eye）MBh.; having（or used in）the meaning of（loc.）;

6.2.3 *-gata* mfn. one who has come within the range of or in connection with（gen.）;

6.2.4 *-tā* f. the state of being liable to（in comp.）;

6.2.5 *-prakaraṇa* N. of wk. ;

6.2.6 *-pīḍā* f. inauspicious position of stars within the ecliptic;

6.2.7 -rādhyāya m. = -ra-phala ;

6.2.8 *-rāntara-gata* mfn. being within the power of（gen.）;

6.2.9 *-rī-kṛta* mfn. within the range of observation; overcome.

6.3 【梵漢辭典,p462】（陽性名詞）牧牛場，活動的範圍，領域，住家處所，轄區，眼界，是也，能力所及的範圍；可感覺的對象；地平線，親近的，給鳥食的地方；（經文）境，境界，行境，所行境，所行之境；行，所行，行處，所行處，所應行，近處，親近處，緣，塵。

7. अभिज्ञ abhijña 形容詞　神通

7.1 【詞尾變化】沒有詞尾變化。

7.2 【摩威梵英,p62】

7.2.1 mf(*ā*)n. knowing , skilful , clever ; understanding , conversant with（gen. or ifc.）;

7.2.2（*ā*）f. remembrance , recollection ; supernatural science or faculty of a Buddha（of which five are enumerated , viz. 1. taking any form at will ; 2. hearing to any distance ; 3. seeing to any distance ; 4. penetrating men's thoughts ; 5. knowing their state and antecedents）.

7.3 【梵漢辭典,p6】（陰性形容詞）了解，成爲～的知己，有～的經驗，熟知～（經文）知，善知，了，了知，解，證，證見。

8. पञ्चेह pañceha 形容詞　這五個

8.1 【詞尾變化】pañceha 根據連音規則是由 pañca-iha 所組成，iha 資料前面已有說明，所以字典查 pañca。

8.2 【摩威梵英,p575】in comp. for pañcan.

8.3 【摩威梵英,p578, pañcan】pl. five RV.

8.4 【梵漢辭典,p832】（數詞）（形容詞）（經文）五。

9. सपर्शयित्वा sparśayitvā 動詞　獲得

9.1 【詞尾變化】sparśayitvā 是佛教的轉寫異體，學者認爲是從√spṛś 變化過來，〔註 42〕所以字典查√spṛś。

〔註 42〕請見江島惠教等編《梵藏漢法華經原典總索引》，東京：靈友會出版，1988 年出版。頁 1127。

9.2 【摩威梵英,p1269】cl. 6.（m. c. sparkśyati; sprakśyati MBh.）, to touch , feel with the hand , lay the hand on（acc. or loc.）, graze , stroke RV. ; to handle , take hold of MBh.; to touch or sip water , wash or sprinkle certain parts of the body with water MBh.; to touch so as to hurt , injure , harm ; to perceive or feel by touch ; to touch , come into contact（lit. ; and fig. in astron. sense）; to reach or penetrate to MBh. ; to come up to , equal ; to act upon , affect; to touch endow or fill with（instr.）RV.; to touch i.e. befall , fall to the lot of , come upon , visit , afflict(acc.)MBh. ; to touch , take hold of , make one's own , appropriate MBh. ; to attain to , obtain , experience , undergo MBh.; to grant , bestow BhP. to be touched or seized or affected by MBh. , to cause to touch（two acc.）, bring into immediate contact with（loc. or instr.）MBh.; to convey to（loc.）RV. ; to fill or cover with(instr.); to perceive by touch , feel; to offer , present , give. MBh..

9.3 【梵漢辭典,p1193】(動詞）觸摸，撫摸，接觸，用（水）洗（身體部位），漱口，感覺，接觸，不愉快的影響，傷害，媲美；對～（對格）產生作用；影響，左右，降臨到～，得手，獲得，經驗；(經文）成，證，得，摩，觸，指，通達。

10. वसन्त्य् vasanty 動詞　停留；依靠

10.1 【詞尾變化】vasanty 根據連音規則是從 vasanti 變化過來，vasanti 是√vas 現在式主動第三人稱複數形，所以字典查√vas。

10.2 資料前面已有說名。

11. अरण्ये araṇye 名詞　山林；荒野

11.1 【詞尾變化】araṇye 是 araṇya 的於格單數形，所以字典查 araṇya。

11.2 資料前面已有說明。

12. सुगतस्य sugatasya putrāḥ 名詞　佛子們

12.1 【詞尾變化】sugatasya 是 sugata 的單數屬格形，而 putrāḥ 則是 putra 的複數主格形，所以字典查 sugata-putra。

12.2 資料前面已有說明。

【筆者試譯】：放棄了欲望不留餘地，

克服了（一切），達到完全清淨的境界，
獲得了五種神通，
（就是）那些住在荒郊野外的佛子們！

【什公漢譯】：又見離欲，常處空閑，深修禪定，得五神通。

【英 譯 本】：Others who have renounced all sensual
desires, by purifying their own self, have cleared their
sphere and obtained the five transcendent faculties,
live in the wilderness, as（true）sons of the Sugata.

【信譯研究】：信譯。因爲鳩摩羅什加了一句「深修禪定」，這是梵本所沒有的。不過按照佛教的說法，神通通常都是由禪定得來。所以還是可以算信譯。

【第廿五頌】

पादैः समैः स्थित्विह केचि धीराः
कृताञ्जली संमुखि नायकानाम्।
अभिस्तवन्तीह हर्षं जनित्वा
गाथासहस्रेहि जिनेन्द्रराजम्॥२५॥

【羅馬譯音】

pādaiḥ samaiḥ sthitviha keci dhīrāḥ
kṛtāñjalī saṁmukhi nāyakānām|
abhistavantīha harṣaṁ janitvā
gāthāsahasrehi jinendrarājam||25||

【句義解析】

pādaiḥ samaiḥ sthitv iha ke-ci dhīrāḥ
kṛtāñjalī saṁmukhi nāyakānām|
abhistavantīha harṣaṁ janitvā
gāthā-sahasrehi jinendra-rājam||25||

【辭彙研究】

1. पादैः pādaiḥ 名詞　腳

1.1 【詞尾變化】pādaiḥ 是 pāda 的工具格複數形，所以字典查 pāda。

1.2 資料前面已有說明。

2. समैः samaiḥ 形容詞　同樣的

2.1 【詞尾變化】samaiḥ 是 sama 的工具格複數形，所以字典查 sama。

2.2 【摩威梵英,p1152】

2.2.1 mf（*ā*）n.（prob. originally identical with prec.）even , smooth , flat , plain , level , parallel RV.; same , equal , similar , like , equivalent , like to or identical or homogeneous with , like in or with regard to anything; always the same , constant , unchanged , fair , impartial towards（loc. or gen.）ib. ; even（not `" odd "'）, a pair; having the right measure , regular , normal , right , straight; equable , neutral , indifferent ; equally distant from extremes , ordinary , common , middling MBh. ; just , upright , good , straight , honest ib. ; easy , convenient; full , complete , whole , entire ;

2.2.2 m. peace ; the point of intersection of the horizon and the meridian line; N. of partic. zodiacal signs; a kind of straight line placed over a numerical figure to mark the process of extracting the square root ib. ;（in music）a kind of time; a grass-conflagration ; a Jina ; N. of a son of Dharma ; of a son of Dhṛitarāṣṭra MBh. ; of a king of the Nandi-vegas（v.l. *śama*）;

2.2.3（*ā*）f. a year see *samā* ;

2.2.4（*am*）n. level ground , a plain MBh.; equability , equanimity , imperturbability MBh. ; likeness , similarity , equality; right measure or proportion（*ena* , `exactly , precisely'）; settlement , compensation; good circumstances;（in rhet.）a partic. figure , sameness of objects compared to one another ;（in geom.）a mean proportional segment（described as a fourth proportional to the two perpendiculars and the link or segment , and used for solving problems in a trapezium）;

2.2.5 = *samā* f. a year;

2.2.6（*samam*）ind. in like manner , alike , equally , similarly RV. ; together with or at the same time with or in accordance with（instr. or comp.）

MBh.; just , exactly , precisely BhP. ; honestly , fairly.

2.3 【梵漢辭典,p1068】（形容詞）平坦的，平滑的，水平的，平行的，類似的，相似的，相等的，同等的，同樣的，同一的，不變的；普通的，中等的；不關心的，中立的，善良的，正確的，正直的，容易的；（經文）同，齊，類，正，平，安，並，等，如，平等，童伊，共同，同等，普等，平齊，齊平，正直，齊等，平正，安平，坦然，平坦，如～平等，猶如，等無有異，俱時，一時俱。

3. स्थित्व sthitv 過去被動分詞　站著；處在

3.1 【詞尾變化】sthitv 學者認爲是從 sthita 變化過來，〔註 43〕所以字典查 sthita。

3.2 資料前面已有說明。

4. धीराः dhīrāḥ 形容詞　堅固的；心意堅定的

4.1 【詞尾變化】dhīrāḥ 是 dhīra 的複數主格形，所以字典查 dhīra。

4.2 資料前面已有說明。

5. कृताञ्जली kṛtāñjalī 形容詞　合掌的

5.1 【詞尾變化】kṛtāñjalī 是由 kṛta-añjalī 所組成，kṛta 資料前面已有說明，añjalī 是從 añjali 變化而來，所以字典查 añjali。

5.2 【摩威梵英,p11】m.（√añj）, the open hands placed side by side and slightly hollowed（as if by a beggar to receive food ; hence when raised to the forehead , a mark of supplication）, reverence , salutation , benediction ; a libation to the Manes（two hands full of water , udakāñjali）VP. ; a measure of corn , sufficient to fill both hands when placed side by side , equal to a kuḍava.

5.3 【梵漢辭典,p616, kṛtāñjalī】（形容詞）爲向～（對格）請願而合掌的；（經文）合掌。

6. संमुखि saṁmukhi 形容詞　在前面的

6.1 【詞尾變化】saṁmukhi 是 saṁ-mukha 的陰性形，而 saṁ 資料前面已有說明，所以字典查 mukha。

〔註 43〕請見江島惠教等編《梵藏漢法華經原典總索引》，東京：靈友會出版，1988 年出版。頁 1125。

6.2 【摩威梵英,p819】

6.2.1 n.（m. g. *ardharcadi* ; ifc. *ā* , or *ī*）the mouth , face , countenance RV.; the beak of a bird , snout or muzzle of an animal MBh.; a direction , quarter（esp. ifc. cf. *diṅ-m-*; mfn. turning or turned towards , facing cf. *adho-m-* also *am* ind. cf. *prān-mukham*）; the mouth or spout of a vessel; opening aperture , entrance into or egress out of(gen. or comp.)MBh. ; the mouth or embouchure（of a river）; the fore part , front , van（of an army）MBh. ; the upper part , head , top , tip or point of anything MBh.; the nipple（of a breast）; the surface , upper side Āryabh. ; the chief , principal , best（ifc. = having any one or anything as chief）MBh.; introduction , commencement , beginning MBh.; source , cause , occasion of（gen. or comp.）MBh. ; a means（*ena* ind. by means of）;（in dram.）the original cause or source of the action Daśar.;（in alg.）the first term or initial quantity of a progression ;（in geom.）the side opposite to the base , the summit; the Veda ; rock salt ; copper ;

6.2.2 m. Artocarpus Locuchs.

6.3 【梵漢辭典,p1101, saṁ-mukha】（形容詞）與～（屬格）面對的或相向的，對～（位格）熱衷的；（經文）前，現前；現見，現在前。（副詞）朝～的方向，朝；臉，朝正面；在前面。

7. नायकानाम् nāyakānām 名詞　導師

7.1 【詞尾變化】nāyakānām 是 nāyaka 的屬格複數形，所以字典查 nāyaka。

7.2 資料前面已有說明。

8. अभिस्तवन्तीह abhistavantīha 動詞　讚誦如

8.1 【詞尾變化】abhistavantīha 根據連音規則是從 abhi-stavanti-iha 變化過來，而 abhi-stavanti 也就是 abhi-√stu 的現在式主動第三人稱複數形，而 abhi 前面已有資料，故字典查√stu。

8.2 【摩威梵英,p1259,√stu】cl. 2., to praise , laud , eulogize , extol , celebrate in song or hymns（in ritual , `to chant' , with loc. of the text from which the Sāman comes）RV, to praise , celebrate ; to cause to praise or celebrate BhP., to wish to celebrate.

8.3 【梵漢辭典,p1216, abhi-√stu】（動詞）讚賞，讚誦；（經文）歎，讚，

讚歎。

9. हर्शं harṣaṁ 形容詞　豎起的；歡喜的

9.1 【詞尾變化】harṣaṁ 根據連音規則，是從 harṣam 變化過來，harṣam 則是 harṣa 的對格單數形，所以字典查 harṣa。

9.2 資料前面已有說明。

10. जनित्वा janitvā 名詞　母親

10.1 【詞尾變化】沒有詞尾變化。

10.2 【摩威梵英,p411, janitva】

10.2.1 mfn. = -*tavya* RV. ;

10.2.2 m. father; m. du. parents i ;

10.2.3（*ā*）f. mother.

10.3 【梵漢辭典,p523】（陰性名詞）母，母親。

11. सहस्रहि sahasrehi 形容詞　如此千的

11.1 【詞尾變化】sahasrehi 根據連音規則爲 sahasra-ihi，所以字典查 sahasra-ihi。

11.2 資料前面已有說明。

12. जिनेन्द्र jinendra 名詞　佛陀；世尊

12.1 【詞尾變化】沒有詞尾變化。

12.2 【摩威梵英,p421】

12.2.1 m. a Buddha; a Jain saint; N. of a grammarian（also called -*dra-buddhi*）, author of a treatise called Nyāsa ;

12.2.2 -*caritra* n. N. of wk. by Amara-candra（also called Padmananda-mahākāvya）; -*buddhi* see before.

12.3 【梵漢辭典,p533】（陽性名詞）諸耆那（Jina）之主，佛陀（Buddha）;（經文）佛，世尊。

【筆者試譯】: 也有這些心意堅定的（行者）站在平地的，
他們合掌站在導師前面，
歡喜地如讚誦母親那樣，
以千句詩歌讚誦法中之王（即佛陀）！

【什公漢譯】: 又見菩薩，安禪合掌，以千萬偈，讚諸法王。

【英 譯 本】：Some are standing firm, the feet put together
and the hands joined in token of of respect towards the
learders, and are praising joyfully the king of the
leading Ginas in thousands of stanzas.

【信譯研究】：信譯。

【第廿六頌】

स्मृतिमन्त दान्ताश्च विशारदाश्च
सूक्ष्मां चरिं केचि प्रजानमानाः।
पृच्छन्ति धर्मं द्विपदोत्तमानां
श्रुत्वा च ते धर्मधरा भवन्ति॥२६॥

【羅馬譯音】

smṛtimanta dāntāśca viśāradāśca
sūkṣmāṁ cariṁ keci prajānamānāḥ|
pṛcchanti dharmaṁ dvipadottamānāṁ
śrutvā ca te dharmadharā bhavanti||26||

【句義解析】

smṛtimanta dāntāś ca viśāradāś ca
sūkṣmāṁ cariṁ ke-ci prajānamānāḥ|
pṛcchanti dharmaṁ dvi-padottamānāṁ
śrutvā ca te dharma-dharā bhavanti||26||

【辭彙研究】

1. स्मृतिमन्त smṛtimanta 形容詞　正念

1.1 【詞尾變化】smṛtimanta 根據學者的看法應爲 smṛtimat 變化而來），所以字典查 smṛtimat。

1.2 【摩威梵英,p1272】mfn. having recollection or full consciousness MBh.; having a good memory MBh.; remembering a former life; prudent , discreet; versed in tradition or law; anything which causes recollection.

1.3 【梵漢辭典,p1185】（形容詞）有記憶的；有（充分）意識的；有記憶力的；精通法律的；（經文）正念，具念，有念，強識，得本心，得正念，具念力，有念力，恆住正念，常一其心，志念堅固，具足憶念。

2. दान्ताश्च dāntāś ca 形容詞　調伏

2.1 【詞尾變化】dāntāś ca 根據連音規則是從 dāntāḥ ca 變化過來，而 dāntāḥ 則是 dānta 的複數主格形，所以字典查 dānta。

2.2 【摩威梵英,p475】

2.2.1 mfn.（√dam）tamed , broken in , restrained , subdued ; mild , patient MBh.; liberal ;

2.2.2 m. a tamed ox or steer; a donor , giver; Ficus Indica or = *damanaka*; N. of a son of Bhīma; of a bull;

2.2.3 pl. of a school of the AV. ;

2.2.4（*ā*）f. of an Apsaras MBh.

2.3 【梵漢辭典,p348】（過去被動分詞）（形容詞）被馴服的；（經文）調，所調，調伏，善調，調順，調柔，淳善，善舜，降伏，受化（者）。

3. विशारदाश्च viśāradāś ca 形容詞　熟練的

3.1 【詞尾變化】viśāradāś ca 根據連音規則是從 viśāradāḥ ca 變化過來，而 viśāradāḥ 則是 viśārada 的複數主格形，所以字典查 viśārada。

3.2 【摩威梵英,p952】

3.2.1 mf（*ā*）n. experienced , skilled or proficient in , conversant with MBh.; learned , wise ; clever（as a speech）BhP. ; of a clear or serene mind; famous , celebrated ; beautifully autumnal; lacking the gift of speech ib. ; bold , impudent ib. ; = śreṣṭha.

3.2.2 m. Mimusops Elengi Kir.; N. of an author and of another person ;

3.2.3（*ā*）f. a kind of Alhagi ;

3.2.4 *-di-man* m. skill , proficiency , conversancy.

3.3 【梵漢辭典,p1456】（形容詞）對～有經驗的；熟練的，進步的或精通的；善於（言詞）的；秋天的；無辯才的；大膽的，不客氣的；（經文）無畏，無怯弱，無所畏，無有怖畏，無有恐懼，得無所畏者，辨，辯才。

4. सूक्श्मां sūkṣmāṁ 形容詞　細微的

4.1【詞尾變化】sūkṣmāṁ 根據連音規則是從 sūkṣmām 變化過來，而 sūkṣmām 是 sūkṣmā 的對格單數形，但 sūkṣmā 是 sūkṣma 的陰性形，所以字典查 sūkṣma。

4.2 【摩威梵英,p1240】

4.2.1 mf（*ā*）n.（prob. connected with *sūci*）minute , small , fine , thin , narrow , short , feeble , trifling , insignificant , unimportant（with *artha* m. `a trifling matter'）MBh.; acute , subtle , keen（understanding or mental operation ; *am* ind.）; nice , exact , precise; subtle , atomic , intangible MBh. ;

4.2.2 m. a partic. figure of rhetoric（`the subtle expression of an intended act '）;（with Śaivas）one who has attained a certain grade of emancipation; a mystical N. of the sound *ī*; N. of Śiva MBh. ; of a Dānava;

4.2.3 m. or n. an atom , intangible matter Sāṃkhyak. MBh.; the subtle all-pervading spirit , Supreme Soul ; the Kataka or clearing-nut plant L. ; = *kṛtaka* , or *kaitava* ;

4.2.4（*ā*）f. sand; small cardamoms; N. of two plants（= *yūthikā* or *karuṇī*）; of one of the 9 Śaktis of Viśṇu;

4.2.5（*am*）n. the cavity or socket of a tooth Viśṇ. ; woven silk ; marrow; the Vedanta philosophy.

4.3 【梵漢辭典,p1230】（形容詞）微妙的，微細的，小的，薄的，狹窄的；短的，瑣碎的，纖細的，幾乎聽不到的（聲音）；銳利的，敏銳的；充足的，正確的，難以捉摸的，原子的；（經文）細，深，微細，微妙，細微，幽微，最細，難知，有細，細軟，細滑，深妙，難解，細物。

5. चरिं cariṁ 形容詞　所行

5.1 【詞尾變化】cariṁ 根據連音規則是從 carim 變化過來，而 carim 是 cari 的對格單數形，所以字典查 cari。

5.2 【摩威梵英,p389】m. an animal ; N. of a man.

5.3 【艾格混梵,p225】（ī chiefly or wholly m. c.）, f.（not recorded in MIndic;= Skt. caryā, Pali cariyā, both also in BHS, see s.vv.）course of conduct, regular system of action（esp. religious）; particularly with reference to the programmatic course of a Bodhisattva, leading to enlightenment;（on its four aspects, or stages see s. v. caryā;) these forms chiefly, but not exclusively, in verse; see also cāri, cārikā; in prose the usual expression is (Bodhisattva-) caryā, e. g. SP 7.1;)

5.4 【梵漢辭典,p315】(陰性名詞)〔(韻律) =caryā〕;(經文)行,所行。

6. प्रजानमाना: prajānamānāḥ 形容詞　了知(佛法)的目的

6.1 【詞尾變化】prajānamānāḥ 是 prajāna-māna 的複數對格形,但 māna 資料前面已有說明,字典查 prajāna。

6.2 【摩威梵英】無此資料,該字可能不是標準梵文。

6.3 【艾格混梵,p357】(from prajāna = Skt. prajānant, knowing) in dharma –tāyai, (for) state of knowing (the dharma).

6.4 【梵漢辭典,p911】(形容詞)(俗語) =prajānat,現在分詞〔Jña〕,(經文)知,了知。

7. पृच्छन्ति pṛcchanti 形容詞　到達

7.1 【詞尾變化】pṛcchanti 爲√praś 的現在式第三人稱複數主動形,所以字典查√praś。

7.2 資料前面已有說明。

8. द्विपदोत्तमानां dvi-padottamānāṁ 名詞　兩足尊

8.1 【詞尾變化】dvi-padottamānāṁ 根據連音規則,是 dvipadottama 的複數屬格形,不過 dvipadottama 根據連音規則,是從 dvi-pada-uttama 所組成,所以字典查 dvi-pada-uttama。

8.2 【摩威梵英,p504, dvi】du. two (nom. dvau see dva).

8.3 【摩威梵英,p583, pada】n. (rarely m.) a step , pace , stride ; a footstep , trace , vestige , mark , the foot itself. RV. (padena , on foot ; pade pade , at every step , everywhere , on every occasion ; trīṇi padāni viṣṇoḥ , the three steps or footprints of Viśṇu, also N. of a constellation or according to some `the space between the eyebrows ' ; sg. viśṇoḥ padam N. of a locality ; padaṃ-dā , padāt padaṃ-gam or cal , to make a step move on ; padaṃ-kṛ , with loc. to set foot in or on , to enter ; with mūrdhni , to set the foot upon the head of 〔gen.〕 i.e. overcome ; with citte or hṛdaye , to take possession of any one's heart or mind ; with loc. or prati , to have dealings with padaṃ ni-dhā with loc. , to set foot in = to make impression upon ; with padavyām , to set the foot on a person's 〔gen. or ibc.〕 track , to emulate or equal ; padam ni-bandh with loc. , to enter or engage in）; a sign , token , characteristic MBh.; a footing , standpoint ; position rank station , site , abode , home RV.; a business affair , matter , object or cause of（gen. or comp.）; a pretext ; a part , portion , division; a square on a chess-board; a plot of ground; the foot as a measure of length; a ray of light（m. L.）; a portion of a verse , quarter or line of a stanza RV. ; a word or an inflected word or the stem of a noun in the middle cases and before some Taddhitas ; any one in a set of numbers the sum of which is required ; a period in an arithmetical progression; a square root; a quadrant ; protection.

8.4 【摩威梵英,p177, uttama】

8.4.1 mfn.（superlative fr. 1. *ud* ; opposed to *avama* , *adhama* , ; cf. *an-uttama*）, uppermost , highest , chief ; most elevated , principal ; best , excellent RV. AV. ; first , greatest ; the highest（tone）; the most removed or last in place or order or time RV. MBh. ;

8.4.2（*am*）ind. most , in the highest degree; at last , lastly;

8.4.3 m. the last person（= in European grammars the first person）; N. of a brother of Dhruva（son of Uttāna-pa1da and nephew of Priya-vrata）; of a son of Priya-vrata and third Manu ; of the twenty-first Vyāsa ;

8.4.4（*ās*）m. pl.N. of people MBh. ;

8.4.5（*ā*）f. a kind of Piḍakā or pustule; the plant Oxystelma Esculentum（Asclepias Rosea Roxb.）; an excellent woman（one who is handsome , healthy , and affectionate）.

8.5 【梵漢辭典,p423, dvipadottama】（陽性名詞）（經文）〔佛號〕兩足尊，兩足之尊，兩足中尊，最上二足尊，兩足世尊；如來。

9. श्रुत्वा śrutvā 動詞　聽聞；學習

9.1 【詞尾變化】śrutvā 是√śru 的絕對分詞不規則變化，所以字典查√śru。

9.2 資料前面已有說明。

10. धरा dharā 形容詞　大地的

10.1 【詞尾變化】沒有詞尾變化。

10.2 【摩威梵英,p510】f. of *-ra* q.v.

10.3 【摩威梵英,p510, dhara】

10.3.1 mf（*ā*）n.（*dhṛ*）bearing , supporting（scil. the world , said of Kṛiśṇa and Śiva）MBh. ; holding , bearing , carrying , wearing , possessing , having , keeping（also in memory）, sustaining , preserving , observing ; a flock of cotton ; a frivolous or dissolute man（= *viṭa*）; a sword ; N. of a Vasu MBh. ; of a follower of the Pāṇḍavas ib. of the king of the tortoises; of the father of Padma-prabha（6th Arhat of pres. Ava-sarpiṇī）;

10.3.2（*ā*）f. `bearer , supporter' , the earth MBh. ; the uterus or womb; a vein or tubular vessel of the body; marrow ; a mass of gold or heap of valuables（representing the earth and given to Brāhmans）; one of the 8 forms of Sarasvatī id. ; N. of one of the wives of Kaṣyapa（mother of the land and water-birds , prob. = the Earth）（v.l. *irā*）;

10.3.3 n. poison（v.l. *dara*）

10.4 【梵漢辭典,p368】（陰性形容詞）大地，子宮。

1. भवन्ति bhavanti 動詞　到達；成爲

11.1 【詞尾變化】bhavanti 是√bhū 的現在式第三人稱複數形，所以字典查√bhū。

11.2 資料前面已有說明。

【筆者試譯】：熟練正念與調伏，
細微的行爲，了知佛法的目的，
成就（證到）兩足尊（世尊）的佛法，
學習與成就如大地般（廣闊）的佛法。

【什公漢譯】：復見菩薩，智深志固，能問諸佛，聞悉受持。

【英 譯 本】：Some thoughtful, meek, and tranquil, who
Have mastered the niceties of the course of duty,
Question the highest of men about the law, and
Retain in their memory what they have learnt.

【信譯研究】：信譯。本段爲意譯。

【第廿七頌】

परिभावितात्मान जिनेन्द्रपुत्रान्
कांश्चिच्च पश्याम्यहु तत्र तत्र।
धर्मं वदन्तो बहुप्राणकोटिनां
दृष्टान्तहेतूनयुतैरनेकैः॥२७॥

【羅馬譯音】

paribhāvitātmāna jinendraputrān
kāṁścicca paśyāmyahu tatra tatra|
dharmaṁ vadanto bahuprāṇakoṭināṁ
dṛṣṭāntahetūnayutairanekaiḥ||27||

【句義解析】

paribhāvitātmāna jinendra-putrān
kāṁś-cic ca paśyāmy ahu tatra tatra|
dharmaṁ vadanto bahu-prāṇa-koṭināṁ
dṛṣṭānta-hetū-nayutair anekaiḥ||27||

【辭彙研究】

1. तत्र तत्र tatra tatra 片語 經常在當中

1.1 【詞尾變化】沒有詞尾變化。

1.2 【摩威梵英】僅有單字資料，資料前面已有說明。

1.3 【梵漢辭典,p1284】(片語)經常在其中，彼等之中或之上；在此處彼處，在彼方此方，到處。

2. वदन्तो vadanto 動詞 向～來說

2.1 【詞尾變化】vadanto 根據連音規則是從 vadantaḥ 變化過來，而 vadantaḥ 是 vadat 的主格複數形，而 vadat 是√vad 的現在主動分詞。所以字典查√vad。

2.2 資料前面已有說明。

3. बहुप्राणकोटिनां bahu-prāṇa-koṭināṁ 複合詞 眾多千億眾

3.1 【詞尾變化】bahu-prāṇa-koṭināṁ 根據連音規則是從 bahu-prāṇa-koṭinām 變化過來，而 bahu-prāṇa-koṭinām 是 bahu-prāṇa-koṭi 的複數屬格。字典查 prāṇa，其餘資料前面都有說明。

3.2 【摩威梵英,p705】

3.2.1 m.（ifc. f. ā）the breath of life , breath , respiration spirit vitality ;

3.2.2 pl. life RV.; a vital organ vital air; air inhaled , wind AV. ; breath（as a sign of strength）. vigour , energy , power MBh. ; a breath（as a measure of time , or the tñtime requisite for the pronunciation of 10 long syllables = 1/6 Vina1d2ika1）; N. of a Kalpa（the 6th day in the light half of Brahmās month）Pur. ;（in Sāṃkhya）the spirit（= *puruṣa*）;（in Vedants）the spirit identified with the totality of dreaming spirits ; poetical inspiration ; myrrh ; a N. of the letter *y* ; of a Sāman; of Brahmā ; of Viśṇu; of a Vasu BhP. ; of a son of the Vasu Dhara; of a Marut; of a son of Dhātṛi ; of a son of Vidhātṛi BhP. ; of a Ṛiśi in the 2nd Manv-antara.

3.3 【梵漢辭典,p922】（陽性名詞）氣息，呼吸，活力，生氣，出息，微風，風，呼吸，氣力，精力，活力，精神，個我，生命力的象徵，感覺器官；（經文）生，命，生命，性命；身命，壽，壽命；眾生。

4. दृष्टान्त dṛṣṭānta 名詞 比喻

4.1 【詞尾變化】沒有詞尾變化。

4.2 【摩威梵英,p492】

4.2.1 m. `the end or aim of what is seen' , example , paragon , standard , allegory , type MBh. ; instance , exemplification（rhet.）; a Śāstra ; a partic. high number ; death ;

4.2.2 -*kalikā* f. N. of wk. ;

4.2.3 -*tas* ind. as a standard or example or precedent MBh. ;

4.2.4 -*vat* mfn. containing examples or comparisons Ja1takam. ;

4.2.5 -*śataka* n. `a hundred examples'N. of wk. MW. ;

4.2.6 dṛṣṭāntaya Nom. P. -*yati* , to adduced as an example;

4.2.7 -*ntita* mfn. adduced as an example or comparison.

4.3 【梵漢辭典,p402】（陽性名詞）範例，模範，前例，實例，例子，用來說明主張的實例，比喻；（經文）譬，喻，譬喻，比，近比，比喻。

5. अनेकैः anekaiḥ 形容詞　各種的；眾多的

5.1 【詞尾變化】anekaiḥ 是 aneka 的工具格複數形，所以字典查 aneka。

5.2 資料前面已有說明。

【筆者試譯】：優秀的佛子們，
我看到處都有些（這樣的人），
向眾多千億的眾生說法，
用非常多樣的譬喻。

【什公漢譯】：又見佛子，定慧具足，以無量喻，爲眾講法。

【英 譯 本】：And I see here and there some sons of the
principal Gina who, after completely developing
their own self, are preaching the law to many kotis
of living beings with many myriads of illustrations and resons.

【信譯研究】：信譯。

【第廿八頌】

प्रामोद्यजाताः प्रवदन्ति धर्मं
समादपेन्तो बहुबोधिसत्त्वान्।
निहत्य मारं सबलं सवाहनं
पराहनन्ती इमु धर्मदुन्दुभिम्॥२८॥

【羅馬譯音】

prāmodyajātāḥ pravadanti dharmaṁ
samādapento bahubodhisattvān|
nihatya māraṁ sabalaṁ savāhanaṁ
parāhanantī imu dharmadundubhim||28||

【句義解析】

prāmodya-jātāḥ pravadanti dharmaṁ
samādapento bahu-bodhisattvān|

nihatya māraṁ sabalaṁ savāhanaṁ

parāhanantī imu dharma-dundubhim||28||

【辭彙研究】

1. प्रामोद्य prāmodya 形容詞　狂喜

1.1 【詞尾變化】沒有詞尾變化。這個字非標準梵文，相當於 pra-moda，所以字典查 pra-moda。

1.2 【摩威梵英,p686, pramoda】

1.2.1 m.（also pl. ; ifc. f. *ā*）excessive joy , delight , gladness MBh.;（also n.）one of the 8 Sāṃkhya perfections Tattvas. ;（with Jainas）joy as exhibited in the virtuous ; Pleasure personified（as a child of Brahmā VP.）; the 4th year in a 60 years' cycle of Jupiter ; a strong perfume BhP. ; a kind of rice; N. of a being attendant upon Skanda MBh. ; of a Nāga; of an author; of sev. men VP. Ra1jat. ;

1.2.2 -*cārin* w.r. for *pramāda-c-* q.v. ;

1.2.3 -*tīrtha* n. N. of a Ti1rtha;

1.2.4 -*nṛtya* n. joyous dancing , a joyful dance ;

1.2.5 -*modāḍhyā* f. a partic. plant = *aja-modā.*

1.3 【梵漢辭典,p921, prāmodya】（中性形容詞）〔起自 pra-moda〕狂喜，歡喜，欣喜，幸福；（經文）喜，勝喜，歡喜，悅，欣，歡，樂，歡悅，喜悅，喜樂，欣樂，（自）慶，和悅予；踴躍。

2. जाता: jātāḥ 形容詞／過去被動分詞　已生

2.1 【詞尾變化】jātāḥ 是 jāta 的複數主格形，所以字典查 jāta。

2.2 【摩威梵英,p417】

2.2.1 mfn.（$\sqrt{}$*jan*）born , brought into existence by（loc.）, engendered by（instr. or abl.）RV.; grown , produced , arisen , caused , appeared; appearing on or in; destined for（dat.）RV.; turning to（dat.）; happened , become , present , apparent , manifest; belonging to（gen.）RV. ; ready at hand ; possessed of（instr.）MBh.; often instead of in comp;

2.2.2 m. a son RV. ; a living being（said of men , rarely of gods）RV.; N. of a son of Brahmā ;

2.2.3 n. a living being , creature RV. ; birth , origin; race , kind , sort , class , species AV ; a multitude or collection of things forming a class MBh. ; individuality , specific condition（*vyakta*）; = *-karman*;（impers. with double instr.）it turned out or happened that ;

2.2.4（*ā*）f. a daughter ;

2.3 【梵漢辭典,p526】（過去被動分詞）（經文）生，所生，已生，生在，深生，起，現，得，生已，現在，起成，成已。

3. प्रवदन्ति pravadanti 動詞　宣說

3.1 【詞尾變化】pravadanti 是 pra-√vad 的現在式第三人稱複數形，所以字典查 pra-√vad。

3.2 【摩威梵英,p690】P. Ā. -vadati , -te（Ved. inf. pra-vaditos）, to speak out , pronounce , proclaim , declare , utter , say , tell RV.; to speak to（acc.）; to raise the voice（said of birds and animals）; to roar , splash（said of water）. ;（cf. a-pravadat）to assert , affirm , state ; to pronounce to be , call , name（2 acc.）MBh.; to offer for sale（with instr. of price）.（v.l.）: Caus. -vādayati , to cause to sound , play（with acc. of the instrument）MBh. ;（without an object）to play , make music.（also -vādyati , with act. meaning MBh）.

3.3 【梵漢辭典,p1366】（動詞）說出，發言，講述，聲明，宣布；出聲，噴出，斷言，肯定，宣示，宣稱；（經文）說，告。

4. समादपेन्तो samādapento 動詞　勸修；教導

4.1 【詞尾變化】samādapento 根據連音規則是從 samādapentaḥ 變化過來，而 samādapentaḥ 則是 sam-ā-√da 的使役法現在式主動分詞主格複數形的俗語轉寫，所以字典查 sam-ā-√da。〔註 44〕

4.2 【摩威梵英】sam-ā-√da 個別單字部分資料前面已有說明。結合者並未有資料。

4.3 【梵漢辭典,p339】（使役動詞）使攝取，勸導，喚起；（經文）教，教化，

〔註 44〕samādapeti 在俗語當中等同 samādāpayati，因此 samādapeta 等於 samādāpayata，其字根即為 sam-ā-√da。請見 Franklin Edgerton 編《Buddhist Hybrid Sanskrit Grammar And Dictionary》，Reprint：1993，By Motilal Banarsidass Publishers Pvt.Ltd., Dehli,India,p.567。

教行，教令，教授，教持，教導，勸，勸導，勸受，勸令，勸型，勸勉，勸化，勸諭，勸修，勸令修行，令修。

5. निहत्य nihatya 動詞　打擊；修正

5.1 【詞尾變化】nihatya 是 ni-√han 的不變格寫法，所以字典查 ni-√han。

5.2 【摩威梵英,p564】

5.2.1 P. *-hanti*（Impv. *-jahi* RV. ; p. *-ghna* TS. ; 3- sg. Ā. *-jighnate* RV. ; p. *jighnamāna* MBh. ; pf. *-jaghāma* RV. ; pl. *-jaghnur* , *-nire* MBh. ; fut. *-haniṣyati* , *-te* , *-haṃsyati* MBh. ; p. *-haniṣyat* RV. ; <u>ind. p. *-hatya*</u> 〔cf. *a-nihatya*〕 ; inf. *-hantave* RV. ; *-hantum* R.）, to strike or fix in , hurl in or upon or against（loc.）RV.; to make an attempt upon , attack , assail（acc. loc. or gen.）AV. MBh. ; to strike or hew down（also -mow L.）, kill , overwhelm , destroy RV.（also applied to planets）; to hit , touch（lit. and fig.）MBh. BhP.〔564,3〕; to beat（a drum）; to punish , visit , afflict; to attach to（Pass. *-hanyate* , to be fixed upon , with loc.）AV. ; to drop , lower , let sink（hands , wings）AV.; to speak with the unaccented tone i.e. with the Anudātta;（in arithm.）to multiply Āryabh. Comm.: Caus. see *ni-ghāta* , *-taya*.

5.3 【梵漢辭典,p482】（動詞）打在～（位格）之中或之上；拋向～（位格）；射中，襲擊，攻擊，打倒，殺害，殺（平常使用之意）；征服，克服命運，處罰；破壞；使無效，使挫折，去除，降低音調的。（經文）滅，除，推滅，滅除，損壞，離。

6. मारं māraṁ 形容詞　魔

6.1 【詞尾變化】māraṁ 根據連音規則，是從 māram 變化過來的，而 māram 則是 māra 的對格單數形，所以字典查 māra。

6.2 【摩威梵英,p811】

6.2.1 mfn.（√*mṛ*）killing , destroying ;

6.2.2 m. death , pestilence AV. ; slaying , killing ; an obstacle , hindrance; the passion of love , god of love ;（with Buddhists）the Destroyer , Evil One（who tempts men to indulge their passions and is the great enemy of the Buddha and his religion ; four Māras are enumerated in Dharmas. 80 , viz. *skandha-* , *kleza-* , *devaputra-* , and *mṛtyu-m-* ; but the later Buddhist theory of races of gods led to the figment of millions of Māras ruled over by a chief Māra）; the thorn-apple;

6.2.3（*ī*）f. killing , slaughter Prasannar. ; pestilence（also personified as the goddess of death and identified with Durga1）AV.

6.3 【梵漢辭典,p712】（形容詞）謀殺，破壞；（陽性）死；惡性傳染病，瘟疫，殺害，障害，愛，愛神，誘惑者，惡魔；（經文）障；惡者，煞者；惡魔，邪魔，魔怨，魔王，眾魔，天魔。

7. सबलं sabalaṁ 形容詞　有力的

7.1 【詞尾變化】sabalaṁ 根據連音規則，是從 sabalam 變化過來，而 sabalam 是 sabala 的對格單數形，所以字典查 sabala。

7.2 【摩威梵英,p1151】

7.2.1（sa-）mfn. powerful , strong RV.; together with strength or power ; accompanied by a force or army. MBh. ; together with Bala（Kṛiśṇa's eldest brother）BhP. ;

7.2.2 m. N. of a son of Manu Bhautya; of a son of Vasiśṭha（and one of the 7 Ṛiśis）; of one of the 7 Ṛiśis under Manu Śāvarṇa ib. ;

7.2.3 -*tā* f.（ŚāṅkhBr.）, -*tva* n.（Śiṣ.）power , strength ;

7.2.4 -*vāhana* mfn. with an army and followers ;

7.2.5 -*siṃha* m. N. of a king Inscr. ;

7.2.6 -*lāt-kāram* ind. with force , forcibly;

7.2.7 -*lānuga* mfn. followed by an army MBh. ; = *sa-balavāhana.*

7.3 【梵漢辭典,p1041】（形容詞）有力的，強壯的；（經文）大力。

8. सवाहनं savāhanaṁ 形容詞　去除

8.1 【詞尾變化】savāhanaṁ 根據連音規則，是從 sa-vāhanam 變化過來，而 sa-vāhanam 是 sa-vāhana 的對格單數形，而 sa 前面資料已有說明，所以字典查 vāhana。

8.2 【摩威梵英,p949】

8.2.1 mfn. drawing , bearing , carrying , conveying , bringing;

8.2.2 m. N. of a Muni;

8.2.3（*ā*）f. an army ;

8.2.4 n. the act of drawing , bearing , carrying , conveying MBh. ; driving;

riding ; guiding（horses）MBh. ; any vehicle or conveyance or draught-animal , carriage , chariot , waggon , horse , elephant; any animal ; `oar' or `sail'.

8.3 【梵漢辭典,p1370】（形容詞）駕馭；運送；帶來，（中性名詞）牽引或乘用的動物，車輛，運輸機關，戰車，載貨馬車；動物；拖曳，運輸，騎乘，駕駛，去除；（形容詞）乘上，驅動；（經文）車，轉，乘，御，向，轉向，運轉，輦輿，挑牽，篙，棹，遣除，遣蕩。

9. पराहनन्ती parāhanantī 動詞　打擊

9.1 【詞尾變化】parāhanantī 是 parā-√han 的現在主動分詞的主格單數形，所以字典查 parā-√han。

9.2 【摩威梵英,p591】P. -hanti（impf. 2. 3. sg. parāhan pf. 3. pl. parā-jaghnur）, to strike down or away , hurl down , overthrow RV. MBh. ; to touch , feel , grope.

9.3 【梵漢辭典,p482】（動詞）丟棄，顛覆（RV）；切除；（經文）擊，按指。

10. दुन्दुभिम् dundubhim 名詞　鼓

10.1 【詞尾變化】dundubhim 是 dundubhi 的單數對格形，所以字典查 dundubhi。

10.2 【摩威梵英,p484】

10.2.1 mf. a sort of large kettledrum RV. MBh.; a sort of poison ; N. of the 56th year in the Jupiter cycle of 60 years; of Kiṛiśṇa MBh. ; of Varuṇa; of Asuras , a Rakśas , a Yakśa; of a son of Andhaka and grandson of Anu ; f. a drum AV.（also *-bhī* MBh.）;

10.2.2（*i*）f. a partic. throw of the dice in gambling ; N. of a Gandharvī MBh. ;

10.2.3 n. N. of a partic. Varsha in Krauṇca-dvīpa.

10.3 【梵漢辭典,p408】（陽性／陰性名詞）鼓，圓桶鼓；（經文）鼓，大鼓，天鼓，妙鼓，妙法鼓。

【筆者試譯】:（心中）生起歡喜地說法，
教導很多菩薩（修行），
（能）打擊與降服大力的魔，
而擊打這個法鼓。

【什公漢譯】：欣樂說法，化諸菩薩，破魔兵眾，而擊法鼓。

【英 譯 本】：Joyfully they proclaim the law, rousing many Bodhisattvas; after conquering the Evil One with his hosts and vehicles, they strike the drum of the law.

【信譯研究】：信譯。

【第廿九頌】

पश्यामि कांश्चित् सुगतस्य शासने
संपूजितान्नरमरुयक्षराक्षसैः।
अविस्मयन्तान् सुगतस्य पुत्रान्
अनुन्नतान् शान्तप्रशान्तचारीन्॥२९॥

【羅馬譯音】

paśyāmi kāṁścit sugatasya śāsane
saṁpūjitānnaramaruyakṣarākṣasaiḥ|
avismayantān sugatasya putrān
anunnatān śāntapraśāntacārīn||29||

【句義解析】

paśyāmi kāṁś-cit sugatasya śāsane
saṁpūjitān nara-maru-yakṣa-rākṣasaiḥ|
avismayantān sugatasya putrān
anunnatān śānta-praśānta-cārīn||29||

【辭彙研究】

1. शासने śāsane 形容詞　教法

1.1 【詞尾變化】śāsane 是 śāsana 的單數於格形，所以字典查 śāsana。

1.2 【摩威梵英,p1069】

1.2.1 mf（*ī*）n. punishing , a punisher , chastiser（see *pāka-* , *pura-* , *rukmi-* , *smara-z-*）; teaching , instructing , an instructor BhP. ;

1.2.2（*ī*）f. an instructress RV.;

1.2.3（*am*）n.（ifc. f. *ā*）punishment , chastisement , correctionMBh. ; government , dominion , rule over（comp.）MBh. ; an order , command , edict , enactment , decree , direction RV. ; a royal edict , grant , charter（usually a grant of land or of partic. privileges , and often inscribed on stone or copper）; a writing , deed , written contract or agreement ; any written book or work of authority , scripture（=*śāstra*）; teaching , instruction , discipline , doctrine（also= `faith' , `religion'）MBh.; a message（see comp.）; self-control.

1.3 【梵漢辭典,p1147】（形容詞）懲罰，給予教訓，（陽性名詞）懲罰者，教師；（中性）懲罰，刑罰，～的統治，發揮勢力，支配；國王頒布的命令，敕命，許可的敕令，授與，教訓，教導，規定，規則，管理，建議，教義，信仰，宗教，指示，下命令；（經文）教，教法，教化，教誡，所證，所說法，正教，聖教，遺教，法，法輪，法教，正教，佛法，正法，佛教，遺法。

2. संपूजितान् saṁpūjitān 形容詞／過去被動分詞　恭敬供養

2.1 【詞尾變化】saṁpūjitān 是 saṁ-pūjita 的複數對格形，saṁ 的資料前面已有說明，所以字典查 pūjita。

2.2 【摩威梵英,p641】

2.2.1 mfn. honoured , received or treated respectfully , worshipped , adored MBh.; honoured by（gen.）or on account of（comp.）MBh. ; acknowledged , recommended MBh.; frequented , inhabited MBh. ; consecrated ; supplied with（comp.）MBh. ;

2.2.2 m. a god . ;

2.2.3 n. N. of a place.

2.3 【梵漢辭典,p1106, saṁpūjita】（過去被動分詞）供養，好供養，好生供養，恭敬，奉事。

3. मरु maru 名詞　天神

3.1 【詞尾變化】沒有詞尾變化。

3.2 【摩威梵英,p790】

3.2.1 m.（prob. fr. √mṛ）a wilderness , sandy waste , desert（often pl.）MBh. ; a mountain , rock MBh.; `the desertlike penance' i.e. abstinence from drinking MBh.; a species of plant; a deer , antelope; N. of a Daitya（usually associated with Naraka）MBh. ; of a Vasu; of a prince（the son of Śīghra）; of a king belonging to the Ikshvāku family BhP. ; of a son of Hary-aśva;

3.2.2 pl. N. of a country（Marwar）and its inhabitants Tār. R. Var.

3.3 【摩威梵英,p790,marut】

3.3.1 m. pl.（prob. the `flashing or shining ones' ; cf. marīci）the storm-gods（Indra's companions and sometimes e.g. = *devāḥ* , the gods or deities in general ; said in the Veda to be the sons of Rudra and Pṛiśni, or the children of heaven or of ocean ; and described as armed with golden weapons i.e. lightnings and thunderbolts , as having iron teeth and roaring like lions , as residing in the north , as riding in golden cars drawn by ruddy horses sometimes called Pṛiśatīḥ q.v. ; they are reckoned in Naigh. v , 5 among the gods of the middle sphere , and in RV. viii , 96 , 8 are held to be three times sixty in number ; in the later literature they are the children of Diti , either seven or seven times seven in number , and are sometimes said to be led by Ma1taris3van）RV.; the god of the wind（father of Hanumat and regent of the north-west quarter of the sky）（cf. comp.）; wind , air , breath（also applied to the five winds in the body）; a species of plant Bhpr. ; gold; beauty; N. of a Sādhya; of the prince Bṛihad-ratha;

3.3.2 f. Trigonella Corniculata ;

3.3.3 n. a kind of fragrant substance（=*granthi-parṇa*）

3.4 【梵漢辭典,p716】

3.4.1（陽性名詞）乾燥的地域，荒漠，多沙的荒地，沙漠；山，岩石。（經文）高巖，絕邊廣川。

3.4.2（陽性名詞）=marut.（經文）天。

4. राक्षसैः rākṣasaiḥ 形容詞　羅剎

4.1 【詞尾變化】rākṣasaiḥ 是 rākṣasa 的工具格複數形，字典查 rākṣasa。

4.2 【摩威梵英,p871】

4.2.1 mf（*i*）n.（fr. *rakṣas*）belonging to or like a Rakshas , demoniacal , infested by demons（with *vivāha* , or *dharma* or *vidhi* m. `one of the 8 forms of marriage' , the violent seizure or rape of a girl after the defeat or destruction of her relatives）;

4.2.2 m. a Rakshas or demon in general , an evil or malignant demon（the Rākśasas are sometimes regarded as produced from Brahmā's foot , sometimes with Rāvaṇa as descendants of Pulastya , elsewhere they are styled children of Khasā or Su-rasa ; according to some they are distinguishable into 3 classes , one being of a semi-divine benevolent nature and ranking with Yakśas &c. ; another corresponding to Titans or relentless enemies of the gods ; and a third answering more to nocturnal demons , imps , fiends , goblins , going about at night , haunting cemeteries , disturbing sacrifices and even devouring human beings ; this last class is the one most commonly mentioned ; their chief place of abode was Laṇkā in Ceylon）; a king of the Rakśas g. *parśv-ādi* ;（with Jainas）one of the 8 classes of Vyantaras ; N. of the 30th Muhūrta ; of one of the astronomical Yogas. ; of a minister of Nanda; of a poet;

4.2.3 m. n. the 49th year in the Jupiter cycle of 6o years;

4.2.4（*ī*）f. a Rākśasī or female demon MBh.; the island of the Rākśasas i.e. Laṇkā or Ceylon Buddh. ; N. of a malignant spirit supposed to haunt the four corners of a house ; of a Yoginī ; night ; a kind of plant（=*caṇḍā*）; a large tooth , tusk.

4.3 【梵漢辭典,p1012】（形容詞）羅刹（Rākṣas）所屬或持有的，惡魔的；（陽性名詞）夜魔，惡魔；（經文）惡鬼；魅，羅刹。

5. अविस्मयन्तान् avismayantān 動詞　不驚慌；不擔心；不驚奇

5.1 【詞尾變化】avismayantān 是 avismayat 的異寫體，[註45] avismayat 是 a-vi-√smi 的現在式主動分詞，其中 a 是否定字首，所以字典查 vi-√smi。

5.2 【摩威梵英,p1002】Ā. -smayate（m.c. also P.）, to wonder , be surprised or astonished at（instr. loc. , or abl.）; to be proud of（instr.）: Caus.

[註45] 請見江島惠教等編《梵藏漢法華經原典總索引》，東京：靈友會出版，1988年出版。頁 115。

-smāyayati , or -smāpayati , -te, to astonish , surprise MBh.: Desid. of Caus. see vi-sismāpayiṣu.

5.3 【梵漢辭典,p1184】（動詞）因～（具格／從格／位格）而狼狽或驚慌的；因～（苦行；具格）而驕傲的；（經文）生奇特想。

6. अनुन्नतान् anunnatān 形容詞　不高傲

6.1 【詞尾變化】anunnatān 是 anunnata 的複數對格形，所以字典查 anunnata。

6.2 【摩威梵英,p34】 mfn. not elevated , not lifted up.

6.3 【梵漢辭典,p113】（過去被動分詞）不高舉，不揚昇；（經文）無高，不高，不高舉，無高倨，無倨傲，黀，未滿；（形容詞）（經文）不高，離慢。

7. शान्त śānta 過去被動分詞　寂靜；平靜

7.1 【詞尾變化】沒有詞尾變化。

7.2 【摩威梵英,p1064】

7.2.1 mfn.（fr. √*śam*）appeased , pacified , tranquil , calm , free from passions , undisturbed MBh. ; soft , pliant ; gentle , mild , friendly , kind , auspicious（in augury ; opp. to *dīpta*）AV.; abated , subsided , ceased , stopped , extinguished , averted（*śāntam* or *dhik śāntam* or *śāntam pāpam* , may evil or sin be averted! may God forfend! Heaven forbid! not so!）MBh.; rendered ineffective , innoxious , harmless（said of weapons）MBh. ; come to an end , gone to rest , deceased , departed , dead , died out; purified , cleansed ;

7.2.2 m. an ascetic whose passions are subdued; tranquillity , contentment（as one of the Rasas q.v.）; N. of a son of Day MBh. ; of a son of Manu ; of a son of Śambara ; of a son of Idhma-jihva BhP. ; of a son of Āpa; of a Devaputra ;

7.2.3（*ā*）f.（in music）a partic.; Emblica Officināis ; Prosopis Spicigera and another species ; a kind of Dūrvā grass ; a partic. drug（=reṇukā）; N. of a daughter of Daśa-ratha（adopted daughter of Loma-pāda or Roma-pāda and wife of Ṛiśya-śṛiṅga）MBh.;（with Jainas）of a goddess who executes the orders of the 7th Arhat ; of a Śakti;

7.2.4 n. tranquillity , peace of mind BhP. ; N. of a Varsha in Jambu-dvīpa; N. of a Tīrtha.

7.3 【梵漢辭典,p1127】(過去被動分詞)(經文)寂,寂定,寂靜,靜寂,寂滅,已寂,湛寂;靜,靜妙,停,息,自息,止息,柔善,盡,冷,無熱,淡泊,恬泊。

【筆者試譯】:我又看見一些佛陀的教法,
讓男人,天神,夜叉,羅刹惡魔們所恭敬供養,
佛子們並不感到奇特,
所修行的(內容)都是不高傲,寂靜與最極靜。

【什公漢譯】:又見菩薩,寂然宴默,天龍恭敬,不以爲喜。

【英 譯 本】:I see some sons of the Sugata, humble, calm,
and quiet in conduct, living under the command of
the Sugatas, and honoured by men, gods, goblins,
and Titans.

【信譯研究】:信譯。

【第卅頌】

वनषण्ड निश्राय तथान्यरूपा
अवभासु कायातु प्रमुञ्चमानाः।
अभ्युद्धरन्तो नरकेषु सत्त्वां-
स्तांश्चैव बोधाय समादपेन्ति॥३०॥

【羅馬譯音】

vanaṣaṇḍa niśrāya tathānyarūpā
avabhāsu kāyātu pramuñcamānāḥ|
abhyuddharanto narakeṣu sattvāṁ-
stāṁścaiva bodhāya samādapenti||30||

【句義解析】

vana-ṣaṇḍa niśrāya tathā nya rūpā

avabhāsu kāyātu pramuñcamānāḥ|
abhyuddharanto narakeṣu sattvāṁs
tāṁś caiva bodhāya samādapenti||30||

【辭彙研究】

1. वन vana 名詞　樹木

1.1 【詞尾變化】沒有詞尾變化。

1.2 【摩威梵英,p917】

1.2.1 n.（once m.）a forest , wood , grove , thicket , quantity of lotuses or other plants growing in a thick cluster（but in older language also applied to a single tree）RV.; plenty , abundance; a foreign or distant land RV; wood , timber RV. ; a wooden vessel or barrel（for the Soma juice）RV.（?）; a cloud（as the vessel in the sky）;

1.2.2（prob.）the body of a carriage RV. ; water ; a fountain , spring; abode; Cyperus Rotundus; = *raśrmi* , a ray of light;

1.2.3（prob.）longing , earnest desire ;

1.2.4 m. N. of a son of Uśīnara BhP. ; of one of the 10 orders of mendicants founded by Śamkaracārya（the members of which affix *vana* to their names cf. *rārmendra-v-*）;

1.2.5（*ā*）f. the piece of wood used for kindling fire by attrition（=araṇi q.v. ; sometimes personified）RV.;

1.2.6（*ī*）f. a wood , forest.

1.3 【梵漢辭典,p1384】（中性名詞）樹木，小樹林，樹叢，聚集，成群，豐富；裝酒的木桶，雲，水，住所；（經文）林，樹，草木，林藪；叢林，園，園林。

2. षण्ड ṣaṇḍa 形容詞　樹林；植物群

2.1 【詞尾變化】沒有詞尾變化。

2.2 【摩威梵英,p1108】

2.2.1 m. n.（often written *khaṇḍa*}, also v.l. or w.r. for *śaṇḍa* , *ṣaṇḍha* , and *saṇḍa*）a group of trees or plants , wood , thicket（always ifc.; cf. *vana* and *vṛkṣa-ṣ-*）; any group or multitude , heap , quantity , collection BhP. ;

2.2.2 m. a bull set at liberty（*-tva* n.）（cf. *nīlaṣ-*}）; a breeding bull ; N. of a serpent-demon;

2.2.3 n. = *liṅga*（used in explaining *pāṣaṇḍa*）BhP.

2.3 【梵漢辭典,p1124】（陽性／中性名詞）（常爲 khaṇḍa 的別音）樹林或植物群（常與 vana, vṛkṣa-及植物名連用）；堆積，數量，收集；（經文）林，叢；密林。

3. निश्राय niśrāya 動名詞　依止

3.1 【詞尾變化】niśrāya 即爲 niśritya，是 ni-√śri 的動名詞，所以字典查 ni-√śri。

3.2 【摩威梵英,p561】P. -śrayati（aor. -aśret）, to lean on or against ; to lay or cast down RV.

3.3 【梵漢辭典,p1199, ni-√śri】（經文）坐，依，依止，爲依止。

3.4 【梵漢辭典,p808, niśrāya】（動名詞）〔=niśritya〕（經文）依，倚，處。

4. तथान्य tathānya 副詞　其他如

4.1 【詞尾變化】tathānya 根據連音規則是由 tatha-anya 所組成。字典查 tatha-anya。

4.2 資料前面已有說明。

5. रूपा rūpā 形容詞　色相；美麗的

5.1 【詞尾變化】rūpā 爲 rūpa 的陰性單數主格形，所以字典查 rūpa。

5.2 資料前面已有說明。

6. अवभासु avabhāsu 名詞　光明下

6.1 【詞尾變化】avabhāsu 是 ava-bhā 的於格複數形，所以字典查 ava-bhā。

6.2 【摩威梵英,p96,ava】ind.（as a prefix to verbs and verbal nonus expresses）off , away , down RV. ;（exceptionaIly as a preposition with abl.）down from AV. ;（for another use of this preposition see ava-kokila.）

6.3 【摩威梵英,p750,bhā】

6.3.1 f.（nom. prob. *bhās*）light , brightness , splendour;

6.3.2 m. the sun.

6.4 【梵漢辭典,p205,ava】〔動詞及名詞的接頭詞〕離開；在下的；（經文）下，（介係詞）〔與從格並用〕在～之下。

6.5 【梵漢辭典,p248,bhā】（陰性名詞）光輝，光明，莊嚴華麗；（經文）光明。

7. कायातु kāyātu 形容詞　身體

7.1 【詞尾變化】kāyātu 疑爲 kāyāsu 的轉寫（據上一個字也是複數於格形來看），kāyāsu 爲 kāya 的複數於格形，所以字典查 kāya。

7.2 資料前面已有說明。

8. प्रमुञ्चमानाः pramuñcamānāḥ 動詞　解放；放射

8.1 【詞尾變化】pramuñcamānāḥ 是 pra-√muc 的現在式主動中間分詞的複數主格形，所以字典查 pra-√muc。

8.2 資料前面已有說明。

9. अभ्युद्धरन्तो abhyuddharanto 動詞　拔出；救濟

9.1 【詞尾變化】abhyuddharanto 是 abhy-ud-√dhṛ 的現在式主動分詞的主格複數形，所以字典查 abhy-ud-√dhṛ。

9.2 【摩威梵英,p78】(√hṛ), Ved. to take out (especially one fire in order to add it to another); to take or draw out , draw (as water) MBh. ; to take up , lift up MBh.; to re-obtain; to elevate , render prosperous MBh.: Caus. (ind. p. -uddhārya) to raise , lift up MBh.

9.3 【梵漢辭典,p381】（經文）濟，拔濟，拔出。

10. नरकेषु narakeṣu 名詞　地獄

10.1 【詞尾變化】narakeṣu 是 naraka 的於格複數形，所以字典查 naraka。

10.2 【摩威梵英,p529】

10.2.1 (Nir. ; *naraka* TĀr.) m. or n. hell , place of torment MBh. ; (distinguished from pātāla q.v. ; personified as a son of Anṛita and Nirṛiti or Nirkṛiti; there are many different hells , generally 21) ;

10.2.2 m. N. of a demon (son of Viśṇu and Bhūmi or the Earth , and therefore called Bhauma , haunting Prāg-jyotisha and slain by Kṛiśṇa) MBh.; of a son of Vipra-citti; = *deva-rātriprabheda* (?) ;

10.2.3 m. or n. N. of a place of pilgrimage MBh. (v.l. *anaraka*) ;

10.3 【梵漢辭典,p768】（陽性名詞）冥界，地界，地獄；（經文）地獄，惡道，不可樂，不可救濟，非行，闇冥。

11. सत्त्वांस् sattvāṁs 名詞 有情眾生

11.1 【詞尾變化】sattvāṁs 因爲和下一句的 tāṁś ca 相連，根據連音規則，是從 sattvān 變化過來，sattvān 是 sattva 的對格複數形，所以字典查 sattva。

11.2 資料前面已有說明。

12. तांश्च tāṁś ca 代名詞 他們

12.1 【詞尾變化】tāṁś ca 根據連音規則是從 tān ca 變化過來，而 tān 是 ta 的複數對格形，所以字典查 ta。

12.2 資料前面已有說明。

13. बोधाय bodhāya 形容詞 了悟的

13.1 【詞尾變化】bodhāya 是 bodha 的單數爲格形，所以字典查 bodha。

13.2 【摩威梵英,p734】

13.2.1 mfn. knowing , understanding ;

13.2.2 m. waking , becoming or being awake , consciousness AV. MBh. ; the opening of blossom , bloom; the taking effect（of spells ; acc. with *pra-yā* , `to begin to take effect'）; exciting（a perfume）; perception , apprehension , thought , knowledge , understanding , intelligence ; designation ; awakening , arousing ; making known , informing , instructing ; Knowledge personified as a son of Buddhi; N. of a man;

13.2.3 pl. N. of a people MBh.

13.3 【梵漢辭典,p288】（形容詞）理解，了悟；（陽性形容詞）覺悟清醒的，覺醒之職狀態，意識，開花的，綻開的；喚起（香氣）的；領悟，知識，理解；表現；（經文）覺，知，菩提。

【筆者試譯】：其他如住在美麗的樹林的（佛子們），
在身體放射出光明下，
拔濟出地獄有情眾生，
勸導他們了悟修行。

【什公漢譯】：又見菩薩，處林放光，濟地獄苦，令入佛道。

【英 譯 本】：Others, again, who have retired to woody
thickets, are saving the creatures in the hells by

emitting radiance from their body, and rouse them
to enlightenment.

【信譯研究】：信譯。

【第卅一頌】

वीर्ये स्थिताः केचि जिनस्य पुत्रा
मिद्धं जहित्वा च अशेषतोऽन्ये।
चंक्रम्ययुक्ताः पवने वसन्ति
वीर्येण ते प्रस्थित अग्रबोधिम्॥३१॥

【羅馬譯音】

vīrye sthitāḥ keci jinasya putrā
middhaṁ jahitvā ca aśeṣato'nye|
caṁkramyayuktāḥ pavane vasanti
vīryeṇa te prasthita agrabodhim||31||

【句義解析】

vīrye sthitāḥ ke-ci jinasya putrā
middhaṁ jahitvā ca aśeṣato 'nye|
caṁkramya-yuktāḥ pavane vasanti
vīryeṇa te prasthita agra-bodhim||31||

【辭彙研究】

1. वीर्ये vīrye 形容詞　精進的

1.1 【詞尾變化】vīrye 是 vīrya 的單數於格形，所以字典查 vīrya。

1.2 資料前面已有說明。

2. स्थिताः sthitāḥ 形容詞　處在於；站立的

2.1 【詞尾變化】sthitāḥ 是 sthita 的複數主格形，所以字典查 sthita。

2.2 資料前面已有說明。

3. मिद्धं middhaṁ 形容詞　懶惰；怠惰

3.1 【詞尾變化】middhaṁ 根據連音規則，是從 middham 變化過來，而 middham 則是 middha 的對格單數形，所以字典查 middha。

3.2 【摩威梵英,p817】n. sloth , indolence（one of the 24 minor evil passions Dharmas. 69）.

3.3 【梵漢辭典,p728】（中性形容詞）精神上的遲鈍，怠惰；（經文）眠，睡，睡眠，悔眠，昏滯。

4. अशेषतोऽन्ये aśeṣato 'nye 複合詞　完全沒有的

4.1 【詞尾變化】aśeṣato 'nye 根據連音規則是從 aśeṣatāḥ anye 變化過來，而 aśeṣatāḥ 是 aśeṣatas 的主格單數形，而 anye 是 anya 主格複數形，所以字典查 aśeṣatas anya。

4.2　資料前面已有說明。

5. चंक्रम्य caṁkramya 動詞　反復繞行

5.1 【詞尾變化】caṁkramya 根據連音規則是從 caṅkramye 變化過來，也就是√kram 的第一人稱單數現在式主動的反覆形，所以字典查√kram。

5.2 【摩威梵英,p319】

5.2.1 cl. 1. *krāmati*（also *kramati*）, *kramate*（also *krāmate* ; also cl. 4. P. *krāmyati* 〔*kramyati*〕 ; aor. *akramīt* RV.; *kramiṣṭa* , *kraṃsate* 〔RV〕 , pl. *cakramanta*〔RV.〕; perf. *cakrāma* , or *cakrame* ; p. *cakramāṇa* RV. ; fut. *kramiśyati* or *kraṃsyate* ind. p. *krāntvā* , *krantvā* , or *kramitvā*,

5.2.2 to step , walk , go , go towards , approach（with *accha* , *adhi* acc. or loc.）RV.; to approach in order to ask for assistance（with loc.）AV.; to go across , go over MBh.; Ved. to climb（as on a tree's branch）; to cover（in copulation）AV; to stretch over , project over , tower above ,（ind. p. *krāntvā*）; to take possession of Pañcat. ; Ā. to undertake , strive after , make effort for（dat.）;（loc.）; Ā. to proceed well , advance , make progress , gain a footing , succeed , have effect MBh.; to be appliable or practicable ;

5.2.3 P. to be liable to the peculiar arrangement of a Vedic text called Krama（i.e. to be doubled , as a letter or word）; Ā. to read according to the Krama arrangement of a Vedic text.（*a-krānta*）: Caus. P. *kramayati* , to cause to step; *kramayati* or *krām-* , to make liable to the peculiar arrangement called Krama（i.e. to double a letter or word）: Intens. *caṅkramyate*（p.

caṅ-kramyamāṇa 〔MBh.〕 or *-kramam-* MBh. and BhP.）or *caṅkramīti*（MBh. ; impf. 2. pl. *caṅkramata* RV.; fut. p. *caṅkramiśyat*; ind. p. *-mitvā* ; cf. *-mita*）, to step to and fro , walk or wander about.

5.3 【梵漢辭典,p607】（動詞）（反復）繞行的；（經文）行，經行，徐步（經行），（靜思）經行，常轉，常轉不住，輪轉不絕。

6. युक्ताः yuktāḥ 形容詞　埋首於；從事～的

6.1 【詞尾變化】yuktāḥ 是 yukta 的複數主格形，所以字典查 yukta。

6.2 資料前面已有說明。

7. पवने pavane 名詞　樹林靜處

7.1 【詞尾變化】pavane 是 pavana 的單數於格形，所以字典查 pavana。

7.2 【摩威梵英,p610】

7.2.1 m. `purifier' , wind or the god of wind , breeze , air（ifc. f. *ā*）MBh.; vital air , breath; the regent of the Nakshatra Svāti and the north-west region ; N. of the number 5（from the 5 vital airs）ib. ; a householder's sacred fire ; a species of grass ; N. of a son of Manu Uttama BhP. ; of a mountain; of a country in Bharata-kshetra ;

7.2.2（*ī*）f. a broom ; the wild citron-tree（v.l. *pacanī*）; N. of a river ;

7.2.3 n. or m. purification , winnowing of corn ; a potter's kiln;

7.2.4 n. an instrument for purifying grain, sieve , strainer AV; blowing ; water ;

7.2.5 mfn. clean , pure.

7.3 【梵漢辭典,p884】（中性名詞）樹林，有樹林的土地；（經文）靜處。

8. वसन्ति vasanti 動詞　停留

8.1 【詞尾變化】vasanti 是√vas 的現在式主動第三人稱複數形，所以字典查√vas。

8.2 資料前面已有說明。

9. वीर्येण vīryeṇa 形容詞　精進的

9.1 【詞尾變化】vīryeṇa 是 vīrya 的複數於格形，所以字典查 vīrya。

9.2 資料前面已有說明。

10. प्रस्थित prasthita 過去被動分詞　啓程；出發

10.1 【詞尾變化】沒有詞尾變化。

10.2 【摩威梵英,p699】

10.2.1 mfn. set forth , prepared , ready（as sacrifice）RV; rising , upright RV. ; standing forth , prominent AV. ; appointed , installed ; set out , departed , gone to（acc. with or without *prati* dat. or loc.）or for the purpose of（dat.）MBh.;

10.2.2（*-vat* mfn. = *pra-tasthe* , ` he has set out '）;

10.2.3（ifc.）reaching to ,（v.l. *prati-ṣṭhita*）;

10.2.4（*am*）impers. a person（instr.）has set out BhP. ;

10.2.5 n. setting out , going away , departure ; N. of partic. Soma vessels（see next）;

10.2.6 *-yājyā* f. a verse pronounced on offering the Prasthita vessels ,

10.2.7（*-homa* m. the oblation connected with it Vait.）

10.3 【梵漢辭典,p936】（過去被動分詞）啓程，出發，行進的，出外旅行；（經文）行，趣，發趣，趣入，求，住。

【筆者試譯】：有些佛子處於精進（狀態），
完全不當怠惰爲母親（譯案：完全不懈怠）
埋首於反覆經行，停留於樹林靜處，
精進致力，向著無上菩提出發。

【什公漢譯】：又見佛子，未嘗睡眠，經行林中，懃求佛道。

【英 譯 本】：There are some sons of the Gina who dwell
in the forest, abiding in vigour, comletely renouncing
sloth, and actively engaged in walking; it
is by energy that they are striving for supreme enlightenment.

【信譯研究】：信譯。

【第卅二頌】

ये चात्र रक्षन्ति सदा विशुद्धं
शीलं अखण्डं मणिरत्नसादृशम्।
परिपूर्णचारी च भवन्ति तत्र

शीलेन ते प्रस्थित अग्रबोधिम्॥ ३ २॥

【羅馬譯音】

ye cātra rakṣanti sadā viśuddhaṁ
śīlaṁ akhaṇḍaṁ maṇiratnasādṛśam|
paripūrṇacārī ca bhavanti tatra
śīlena te prasthita agrabodhim||32||

【句義解析】

ye cātra rakṣanti sadā viśuddhaṁ
śīlaṁ akhaṇḍaṁ maṇi-ratna-sādṛśam|
paripūrṇa-cārī ca bhavanti tatra
śīlena te prasthita agra-bodhim||32||

【辭彙研究】

1. चात्र cātra 複合詞　而於此處

1.1 【詞尾變化】cātra 根據連音規則即 ca-atra 的組合，所以字典查 atra。

1.2 資料前面已有說明。

2. रक्षन्ति rakṣanti 動詞　守護

2.1 【詞尾變化】rakṣanti 是√rakṣ 的現在式主動的第三人稱複數形，所以字典查√rakṣ。

2.2 【摩威梵英,p859】cl. 1. to guard , watch , take care of , protect , save , preserve（`from' abl.）RV.; to tend（cattle）Mn. MBh.; to rule（the earth or a country）MBh. ; to keep（a secret）; to spare , have regard to（another's feelings）; to observe（a law , duty）RV. MBh. ; to guard against , ward off , keep away , prevent , frustrate , injure AV.; to beware of Kathās. ; to heed , attend to（loc.）RV.; to conceal , hide RV. ; to conceal one's self , be afraid, to guard , watch , save or protect from（abl.）,to wish to guard , intend to protect from（abl.）MBh.

2.3 【梵漢辭典,p1912】（動詞）防衛，保護；守備，看顧（家畜），照顧，節約，保存，保守，救護，～（從格）的保存；遵奉（法規等）；統治（國家），支配；警戒～（對格），對～提防；（經文）護，能護，守護，防護，救護，爲救護，作守護，防援，防制；持，護持。

3. सदा sadā 副詞 始終地

3.1 【詞尾變化】沒有詞尾變化。

3.2 【摩威梵英,p1139】ind. always , ever , every time , continually , perpetually（with na ' , never'）RV.

3.3 【梵漢辭典,p1045】（副詞）始終地，恆常地，永遠地：+na 決不做～（經文）永，恆，常，恆時。

4. विशुद्धं viśuddhaṁ 過去被動分詞 完全清淨

4.1 【詞尾變化】viśuddhaṁ 根據連音規則是從 viśuddham 變化過來，而 viśuddham 是 viśuddha 的單數對格形，所以字典查 viśuddha。

4.2 資料前面已有說明。

5. शीलं śīlaṁ 名詞 誡律

5.1 【詞尾變化】śīlaṁ 根據連音規則是從 śīlam 變化過來，而 śīlam 則是 śīla 的單數對格形，所以字典查 śīla。

5.2 【摩威梵英,p1079】

5.2.1 n.（and m. g. *ardharcādi* ; ifc. f. *ā*）habit , custom , usage , natural or acquired way of living or acting , practice , conduct , disposition , tendency , character , nature（often ifc. = `habituated' or `accustomed' or `disposed' or `addicted to' , `practising' ; cf. *guṇa-*, *dāna-* , *puṇya-ś-*）VS. good disposition or character , moral conduct , integrity , morality , piety , virtue Mn. MBh.;（with Buddhists *śīla* ' , moral conduct ' , is one of the 6 or 10 perfections or Pāramitās 〔q.v.〕 and is threefold , viz. *sambhāra* , *kuśala-saṃgrāha* , *sattvārtha-kriyā*）; a moral precept（with Buddh. there are 5 fundamental precepts or rules of moral conduct cf. *pañca-śīla*）; form , shape , beauty ;

5.2.2 m. a large snake in this sense prob. fr. 1. *śī*）; N. of a man Buddh. ; of a king Rājat. ;

5.3 【梵漢辭典,p1171】（中性／陽性名詞）習慣，風俗，氣質，性向，性格，舉止，好的行爲或習慣，高尚的品行，廉潔，道德性；（形容詞）習慣於，有～氣質的，有～傾向的，專心於～，實行～；（經文）尸羅，習，性，自性，稟性，戒，持戒，淨戒，受持禁戒，善戒，戒行，戒律；善行，常樂，具，威儀，界。

6. अखण्डं akhaṇḍaṁ 形容詞　完整的

6.1 【詞尾變化】akhaṇḍaṁ 根據連音規則，是從 akhaṇḍam 變化過來，而 akhaṇḍam 是 akhaṇḍa 的單數對格形，所以字典查 akhaṇḍa。

6.2 【摩威梵英,p4】

6.2.1 mfn. not fragmentary , entire , whole;

6.2.2（*am*）, n. time ;（*a-khaṇḍā dvā daśī*）, the twelfth day of the first half of the month.

6.3 【梵漢辭典,p60】（形容詞）不分，完全；（經文）不破；無缺漏，無有缺漏。

7. सादृशम् sādṛśam 形容詞　譬如

7.1 【詞尾變化】sādṛśam 是 sādṛśa 的單數對格形，所以字典查 sādṛśa。

7.2 【摩威梵英,p1200】

7.2.1 mf（*ī*, once in R. *ā*）n. like , resembling , similar to（gen. instr. , loc , or comp.）or in（instr. loc. , or comp.）RV. ; conformable , suitable , fit , proper , right , worthy MBh. ;

7.2.2（*am*）ind. suitably , well.

7.3 【梵漢辭典,p1050】（形容詞）相似的，如～的（=sadṛśa）；（經文）如。

8. परिपूर्ण paripūrṇa 形容詞／過去被動分詞　被～填滿的

8.1 【詞尾變化】沒有詞尾變化。

8.2 【摩威梵英,p597】

8.2.1 mfn. quite full; completely filled or covered with , occupied by（comp.）MBh. ; accomplished , perfect , whole , complete ib. ; fully satisfied , content ;

8.2.2 -candra-vimala-prabha m. N. of a Samādhi. ;

8.2.3 -*tā* f. -*tva* n. completion , fulness , satiety , satisfaction;

8.2.4 -*bhāṣin* mfn. speaking perfectly i.e. very wisely ;

8.2.5 -*mānasa* mfn. satisfied in mind;

8.2.6 -*mukha* mf（*ī*）n. having the face entirely covered or smeared or painted with（comp.）;

8.2.7 -*sahasra-candra-vatī* f. `possessing a thousand full moons ' , N. of Indra's wife;

8.2.8 -*vyañjanatā* f. having the sexual organs complete（one of the 80 secondary marks of a Buddha）;

8.2.9 -*ṇārtha* mfn. having attained one's aim ; full of meaning , wise（as a speech）MBh.;

8.2.10 -*ṇendu* m. the full moon.

8.3 【梵漢辭典,p862】（過去被動分詞）被～充滿或塡滿的；（經文）滿，圓滿，善圓滿，已滿，盈滿，遍滿，充滿，普滿，彌滿，滿足，已滿足，具，已具足，皆具足，備；圓，圓融。

9. शीलेन śīlena 名詞　誡律

9.1 【詞尾變化】śīlena 是 śīla 的單數工具格形，所以字典查 śīla。

9.2 資料前面已有說明。

【筆者試譯】：而在這裡始終守護完全清淨的
完整的戒律，就像珍珠玉石寶物那樣，
所做所爲都非常圓滿，也成就圓滿的戒行，
向著無上菩提邁進。

【什公漢譯】：又見具戒，威儀無缺，淨如寶珠，以求佛道。

【英 譯 本】：Others complete their course by keeping a
constant purity and an unbroken morality like precious
stones and jewels; by morality do these strive
for supreme enlightenment.

【信譯研究】：信譯。

【第卅三頌】

क्षान्तीबला केचि जिनस्य पुत्रा
अधिमानप्राप्तान क्षमन्ति भिक्षुणाम्।
आक्रोश परिभाष तथैव तर्जनां

क्षान्त्या हि ते प्रस्थित अग्रबोधिम्॥३३॥

【羅馬譯音】

kṣāntībalā keci jinasya putrā
adhimānaprāptāna kṣamanti bhikṣuṇām|
ākrośa paribhāṣa tathaiva tarjanāṁ
kṣāntyā hi te prasthita agrabodhim||33||

【句義解析】

kṣāntībalā ke-ci jinasya putrā
adhimāna-prāptāna kṣamanti bhikṣuṇām|
ākrośa paribhāṣa tathaiva tarjanāṁ
kṣāntyā hi te prasthita agra-bodhim||33||

【辭彙研究】

1. क्षान्तीबला kṣāntībalā 形容詞　具有熱力的

1.1 【詞尾變化】kṣāntībalā 即 kṣāntibala），也就是 kṣānti-bala，字典查 kṣānti-bala。

1.2 【摩威梵英,p326, kṣānti】f. patient waiting for anything ; patience , forbearance , endurance , indulgence MBh.; the state of saintly abstraction;（in music）N. of a Śruti ; N. of a river VP.

1.3 【摩威梵英, bala】資料前面已有說明。

1.4 【梵漢辭典,p623, kṣānti】（陰性形容詞）燒焦的，熱，發熱。

1.5 【梵漢辭典, bala】資料前面已有說明。

2. अधिमान adhimāna 形容詞　驕傲；憍慢

2.1 【詞尾變化】adhimāna 是 adhi-māna，所以字典查 adhi-māna 兩個字。

2.2 【摩威梵英,p20,adhi】ind. , as a prefix to verbs and nouns , expresses above , over and above , besides. As a separable adverb or preposition ;（with abl.）Ved. over ; from above , from ; from the presence of ; after ; for ; instead of RV.（with loc.）Ved. over ; on ; at ; in comparision with ;（with acc.）over , upon , concerning.

2.3 【摩威梵英,p809,māna】

2.3.1 m.（*man*）opinion , notion , conception , idea Tattvas.（cf. *ātma-m-*）; purpose , wish , design; self-conceit , arrogance , pride（with Buddhists one of the 6 evil feelings; or one of the 10 fetters to be got rid of.）;

2.3.2（also n.）consideration , regard , respect , honour MBh.; a wounded sense of honour , anger or indignation excited by jealousy（esp. in women）, caprice , sulking; N. of the father of Agastya（perhaps also of Agastya himself Pāṇ. the family of Māna）RV. ;（in astron.）N. of the tenth house（W. also a blockhead; an agent ; a barbarian）.

2.4 【梵漢辭典,p32】（陽性／中性形容詞）（經文）（我）慢，過慢，增上慢。

3. प्राप्तान prāptāna 複合詞　獲得這個

3.1 【詞尾變化】prāptāna 即等於 prāpta-ana，所以字典查 prāpta-ana。

3.2 資料前面已有說明。

4. क्षमन्ति kṣamanti 動詞　能忍

4.1 【詞尾變化】kṣamanti 是√kṣam 的現在式主動第三人稱複數形，所以字典查√kṣam。

4.2 【摩威梵英,p326】

4.2.1 cl. 1. Ā. *kṣamate*（ep. also P. *-ti* ; Ved. cl. 2. P. *kṣamiti* ; cl. 4. P. *kṣāmyati*〔cf. Impv. Ā. 3. sg. *kṣamyatām* BhP〕; perf. *cakṣame* MBh. pl. *-mire*; 1. du. *cakṣaṇvahe.*

4.2.2 1. pl. *-ṇmahe*; fut. 2nd *kṣaṃsyate* , *-ti* , *kṣamiṣyati* ; aor. 2. sg. *akṣaṃsthās*; inf. kṣantum MBh. , to be patient or composed , suppress anger , keep quiet RV. MBh.; to submit to（dat.）; to bear patiently , endure , put up with（acc.）, suffer MBh.; to pardon , forgive anything（acc.）to（gen. or dat.）MBh.（e.g. kṣamasva me *tad* , forgive me that）; to allow , permit , suffer Sa1h.;（with Pot.）; to bear any one , be indulgent to MBh.（Pass.）; to resist; to be able to do anything（inf.）; to seem good: Caus. P. Ā. *kṣamayati* , *kṣāmayate* , to ask any one（acc.）pardon for anything（acc.）MBh.;（perf. *kṣamayām āsa*）to suffer or bear patiently（cf. *kṣamāpaya*）;

4.3 【梵漢辭典,p620】（動詞）忍耐，抑制憤怒；服從～（於格）；有忍受的，能容忍的；相對於～（於格／屬格）寬恕～（對格）；將～（對格）給予（屬格）容許～對～（對格）總榮的；能得，可能；使一致，適當，看好；（經文）忍，能忍，忍受，堪忍，修忍，忍聽，安忍，能堪忍，能忍受，堪能忍受，修型忍，能修行忍，勤修行忍。

5. भिक्षुणाम् bhikṣuṇām 形容詞　於比丘們的

5.1 【詞尾變化】bhikṣuṇām 是 bhikṣu 的複數於格形，所以字典查 bhikṣu。

5.2 資料前面已有說明。

6. आक्रोश ākrośa 名詞　辱罵

6.1 【詞尾變化】沒有詞尾變化。

6.2 【摩威梵英,p128】m. assailing with harsh language , scolding , reviling , abuse ; N. of a prince MBh.

6.3 【梵漢辭典,p62】（陽性名詞）壞話；咒罵；（經文）罵，惡口，毀僻，呵罵，輕毀，悔恨罵辱。

7. परिभाष paribhāṣa 名詞　呵罵毀辱

7.1 【詞尾變化】沒有詞尾變化。

7.2 【摩威梵英,p598】f. speech , discourse, words, MBh;BhP.;blame,censure, reproof（only pl.）;any explantory rule or general definition,（in gram.）a rule or maxim which teaches the proper interpretation or application of other rules,;（in medic.）prognosis; a table or list of abbreviatins or signs used in any work;（also pl.）N. of sev. wks;

7.3 【梵漢辭典,p850】（陽性名詞）（經文）責，罵辱，呵罵毀辱。

8. तथैव tathaiva 副詞　如是

8.1 【詞尾變化】tathaiva 根據連音規則即 tathā eva 的變化。字典查 tathā eva。

8.2 資料前面已有說明。

9. तर्जनां tarjanāṁ 名詞　責罵

9.1 【詞尾變化】tarjanāṁ 根據連音規則，是從 tarjanām 變化過來，而 tarjanām 是 tarjanā 的對格單數形，所以字典查 tarjanā。

9.2 【摩威梵英,p】

9.3 【梵漢辭典,p1279】（陰性名詞）責罵；（經文）輕蔑，嗔罵。

10. क्षान्त्या हि kṣāntyā hi 片語　由於忍辱

10.1 【詞尾變化】kṣāntyā 是 kṣānti 的單數工具格形，所以字典查 kṣānti。hi 則是接尾詞，資料前面已有說明。

10.2 【摩威梵英,p326】f. patient waiting for anything ; patience , forbearance , endurance , indulgence MBh.; the state of saintly abstraction. ;（in music）N. of a Śruti ; N. of a river.

10.3 【梵漢辭典,p622】（陰性名詞）〔=kṣānta（中性名詞）〕（經文）忍，忍辱，安忍，堪忍，能堪忍，和忍，忍加行。

【筆者試譯】：有些非常精進的佛子
能夠忍受來自那些憍慢比丘們的，
辱罵，毀謗這樣的苛責，
向無上菩提出發而修忍辱之行。

【什公漢譯】：又見佛子，住忍辱力，增上慢人，惡罵捶打，
皆悉能忍，以求佛道。

【英 譯 本】：Some sons of the Gina, whose strength consists
in forbearance, patiently endure abuse, censure,
and threats from proud monks. They try to attain
enlightenment by dint of forbearance.

【信譯研究】：信譯。不過這裡鳩摩羅什用六句偈翻譯梵本四句頌。

【第卅四頌】

कांश्चिच्च पश्याम्यहु बोधिसत्त्वान्
क्रीडारतिं सर्व विवर्जयित्वा।
बालान् सहायान् परिवर्जयित्वा
आर्येषु संसर्गरतान् समाहितान्॥३४॥

【羅馬譯音】

kāṁścicca paśyāmyahu bodhisattvān
krīḍāratiṁ sarva vivarjayitvā|
bālān sahāyān parivarjayitvā

āryeṣu saṁsargaratān samāhitān||34||

【句義解析】

kāṁś-cic ca paśyāmy ahu bodhisattvān
krīḍā-ratiṁ sarva vivarjayitvā|
bālān sahāyān parivarjayitvā
āryeṣu saṁsarga-ratān samāhitān||34||

【辭彙研究】

1. क्रीडा krīḍā 名詞 娛樂；嬉戲

1.1 【詞尾變化】沒有詞尾變化。

1.2 【摩威梵英,p321, krīḍā】f. of -ḍa q.v.

1.3 【摩威梵英,p321, krīḍa】

1.3.1 mfn. playing , sporting（said of the winds）RV; m. sport , play L. ;

1.3.2（Ā）f. sport , play , pastime , amusement , amorous sport（often in comp. e.g. *krīḍā-mudaḥ* f. pl. the pleasures of playing or of amorous sport; *kṛṣṇa-k-* , sport with Kṛiśṇa; *jala-k-* , playing about in water MBh. ; *toya-k-*）; working miracles for one's amusement; disrespect shown by jest or joke ; a play-ground MBh.;（in music）a kind of measure.

1.4 【梵漢辭典,p610】（陰性名詞）遊戲，競技，玩笑，玩賞；（經文）戲，遊戲，嬉戲，戲娛樂。

2. रतिं ratiṁ 形容詞 快樂；享樂

2.1 【詞尾變化】ratiṁ 根據連音規則是從 ratim 變化過來，而 ratim 是 rati 的單數對格形，所以字典查 rati。

2.2 【摩威梵英,p867】f. rest , repose; pleasure , enjoyment , delight in , fondness for（loc. or comp. ; ratim with āp , labh , upa-labh , adhi-gam , vidkṛ or bandh and loc. , `to find pleasure in'）MBh.; the pleasure of love , sexual passion or union , amorous enjoyment（often personified as one of the two wives of Kāma-deva , together with Prīti q.v.）MBh.; the pudenda ; = rati-gṛha , pleasure-house ; N. of the sixth Kala of the Moon; of an Apsaras MBh. ; of the wife of Vibhu（mother of Priṭhu-sheṇa）BhP. ; of a magical incantation recited over weapons ; of the letter n; of a metre.

2.3 【梵漢辭典,p1021】（陰性名詞）休息；快樂；享樂；滿足；～（位格）的快樂；性的享樂，性交；（經文）樂，可樂，愛樂，欣樂，快樂，喜樂，喜，歡喜，欣，欣慰，嬉，愛，遊戲，大適悅，恍惚，塵愛，染著。

3. विवर्जयित्वा vivarjayitvā 形容詞 捨離

3.1 【詞尾變化】vivarjayitvā 爲 vi-√vṛj 的使役動詞動名詞，所以字典查 vi-√vṛj。

3.2 資料前面已有說明。

4. बालान् bālān 形容詞 未成年人；無知的人

4.1 【詞尾變化】bālān 是 bāla 的對格複數形，所以字典查 bāla。

4.2 【摩威梵英,p728】

4.2.1 mf（*ā*）n. young , childish , infantine , not full-grown or developed（of per. sons and things）MBh.; newly risen , early（as the sun or its rays）; new or waxing（as the moon）; puerile , ignorant , simple , foolish; pure（as an animal fit for sacrifice）;

4.2.2 m.a child , boy（esp. one under 5 years）MBh. ;（in law）a minor（minors are classified as *kunāra* , or boys under 5 years of age ,*śiśu* under 8 , *pogaṇḍa* from the 5th to the end of the 9th or till the 16th year , and *kiśora* from the 10th to the 16th year）; a fool , simpleton ; any young animal; a colt , foal ; a five years old elephant; Cypriuus Denticulatus or Rohita ; N. of a Rakshas VP. ; of a prince ;

4.2.3（*ā*）f. a female child , girl , young woman（esp. one under 16 years）MBh.; a one year old cow; small cardamoms; Aloe Indica; a kind of metre; a partic. mystical prayer; N. of the mother of Va1lin and Su-griva（said to have been formed by Prajā-pati out of some dust which had fallen into his eyes）;

4.2.4 n. Andropogon Muricatus ; heat.

4.3 【梵漢辭典,p240】（形容詞）年輕的，未完全成長的；剛生起的（太陽），曙（光），新（月）；孩子氣的，稚氣的，愚蠢的；（經文）幼稚，愚，癡，愚癡，凡愚；（陽性形容詞）兒童，少年，未成年者；蠢的，傻的；（經文）童子，幼童，童幼，童稚，嬰兒，小兒，孺兒，愚，愚人，愚小，愚夫，無智人。

5. सहायान् sahāyān 名詞　伴侶

5.1 【詞尾變化】sahāyān 是 sahāya 的複數對格形，所以字典查 sahāya。

5.2 【摩威梵英,p1195】

5.2.1 m.（ifc. f. *ā* prob. fr. *saha* + *aya* cf. *sahāyana* ; but accord. to some , a Prākṛit form of *sakhāya* see *sakhi*）, one who goes along with（another）, a companion , follower , adherent , ally , assistant , helper in or to（loc. or comp. ; ifc. `having as a companion or assistant , accompanied or supported by '）MBh.;

5.2.2（ibc.）companionship , assistance（see comp.）; N. of Śiva MBh. ; the ruddy goose ; a kind of drug or perfume.

5.3 【梵漢辭典,p1055】（陽性名詞）～（位格）的同伴，同僚，輔助；（形容詞）有～做伴的；由～陪伴或支持；（經文）伴，佐，助伴，伴類，眷屬，親友，朋黨，助，同伴，同事；侶，朋，等侶，伴侶，知識。

6. प्रवर्जयित्वा parivarjayitvā 動詞　避開

6.1 【詞尾變化】parivarjayitvā 爲 pari-√vṛj 的使役動詞動名詞，所以字典查 pari-√vṛj。

6.2 【摩威梵英,p601】P. -vṛṇakti（Impv. -vṛṅdhi , -vṛṇaktu ; aor. Subj. -varjati Pot. -vṛjyāt）, to turn out of the way of（acc.）, avoid , shun , spare , pass over RV. ; to cast out , expel;（Ā.）to surround , enclose BhP.: Caus. -varjayati , -te（ind. p. -varjya）, to keep off , remove AV. ; to avoid , shun , quit , abandon , not heed , disregard MBh. &c.

6.3 【梵漢辭典,p1475】（動詞）岔開；避開；躲開；無～（具格）而爲的，節約；除外，驅逐；包圍；（使役）迴避，避開，拋棄，擱置；不顧，忽略；（經文）棄，捨離，遠離。

7. आर्येषु āryeṣu 形容詞　高貴的人

7.1 【詞尾變化】āryeṣu 是 ārya 的複數於格形，所以字典查 ārya。

7.2 【摩威梵英,p152】

7.2.1 m.（fr. *arya* ,√ *ṛ*）, a respectable or honourable or faithful man , an inhabitant of *Āryāvarta* ; one who is faithful to the religion of his country ; N. of the race which immigrated from Central Asia into *Āryāvarta*（opposed to *an-Ārya* , *dasyu* , *dāsa*）; in later times. of the first three castes（opposed to *śūdra*）RV. MBh.; a man highly esteemed , a respectable , honourable man; a master , an owner; a friend ; a Vaiśya ; Buddha ;（with Buddhists〔Pāli *ayyo* , or *ariyo*〕）a man who has thought on the four chief truths of Buddhism and lives accordingly , a Buddhist priest ; a son of Manu *Sāvarṇa* ;（mf（*ā* and *ārī*）n.）Āryan , favourable to the Āryan people RV.; behaving like an Āryan , worthy of one , honourable , respectable , noble; of a good family ; excellent ; wise ; suitable ;

7.2.2（*ā*）f. a name of Pārvatī ; a kind of metre of two lines（each line consisting of seven and a half feet ; each foot containing four instants , except the sixth of the second line , which contains only one , and is therefore a single short syllable ; hence there are thirty instants in the first line and twenty-seven in the second）;

7.3 【梵漢辭典,p160】（形容詞）重信義的，關於自己的種族；可尊敬，高貴的；（經文）貴；聖；聖者，妙聖，賢聖善。

8. संसर्ग saṁsarga 形容詞　混合

8.1 【詞尾變化】沒有詞尾變化。

8.2 【摩威梵英,p1120】

8.2.1 mfn. commingling , combining（intr.）;

8.2.2 m.（ifc. f. *ā*）mixture or union together , commixture , blending , conjunction , connection , contact , association , society , sexual union , intercourse with（gen. instr. with and without *saha* loc. , or comp.）MBh. ; confusion ,indulging in , partaking of（comy.）BhP. ; sensual attachment; a partic. conjunction of celestial bodies AV. ; a partic. combination of two humours which produces diseases（cf. *saṃ-nipāta*）; community of goods ; duration MBh. ; point of intersection; acquaintance , familiarity ; co-existence（= *samavāya*）ib. ;

8.2.3（*ī*）f. see below *-ja* mfn. produced by union or contact;

8.2.4 *-tas* ind. through union or connection , in consequence of intercourse or familiarity;

8.2.5 -*doṣa* m. the fault or evil consequences of association（with bad people）ib.;

8.2.6 -*vat* mfn. being in contact, connected with（comp.; also -*tva* n.）;

8.2.7 *vidtā* f. the art of intercourse with men, social science MBh.;

8.2.8 -*gābhāva* m.（in Nyāya）a partic. form of the category of non-existence（said to be of three kinds, prior, incidental, and final, or absence of birth, destruction of present being, and necessary cessation of existence）;

8.2.9 -*prakaraṇa* n. N. of wk.

8.3 【梵漢辭典,p1109】（陽性形容詞）與～（具格／屬格）結合，聯合或接觸；參與或沉溺餘，與～混合；（與感官世界的）接觸，感官的沉迷；（經文）雜，近，會，觸，相觸，合，合時，親，親近；所合，相雜，共合，群眾，憒鬧，和合，聚集，習俗，喧嘩，交會，擾亂，合集，雜談說，相雜住，合何處，所耽著，所執著。

9. रतान् ratān 形容詞／過去被動分詞　歡喜，滿足

9.1 【詞尾變化】ratān 是 rata 的對格複數形，所以字典查 rata。

9.2 資料前面已有說明。

10. समाहितान् samāhitān 三昧；平和

10.1【詞尾變化】samāhitān 是 samāhita 的複數對格形，所以字典查 samāhita。

10.2 【摩威梵英,p1160】

10.2.1 mfn. put or held together joined assembled, combined, united（pl. `all taken together'）MBh.; joined or furnished or provided with（instr. or comp.）ib.; put to, added（as fuel to fire）AV.; put or placed in or upon, directed, applied, fixed, imposed, deposited, entrusted, delivered over; composed, collected, concentrated（as the thoughts upon, with loc.）; one who has collected his thoughts or is fixed in abstract meditation, quite devoted to or intent upon（with loc.）, devout, steadfast, firm MBh.; put in order, set right, adjusted; suppressed, repressed, lowered（as speech）; made, rendered; completed, finished, ended MBh.; concluded, inferred, demonstrated, established; granted, admitted, recognised, approved;

corresponding or equal to , like , resembling（comp.）; harmonious , sounding faultlessly ; m. a pure or holy man ;

10.2.2 n. great attention or intentness ;（in rhet.）a partic. kind of comparison;

10.2.3 -*dhī* mfn. one who has concentrated his thoughts in devotion , Bhp. ; -*mati* mfn. one who has an attentive mind;

10.2.4 -*manas* mfn. having the mind absorbed in（anything）;

10.2.5 -*mano-buddhi* mfn. having the mind or thoughts collected or composed ;

10.2.6 -*tātman*（*saṃāh-*）mfn. one whose spirit is united with（instr.）

10.3 【梵漢辭典,p1073】（過去被動分詞）（經文）定，和，得定，定心，安布，不離，等引，寂靜，無不定，平等住，住平等，棲正定，入禪定，於定已入，定淨（菩薩），安住三昧；三昧。

【筆者試譯】：我又看見一些菩薩們，
放棄了嬉戲享樂，
避開了無知的人做伴侶
親近品行高貴的人，於內心平和感到歡喜。

【什公漢譯】：又見菩薩，離諸戲笑，及癡眷屬，親近智者。

【英 譯 本】：Further, I see Bodhisattvas, who have forsaken
all wanton pleasures, shun unwise companions
and delight in having intercourse with genteel men
（âryas）;

【信譯研究】：信譯。

【第卅五頌】

विक्षेपचित्तं च विवर्जयन्तान्
एकाग्रचित्तान् वनकन्दरेषु।
ध्यायन्त वर्षाण सहस्रकोट्यो
ध्यानेन ते प्रस्थित अग्रबोधिम्॥३५॥

【羅馬譯音】

vikṣepacittaṁ ca vivarjayantān
ekāgracittān vanakandareṣu |
dhyāyanta varṣāṇa sahasrakoṭyo
dhyānena te prasthita agrabodhim||35||

【句義解析】

vikṣepa-cittaṁ ca vivarjayantān
ekāgra-cittān vana-kandareṣu |
dhyāyanta varṣāṇa sahasra-koṭyo
dhyānena te prasthita agra-bodhim||35||

【辭彙研究】

1. विक्षेप vikṣepa 形容詞　散亂的

1.1 【詞尾變化】沒有詞尾變化。

1.2 【摩威梵英,p956】

1.2.1 m. the act of throwing asunder or away or about , scattering , dispersion; casting , throwing , discharging; moving about or to and fro , waving , shaking , tossing MBh. ; drawing（a bow-string）; letting loose , indulging （opp. to *saṃyama*）BhP. ; letting slip , neglecting（time）; inattention , distraction , confusion , perplexity; extension , projection Vedāntas.（see -*śakti*）; abusing , reviling; compassion , pity; celestial or polar latitude; a kind of weapon MBh.; a camp , cantonment（?）Buddh. ; a kind of disease; sending , dispatching ; refuting an argument;

1.2.2 -*dhruva* m.（in astron.）the greatest inclination of a planet's orbit;

1.2.3 -*lipi* m. a kind of writing;

1.2.4 -*vṛtta* n. = *kṣepa-v-* ;

1.2.5 -*śakti* f.（in phil.）the projecting power（of *Māyā* or *ā-vidyā* i.e. that power of projection which raises upon the soul enveloped by it the appearance of an external world）Vedāntas.（-*ti-mat* mfn. endowed with the above power ib.）;

1.2.6 -*pādhipati* m. the chief of a camp or cantonment（?）Buddh.

1.3 【梵漢辭典,p1430】（陽性形容詞）散落，扔，投擲，動搖，坡動，擲出，疏忽，分心，投射力〔以幻術或無明使原本不存在的現象世界變成現實的力量：吠檀多派（Vedānta 哲學）〕；（經文）揚，動，散，亂，擾動，散亂，散動，壞亂，紛亂，雜亂，憒亂，動亂，動搖，煩擾，煩惱，錯亂，狂亂，亂心，亂意，心亂。

2. चित्तं cittaṁ 形容詞　注意；思考

2.1 【詞尾變化】cittaṁ 根據連音規則是從 cittam 變化過來，cittam 則是 citta 的單數對格形，所以字典查 citta。

2.2 資料前面已有說明。

3. विवर्जयन्तान् vivarjayantān 動詞　捨離

3.1 【詞尾變化】vivarjayantān 爲 vi-√vṛj 的使役動詞，所以字典查 vi-√vṛj。

3.2 資料前面已有說明。

4. एकाग्र ekāgra 形容詞　全神貫注的

4.1 【詞尾變化】沒有詞尾變化。

4.2 【摩威梵英,p230】

4.2.1 mfn. one-pointed , having one point , fixing one's attention upon one point or object , closely attentive , intent , absorbed in MBh. BhP.; undisturbed , unperplexed ; known , celebrated ;

4.2.2（*am*）n.（in math.）the whole of the long side of a figure which is subdivided ;

4.2.3（*am*）ind. with undivided attention MBh. ;

4.2.4 -*citta* mfn. having the mind intent on one object ;

4.2.5 -*tas* ind. with undivided attention ;

4.2.6 -*tā* f. -*tva* n. intentness in the pursuit of one object , close and undisturbed attention ;

4.2.7 -*dṛṣṭi* mfn. fixing one's eyes on one spot;

4.2.8 -*dhī* mfn. fixing one's mind on one object , closely attentive;

4.2.9 -*mati* mfn. id. ;

4.2.10（*is*）m. N. of a man;

4.2.11 -*manas* mfn. fixing one's mind on one object , closely attentive MBh.

4.3 【梵漢辭典,p429】（形容詞）有一個尖端的，專注於一個對象，全神貫注的，專心的，迷醉於～；完全由～充滿的；（經文）一境；一緣；一心。

5. चित्तान् cittān 過去被動分詞／形容詞　注意；思考

5.1 【詞尾變化】cittān 是 citta 的複數對格形，所以字典查 citta。

5.2 資料前面已有說明。

6. कन्दरेषु kandareṣu 名詞　洞穴；峽谷

6.1 【詞尾變化】kandareṣu 是 kandara 的複數於格形，所以字典查 kandara。

6.2 資料前面已有說明

7. ध्यायन्त dhyāyanta 動詞　禪定

7.1 【詞尾變化】dhyāyanta 是√dhyai 變化過來，所以字典查√dhyai。

7.2 【摩威梵英,p521】cl. 1. dhyāyati（ep. also -te , or cl. 2. dhyāti ; Impv. dhyāhi ; Pot. dhyāyāt ; -yīta ; perf. dadhyau ; aor. adhyāsīt; 3. pl. dhyāsur MBh. ; fut. dhyāsyati ; dhyātā ; ind. p. dhyātvā ib. ; -dhyāya MBh. ; dhyāyam）to think of , imagine , contemplate , meditate on , call to mind , recollect（with or scil. manasā or -si , cetasā , dhiyā , hṛdaye）MBh. ; to brood mischief against（acc.）;（alone）to be thoughtful or meditative MBh.; to let the head hang down（said of an animal）Car.: Pass. dhyāyate , to be thought of ,; Caus. dhyāpayati : Desid. didhyāsate: Intens. dādhyāyate , dādhyāti , dādhyeti.

7.3 【梵漢辭典,p386】（動詞）（史詩）沉思，冥想～（對格），思考，深思；（經文）修習定，修靜慮，思量，審慮，攝念，禪思。

8. वर्षाण varṣāṇa 形容詞　年；歲

8.1 【詞尾變化】varṣāṇa 在詩歌裏面可做 varṣa-aṇa 來解釋，而 aṇa 在梵文詩歌裏面作詩歌的獨特字根（【摩威梵英,p11】），所以字典查 varṣa。

8.2 資料前面已有說明。

9. कोट्यो koṭyo 形容詞　萬億

9.1 【詞尾變化】koṭyo 根據連音規則是從 koṭyāḥ 變化過來，koṭyāḥ 是 koṭi 的單數屬格形，所以字典查 koṭi。

9.2 【摩威梵英,p312】f. the curved end of a bow or of claws , end or top of anything , edge or point（of a sword）, horns or cusps（of the moon）MBh.; the highest point , eminence , excellence; `a point or side in an argument or disputation' ,（if there are two）`alternative' see -dvaya below ; the highest number in the older system of numbers（viz. a Krore or ten millions）MBh. ; the complement of an arc to 90 degrees ; the perpendicular side of a right-angled triangle; Medicago esculenta.

9.3 【梵漢辭典,p604】（陰性形容詞）彎曲的前端（弓，禽獸的爪等）；尖端，極端，高度，最高度，優秀；（數詞）千萬；（經文）際，邊際；邊，邊際；上，頂；〔數詞〕千萬，億，萬億，百仟，十萬，京。

10. ध्यानेन dhyānena 名詞　禪定

10.1 【詞尾變化】dhyānena 是 dhyāna 的單數工具格形，所以字典查 dhyāna。

10.2 【摩威梵英,p521】

10.2.1 n. meditation , thought , reflection ,（esp.）profound and abstract religious meditation ,（*-nam āpad* , *ā-sthā* or *-naṃ-gam* , to indulge in religious meditation）MBh.（with Buddhists divided into 4 stages; but also into 3）; mental representation of the personal attributes of a deity ; insensibility , dulness;

10.2.2（*-na*） m. N. of a partic. personification; of the 11th day of the light half in Brahma's month.

10.3 【梵漢辭典,p386】（中性名詞）靜慮，宗教的冥想；（經文）定，思惟，靜慮，修定；定。

【筆者試譯】：捨棄散亂的心，
住在山洞樹林之間，全神貫注地思惟，
投入了百千萬億年修行禪定，
向著無上菩提出發而修行禪定。

【什公漢譯】：一心除亂，攝念山林，億千萬歲，以求佛道。

【英 譯 本】：Who, with avoidance of any distraction of
thoughts and with attentive mind, during thousands
of kotis of years have meditated in the caves of the
wilderness; these strive for enlightenment by dint of meditation.

【信譯研究】：信譯。

【第卅六頌】

ददन्ति दानानि तथैव केचित्

सशिष्यसंघेषु जिनेषु संमुखम्।

खाद्यं च भोज्यं च तथान्नपान्नं

गिलानभैषज्य बहू अनल्पकम्॥ ३ ६॥

【羅馬譯音】

dadanti dānāni tathaiva kecit

saśiṣyasaṁgheṣu jineṣu saṁmukham|

khādyaṁ ca bhojyaṁ ca tathānnapānnaṁ

gilānabhaiṣajya bahū analpakam||36||

【句義解析】

dadanti dānāni tathaiva ke-cit

saśiṣya-saṁgheṣu jineṣu saṁmukham|

khādyaṁ ca bhojyaṁ ca tathā nna-pānnaṁ

gilāna-bhaiṣajya bahū analpakam||36||

【辭彙研究】

1. सशिष्य saśiṣya 形容詞　與弟子一起的

1.1 【詞尾變化】沒有詞尾變化。

1.2 【梵英辭典,p1191】mfn. attended by pupils.

1.3 【梵漢辭典,p1148】（形容詞）與弟子一起的。

2. संघेषु saṁgheṣu 形容詞　群體；僧伽

2.1 【詞尾變化】saṁgheṣu 是 saṁgha 的於格複數形，所以字典查 saṁgha。

2.2 資料前面已有說明。

3. जिनेषु jineṣu 名詞　勝者

3.1 【詞尾變化】jineṣu 是 jina 的於格複數形，所以字典查 jina。

3.2 【梵英辭典,p421】

3.2.1 mfn.（*ji*）victorious;

3.2.2 m. `Victor' , a Buddha Buddh.; an Arhat（or chief saint of the Jainas ; 24 Jinas are supposed to flourish in each of the 3 Avasarpiṇīs , being born in Āryāvarta）Jain.;（hence）the number `24'; metrically for *jaina* ; Vishṇu; N. of Hemac.（?）; of a Bodhi-sattva ; of a son of Yadu.

3.3 【梵漢辭典,p532】（陽性名詞）（勝者）佛陀，耆那教（Jina）的聖者；（經文）勝，勝者，最聖，最勝者；大覺，佛，佛陀，如來；大聖。

4. संमुखम् saṁmukham 形容詞　面對；面向

4.1 【詞尾變化】saṁmukham 是 saṁmukha 的對格單數形，所以字典查 saṁmukha。

4.2 【梵英辭典,p1111,saṁ】（in comp.）= sam q.v.

4.3 【梵英辭典,p1180,sammukha】

4.3.1 mf（*ī* rarely *ā*）n. facing , fronting , confronting , being face to face or in front of or opposite to（gen. or ifc. or ibc.）, present , before the eyes; being about to begin or at the beginning of（comp.）; directed or turned towards; inclined or favourable to（gen. or comp.）, propitious; intent upon（loc. or comp.）; adapted to circumstances , fit , suitable; with the mouth or face;

4.3.2（*am*）ind. towards , near to（*atmanaḥ* , `one's self'）; opposite , in front or in presence of（gen.）MBh. ;

4.3.3（*e*）ind. opposite , before , face to face , in front or in presence or in the beginning of(gen. or comp. ; with *bhū* , `to oppose , resist' ; with *sthā* , to look any one in the face）.

4.4 【梵漢辭典,p1101】（形容詞）面對的；朝；朝正面。（經文）前，現前。

5. खाद्यं khādyaṁ 形容詞／名詞　可吃的東西

5.1 【詞尾變化】khādyaṁ 根據連音規則是由 khādyam 變化過來，而 khādyam 是 khādya 的對格單數形，所以字典查 khādya。

5.2 【梵英辭典,p339】

5.2.1 n. `eatable , edible' , food , victuals MBh.;

5.2.2 m.（=*khadira*）Acacia Catechu Gal.

5.3 【梵漢辭典,p590】（未來被動分詞）供食用的（中性名詞）食物；糧食，（經文）膳，餚膳。

6. भोज्यं bhojyaṁ 形容詞／未來被動分詞　可食的

6.1 【詞尾變化】bhojyaṁ 根據連音規則是由 bhojyam 變化過來，而 bhojyam 是 bhojya 的對格單數形，所以字典查 bhojya。

6.2 【梵英辭典,p768】

6.2.1 mfn. to be enjoyed or eaten , eatable , what is enjoyed or eaten ,（esp.）what may be eaten without mastication MBh.; to be enjoyed or used MBh.; to be enjoyed sexually; to be enjoyed or felt MBh.; to be suffered or experienced; to be fed , one to whom food must be given MBh. ;（fr. Caus.）to be made to eat , to be fed MBh.;

6.2.2 m. pl. N. of a people.（prob. w.r. for *bhoja*）;

6.2.3（*ā*）f. a procuress; a princess of the Bhojas MBh. BhP.;

6.2.4 n. anything to be enjoyed or eaten , nourishment , food MBh.; the act of eating , a meal MBh.; a festive dinner ; a dainty; a feast a store of provisions , eatables ib. , enjoyment , advantage , profit.

6.3 【梵漢辭典,p272】（未來被動分詞）可食的，能吃的，可享受或使用的；可享受性慾的；可被體驗或感受的；可養育的；（經文）應食，（炊熟）方得成食，應食熟食，炊熟方得成食。（中性形容詞）可食之物，糧食，食物，吃，享受，利益；（經文）食，飲食。

7. तथान्न tathā nna 形容詞　這樣地吃

7.1 【詞尾變化】tathā nna 根據連音規則即 tathā anna 的結合，tathā 資料前面已有說明，字典查 anna。

7.2 【梵英辭典,p45】mfn.（$\sqrt{}$ad）, eaten ;（annam）n. food or victuals , especially boiled rice ; bread corn ; food in a mystical sense（or the lowest form in which the supreme soul is manifested , the coarsest envelope of the Supreme Spirit）; water ; earth.

7.3 【梵漢辭典,p102】（過去被動分詞）所吃的；（經文）所食；（中性形容詞）食物，米，稻穀；（經文）食，飲食，喫物，喫食。

8. पान्नं pānnaṁ 動詞　喝；飲

8.1 【詞尾變化】pānnaṁ 根據連音規則是由 pānnam 變化過來，而 pānnam 是 pānna 的對格單數形，但根據連音規則，應爲 pāna 的變化而來。而 pāna 是$\sqrt{}$pā 的現在中間分詞形，所以字典查$\sqrt{}$pā。

8.2 【梵英辭典,p612】cl. 1. to drink , quaff, suck , sip , swallow（with acc. , rarely gen.）RV.;（met.）to imbibe , draw in , appropriate , enjoy , feast upon（with the eyes , ears &c.）Mn. MBh.; to drink up , exhaust , absorb BhP.; to drink intoxicating liquors Buddh.: Pass. pīyate AV.: Caus. pāyayati , -te , to cause to drink , give to drink , water（horses or cattle）RV., to wish to drink , thirst, to wish or intend to give to drink, to drink greedily or repeatedly.

8.3 【梵漢辭典,p821】（動詞）喝，暢飲，吸收；吸食，啜飲，吸入，享受，吸盡，用盡，帶走，攝取；（經文）飲，受潤。

9. गिलान gilāna 形容詞　疾病的

9.1 【詞尾變化】沒有詞尾變化。

9.2 【梵英辭典】無此資料，疑爲混合梵文。

9.3 【艾格混梵,p212】（=Pāli, both ; Skt. glāna, BHS glāna and glānaka）, weak, exhausted, sick.

9.4 【梵漢辭典,p460】（陽性名詞）（俗語）〔<glāna〕（經文）疾病者；病，重疾。

10. भैषज्य bhaiṣajya 名詞　醫療藥品

10.1 【詞尾變化】沒有詞尾變化。

10.2 【梵英辭典,p762】

10.2.1 m. patr. fr. *bhiṣaj* , or *bhiṣaja* g. *gargādi*;

10.2.2 n. curativeness , healing efficacy ; a partic. ceremony performed as a remedy for sickness; any remedy , drug or medicine（`against' gen.）; the administering of medicines.

10.3 【梵漢辭典,p252】（中性名詞）有療效的；藥物，給～（屬格）的藥物；（經文）藥，良藥，妙藥，湯藥，醫藥，藥餌，藥草，醫王，含消藥。

11. बहू bahū 形容詞　多量的；眾多的

11.1 【詞尾變化】bahū 是 bahu 的雙數主格形。所以字典查 bahu。

11.2 資料前面已有說明。這裡採用雙性，大致上是指男女性。

12. अनल्पकम् analpakam 形容詞　眾人

12.1 【詞尾變化】analpakam 是 analpaka 的對格單數形，所以字典查 analpaka。

12.2 資料前面已有說明。

【筆者試譯】：有些（人）則奉獻出佈施品，
給勝（聖）者，僧伽與弟子們一起，
提供了這些可吃的，可以喝的，與需要炊熟的食物，
大量的疾病的醫療用品給眾人。

【什公漢譯】：或見菩薩，餚饍飲食，百種湯藥，施佛及僧。

【英 譯 本】：Some, again, offer in presence of the Ginas
and the assemblage of disciples gifts（consisting）in
food hard and soft, meat and drink, medicaments
for the sick, in plenty and abundance.

【信譯研究】：信譯。

【第卅七頌】

वस्त्राण कोटीशत ते ददन्ति
सहस्रकोटीशतमूल्य केचित्।
अनर्घमूल्यांश्च ददन्ति वस्त्रान्
सशिष्यसंघान जिनान संमुखम्॥३७॥

【羅馬譯音】

vastrāṇa koṭīśata te dadanti
sahasrakoṭīśatamūlya kecit|
anarghamūlyāṁśca dadanti vastrān
saśiṣyasaṁghāna jināna saṁmukham||37||

【句義解析】

vastrāṇa koṭī-śata te dadanti
sahasra-koṭī-śata-mūlya ke-cit|
anargha-mūlyāṁś ca dadanti vastrān
saśiṣya-saṁghāna jināna saṁmukham||37||

【辭彙研究】

1. वस्त्राण vastrāṇa 名詞 衣服

1.1 【詞尾變化】vastrāṇa 是 vastra 的複數主格形，所以字典查 vastra。

1.2 資料前面已有說明。

2. मूल्य mūlya 名詞 價值

2.1 【詞尾變化】沒有詞尾變化。

2.2 【摩威梵英,p827】

2.2.1 mfn. being at the root; to be torn up by the root ; = mūlenānāmyam and = mūlena samaḥ; to be bought for a sum of money , purchasable ;

2.2.2 n.（ifc. f. *ā*）original value , value , price , worth , a sum of money given as payment MBh. ; wages , salary , payment for service rendered ; earnings , gain; capital , stock ; an article purchased.

2.3 【梵漢辭典,p749】（形容詞）生存或附著於根的；（中性名詞）價格，市價，工資，報酬，所得；本金；（經文）價，價值，價直，直，值，利，財利。

3. मूल्यांश्च mūlyāṁś ca 形容詞 所帶來的金額總值

3.1 【詞尾變化】mūlyāṁś ca 根據連音規則是 mūlyān ca 變化過來，而 mūlyān 則是對格複數形。

3.2 資料前面已有說明。

4. अनर्घ anargha 形容詞 極貴重的

4.1 【詞尾變化】沒有詞尾變化。

4.2 【摩威梵英,p26】

4.2.1 mfn. priceless , invaluable ;

4.2.2 m. wrong value.

4.3 【梵漢辭典,p89】（陽性名詞）不正當的價格，虛價；（形容詞）不被定價的，極貴重的；（經文）無價；賤。

【筆者試譯】：你（又）布施了無量的衣服，
這些也是價值無量的好衣服，
布施了如此價值極其貴重的衣服，

給勝（聖）者，僧伽與弟子們一起。

【什公漢譯】：名衣上服，價直千萬，或無價衣，施佛及僧。

【英 譯 本】：Others offer in presence of the Ginas and the assemblage of disciples hundreds of kotis of clothes, worth thousands of kotis, and garments of priceless value.

【信譯研究】：信譯。

【第卅八頌】

विहार कोटीशत कारयित्वा
रत्नामयांश्चो तथ चन्दनामयान्।
प्रभूतशय्यासनमण्डितांश्च
निर्यातयन्तो सुगतान संमुखम्॥३८॥

【羅馬譯音】

vihāra koṭīśata kārayitvā
ratnāmayāṁśco tatha candanāmayān|
prabhūtaśayyāsanamaṇḍitāṁśca
niryātayanto sugatāna saṁmukham||38||

【句義解析】

vihāra koṭī-śata kārayitvā
ratnā-mayāṁś co tatha candanā-mayān|
Prabhūta-śayyāsana-maṇḍitāṁś ca
niryātayanto sugatāna saṁmukham||38||

【辭彙研究】

1. विहार vihāra 名詞 寺院

1.1 【詞尾變化】沒有詞尾變化。

1.2 【摩威梵英,p1003】

1.2.1 m.（once in BhP. n.）distribution , transposition（of words）; arrangement or disposition（of the 3 sacred fires ; also applied to the fires themselves or the space between them）; too great expansion of the organs of speech（consisting in too great lengthening or drawling in pronunciation , opp. to *saṁ-hāra* q.v.）; walking for pleasure or amusement , wandering , roaming MBh.; sport , play , pastime , diversion , enjoyment , pleasure MBh.; a place of recreation , pleasure-ground MBh;（with Buddhists or Jainas）a monastery or temple（originally a hall where the monks met or walked about ; afterwards these halls were used as temples）; consecration for a sacrifice;

1.2.2 N. of the country of Magadha（called Bihar or Behār from the number of Buddhist monasteries）; the shoulder ; a partic. bird（= *bindurekaka*）; = *vaijayanta* ;

1.2.3 -*kārikā* f. pl. N. of wk. ;

1.2.4 -*krīḍā-mṛga* m. a toy-antelope to play with BhP. ;

1.2.5 -*gṛha* n. a pleasure-house , play-house , theatre MW. ;

1.2.6 -*dāsī* f. a female attendant of a convent or temple. ;

1.2.7 -*deśa* m. a place of recreation , pleasure-ground MBh.;

1.2.8 -*bhadra* m. N. of a man ;

1.2.9 -*bhūmi* f. = -*deśa* ; a grazing-ground , pasturage Kir. ;

1.2.10 -*yātrā* f. a pleasure-walk MBh. ;

1.2.11 -*vat* mfn. possessing a place of recreation MBh. ;（ifc.）delighting in;

1.2.12 -*vana* n. a pleasure-grove ;

1.2.13 -*vāpī* f. `pleasure-pond'N. of wk. ;

1.2.14 -*vāri* n. water for sporting or playing about in Ragh. ;

1.2.15 -*śayana* n. a plñpleasure-couch ;

1.2.16 -*śaila* m. a pleasure-mountain ;

1.2.17 -*sthaī* f.（Vas.）, -*sthāna* n.（BhP.）;

1.2.18 -*rājira* n.（= -*radeśa*）; -*rāvasatha* m.（= -*ra-gṛha*）MBh.

1.3 【梵漢辭典,p1423】（陽性／中性名詞）（言詞的）安排，移轉；三聖火（的配置）或其彼此的空間；步履搖晃，散步；因～而愉快的或享樂的；休養的場所；（佛陀止住的園林），佛教徒的（或者那教的）僧院或寺院；歡喜的；（經文）行，行住，遊，遊步，住，安住，所住，住處，境，靜住，修業，所在，靜室，舍，房舍，寺，寺門，寺舍，寺館，塔寺，伽藍，僧房。

2. कारयित्वा kārayitvā 動詞　作爲；實行

2.1 【詞尾變化】kārayitvā 是√kṛ 的使役動詞絕對格（不變格）變化形，所以動詞查√kṛ

2.2 資料前面已有說明。

3. मयांश्चो mayāṁś co 形容詞　爲～所形成

3.1 【詞尾變化】mayāṁś co 根據連音規則是從 mayān co，當中 mayān 是 maya 的複數對格形，所以字典查 maya 與 co。

3.2 maya 的部分前面資料已有說明。

3.3 【摩威梵英,co】無此字，疑爲非標準梵文。

3.4 【艾格混梵,p234,co】=ca, and: SP 13.15.

3.5 【梵漢辭典,p335,co】（ca-u）（經文）及。

4. तथ tatha 副詞　如此

4.1 【詞尾變化】即 tathā，〔註 46〕字典查 tathā。

4.2 資料前面已有說明。

5. चन्दना candanā 名詞　旃檀香

5.1 【詞尾變化】candanā 後面接 mayān，根據學者說法，這裡 candanā 是 candana 的異寫，所以字典查 candana。〔註 47〕

5.2 資料前面已有說明。

6. प्रभूत prabhūta 動詞　從～而生

6.1 【詞尾變化】prabhūta 是 pra-√bhū 的過去被動分詞，所以字典查 pra-√bhū。

6.2 【摩威梵英,p684】

6.2.1 mfn. come forth , risen , appeared ;（ifc.）become , transformed into;

〔註 46〕請見江島惠教等編《梵藏漢法華經原典總索引》，東京：靈友會出版，1988 年出版。頁 404。

〔註 47〕請見江島惠教等編《梵藏漢法華經原典總索引》，東京：靈友會出版，1988 年出版。頁 362。

abundant , much , numerous , considerable , high , great; abounding in （comp.）; able to（inf.）; governed , presided over ; mature , perfect ;

6.2.2 m. a class of deities in the 6th Manvantara Hariv.（v.l. *pra-sūta*）;

6.2.3 n.（in phil.）a great or primary element（= *mahā-bhūta*）;

6.2.4 *–jihvatā* f. having a long tongue（one of the 32 signs of perfection of a Buddha）;

6.2.5 *–tā* f. quantity , plenty , multitude , large number;

6.2.6 *-tva* n. id.; sufficiency.（v.l. for *prabhū-tva*）;

6.2.7 *-dhana-dhānya-vat* mfn. rich in money and corn;

6.2.8 *-nāgāśva-ratha* mfn. having many elephants and horses and chariots MBh. ;

6.2.9 *-bhrānta* n. much roaming ;

6.2.10 *-yavasendhana* mfn. abounding in fresh grass and fuel ib. ;

6.2.11 *-ratna* m. N. of a Buddha SaddhP. ;

6.2.12 *-rūpa* n. great beauty;

6.2.13 *-vayas* mfn. advanced in years , old ;

6.2.14 *-varśa* n. pl. many years ;

6.2.15 *-śas* ind. many times , often;

6.2.16 *-totka* m. ardently desirous of or longing for.

6.3 【梵漢辭典,p278】從～（從格）而生的，變形成；豐富的，多的，廣的，多數的，顯著的，大的；得爲。

7. शय्यासन śayyāsana 名詞　臥鋪與座席

7.1 【詞尾變化】沒有詞尾變化。

7.2 【摩威梵英,p1056】(-sayyās-) and a seat（-stha mfn. occupying a couch or seat ib.）; lying and sitting（-bhoga m. enjoyment of lying and sitting; cf. śayanāsana-sevana）.

7.3 【梵漢辭典,p1165】(中性名詞)(雙數)臥鋪與座席；(經文)臥具；床臥。

8. मण्डितांश्च maṇḍitāṁś ca 形容詞　莊嚴，裝飾

8.1 【詞尾變化】根據連音規則 maṇḍitāṁś ca 是從 maṇḍitān ca 變化過來的，而 maṇḍitān 是 maṇḍita 的複數對格形，所以字典查 maṇḍita。

8.2 【摩威梵英,p775】

8.2.1 mfn. adorned , decorated MBh;

8.2.2 m.（with Jainas）N. of one of the 11 Gaṇsdhipas.

8.3 【梵漢辭典,p703】（形容詞）是 Maṇḍ 的（過去被動分詞）（經文）嚴，莊嚴，裝飾。

9. निर्यातयन्तो niryātayanto 動詞　贈送；布施

9.1 【詞尾變化】niryātayanto 據學者看法是 niryātayante 的異寫。〔註 48〕niryātayante 則是 nir-√yat 的使役動詞現在是第三人稱複數形，所以字典查 nir-√yat。

9.2 【摩威梵英,p556】Caus. *-yātayati* , to snatch away , carry off , take or fetch out of（abl.）, get , procure MBh ; to give back , restore , make restitution MBh; to give as a present;（*vairam*）to return or show enmity , take revenge MBh; to forgive , pardon , set free.

9.3 【梵漢辭典,p1507】（動詞）拿掉，去除；自～（從格）帶來；交給，歸還，贈送，（對敵人）回擊（=復仇），費（時）；（經文）施，布施，奉施，奉上，奉進，奉事，奉屬，獻；貢上，與，送與，屬，捨，以用布施，咸持供養。

10. सुगतान sugatāna 名詞　佛教之師們

10.1 【詞尾變化】sugatāna 是 sugata 對格複數形異寫，字典查 sugata。

10.2 資料前面已有說明。

【筆者試譯】：一所寺院用無量裝飾物，
有珍寶所做成的，也有如此旃檀香木所做成的，
也有許多莊嚴的臥鋪與座席，
這些也都要布施給佛教的法師們。

【什公漢譯】：千萬億種，栴檀寶舍，眾妙臥具，施佛及僧。

【英 譯 本】：They bestow in presence of the Sugatas hundreds
of kotis of monasteries which they have caused
to be built of precious substances and sandal-wood,
and which are furnished with numerous lodgings（or couches）.

〔註 48〕請見江島惠教等編《梵藏漢法華經原典總索引》，東京：靈友會出版，1988 年出版。頁 564。

【信譯研究】：信譯。

【第卌九頌】

आराम चौक्षांश्च मनोरमांश्च

फलैरुपेतान् कुसुमैश्च चित्रैः।

दिवाविहारार्थ ददन्ति केचित्

सश्रावकाणां पुरुषर्षभाणाम्॥३९॥

【羅馬譯音】

ārāma caukṣāṁśca manoramāṁśca

phalairupetān kusumaiśca citraiḥ|

divāvihārārtha dadanti kecit

saśrāvakāṇāṁ puruṣarṣabhāṇām||39||

【句義解析】

ārāma caukṣāṁś ca mano-ramāṁś ca

phalair upetān kusumaiś ca citraiḥ|

divā-vihārārtha dadanti ke-cit

saśrāvakāṇāṁ puruṣa-rṣabhāṇām||39||

【辭彙研究】

1. आराम ārāma 名詞　歡喜，庭園

1.1. 【詞尾變化】無詞尾變化。

1.2. 【摩威梵英,p150】

1.2.1. m. delight , pleasure; place of pleasure , a garden , grove MBh.;

1.2.2. N. of a particular Daṇḍaka metre.

1.3. 【梵漢辭典,p149】（陽性名詞）歡喜，快樂，庭園，果園；（經文）喜，玩，好樂，樂戲；苑，園，林，園林，園苑，妙園林，共喜園；（形容詞）（經文）著，貪，愛，可愛，愛樂，深生愛樂。

2. चौकषांश्च caukṣāṁś ca 形容詞　純潔，清淨（的人）

2.1. 【詞尾變化】caukṣāṁś ca 根據連音規則，是從 caukṣān ca 變化過來的，

而 caukṣān 是 caukṣa 的對格複數形，所以字典查 caukṣa。

2.2. 【摩威梵英,p403】

2.2.1. mfn.（fr. cukṣā g. chattrādi）= cokṣa , pure , clean（persons）MBh.;

2.2.2. m. pl. N. of a family Pravar. i ,（i and）7.

2.3. 【梵漢辭典,p320】（形容詞）〔=cokṣa〕清淨的，聖潔的；（經文）潔，鮮，淨，新淨，清淨，淨好，好，勝。

3. मनोरमांश्च mano-ramāṁś ca 形容詞　令人欣喜，令人愉快的

3.1. 【詞尾變化】mano-ramāṁś ca 根據連音規則，是從 mano-ramān ca 變化過來，而 mano-ramān 則是 mano-rama 的複數對格形，所以字典查 mano-rama。

3.2. 資料前面已有說明。

4. फलैर् phalair 名詞（樹上的）很多的果實

4.1. 【詞尾變化】phalair 根據連音規則，其變化是因爲 phalaiḥ 與後面的 upetān 相連而變化成 phalair，而 phalaiḥ 則是 phala 的複數工具格形，因此字典查 phala。

4.2. 資料前面已有說明。

5. उपेतान् upetān 形容詞　具足的；滿足的

5.1. 【詞尾變化】upetān 是從 upeta 的複數對格形，因此字典查 upeta。

5.2. 資料前面已有說明。

6. कुसुमैश्च kusumaiś ca 名詞　花

6.1. 【詞尾變化】kusumaiś ca 根據連音規則，是從 kusumaiḥ ca 變化過來，而 kusumaiḥ 則是 kusuma 的工具格複數形，所以字典查 kusuma。

6.2. 【摩威梵英,p298】

6.2.1. n.（fr. √kus; g. ardharcādi）, a flower , blossom;

6.2.2. N. of the shorter sections of Deveśvara's Kavi-kalpa-latā（the longer chapters being called stabaka）; fruit. ; the menstrual discharge; a particular disease of the eyes;

6.2.3. m. a form of fire; N. of an attendant of the sixth Arhat of the present Avasarpiṇī ; N. of a prince Buddh.

6.3. 【梵漢辭典,p641】（中性名詞）花；（經文）華，花，眾妙。

7. चित्रैः citraiḥ 形容詞 華麗的裝飾

7.1. 【詞尾變化】citraiḥ 爲 citra 的工具格複數型，所以字典查 citra。

7.2. 【摩威梵英,p396】

7.2.1. mf（ā）n. conspicuous , excellent , distinguished RV. ; bright , clear , bright-coloured RV. ; clear（a sound）RV. ; variegated , spotted , speckled（with instr. or in comp.）; agitated（as the sea , opposed to sama）; various , different , manifold MBh.;（execution）having different varieties（of tortures）; strange , wonderful ; containing the word *citrā* ;

7.2.2.（ām）ind. so as to be bright; in different ways;（to execute）with different tortures;

7.2.3.（ās）m. variety of colour; *Plumbago śeylanica* ; *Ricinus* communis; *Jonesia Aśoka*; a form of Yama Tithya1d. ; N. of a king RV.（ciītra）; of a *Jābāla-gṛihapati*; of a king ;

7.2.4.（ā）f. Spica virginis , the 12th（in later reckoning the 14th）lunar mansion AV; a kind of snake; N. of a plant; a metre of 4 X 16 syllabic instants ; another of 4 x 15 syllables ; another of 4 x 16 syllables ; a kind of stringed instrument ; a kind of *Mūrchanā*（in music）; illusion , unreality; `born under the asterism *Citrā* N. of *Arjuna's* wife（sister of *Kṛishṇa* =*subhadrā*）; of a daughter of Gada（or *Kṛishṇa*）; of an *Apsaras* ; of a river *Divyāv*.; of a rock BhP.; f. pl. the asterism Citrā;

7.2.5.（ām）n. anything bright or coloured which strikes the eyes RV; a brilliant ornament , ornament RV; a bright or extraordinary appearance , wonder;（with *yadi* or *yad* or fut.）strange , curious; strange!; the ether , sky ; a spot MBh.; a sectarial mark on the forehead; = kuṣṭha ; a picture , sketch , delineation MBh.（*sa*- mfn. = -*ga*）; variety of colour ; a forest（*vana* for *dhana*）of variegated appearance; various modes of writing or arranging verses in the shape of mathematical or other fanciful figures（syllables which occur repeatedly being left out or words being represented in a shortened form）; punning in the form of question and answer , facetious conversation , riddle.

7.3. 【梵漢辭典,p331】

7.3.1.（形容詞）明顯的，易見的，顯著的，發亮的；清楚的，可聽到的（聲音）；雜色的，有斑點的，斑駁的；各種的，多樣的，各種拷問（刑罰）；奇異的，令人驚訝的；四處奔跳的；（經文）種種；種種不同，雜類；雜飾，雜色，妙色；有殊，稀奇；癩病；

7.3.2.（中性）鮮豔的色彩，華麗的裝飾；寶石；繪畫；令人驚奇的現象，驚異；（經文）畫，錦；布彩；印文；嚴飾。

7.3.3.（中性）（形容詞）（經文）色；諸，種種。

8. दिवा divā 副詞　白天；（每天）

8.1. 【詞尾變化】沒有詞尾變化。

8.2. 【摩威梵英,p478】ind. by day（often opposed to *náktam*）RV. ; used also as subst;（with *rātris*）MBh.; esp. in beginning of comp.

8.3. 【梵漢辭典,p394】（副詞）在日中；〔有時爲一句中之主詞〕日；（經文）晝，日，晝時。

9. विहारार्थ vihārārtha 名詞　僧院的利用

9.1. 【詞尾變化】vihārārtha 根據連音規則，是由 vihāra-artha 兩個字所形成，所以字典要查 vihāra-artha。

9.2. 資料前面已有說明。

10. सश्रवकाणां saśrāvakāṇāṁ 複合形容詞　這些聽法的僧人們

10.1. 【詞尾變化】saśrāvakāṇāṁ 根據連音規則，是從 saśrāvakāṇām 變化過來，而 saśrāvakāṇām 是由 sa-śrāvakāṇām 所組合而成，其中 śrāvakāṇām 是 śrāvaka 的複數所有格形，所以字典查 sa-śrāvaka 兩個字。

11. पुरुष puruṣa 名詞　人；男人

11.1. 【詞尾變化】沒有詞尾變化。

11.2. 資料前面已有說明。

12. र्षभाणाम् rṣabhāṇām 形容詞　最傑出的

12.1. 【詞尾變化】rṣabhāṇām 根據連音規則是由 puruṣa 與 ṛṣabhāṇām 結合變化而成，而 ṛṣabhāṇām 是 ṛṣabha 的複數所有格形，所以字典查 ṛṣabha。

12.2. 【摩威梵英,p226】

12.2.1. m., a bull（as impregnating the flock ; cf. *vṛṣabha* and *ukṣan*）RV. AV.;

any male animal in general; the best or most excellent of any kind or race（cf. *puruṣarṣabha*）MBh.; the second of the seven notes of the Hindū gamut（abbreviated into *Ṛi*）; a kind of medicinal plant; a particular antidote; a particular; the fifteenth; N. of several men ; of an ape ; of a *Nāga* ; of a mountain ; of a *Tīrtha* ;

12.2.2.（*ās*）m. pl. the inhabitants of *Krauṇca-dvīpa*; N. of a people ;

12.3.（*ī*）f. a woman with masculine peculiarities（as with a beard）; a widow ; Carpopogon Pruriens Car. ; another plant ;

12.4. 【梵漢辭典,p1032】（陽性名詞）公牛，公的，在～之中是最高級的，最高尚的或最傑出的；（經文）牛，大牛王，超群，勝群，神仙，神仙曲，第二音。

【筆者試譯】：令人欣喜而清淨的庭園，
有各種果實與花朵的樹木，
如此用做白晝修行用的僧院，
有些人也供養這些前來聽佛法的與最傑出的佛陀使用。

【什公漢譯】：清淨園林，華菓茂盛，流泉浴池，施佛及僧。

【英 譯 本】：Some present the leaders of men and their
disciples with neat and lovely gardens abounding
with fruits and beautiful flowers, to serve as places
of daily recreation.

【信譯研究】：信譯。不過鳩摩羅什增加了一句「流泉浴池」，這是本偈原文所沒有的。或許爲了補足漢失的韻腳作爲對等緣故。

【第四十頌】

ददन्ति दानानिममेवरूपा
विविधानि चित्राणि च हर्षजाताः।
दत्वा च बोधाय जनेन्ति वीर्यं
दानेन ते प्रस्थित अग्रबोधिम्॥४०॥

【羅馬譯音】

dadanti dānānimamevarūpā
vividhāni citrāṇi ca harṣajātāḥ|
datvā ca bodhāya janenti vīryaṁ
dānena te prasthita agrabodhim||40||

【句義解析】

dadanti dānān imam eva-rūpā
vividhāni citrāṇi ca harṣa-jātāḥ|
datvā ca bodhāya janenti vīryaṁ
dānena te prasthita agra-bodhim||40||

【辭彙研究】

1. दानान् dānān 名詞（陽性）財產

1.1 【詞尾變化】dānān 是 dāna 的複數對格形，所以字典查 dāna。

1.2 【摩威梵英,p474】

1.2.1 n. the act of giving RV. MBh.; giving in marriage; giving up; communicating , imparting , teaching; paying back , restoring; adding , addition; donation , gift RV.; oblation; bribery.

1.2.2 n. cutting off. splitting , dividing; pasture , meadow RV. ; rut-fluid（which flows from an elephant's temples）MBh.;

1.2.3 m. distribution of food or of a sacrificial meal ; imparting , communicating , liberality ; part , share , possession ; distributor , dispenser RV.n. purification L.

1.3 【梵漢辭典,p346】

1.3.1（陰性名詞）給予，嫁（女兒），贈與，奉獻（供品），將～教導給；拋棄；繳納（負債）；佈施品；喜捨，贈賄；附加；貢獻品；供品；（經文）施，佈施，施他，惠施，行施，能施，與，捨離，能捨；供養。

1.3.2（陽性名詞）（尤指食物的）分配，進餐，祭祀的饗宴；寬宏仁慈；應得之份；財產。（中性名詞）分泌物（大象發春期中從太陽穴滲出的一種芳香）。

1.3.3（中性名詞）（經文）施；與；佈施。

2. इमम् imam 代名詞　這；其

2.1 【詞尾變化】imam 是 ayam 的單數對格形，所以字典查 ayam。

2.2 【摩威梵英,p84】this one. see idám.

2.3 【摩威梵英,p165,idam】

2.3.1 ayám , iyám, idám; a kind of neut. of the pronom; the regular forms are partly derived from the pronom.; the Veda exhibits various irregular formations e.g. fr. pronom.; the RV. has in a few instances the irregular accentuation *ásmai* ;this , this here , referring to something near the speaker ; known , present ;*idam* often refers to something immediately following , whereas *etad* points to what precedes. *idam* occurs connected with *yad, tad, etad, kim*, and a personal pronoun , partly to point out anything more distinctly and emphatically , partly pleonastically.

2.3.2 ind.〔Ved. and in a few instances in classical Sanskṛit〕here , to this place ; now , even , just ; there ; with these words RV. AV.; in this manner.

2.4 【梵漢辭典,p228】（代名詞）（主格）（單數）（陽性）這，此（常做「此處」）；（經文）是，此，其。

3. रूपा rūpā 名詞　優美的東西

3.1 【詞尾變化】rūpā 爲 rūpa 的陰性形，字典查 rūpa。

3.2 【摩威梵英,p886】n.（perhaps connected with *varpa* , *varpas* ; ifc. f. *ā* , rarely *ī*），其餘資料前面已有說明。

3.3 【梵漢辭典】前面已有資料說明。

4. विविधानि vividhāni 形容詞　多種類的，形形色色的

4.1 【詞尾變化】vividhāni 是 vividha 的主格複數形，所以字典查 vividha。

4.2 資料前面已有說明。

5. चित्राणि citrāṇi 形容詞（中性）華麗的裝飾

5.1 【詞尾變化】citrāṇi 爲 citra 的對格複數型，所以字典查 citra。

5.2 資料前面已有說明。

6. हर्ष harṣa 形容詞（陽性）戰慄；歡喜，快樂

6.1 【詞尾變化】沒有詞尾變化。

6.2 資料前面已有說明。

7. जाताः jātāḥ 形容詞　所生，生起的

7.1 【詞尾變化】jātāḥ 是 jāta 的複數主格形，所以字典查 jāta。

7.2 資料前面已有說明。

8. दत्वा dat（t）vā 動名詞　給予；贈與

8.1 【詞尾變化】datvā 梵英與梵漢辭典並未有此字，但於土田版之《改訂梵文法華經》中作" dattvā"，〔註 49〕係爲√dā 之動名詞形，故採用之。

8.2 資料前面已有說明。

9. बोधाय bodhāya 形容詞　覺悟；覺知

9.1 【詞尾變化】bodhāya 是 bodha 的單數爲格形，所以字典查 bodha。

9.2 資料前面已有說明。

10. जनेन्ति janenti 動詞　生

10.1 【詞尾變化】janenti 據學者看法是 jananti 的異寫），而 jananti 是√jan 的陽性現在式第三人稱複數形，所以字典查√jan。

10.2 【摩威梵英,p410】cl. 1.〔RV. AV.〕 and cl. 3 to generate , beget , produce , create , cause RV. AV.; to produce（a song of praise , &c.）RV. ;（cl. 10 or Caus.）to cause to be born AV.; to assign , procure RV. twice cl. 1. A1. to be born or produced , come into existence RV. AV.; to grow（as plants , teeth）AV.; to be born as , be by birth or nature（with double nom.）MBh. ; to be born or destined for acc. RV.; to be born again; to become , be RV.; to be changed into（dat.）; to take place , happen; to be possible or applicable or suitable; to generate , produce, to be born or produced.

10.3 【梵漢辭典,p521】（動詞）由妻生（子）；自～（從格）生的；始發生，使產生，創作（歌曲等）；使結果實；使～（對格）變成（對格）；出生，生產，發起，成長；再生；變成，歸～（屬格）所有；產生，可能的，使適當的，可允許的；（經文）發，造，起，生，出生，誕生。

11. वीर्यं vīryaṁ 名詞　英雄的行爲；精進

11.1 【詞尾變化】vīryaṁ 根據連音規則，是從 vīryam 變化過來，而 vīryam

〔註 49〕請見荻原雲來、土田勝彌編著《改訂梵文法華經》，東京：山喜房書局出版，1994 年出版。頁 12。

則是 vīrya 的單數主格。所以字典查 vīrya。

11.2　資料前面已有說明。

12. दानेन dānena 名詞　財產

12.1 【詞尾變化】dānena 是 dāna 的單數工具格形，所以字典查 dāna。

12.2　資料前面已有說明。

13. प्रस्थित prasthita 過去被動分詞／形容詞　啓程；出發

13.1 【詞尾變化】沒有詞尾變化。

13.2　資料前面已有說明。

【筆者試譯】：捐出了這些如此優美的東西，
各色各樣有華美裝飾令人欣喜不已，
（這樣的佈施）來鼓勵致力修成正果，這般英雄行爲！
用這樣的佈施祈求無上菩提！

【什公漢譯】：如是等施，種果微妙，歡喜無厭，求無上道，

【英 譯 本】：When they have, with joyful feelings, made
such various and splendid donations, they rouse
their energy in order to obtain enlightenment; these
are those who try to reach supreme enlightenment
by means of charitableness.

【信譯研究】：信譯。

【第四十一頌】

धर्मं च केचित् प्रवदन्ति शान्तं
दृष्टान्तहेतूनयुतैरनेकैः।
देशेन्ति ते प्राणसहस्रकोटिनां
ज्ञानेन ते प्रस्थित अग्रबोधिम्॥४१॥

【羅馬譯音】

dharmaṁ ca kecit pravadanti śāntaṁ
dṛṣṭāntahetūnayutairanekaiḥ|

deśenti te prāṇasahasrakoṭināṁ
jñānena te prasthita agrabodhim||41||

【句義解析】

dharmaṁ ca ke-cit pravadanti śāntaṁ
dṛṣṭānta-hetū-nayutair anekaiḥ|
deśenti te prāṇa-sahasra-koṭināṁ
jñānena te prasthita agra-bodhim||41||

【辭彙研究】

1. धर्मं dharmaṁ 名詞（佛）法

1.1【詞尾變化】dharmaṁ 根據連音規則是從 dharmam 變化過來，而 dharmam 是 dharma 的單數對格形，所以字典查 dharma。

1.2 【摩威梵英,p510】m. that which is established or firm , steadfast decree , statute , ordinance , law ; usage , practice , customary observance or prescribed conduct , duty ; right , justice（often as a synonym of punishment）; virtue , morality , religion , religious merit , good works AV. ; Law or Justice personified（as *Indra* ; as *Yama* MBh. ; as born from the right breast of *Yama* and father of *Śama* , *Kāma* and *Harsha*; as *Vishṇu Hariv.* ; as *Prajā-pati* and son-in-law of *Daksha Hariv.*; as one of the attendants of the Sun ; as a Bull; as a *Dove Kathās.*）; the law or doctrine of Buddhism（as distinguished from the *sañgha* or monastic order）; the ethical precepts of Buddhism（or the principal *dharma* called *sūsra* , as distinguished from the *abhi-dharma* or , further dharma and from the *vinaya* or `discipline , these three constituting the canon of Southern Buddhism）; the law of Northern Buddhism（in 9 canonical scriptures , viz. *Prajñā-pāramitā* , *Gaṇḍa-vyūha* , *Daśa-bhūmīśvara* , *Samadhirāja* , *Laṇkāvatāra* , *Saddharma-puṇḍarika* , *Tathagata-guhyaka* , *Lalita-vistara* , *Suvarṇa-prabhāsa*）; nature , character , peculiar condition or essential quality , property , mark , peculiarity; a partic. ceremony; sacrifice; the ninth mansion; an Upanishad; associating with the virtuous; religious abstraction , devotion;a bow; a Soma-drinker; N. of the 15th

Arhat of the present *Ava-sarpiṇī*; of a son of Anu and father of *Ghṛita Hariv*; of a son of *Gāndhāra* and father of *Dhṛita*; of a son of *Haihaya* and father of *Netra* BhP. ; of a son of *Pṛithu-śravas* and of *Uśanas*; of a son of *Su-vrata* VP.; of a son of *Dīrgha-tapas*; of a king of *Kaśmīra*; of another man; of a lexicographer.

1.3 【梵漢辭典,p369】（陽性名詞）固定的秩序，慣例，習慣，風俗，法則；規定；規則；義務；德，美德，善行；宗教；說教；正義；公正；與～（屬格）相關的法律；性質，性格，本質，特殊屬性，特質；事物；（經文）法，正法，教法，適法，善法，實法，妙法，如法，法門。

2. प्रवदन्ति pravadanti 動詞　開始讚揚

2.1 【詞尾變化】pravadanti 是由 pra-vadanti 所組成，也就是 pra-√vand 的現在式第三人稱複數形，所以字典查 pra-√vand。

2.2【摩威梵英,p919,√vand】cl. 1. A1. to praise , celebrate , laud , extol RV. AV.; to show honour , do homage , salute respectfully or deferentially , venerate , worship , adore RV.; to offer anything（acc.）respectfully to, to be praised or venerated RV., to show honour to any one , greet respectfully.

2.3 【摩威梵英,p652,pra】ind. before ; forward , in front , on , forth（mostly in connection with a verb , esp. with a verb of motion which is often to be supplied ; sometimes repeated before the verb; rarely as a separate word）; as a prefix to subst. = forth , away cf. *pra-vṛtti* , *pra-sthāna* ; as pref. to adj. = excessively , very , much cf. *pra-caṇḍa* , *pra-matta* ; in nouns of relationship = great- cf. *pra-pitāmaha* , *pra-pautra* ;（`according to native lexicographers it may be used in the senses of *gati* , *ā-rambha* , *ut-karṣa* , *sarvato-bhāva*, *prāthamya* , *khyāti* , *ut-patti* , *vy-avahāra*）RV.

2.4 【梵漢辭典,p1386】

2.4.1 √vand（動詞）讚揚，讚歎；恭敬問候，對～表示敬意，尊敬，崇拜；（經文）禮，禮拜，禮敬，作禮，敬禮，致禮，供養，我禮，稽首，稽首禮。

2.4.2 pra-√vand，開始讚揚，高聲讚歎。

3. शान्तं śāntaṁ 形容詞；過去被動分詞　寂靜，止息

3.1 【詞尾變化】śāntaṁ 根據連音規則，是從 śāntam 變化過來，śāntam 是

śānta 的單數對格形，所以字典查 śānta。

3.2 資料前面已有說明。

4. दृष्टान्त dṛṣṭānta 名詞 譬如；模範

4.1 【詞尾變化】沒有詞尾變化。

4.2 資料前面已有說明。

5. हेतू hetū 名詞 正因；原因

5.1 【詞尾變化】hetū 爲 hetu 的雙數主格，所以字典查 hetu。

5.2 資料前面已有說明。

6. नयुतैर् nayutair 形容詞 千億

6.1 【詞尾變化】nayutair 根據連音規則，是由 nayutaiḥ 變化過來，nayutaiḥ 則是 nayuta 的複數工具格形，所以字典查 nayuta。

6.2 資料前面已有說明。

7. अनेकैः anekaiḥ 形容詞 各種的；眾多

7.1 【詞尾變化】anekaiḥ 是 aneka 的複數工具格形，所以字典查 aneka。

7.2 資料前面已有說明。

8. देशेन्ति deśenti 動詞 宣說；指出

8.1 【詞尾變化】deśenti 據學者看法是 deśanti 的異寫，〔註 50〕而 deśanti 爲 √diś 的第三人稱現在式複數形。所以字典查√diś。

8.2 【摩威梵英,p479】cl. 3. P. to point out , show , exhibit RV.; to produce , bring forward（as a witness in a court of justice）; to promote , effect , accomplish ; to assign , grant , bestow upon; to pay（tribute）; to order , command , bid（inf.）, to show , point out , assign MBh.; to direct , order , command; teach , communicate , tell , inform confess Buddh, to wish to show;to show , exhibit , manifest RV. ; to order , command, to show or approve one's self. AV. VS.

8.3 【梵漢辭典,p392】（VI, III）指示，顯示；提出（證據）；分派，授與；成就；奉獻（貢品）；引導，命令；吩咐；（經文）說，宣說，演說，宣通。

9. कोटिनां koṭināṁ 形容詞，數詞 一億；兆；京

〔註 50〕請見江島惠教等編《梵藏漢法華經原典總索引》，東京：靈友會出版，1988 年出版。頁 495。

9.1【詞尾變化】koṭināṁ 根據連音規則，是從 koṭinām 變化過來，而 koṭinām 則是 koṭi 的複數所有格形，所以字典查 koṭi。

9.2　資料前面已有說明。

10. ज्ञानेन jñānena 名詞　知識；智慧，知見

10.1 【詞尾變化】jñānena 是 jñāna 的單數工具格形，所以字典查 jñāna。

10.2　資料前面已有說明。

【筆者試譯】：有些人開始讚揚寂靜佛法，

用種種不可數的正因（案：正法因果）與譬喻來說明，
教示了那些百千萬億的眾生，
這樣的知識來追求無上菩提。

【什公漢譯】：或有菩薩，說寂滅法，種種教詔，無數眾生。

【英 譯 本】：Others set forth the law of quietness, by many
myriads of illustrations and proofs; they preach it
to thousands of kotis of living beings; these are
tending to supreme enlightenment by science.

【信譯研究】：信譯。這裡，梵本頌偈「追求無上菩提」在其他頌偈內多所重複，鳩摩羅什在此將它省略。不言而喻，所以也算信譯。

【第四十二頌】

निरीहका धर्म प्रजानमाना
द्वयं प्रवृत्ताः खगतुल्यसादृशाः।
अनोपलिप्ताः सुगतस्य पुत्राः
प्रज्ञाय ते प्रस्थित अग्रबोधिम्॥४२॥

【羅馬譯音】

nirīhakā dharma prajānamānā
dvayaṁ pravṛttāḥ khagatulyasādṛśāḥ|
anopaliptāḥ sugatasya putrāḥ

prajñāya te prasthita agrabodhim||42||

【句義解析】

nirīhakā dharma prajānamānā
dvayaṁ pravṛttāḥ khaga-tulya-sādṛśāḥ|
anopaliptāḥ sugatasya putrāḥ
prajñāya te prasthita agra-bodhim||42||

【辭彙研究】

1. निरीहका nirīhakā（n）形容詞　無分別（常與「空」連用）

1.1 【詞尾變化】nirīhakā，荻原雲來、土田勝彌認為應為 nirīhakān），而戶田宏文從尼泊爾國立公文書館所藏的梵本 No.4-21（貝葉第 7 頁 b 面）處看來，也認為該處應為 nirīhakān。）所以這裡採認應為" nirīhakān"。nirīhakān 是 nirīhaka 的複數對格形，所以字典查 nirīhaka。

1.2 【摩威梵英】無此字。

1.3 【艾格混梵,p299】

1.3.1 adj.（=Pali id.; Skt. nirīha）, indifferent; often associated with śūnẏa: SP 14.5（vs）; LV 176.14;437.4（vss）; Mv ii.147.17（prose）; AsP 465.19（prose）; ka-tva, abstr., Śikṣ 262.3（vs）; ka-tā, AsP 465.20（prose）. See next.

1.3.2 adj.,=prec.（perhaps corruption for °aka?）:kathaṃ loko nirīhikaḥ Laṅk 25.9（vs, no v.l.）

1.4 【梵漢辭典,p795】（形容詞）（經文）不動，無作，無作用，無生起，生滅無體，遠離，無思，無分別，無貪著步分別。

2. प्रजानमाना prajānamānā 形容詞　從～而生

2.1 【詞尾變化】prajānamānā 疑似為 prajanamānā 的異寫，prajanamānā 則是 pra+√jan 的現在式中間分詞（形容詞）陰性的單數主格形，故字典查 pra+√jan。

2.2 【摩威梵英】pra 與√jan 資料前面已各有說明。

2.3 【梵漢辭典,p521】pra-√jan（動詞）自～（從格）而生的，受生的，發生；出產，生產；變成胎兒；使再生；（經文）有，生，成，續生。

3. द्वयं dvayaṁ 形容詞　兩倍的

3.1 【詞尾變化】dvayaṁ 根據連音規則是從 dvayam 變化過來，而 dvayam 則是 dvaya 的單數主格形。

3.2 【摩威梵英,p503】

3.2.1 n.（fr. and in comp = *dvi*）twofold , double , of 2 kinds or sorts RV. AV. Br. MBh.;

3.2.2（*ī*）f. couple , pair; two things , both（e. g. *tejo-* , the 2 luminaries）MBh.; twofold nature , falsehood RV.; the masc. and fem. gender;

3.2.3（*am*）ind. between

3.3 【梵漢辭典,p421】（形容詞）兩倍的，雙倍的，兩種類的，一對的；（經文）雙，兩，二，二種，二法，二邊，二種法。

4. प्रवृत्ताः pravṛttāḥ 形容詞　現起的；產生的

4.1 【詞尾變化】pravṛttāḥ 是 pravṛtta 的複數主格形，所以字典查 pravṛtta。

4.2 【摩威梵英,p694】

4.2.1 mfn. rotund , globular ; driven up（as a carriage）; circulated（as a book）; set out from（*-tas*）, going to , bound for MBh.; issued from（abl.）, come forth , resulted , arisen , produced , brought about , happened , occurred ; come back , returned MBh. ; commenced , begun MBh. ;

4.2.2（also *-vat* mfn.）having set about or commenced to（inf.）; purposing or going to , bent upon（dat. loc. , or comp.）; engaged in , occupied with , devoted to（loc. or comp.）MBh.; hurting , injuring , offending MBh. ; acting , proceeding , dealing with（loc.）MBh.; existing; who or what has become（with nom.）;

4.2.3（with *karman* n. action）causing a continuation of mundane existence; w.r. for *pra-cṛtta* and *pra-nṛtta* ;

4.2.4（*-vṛtta*）m. = *-varta* , a round ornament;

4.2.5（*ā* f. N. of a female demon）; *-karman* n. any act leading to a future birth;

4.2.6 *-cakra* mfn. `whose chariot wheels run on unimpeded' , having universal power（*-kra-tā* f.）;

4.2.7 *-tva* n. the having happened or occurred;

4.2.8 *-pānīya* mfn.（a well）with abundant water MBh. ;

4.2.9 *-pāraṇa* n. a partic. religious observance or ceremony（v.l.）;

4.2.10 -*vāc* mfn. of fluent speech , eloquent MBh. ;

4.2.11 -*samprahāra* mfn. one who has begun the fight（-*ra-tva* n.）Katha1s. ;

4.2.12 -*ttāśin* m. N. of a partic. class of ascetics.

4.3 【梵漢辭典,p971】（過去被動分詞）（形容詞）從 pra-√ vṛt 變化過來，（經文）起，現起，發起，生，現入；遭遇；轉，流轉；通利，欲；觀，轉。

5. खग khaga 形容詞　飛行的；移到空中的

5.1 【詞尾變化】沒有詞尾變化。

5.2 【摩威梵英,p334】

5.2.1 mfn. moving in air MBh.;

5.2.2 m. a bird MBh. ; N. of *Garuḍa*（cf. -*ga-pati*）; any air-moving insect（as a bee）; a grasshopper ; the sun ; a planet; air , wind MBh.; a deity; an arrow ;

5.2.3 -*pati* m. `chief of birds' , Garuḍa（Vishṇu's vehicle）;

5.2.4 -*pati-gamanā* f. N. of a goddess;

5.2.5 -*pattra* mfn. furnished with bird's feathers（as an arrow）MBh. ;

5.2.6 -*rāj* m. = -*pati*;

5.2.7 -*vaktra* m. Artocarpus Lakucha ;

5.2.8 -*vatī* f. the earth ;

5.2.9 -*śatru* m. `enemy of birds' , Hemionitis cordifolia ;

5.2.10 -*sthāna* n. `a bird's nest' , the hollow of a tree ;

5.2.11 -*gādhipa* m. = -*ga-pati* ;

5.2.12 -*gāntaka* m. `destroyer of birds' , a hawk , falcon ;

5.2.13 -*gābhirāma* m. N. of *Śiva* ;

5.2.14 -*gāsana* m. `seat of the sun' N. of the mountain Udaya（the eastern mountain on which the sun rises）; `sitting on a bird（i.e. on the *Garuḍa*）' , Vishṇu ;

5.2.15 -*géndra* m. the chief of the birds ; a vulture ; Garuḍa ; N. of a prince ;

5.2.16 -géndra-dhvaja m. N. of Vishṇu BhP.;

5.2.17 -*géśvara* m. `the chief of the birds' , a vulture ; Garuḍa.

5.3 【梵漢辭典,p590】

5.3.1（形容詞）移向空中；飛行；（經文）行空，空中。

5.3.2（陽性名詞）鳥，飛蟲（蜜蜂等）；太陽，行星，空氣，風；（經文）鳥。

6. तुल्य tulya 形容詞　均衡的；對等的

6.1 【詞尾變化】沒有詞尾變化。

6.2 【摩威梵英,p451】

6.2.1 mf（*ā*）n.（in comp. accent）equal to , of the same kind or class or number or value , similar , comparable , like; fit for（instr.）;

6.2.2 n. N. of a dance ;

6.2.3（*am*）ind. equally , in like manner MBh.; contemporaneously.

6.3 【梵漢辭典,p1306】

6.3.1（形容詞）均衡的，對等的，相似的，相等的；同一種姓（階級）的；同價值的；不關心的；（經文）等，等者，與等，平等，同，同於，同一；如；稱，所稱，稱量，等量；相似，相似者；中；衡；如量，如，猶如；

6.3.2（副詞）相等地，同樣地；於同時代。

7. सादृशाः sādṛśāḥ 形容詞　對～適當的，如，似

7.1 【詞尾變化】sādṛśāḥ 是 sādṛśa 的複數主格形，所以字典查 sādṛśa。

7.2 資料前面已有說明。

8. अनोपलिप्ताः anopaliptāḥ 形容詞；過去被動分詞　不污損；不著

8.1 【詞尾變化】anopaliptāḥ 是 anopalipta 的複數主格形，所以字典查 anopalipta。

8.2 【摩威梵英】無此字。

8.3 【艾格混梵,p37】neg. ppp.（=an-upa; Pali has an-ūpa in vss, and so also BHS; in BHS not exclusively m.c., see §3.71）, *not defiled*: Mv ii.419.4（prose）; Śikṣ 46.16（so ms.; vs but not m.c.）; may be m.c. in Mv iii.118.9 =326.6; SP 14.6（vs）; LV 224.5; Samādh p.59 1.9 f.

8.4 【梵漢辭典,p102】

8.4.1（過去被動分詞）（形容詞）地方俗語〔從 an-upalipta 變化過來〕；（經文）無所著，不著（泥水）。

8.4.2（經文）不染，無所著，無染著，無所染，無雜穢，不爲～之所染。

9. सुगतस्य sugatasya 名詞　聖人；佛陀

9.1 【詞尾變化】sugatasya 是 sugata 的單數所有格形，所以字典查 sugata。

9.2 資料前面已有說明。

10. पुत्राः putrāḥ 名詞　兒子們

10.1 【詞尾變化】putrāḥ 是 putra 的複數主格形，所以字典查 putra。

10.2 資料前面已有說明。

11. प्रज्ञाय prajñāya 名詞　智慧，精通

11.1【詞尾變化】prajñāya 是 prajñā 加上 āya 而成，所以字典查 prajñā 與 āya。

11.2 【摩威梵英,p702, prajñā】

11.2.1 P. *-jānāti* , to know , understand（esp. a way or mode of action）, discern , distinguish , know about , be acquainted with（acc.）RV.; to find out , discover , perceive , learn MBh., Caus. *-jñāpayati* , to show or point out（the way）; to summon , invite.

11.2.2 mf（*ā*）n. wise , prudent;（ifc.）knowing , conversant with;

11.2.2.1 *-tā*（*-jñā-*）f. knowledge.

11.2.3 f. wisdom , intelligence , knowledge , discrimination , judgment; device , design; a clever or sensible woman; Wisdom personified as the goddess of arts and eloquence; a partic. or energy;（with Buddh.）true or transcendental wisdom（which is three fold Dharmas）; the energy of *ādi-buddha*（through the union with whom the latter produced all things）

11.2.4 mf（*ā* and *ī*）(fr. *jñā*) intellectual (opp. to *śārīra* , *taijasa*) ; intelligent , wise , clever MBh. ;

11.2.4.1 m. a wise or learned man MBh.; intelligence dependent on individuality *Vedāntas*. ; a kind of parrot with red stripes on the neck and wings ;

11.2.4.2（*ā*）f. intelligence , understanding ;

11.2.4.3（*ī*）f. the wife of a learned man ;

11.2.4.4 *-kathā* f. a story about a wise man MW. ;

11.2.4.5 *-tā* f.（Mis.）, *-tva* n.（*Vedāntas.*）wisdom , learning , intelligence ;

11.2.4.6 *-bhūta-nātha* , m. N. of a poet Cat. ;

11.2.4.7 *-māna* m. respect for learned men;

11.2.4.8 *-mānin, -m-mānin̐, -vādika*（MBh.）. mfn. thinking one's self wise.

11.3【摩威梵英,p147, āya】m.（fr. ā-i）, arrival , approach RV ; income , revenue ; gain , profit MBh. ; the eleventh lunar mansion; a die Jyot. ; the number four ; N. of a kind of formulas inserted at particular occasions of a sacrifice; the guard of the women's apartments .

11.4 【梵漢辭典,p912, prajñā】（陰性名詞）教訓，報知；識別，判斷，智能，了解，智慧，明瞭；目的，決心；（經文）慧，妙慧，勝慧，覺慧，智，智慧。

11.5 【梵漢辭典,p227, āya】

11.5.1（陽性）到來，接近；收入，所得；（經文）來；出，聚；生，生長。

11.5.2（陽性）（文法）作爲詞根的接尾詞 ——āya。

【筆者試譯】：從（觀察）法而生的無二分別的佛法，
（對佛法有決定性信心）迅速地產生了，
清淨的佛子們，
要以追求這樣的智慧來達成無上佛道。

【什公漢譯】：或見菩薩，觀諸法性，無有二相，猶如虛空，
又見佛子，心無所著，以此妙慧，求無上道。

【英 譯 本】：（There are）sons of the Sugata who try to
reach enlightenment by wisdom; they understand
the law of indifference and avoid acting at the
antinomy（of things）, unattached like birds in the sky.

【信譯研究】：信譯。梵文原文裡面並沒有「空」或是「無所著」等名詞，應該是譯者爲解說清楚才增加的。因此這裡鳩摩羅什將原文的四句頌以八句漢頌來對譯。

【第四十三頌】

भूयश्च पश्याम्यहु मञ्जुघोष
परिनिर्वृतानां सुगतान शासने।

उत्पन्न धीरा बहुबोधिसत्त्वाः
कुर्वन्ति सत्कारु जिनान धातुषु॥४३॥

【羅馬譯音】

bhūyaśca paśyāmyahu mañjughoṣa
parinirvṛtānāṁ sugatāna śāsane|
utpanna dhīrā bahubodhisattvāḥ
kurvanti satkāru jināna dhātuṣu||43||

【句義解析】

bhūyaś ca paśyāmy ahu Mañjughoṣa
parinirvṛtānāṁ sugatāna śāsane|
utpanna dhīrā bahu-bodhisattvāḥ
kurvanti sat-kāru jināna dhātuṣu||43||

【辭彙研究】

1. भूयश्च bhūyaś 分詞（絕對格）出現，生成

1.1 【詞尾變化】bhūyaś ca 根據連音規則是從 bhūyaḥ ca，而 bhūyaḥ 是√bhū 的絕對格分詞陽性主格單數變化，所以字典查√bhū。

1.2 資料前面已有說明。

2. पश्याम्य् paśyāmy 動詞（IV）我看見

2.1 【詞尾變化】paśyāmy 即 paśyāmi，〔註 51〕paśyāmi 即√paś 的第一人稱單數現在式動詞，所以字典查√paś。

2.2 資料前面已有說明。

3. अहु ahu 代名詞 我

3.1 【詞尾變化】ahu 即 ahaṃ，並非梵文，是 Prakrit 的寫法。

3.2 資料前面已有說明。

4. परिनिर्वतानां parinirvṛtānāṁ 形容詞 完全快樂；完全寂靜

4.1 【詞尾變化】parinirvṛtānāṁ 是由 pari-nirvṛtānāṁ 兩個字組成。pari 是

〔註 51〕請見江島惠教等編《梵藏漢法華經原典總索引》，東京：靈友會出版，1988 年出版。頁 621。

副詞，沒有詞尾變化。nirvṛtānāṁ 根據連音規則是從 nirvṛtānām 變化過來。而 nirvṛtānām 是 nirvṛta 的陽性所有格複數變化形，所以字典查 nirvṛta。

4.2 【摩威梵英,p591,pari】ind. round , around , about , round about ; fully , abundantly , richly RV. ; as a prep.（with acc.）about（in space and time）RV. AV. ; against , opposite to , in the direction of , towards; beyond , more than AV. ; to the share of; successively , severally;（with abl.）from , away from , out of RV. AV.; outside of , except; after the lapse of MBh.; in consequence or on account or for the sake of RV. AV. ; according to RV.

4.3 【摩威梵英,p558, nirvṛta】

4.3.1 mfn. satisfied , happy , tranquil , at ease , at rest MBh.; extinguished , terminated , ceased; emancipated;

4.3.2 n. a house.

4.4 【梵漢辭典,p850,pari】（副詞）在周圍；充分地，完全，專心，非常地。（介詞）〔與對格連用〕～的時候，～的時間，～一帶〔地點〕；面對，朝向，在上面，在此以上；〔與從格連用〕，自～，～之故，跟隨～。（經文）普。

4.5 【梵漢辭典,p803,nirvṛta】（過去被動分詞）（經文）滅，滅度，得滅度，寂滅，寂靜，寂滅相；為足，快安樂，安穩。

5. सुगतान sugatāna 形容詞／名詞 藉由佛；佛的

5.1 【詞尾變化】sugatāna 這個字經過學者研究，字根應為 sugata。〔註 52〕疑似 sugatena 的誤寫，雙方讀音近似緣故。sugatena 為 sugata 的陽性工具格單數，故字典要查 sugata。

5.2 資料前面已有說明。

6. शासने śāsane 形容詞 於、在教訓；教導

6.1 【詞尾變化】śāsane 是 śāsana 的陽性單數位格形，故字典查 śāsana。

6.2 資料前面已有說明。

7. उत्पन्न utpanna 過去被動分詞；形容詞 出現；生

〔註 52〕請見江島惠教等編《梵藏漢法華經原典總索引》，東京：靈友會出版，1988 年出版。頁 1098。

7.1 【詞尾變化】沒有詞尾變化。

7.2 【摩威梵英,p180】mfn. risen , gone up ; arisen , born , produced ; come forth , appeared ; ready Yājñ. ; mentioned , quoted（esp. fr. the Veda）Jaim.

7.3 【梵漢辭典,p1357】（過去被動分詞）出生，產生；（經文）生，已生，生已，受生，所生；出，出現，出生；起，生起，已起；遭，發（心）已。

8. धीरा dhīrā 形容詞　不變的，堅固的，不退的

8.1 【詞尾變化】根據《摩威梵英辭典》頁 517 說明，dhīrā 即 dhīra。所以字典查 dhīra。

8.2 資料前面已有說明。

9. कुर्वन्ति kurvanti 動詞（VIII）禮敬；朝拜

9.1 【詞尾變化】kurvanti 是√kṛ 現在式第三人稱複數形，所以字典查√kṛ。

9.2 資料前面已有說明。

10. कारु kāru 名詞　成就者；製作者

10.1 【詞尾變化】沒有詞尾變化。

10.2 【摩威梵英,p275】

10.2.1 us mf.（fr. √1. kṛ）, a maker , doer , artisan , mechanic Mn. Yājñ. ;（us）

10.2.2 m. \`architect of the gods' N. of Viśva-karman; an art , science;

10.2.3 mfn.（only etymological）horrible.

10.2.4 m.（fr. √2. kṛ）, one who sings or praises , a poet RV. AV. ;

10.2.5（avas）m. pl., N. of a family of Ṛishis GopBr.

10.3 【梵漢辭典,p575】

10.3.1（陽／陰性名詞）勞動者，技工；手工藝者，工匠。

10.3.2（陽性名詞）詩人，歌手。

10.3.3（形容詞）可怕的，驚人的。

11. जिनान jināna 名詞　勝者，指佛陀

11.1 【詞尾變化】jināna 經學者研究疑似爲 jinena 異寫，〔註 53〕jinena 爲 jina 的陽性單數工具格形，故字典查 jina。

〔註 53〕請見江島惠教等編《梵藏漢法華經原典總索引》，東京：靈友會出版，1988 年出版。頁 388。

11.2　資料前面已有說明。

12. धातुषु dhātuṣu 名詞　舍利

12.1 【詞尾變化】dhātuṣu 是 dhātu 的複數於格形，字典查 dhātu。

12.2　資料前面已有說明。

【筆者試譯】：文殊師利！我又聽見了和雅甜美的聲音，
佛陀由正法獲得了寂滅之樂，
眾多不退轉的大菩薩們，
向著佛陀成就者的舍利禮拜。

【什公漢譯】：文殊師利，又有菩薩，佛滅度後，供養舍利。

【英 譯 本】：Further, I see, O Mañgughosha, many Bodhisattvas
who have displayed steadiness under the rule of
the departed Sugatas, and now are worshipping the
relics of the Ginas.

【信譯研究】：信譯。

【第四十四頌】

स्तूपान पश्यामि सहस्रकोट्यो
अनल्पका यथरिव गङ्गवालिकाः।
येभिः सदा मण्डित क्षेत्रकोटियो
ये कारिता तेहि जिनात्मजेहि॥४४॥

【羅馬譯音】

stūpāna paśyāmi sahasrakoṭyo
analpakā yathariva gaṅgavālikāḥ|
yebhiḥ sadā maṇḍita kṣetrakoṭiyo
ye kāritā tehi jinātmajehi||44||

【句義解析】

stūpāna paśyāmi sahasra-koṭyo

analpakā yathariva Gaṅga-vālikāḥ|
yebhiḥ sadā maṇḍita kṣetra-koṭiyo
ye kāritā tehi jinātmajehi||44||

【辭彙研究】

1. अनल्पका analpakā 形容詞　不少，眾多

1.1 【詞尾變化】analpakā 就是 an-alpakā 組合而成，而 an 爲否定意思，根據學者研究，alpakā 即 alpaka），所以字典查 alpaka。

1.2 【摩威梵英,p】

1.2.1 mf（ikā）n. small , minute , trifling;

1.2.2（ām）ind. little;

1.2.3（āt）abl. ind. shortly after;

1.2.4 m. the plants Hedysarum Alhagi and Premna Herbacea.

1.3 【梵漢辭典,p71】（形容詞）（陰性：-ikā）〔=alpa（形）〕；（經文）少，少分，少許，甚少。（陽性）侏儒，（中性）很少，～m（副詞）僅，～āt（從格）無間。

2. यथरिव yathariva 副詞　如～一樣

2.1 【詞尾變化】《摩威梵英》找不到，所以知道 yathariva 是佛教混合梵文，Prakrit，從 yathaiva 變化過來，yathaiva 根據連音規則，就是 yathā-eva 的組合。

2.2 【艾格混梵,p442】（Pali id.,=yathaiva）, just as.

2.3 【梵漢辭典,p1510】（副詞）（俗語）〔（韻律）<yathava（thā-eva）〕（經文）如～。

3. वालिका: vālikāḥ 名詞　沙

3.1 【詞尾變化】vālikāḥ 是 vālikā 的陰性複數主格形，所以字典查 vālikā。

3.2 資料前面已有說明。

4. येभि: yebhiḥ 關係代名詞　作爲～；關於～

4.1 【詞尾變化】yebhiḥ 是 ye 的複數工具格形，而 ye 即 ya。

4.2 資料前面已有說明。

5. कारिता kāritā 過去被動分詞　所做的

5.1 【詞尾變化】kāritā 是 kārita 的陰性形，意思等同於 kārita。所以字典查

kārita。

5.2 【摩威梵英,p274】

5.2.1 mfn. ifc. caused to be made or done , brought about , effected MBh. ;

5.2.2（*ā*）f.（scil. *vṛddhi*）forced to be paid , interest exceeding the legal rate of interest;

5.2.3（*am*）n. the Caus. form of a verb.

5.3 【梵漢辭典,p569】

5.3.1（過去被動詞）所做的，所爲的；由～引起的，由～產生的，與～有關的。（經文）起，造立，建立，作，所作，教他作。

5.3.2 Kāritā 另有（陰性形容詞）意義，被強迫償還（給債主的額外）利息；（經文）所作。

6. तेहि tehi 複合詞 因爲他們

6.1 【詞尾變化】tehi 即爲 te-hi 的組合，而 te 爲代名詞，tad 第三人稱複數主格，hi 爲不變詞，通常在字首之後，意爲由於～，因爲～之故。

6.2 資料前面已有說明。

7. जिनात्मजेहि jinātmajehi 名詞 菩薩們

7.1 【詞尾變化】該字無見於梵英辭典，應非梵文。據學者研究 jinātmajehi 就是 jinātmaja 的 Prakrit（或是巴利文）的複數工具格變化法，梵漢字典查 jinātmaja。

7.2 【梵漢辭典,p533】(na-āt)（陽性）（經文）佛子，最勝子，菩薩。

【筆者試譯】：我又看見無量無數的佛塔寺廟，
像恆河沙數量一樣地多。
在無數的國土當中（這些寺廟）總是用美麗的飾物來裝飾著，
因爲是由這些佛子菩薩們所做的。

【什公漢譯】：又見佛子，造諸塔廟，無數恒沙，嚴飾國界。

【英 譯 本】：I see thousands of kotis of Stûpas, numerous
as the sand of the Ganges, which have been raised
by these sons of the Gina and now adorn kotis of
grounds.

【信譯研究】：信譯。

【第四十五頌】

रत्नान सप्तान विशिष्ट उच्छ्रिताः

सहस्र पञ्चो परिपूर्ण योजना।

द्वे चो सहस्रे परिणाहवन्त-

श्छत्रध्वजास्तेषु सहस्रकोटयः॥४५॥

【羅馬譯音】

ratnāna saptāna viśiṣṭa ucchritāḥ

sahasra pañco paripūrṇa yojanā|

dve co sahasre pariṇāhavanta-

śchatradhvajāsteṣu sahasrakoṭayaḥ||45||

【句義解析】

ratnāna saptāna viśiṣṭa ucchritāḥ

sahasra pañco paripūrṇa yojanā|

dve co sahasre pariṇāhavantaś

chatra-dhvajās teṣu sahasra-koṭayaḥ||45||

【辭彙研究】

1. सप्तान saptāna 形容詞　七（個／的）

1.1. 【詞尾變化】saptāna 爲 sapta-ana 的組合，ana 爲「這」、「此」，資料前面已有說明，字典查 sapta。

1.2. 【摩威梵英,p1149】

1.2.1. seven ;

1.2.2. mfn. = -tamá;

1.2.3. m. N. of Vishṇu Vishṇ.

1.3. 【梵漢辭典,p1131】（數詞／形容詞）七，七的。

2. उच्छ्रिताः ucchritāḥ 形容詞／過去被動分詞　高聳的，高舉的

2.1. 【詞尾變化】ucchritāḥ 是 ucchrita 的陽性複數主格形，所以字典查

ucchrita。

2.2. 【摩威梵英,p174】

2.2.1. mfn. raised , lifted up , erected; rising , arising , mounting MBh. ; high , tall; advancing , arisen , grown powerful or mighty MBh.; wanton , luxuriant Hariv.; excited; increased , grown , enlarged , large , huge; born , produced;

2.2.2. m. Pinus Longifolia.

2.3. 【梵漢辭典,p1315】（過去被動分詞／形容詞）舉起的，抬高的；高的（經文）豎，豎立，起，建，建立；高，高峻，高聳；懸。

3. पञ्चो परिपूर्ण pañco paripūrṇa 複合詞　以上充滿

3.1. 【詞尾變化】pa˝co paripūrṇa 根據連音規則，是從 pa˝ca uparipūrṇa 結合變化而來，而 pa˝ca 為五，資料前面已有說明。而 uparipūrṇa 是由 upari-pūrṇa 結合而成，

3.2. 【摩威梵英,p205,upari】

3.2.1. ind.（as a separable adverb）above , upon , on , upwards , towards the upper side of; besides , in addition to , further; afterwards;higher and higher ; repeatedly , continuously RV. over , above , upon , on , at the head of , on the upper side of , beyond; in connection with , with reference to , with regard to , towards; after RV.

3.3. 【摩威梵英,p642, pūrṇa】

3.3.1. mfn. filled , full , filled with or full of（instr. or gen. or comp.）RV.; abundant , rich; fulfilled , finished , accomplished , ended , past MBh. ; concluded（as a treaty）; complete , all , entire MBh.; satisfied , contented ;

3.3.2.（ifc.）perfectly familiar with; drawn , bent to the full（as a bow）MBh.;（in augury）fullsounding , sonorous and auspicious; uttering this cry; strong , capable , able; selfish , self-indulgent;

3.3.3. m. a partic. form of the sun; a kind of tree;（in music）a partic. measure ; N. of a *Nāga* MBh. ; of a *Deva-gandharva*; of a Buddhist ascetic;

3.3.4. *ā* f. N. of the 15th Kala1 of the month. ; of the 5th , 10th and ; N. of a woman;（with Śiktas）of an authoress of Mantras; of 2 rivers ; ii. fulness , plenty , abundance; water; the cipher or figure

3.4. 【梵漢辭典,p1342,upari】

3.4.1.（副詞）在上，在其上，在上方；向上，向上方；更，接著，其後，〔～～〕逐漸地；常在上方，幾次地，重複地。（經文）更。

3.4.2.（介係詞）在～之上，超越～，在～的彼方；以上（就數字來說），在～之後〔就時間來說〕，與～有關，因為～之故，遠在～之上的。（經文）上。

3.5. 【梵漢辭典,p990, pūrṇa】

3.5.1.（過去被動分詞）被裝滿的，已滿的。（經文）滿，充滿，盛滿，溢滿，充遍，盈，滿足，具足。

3.5.2.（陽性／名詞）〔樹的一種〕;〔拍子的一種〕;〔某 Nāga 之名〕。（經文）〔人名〕圓滿。

3.5.3.（陽性／名詞）（經文）〔佛弟子之名〕滿慈子，滿見子，滿嚴飾女子。即富樓那尊者。

4. योजना yojanā 名詞　由旬（長度的單位）

4.1. 【詞尾變化】yojanā 是 yojana 的陰性形，所以字典查 yojana。

4.2. 【摩威梵英,p858】

4.2.1. n. joining , yoking , harnessing ; that which is yoked or harnessed , a team , vehicle（also applied to the hymns and prayers addressed to the gods）RV. ; course , path ib. ;

4.2.2.（sometimes m. ; ifc. f. *ā*）a stage or Yojana（i.e. a distance traversed in one harnessing or without unyoking ; esp. a partic. measure of distance , sometimes regarded as equal to 4 or 5 English miles , but more correctly = 4 *Krośas* or about 9 miles ; according to other calculations = 2 1/2 English miles , and according to some = 8 *Krośas*）RV.; instigation , stimulation; mental concentration , abstraction , directing the thoughts to one point（= *yoga*）; the Supreme Spirit of the Universe; a finger ;

4.2.3. n. and（*ā*）f. use , application , arrangement , preparation RV. MBh.; erecting , constructing , building; junction , union , combination ;

4.2.4.（*ā*）f. application of the sense of a passage , grammatical construction S3am2k.

4.3. 【梵漢辭典,p1518】（中性名詞）套軛（於牛馬）;（連結在車子的）一列動物，車（RV），〔少用〕；路（吠陀）；〔距離的單位，4 krośa，大約九哩〕；準備，整頓〔或-ā（陰性）〕；煽動，建設，全神貫注；與～結合，合併；（經文）合，應，和合；建立，修造；三十里，驛，四十里，由旬，由延。

5. द्वे dve 數詞／形容詞　二

5.1. 【詞尾變化】dve 是 dva 的中性與陰性的對格，字典查 dva。這個字只有雙數。

5.2. 【摩威梵英,p503】original stem of *dvi*,two RV.; both（with api）; loc. *dvayos* in two genders（masc. and fem.）or in two numbers（sing. and pl.）

5.3. 【梵漢辭典,p419】（形容詞），（數詞），（雙數）二；〔±api〕雙方，二之數字〔即單數及複數等〕（文法）；（經文）二，二種。

6. चो सहस्रे co sahasre 片段語詞　和千數的

6.1. 【詞尾變化】co sahasre 原來是由 ca + u + sahasra 的單樹於格變化，sahasre 形成。這裡面 ca, sahasra 前面資料都有說明，唯獨 u 尚未說明。字典查 u。

6.2. 【摩威梵英,p171】

6.2.1. ind. an enclitic copula used frequently in the Vedas；

6.2.2. (as a particle implying restriction and antithesis, generally after pronominals, prepositions, particles, and before nu and su , equivalent to）and , also , further.

6.2.3. on the other hand（especially in connexion with a relative , e.g. ya u , he on the contrary who &c.）This particle may serve to give emphasis , like id and eva , especially after prepositions or demonstrative pronouns , in conjunction with nu , vai , hi , cid. It is especially used in the figure of speech called Anaphora , and particularly when the pronouns are repeated. It may be used in drawing a conclusion , like the English `now' , and is frequently found in interrogative sentences. Pāini calls this particle u˜ to distinguish it from the interrogative u. In the Pada-pāṭha it is written ūm. In the classical language u occurs only after atha , na , and kim , with a slight modification of the sense , and often only as an expletive（see kim）

6.2.4. u - u or u - uta , on the one hand - on the other hand

6.2.5. partly - partly

6.2.6. as , well - as.

6.3. 【梵漢辭典,p1312】（附屬語）（質詞）且，又，亦；但，然，現在，正好；立即地，（此字用在代名詞，關係代名詞，疑問詞，若干質詞等結束的後面，如 atha-u, na-u, kim-u 的方式使用）。

7. परिणाहवन्तश् pariṇāhavantaś 形容詞　廣大的

7.1. 【詞尾變化】pariṇāhavantaś 和下面的 chatra 有連音規則變化關係，原來是從 pariṇāhavantaḥ chatra 變化而來。而 pariṇāhavantaḥ 是 pariṇāhavat 的複數主格形，所以字典查 pariṇāhavat。但此字不見於【摩威梵英字典】，應非標準梵文，亦不見於【艾格混梵字典】，是俗語還是異寫法無法確定，但由學者對照研究推知。〔註 54〕

7.2. 【梵漢辭典,p858】（形容詞）大的；（經文）廣。

8. छत्र-ध्वजास् chatra-dhvajās 形容詞　傘蓋與寶幢

8.1. 【詞尾變化】chatra-dhvajās 是兩件東西，其中 dhvajās 後面因爲後面 teṣu 的關係形成連音規則，原來是 dhvajāḥ 變化過來，也就是 dhvaja 的陽性複數主格形，資料前面已有說明。而 chatra 無詞尾變化，故此處字典查 chatra。

8.2. 【摩威梵英,p404】

8.2.1. m.（often spelt *chatra*）a mushroom ; Andropogon Schoenanthus ; a parasol-shaped bee-hive ;

8.2.2. n. a parasol , Chattar（ensign of royal or delegated power Jain.）; an umbrella; a particular constellation; `shelter（of pupils）' , a teacher（a meaning derived fr. *chāttra*）;

8.2.3.（*ā*）f. N. of a plant growing in Kaśmir ; Anethum Sowa; Asteracantha longifolia; Rubia Munjista; a mushroom;

8.3. 【梵漢辭典,p324】（中性名詞）〔=chattra〕，（遮蔽物）即陽傘〔王位的徽章之一〕；（經文）蓋，傘，傘蓋，繒蓋，寶蓋。

〔註 54〕請見江島惠教等編《梵藏漢法華經原典總索引》，東京：靈友會出版，1988 年出版。頁 598。案江島教授等人是根據藏文對照比較後做出的結論。

9. तेषु teṣu 代名詞　如此地

9.1. 【詞尾變化】teṣu 是 tad 的中性於格複數形，所以字典查 tad。

9.2. 資料前面已有說明。

10. कोटयः koṭayaḥ 形容詞　千萬億；無量之數

10.1. 【詞尾變化】koṭayaḥ 是 koṭi 的陰性複數主格形，所以字典查 koṭi。

10.2. 資料前面已有說明。

【筆者試譯】：特別的七種寶物被抬起，
足足有五千由旬那麼高！
兩個一千由旬那麼廣大！
又有難以計算許多的傘蓋和幢幡。

【什公漢譯】：寶塔高妙，五千由旬，縱廣正等，二千由旬。

【英 譯 本】：Those magnificent Stûpas, made of seven
precious substances, with their thousands of kotis of
umbrellas and banners, measure in height no less
than 5000 yoganas and 2000 in circumference.

【信譯研究】：信譯。

【第四十六頌】

सवैजयन्ताः सद शोभमाना
घण्टासमूहै रणमान नित्यम्।
पुष्पैश्च गन्धैश्च तथैव वाद्यैः
संपूजिता नरमरुयक्षराक्षसैः॥४६॥

【羅馬譯音】

savaijayantāḥ sada śobhamānā
ghaṇṭāsamūhai raṇamāna nityam|
puṣpaiśca gandhaiśca tathaiva vādyaiḥ
saṁpūjitā naramaruyakṣarākṣasaiḥ||46||

【句義解析】

savaijayantāḥ sada śobhamānā
ghaṇṭā-samūhai raṇamāna nityam|
puṣpaiś ca gandhaiś ca tathaiva vādyaiḥ
saṁpūjitā nara-maru-yakṣa-rākṣasaiḥ||46||

【辭彙研究】

1. सवैजयन्ताः savaijayantāḥ 名詞　這些神旗；勝幡

1.1. 【詞尾變化】savaijayantāḥ 是 sa-vaijayantāḥ 所組成，sa 是代名詞，意爲「其」；而 vaijayantāḥ 爲 vaijayanta 的主格複數形，所以字典查 sa-vaijayanta。

1.2. 資料前面已有說明。

2. सत sada 形容詞　坐落於此的

2.1. 【詞尾變化】沒有詞尾變化。

2.2. 【摩威梵英,p1138】

2.2.1. mfn. = prec.（cf. *barhi-* , *samanī-ṣada* ; *sabhā-sada*）;

2.2.2. m. fruit（cf. *śada*）; a partic.; N. of a son of *Dhṛita-rāśṭra* MBh.（if sadaḥ-suvāc is not one word）;

2.2.3. n. a partic. part of the back of a sacrificial animal.

2.3. 【梵漢辭典,p1045】〔=sad〕,（形容詞）坐在～的，住於～的；（陽性名詞）果實；（中性名詞）〔祭祀牲獸脊梁的一部分〕。

3. शोभमाना śobhamānā 動詞／現在中間分詞　正美麗著；亮麗著

3.1. 【詞尾變化】śobhamānā 是√śubh 的現在式中間分詞，所以字典查√śubh。

3.2. 資料前面已有說明。

4. घण्टा ghaṇṭā 名詞　鈴；鐘

4.1. 【詞尾變化】沒有詞尾變化。

4.2. 【摩威梵英,p375】

4.2.1. f. of *-ṭa* q.v.

4.2.2. m.（for *hantra*?）N. of *Śiva* MBh.（cf. *ghaṭin*）; a kind of dish（sort of sauce , vegetables made into a pulp and mixed with turmeric and mustard seeds and capsicums ; cf. *matsya-*）; N. of a Dānava;

4.2.3.（*ā*）f. a bell MBh.（ifc. f. *ā* MBh.）; a plate of iron or mixed metal struck as a clock（cf. *ghaṭī*）; Bignonia suaveolens; Lida cordifolia or rhombifolia; Uraria lagopodioides; Achyranthes aspera;

4.2.4.（ī）f. see *kṣudra-* , *mahā-* ; N. of *Durgā* MBh.

4.3. 【梵漢辭典,p456】（陰性名詞）鈴，鐘；（經文）鐸，鐘，鈴，金鈴，寶鈴，鈴鐸。

5. समूहै samūhai 名詞　集合，集成

5.1. 【詞尾變化】samūhai 根據學者研究，是從 samūha 變化過來的。所以字典查 samūha。〔註 55〕若與後面的 r 結合，就是 samūhair，則可看做是 samūhaiḥ 的連音規則變化，就是 samūha 的陽性工具格複數形。

5.2. 【摩威梵英,p1170】

5.2.1. m.（ifc. f. *ā*）a collection , assemblage , aggregate , heap , number , multitude AV.; an association , corporation , community; sum , totality , essence MBh. ; N. of a divine being（?）MBh. ;

5.2.2.（*ā*）f. a partic. mode of subsistence;

5.2.3.（*-ha*）*-kārya* n. the business or affairs of a community;

5.2.4. *-kṣāraka* m. civet;

5.2.5. *-gandha* m. civet.

5.3. 【梵漢辭典,p1117】（陽性名詞）（吠陀）累積；（雅語）集合體，塊，多數，聚集，集成（普通之意）；團體（少用）；總計，本質（少用）；（經文）合成；集，聚，積聚，共積聚。

6. रणमान raṇamāna 動詞／現在中間分詞　發出叮噹響

6.1. 【詞尾變化】raṇamāna 爲√raṇ 的現在中間分詞，所以字典查√raṇ。

6.2. 【摩威梵英,p863】

6.2.1. or *ran* cl. 1. 4. to rejoice , be pleased , take pleasure in（loc. , rarely acc.）RV. ; to gladden , delight , gratify ib.: Caus., to cheer , gladden , exhilarate with（instr. or loc.）RV. ; to be at ease , be pleased or satisfied with , delight in（loc.）ib. AV.RV.

6.2.2. cl. 1. P., to sound , ring , rattle , jingle: Caus., to make resound BhP.

〔註 55〕請見江島惠教等編《梵藏漢法華經原典總索引》，東京：靈友會出版，1988 年出版。頁 1055。

6.3. 【梵漢辭典,p1015】(動詞)使滿足(RV)使～歡喜;使鈴鐺叮噹響;(經文)擊,發響,出音,吼,有諍,諍競。

7. नित्यम् nityam 副詞　恆久地;不變地

7.1. 【詞尾變化】

7.1.1. nityam 是 nitya 的陽性單數對格形,所以字典查 nitya。

7.1.2. 不過,若是 nitya 後面加上 m 則是 nitya 的副詞。

7.2. 【摩威梵英,p547】

7.2.1. mf(*ā*) n. innate , native MBh. ; one's own RV. ; continual , perpetual , eternal RV.; ifc. constantly dwelling or engaged in , intent upon , devoted or used to MBh.; ordinary , usual , invariable , fixed , necessary , obligatory.;

7.2.2. m. the sea , ocean ;

7.2.3. (*ā*) f. a plough-share; N. of *Durgā*; of a *Śakti Tantras*. ; of the goddess *Manasā*;

7.2.4. n. constant and indispensable rite or act;

7.2.5. (*-am*) ind. always , constantly , regularly , by all means RV.

7.3. 【梵漢辭典,p811】

7.3.1. (形容詞)內部的,天生的,自身的(吠陀);經常的,恆久的,永久的,不變的,不壞的;於～常在的,獻身於～;正式的,本質的,必須的;(經文)常,恆,常常,恆常,恆不滅。

7.3.2. ～m(副詞)恆久地,不易地,常存地,不變地;(經文)於一切時,常,恆,恆時,常住。

8. पुष्पैश् च puṣpaiś ca 名詞　花;華

8.1. 【詞尾變化】puṣpaiś ca 根據連音規則是從 puṣpaiḥ 變化過來,而 puṣpaiḥ 則是 puṣpa 的陽性複數工具格形,所以字典查 puṣpa。

8.2. 資料前面已有說明。

9. गन्धैश् च gandhaiś ca 名詞　薰香;香味

9.1. 【詞尾變化】gandhaiś ca 根據連音規則,是從 gandhaiḥ ca 變化過來,而 gandhaiḥ 是 gandha 的複數工具格形,所以字典查 gandha。

9.2. 【摩威梵英,p345】

9.2.1. m. smell , odour RV. AV.(ifc. f. *ā* MBh.); a fragrant substance , fragrance , scent , perfume ; sulphur ; pounded sandal-wood; a sectarial mark on the forehead（called so in the south of India）; myrrh; Hyperanthera Moringa;（ifc.）the mere smell of anything , small quantity , little MBh.; connection , relationship; a neighbour; pride , arrogance MBh.;

9.2.2.（*ā*）f. = *-palāśī* ; Desmodium gangeticum; = *-mohinī*; a metre of 17+18+17+18 syllables ;

9.2.3.（*am*）n. smell; black aloe-wood.

9.3. 【梵漢辭典,p446】（陽／中性名詞）（附著物）香，芳香，香氣；薰香（一般爲複數）；～的氣味或痕跡，與～相似的；驕矜，傲慢；（經文）香；氣；氣味。

10. तथैव tathaiva 代名詞　如此

10.1. 【詞尾變化】tathaiva 即 tatha 加上 eva 之意。

10.2. 資料前面已有說明。

11. वाद्यैः vādyaiḥ 名詞　樂器；音樂

11.1. 【詞尾變化】vādyaiḥ 是 vādya 的陽性複數工具格，所以字典查 vādya。

11.2. 【摩威梵英,p940】

11.2.1. mfn. to be said or spoken or pronounced or uttered; to be sounded or played（as a musical instrument）;

11.2.2. n. a speech; instrumental music ;

11.2.3. m. or n. a musical instrument.

11.3. 【梵漢辭典,p1368】

11.3.1.（未來被動分詞）（形容詞）〔起自 Vad〕可說的或可演講的；可發出聲音，或可演奏的（樂器）。

11.3.2.（中性形容詞）談話（少用）；～的演奏（樂器），

11.3.3.（陽性／中性名詞）樂器；

11.3.4.（經文）樂，音樂，伎樂，妓樂，樂器。

12. संपूजिता saṁpūjitā 過去被動分詞／形容詞　供養，敬奉的

12.1. 【詞尾變化】saṁpūjitā 爲 saṁ 加上 pūjitā，而 pūjitā 爲 pūjita 的陰性化詞，爲√pūj 的過去被動分詞。字典查 saṁ-√pūj。

12.2. 資料前面已有說明。

13. मरु maru 名詞　天

13.1. 【詞尾變化】沒有詞尾變化。但配合前後文，取「天」的意思。

13.2. 【摩威梵英,p790】

13.2.1. m.（prob. fr. √*mṛ*) a wilderness , sandy waste , desert（often pl.）MBh.; a mountain , rock MBh. ; ` the desertlike penance ' i.e. abstinence from drinking MBh.; a species of plant; a deer , antelope; N. of a Daitya（usually associated with Naraka）MBh. ; of a Vasu; of a prince（the son of Śīghra）; of a king belonging to the Ikshvā ku family BhP. ; of a son of Hary-aśva ;

13.2.2. pl. N. of a country（Marwar）and its inhabitants.

13.3. 【梵漢辭典,p716】

13.3.1.（陽性名詞）乾燥的地域，荒漠，多殺的荒地，沙漠；山，岩石；（經文）高巖，絕邊廣川。

13.3.2.（陽性）=marut，（經文）天。

14. यक्ष yakṣa 名詞　夜叉

14.1. 【詞尾變化】沒有詞尾變化。

14.2. 【摩威梵英,p838】

14.2.1. n. a living supernatural being , spiritual apparition , ghost , spirit RV. AV. VS.（accord. to some native Comms. = *yaj□a* , *pujā* , *pūjita*）;

14.2.2. m. N. of a class of semi-divine beings（attendants of *Kubera* , exceptionally also of *Vishṇu* ; described as sons of *Pulastya* , of *Pulaha* , of *Kaṣyapa* , of *Khasā* or *Krodhā* ; also as produced from the feet of *Brahmā* ; though generally regarded as beings of a benevolent and inoffensive disposition , like the *Yakṣa* in *Kālidāsa's Megha-dūta* , they are occasionally classed with *Piṣā* cas and other malignant spirits , and sometimes said to cause demoniacal possession ; as to their position in the Buddhist system）MBh.;（with Jainas）a subdivision of the *Vyantaras* ; N. of *Kubera*; of a *Muni* ; of a son of *Śvaphāka*; of *Indra's* palace ; a dog ;

14.2.3.（*ā*）f. N. of a woman;

14.2.4.（*ī*）f. a female *Yakṣa* MBh.; N. of *Kubera's* wife.

14.3. 【梵漢辭典,p1501】（中性）顯現，形態，超自然的存在，妖怪（吠陀）

（陽性名詞）Kubera 神的侍者，半神類名稱；（經文）夜叉，勇健，能噉，能噉鬼，神，鬼神，傷者，藥叉。

15. राक्षसैः rākṣasaiḥ 名詞　羅刹鬼

15.1. 【詞尾變化】rākṣasaiḥ 為 rākṣasa 的陽性複數工具格形，所以字典查 rākṣasa。

15.2. 資料前面已有說明。

【筆者試譯】：旗幡與旗幡相連著，正亮麗著，
鐘鈴聲響不斷地交錯著，
伴隨著眾華、薰香與如此的樂音，
人，天人與非人夜叉，羅刹鬼們都敬拜供養著（佛陀）！

【什公漢譯】：一一塔廟，各千幢幡，珠交露幔，寶鈴和鳴。
諸天龍神，人及非人，香華伎樂，常以供養。

【英 譯 本】：They are always decorated with flags; a multitude
of bells is constantly heard sounding; men,
gods, goblins, and Titans pay their worship with
flowers, perfumes, and music.

【信譯研究】：信譯。但鳩摩羅什以八句偈來翻譯原文。

【第四十七頌】

कारापयन्ती सुगतस्य पुत्रा
जिनान धातुष्विह पूजमीदृशीम्।
येभिर्दिशायो दश शोभिता यः
सुपुष्पितैर्वा यथ पारिजातैः॥४७॥

【羅馬譯音】

kārāpayantī sugatasya putrā
jināna dhātuṣviha pūjamīdṛśīm|
yebhirdiśāyo daśa śobhitā yaḥ
supuṣpitairvā yatha pārijātaiḥ||47||

【句義解析】

kārāpayantī sugatasya putrā
jināna dhātuṣv iha pūjam īdṛśīm|
yebhir diśāyo daśa śobhitāyaḥ
supuṣpitair vā yatha pārijātaiḥ||47||

【辭彙研究】

1. कारापयन्ती kārāpayantī 動詞　安置；監護

1.1. 【詞尾變化】kārāpayantī 是由 kāra-ā 與 payantī 結合而成，形成 kāra-ā（形容詞副詞化）-√pā。但√pā 前面資料已有說明，所以字典找 kāra。

1.2. 【摩威梵英,p274】

1.2.1. mf（ī）n.（√1. *kṛ*）, making , doing , working , a maker , doer; an author; m.（ifc.）an act , action; the term used in designating a letter or sound or indeclinable word; effort , exertion; determination; religious austerity; a husband , master , lord;（*as* or *ā*）m. or f. act of worship , song of praise;（*ī*）f. N. of a plant.

1.2.2. m.（= 2. %{kara}）tax , toll , royal revenue Pa1n2. 6-3 , 10 ; a heap of snow or a mountain covered with it L. ;（mfn.）produced by hail.

1.2.3. m.（2. *kṛ*）, a song or hymn of praise; a battle song RV.

1.2.4. m.（2. *kṝ*）, killing , slaughter.

1.3. 【梵漢辭典,p566】

1.3.1.（形容詞,-ī）作，爲，產生，形成，履行；（陽性名詞）作者，製造者，著作者，作爲，動作，禮拜，静哩，讚歌，軍歌；（經文）作，用，作用，功力，主。

1.3.2. 行動，動作，音，字；質詞（不變化詞）；（經文）作聲，字。

2. धातुष्व् dhātuṣv 名詞　舍利

2.1. 【詞尾變化】dhātuṣv 疑似 dhātu 的複數於格形 dhātuṣu。所以字典查 dhātu。〔註 56〕

2.2. 資料前面已有說明。

〔註 56〕請見江島惠教等編《梵藏漢法華經原典總索引》，東京：靈友會出版，1988 年出版。頁 524。

3. पूजम् pūjam 形容詞　恭敬；奉事

3.1. 【詞尾變化】pūjam 是 pūjā 的單數對格形，所以字典查 pūjā。

3.2. 【摩威梵英,p641】f. honour , worship , respect , reverence , veneration , homage to superiors or adoration of the gods MBh.

3.3. 【梵漢辭典,p984】（陰性形容詞）尊敬，敬重；敬意，崇拜，尊崇；禮拜，供養；慇勤接待；（經文）供，供養，供具，恭敬供養，奉事，奉獻，愛敬，思遇，所宗，供，利養，供養。

4. ईदृशीम् īdṛśīm 形容詞　如此

4.1. 【詞尾變化】īdṛśīm 是 īdṛśī 的單數對格，也就是 īdṛśa 的陰性形。所以字典查 īdṛśa。

4.2. 資料前面已有說明。

5. येभिर् yebhir 關係代名詞　作爲～；身爲～

5.1. 【詞尾變化】yebhir 根據連音規則從 yebhiḥ 變化過來，爲 ya+ebhiḥ 所形成，即 ya+ayam 的陽性工具格複數形。所以字典查 ya 與 ayam。

5.2. 資料前面已有說明。

6. दिशायो diśāyo 形容詞　方向；方角

6.1. 【詞尾變化】diśāyo 根據連音規則是疑似從 diśāyāḥ 變化過來，也就是 diśā 的陰性從格單數形。〔註 57〕

6.2. 資料前面已有說明。

7. शोभितायः śobhitāyaḥ 形容詞　美麗；莊嚴

7.1. 【詞尾變化】śobhitāyaḥ 疑似爲 śobhitāya，也就是 śobhita 的陽性單數爲格形，字典查 śobhita。〔註 58〕

7.2. 【摩威梵英,p1092】mfn.（mostly ifc.）splendid , beautiful , adorned or embellished by MBh.

7.3. 【梵漢辭典,p1187】（經文）莊嚴，眾寶莊嚴，特殊妙好。

8. सुपुष्पितैर् supuṣpitair 形容詞　充滿美麗的花卉

〔註 57〕請見江島惠教等編《梵藏漢法華經原典總索引》，東京：靈友會出版，1988 年出版。頁 472。

〔註 58〕請見江島惠教等編《梵藏漢法華經原典總索引》，東京：靈友會出版，1988 年出版。頁 989。

8.1. 【詞尾變化】supuṣpitair 根據連音規則是從 supuṣpitaiḥ 變化過來，supuṣpita 的陽性工具格複數，字典查 supuṣpita。

8.2. 【摩威梵英,p1228】mfn. having beautiful flowers , abounding with flowers （*e* ind. `on a place abounding with flowers'）MBh.; having the hair bristling（with delight）.

8.3. 【梵漢辭典,p1238】（名稱動詞）（過去被動分詞）（形容詞）充滿花卉的；（經文）華開敷；生妙花。

9. वा vā 質詞　正好是；如同

9.1. 【詞尾變化】沒有詞尾變化。

9.2. 【摩威梵英,p934】

9.2.1. ind. or RV.（often used in disjunctive sentences ; *vā-vā* , `either'- `or ' , `on the one side'' - `on the other' ; *na vā* - *vā* or *na* - *vā* , `neither'- ` nor' ; *vā na-vā* , `either not'-` or '' ; *yadi vā-vā* , `whether'-` or ' ; in a sentence containing more than two members *vā* is nearly always repeated , although if a negative is in the first clause it need not be so repeated ; *vā* is sometimes interchangeable with *ca* and *api* , and is frequently combined with other particles , esp. with *atha* , *atho* , *uta* , *kim* , *yad* , *yadi* q.v. 〔e.g. *atha vā* , `or else'〕 ; it is also sometimes used as an expletive）; either-or not , optionally（in gram. *vā* is used in a rule to denote its being optional）; as , like（= *iva*）MBh.; just , even , indeed , very（= *eva* , laying stress on the preceding word）; but even if , even supposing（followed by a future）; however , nevertheless;（after a rel. or interr.）possibly , perhaps , I dare say MBh.（e.g. *kiṃ vā śakuntalety asya mātur ākhyā* , ` is his mother's name perhaps *Śakuntalā*? ' ; *ko vā* or *ke vā* followed by a negative may in such cases be translated by `every one , all' e.g. *ke vā na syuḥ paribhava-padaṃ niṣphalāram-bha-yatnāḥ* '' everybody whose efforts are fruitless is an object of contempt'）.

9.3. 【梵漢辭典,p1364】

9.3.1.（附屬）（質詞）〔一般出現於字後，但隨韻律之不同偶爾也出現在字前〕；是～或～，任意地；〔=iva〕，如～，與～同樣地，猶如～地；（經文）如，〔=eva〕正好；但是，然而（少用）；

9.3.2. 連，即使是，可能，但願；（經文）若，或，及，麼然。

10. पारिजातैः pārijātaiḥ 名詞　珊瑚樹

10.1. 【詞尾變化】pārijātaiḥ 是 pārijāta 的陽性複數工具格形，所以字典查 pārijāta。

10.2. 【摩威梵英,p621】

10.2.1. m. the coral tree , Erythrina Indica（losing its leaves in June and then covered with large crimson flowers）MBh.; the wood of this tree ; N. of one of the 5 trees of paradise produced at the churning of the ocean and taken possession of by Indra from whom it was afterwards taken by *Kṛṣṇa*）MBh.; fragrance ; N. of sev. wks.（esp. ifc. ; cf. *dāna-*）; of a *Nāga* MBh. ; of a Ṛśi ib. ; of an author of Mantras（with Śiktas）;

10.2.2. *-ka* m. the coral tree or its wood; N. of a Ṛśi MBh. ; of other men（*-ratnākara* m. N. of wk.）;

10.2.3. m. or n. N. of a drama（= *-ta-karaṇa*）;

10.2.4. *-maya* mf（*ī*）n. made of flowers of the celestial;

10.2.5. *-ratnākara* m. N. of wk.（prob. = *-taka-ratn-*）;

10.2.6. *-vat* mfn. possessing the celñcelestial;

10.2.7. *-vṛtta-kkaṇḍa* n. *-vyākaraṇa* n. N. of wks. ;

10.2.8. *-sarasvatī-mantra* m. pl. N. of Partic. magical formulas;

10.2.9. *-haraṇa* n. `robbing the *Pāri* tree 'N. of chs. of Hariv. and VP. , also of a comedy by Gopa1la.dasa ;

10.2.10.（*ṇa-campū*）f. N. of a poem）; *-tācala-māhātmya* n. N. of wk.

10.3. 【梵漢辭典,p854】（陽性名詞）珊瑚樹〔具有深紅花的植物，學名 *Erythrina indica*〕；*Pārijāta* 樹的木材；〔天國中的神話之樹（據說在大海翻攪時所生，屬 *Indra* 神所有，後來由 *Kṛṣṇa* 神自 *Indra* 神取來）〕；（經文）圓生樹，圓綵樹，天樹王。

【筆者試譯】：安置了佛子們，
在佛陀舍利此處恭敬奉事，
這些人從十方前來裝飾（佛舍利塔廟）
如同佈滿了美麗花卉般地裝飾，像顆珊瑚樹那樣。

【什公漢譯】：文殊師利，諸佛子等，為供舍利，嚴飾塔廟，
國界自然，殊特妙好，如天樹王，其華開敷。

【英 譯 本】：Such honour do the sons of the Sugata render
to the relics of the Ginas, so that all directions of
space are brightened as by the celestial coral trees
in full blossom.

【信譯研究】：信譯。但鳩摩羅什用八句中文詩句翻譯，而這裡加了一句梵文本上所沒有的「文殊師利」，但不妨礙經意。

【第四十八頌】

अहं चिमाश्चो बहुप्राणकोट्य
इह स्थिताः पश्यिषु सर्वमेतत्।
प्रपुष्पितं लोकमिमं सदेवकं
जिनेन मुक्ता इयमेकरश्मिः॥४८॥

【羅馬譯音】

ahaṁ cimāśco bahuprāṇakoṭya
iha sthitāḥ paśyiṣu sarvametat|
prapuṣpitaṁ lokamimaṁ sadevakaṁ
jinena muktā iyamekaraśmiḥ||48||

【句義解析】

ahaṁ cimāś co bahu-prāṇa-koṭya
iha sthitāḥ paśyiṣu sarvam etat|
prapuṣpitaṁ lokam imaṁ sadevakaṁ
jinena muktā iyam eka-raśmiḥ||48||

【辭彙研究】

1. अहं ahaṁ 代名詞 我

1.1. 【詞尾變化】根據連音規則 ahaṁ 因為後面接 cimāś，是從 aham 變過來

的。所以字典查 aham。

1.2. 資料前面已有說明。

2. चिमाश् चो cimāś co 與這些

2.1. 【詞尾變化】cimāś co 根據連音規則，是從 cimāḥ co 變化過來，co 據學者研究，就是等於 ca，〔註 59〕而 cimāḥ 部分，日本學者荻原雲來與土田勝彌認爲 cimāḥ 應該是 c'imāḥ，〔註 60〕戶田宏文校訂的尼泊爾國立公文書館所藏的梵文法華經（No.4-21）寫本也是這樣的寫法。〔註 61〕今採此說。而 c'imāḥ 疑爲 caimāḥ，即 ca 與 imāḥ 的結合。imāḥ 爲 idam 的複數主格形。所以字典查 idam。

2.2. 資料前面已有說明。

3. स्थिताः sthitāḥ 過去被動分詞 站立；在

3.1. 【詞尾變化】sthitāḥ 爲 sthita 的主格複數形，字典查 sthita。

3.2. 資料前面已有說明。

4. पश्यिषु paśyiṣu 動詞 看見

4.1. 【詞尾變化】paśyiṣu 根據學者研究，字根爲√paś，〔註 62〕字典查√paś。

4.2. 資料前面已有說明。

5. सर्वम् sarvam 形容詞 一切的

5.1. 【詞尾變化】sarvam 是 sarva 的陽性單數對格形，字典查 sarva。

5.2. 資料前面已有說明。

6. एतत् etat 代名詞 此

6.1. 【詞尾變化】etat 是 etad 的單數主格形，所以字典查 etad。

6.2. 資料前面已有說明。

7. प्रपुष्पितं prapuṣpitaṁ 過去被動分詞／形容詞 開滿花的

7.1. 【詞尾變化】根據連音規則，prapuṣpitaṁ 是從 prapuṣpitam 變化過來，

〔註 59〕請見江島惠教等編《梵藏漢法華經原典總索引》，東京：靈友會出版，1988 年出版。頁 375。

〔註 60〕請見荻原雲來、土田勝彌所編《改訂梵文法華經》，東京：山喜房佛書林，1994 年出版。頁 13。

〔註 61〕請見户田宏文所編《Sanskrit Lotus Sutra Manuscript from the National Archives of Nepal（Romanized Text）》，東京：創價學會，2001 年出版。頁 18。

〔註 62〕請見江島惠教等編《梵藏漢法華經原典總索引》，東京：靈友會出版，1988 年出版。頁 621。

而 prapuṣpitam 是 pra 與 puṣpitam 兩個字結合，而 puṣpitam 是 puṣpita 的中性單數主格形。puṣpita 則是√puṣp，也就是√puṣpa 的異寫體的過去被動分詞。所以字典查 pra-√puṣpa。

7.2. 資料前面已有說明。

8. लोकम् lokam 名詞 地方

8.1. 【詞尾變化】lokam 是 loka 的陽性單數對格形，所以字典查 loka。

8.2. 資料前面已有說明。

9. इमं imaṁ 代名詞 這個

9.1. 【詞尾變化】imaṁ 根據連音規則是從 imam 變化過來，是 idam 的陽性單數對格形，所以字典查 idam。

9.2. 資料前面已有說明。

10. सदेवकं sadevakaṁ 形容詞 這天人的

10.1. 【詞尾變化】sadevakaṁ 根據連音規則是從 sadevakam 變化過來，而 sadevakam 是 sadevaka 的陽性單數對格形。而 sadevaka 爲 sa 與 devaka 的結合，sa 前面已有說明，故字典查 devaka。

10.2. 【摩威梵英,p495】

10.2.1. mf（*ikā*）n. who or what sports or plays; divine , celestial id. ;

10.2.2. m.（*div*）a god , deity（at the end of an adj. comp.）MBh.; N. of a man（?）RV.; of a *Gandharva*（at once a prince , son of *Āhuka* and father of *Devakī*〔below〕MBh. ;）of a son of *Yudhi-shṭhira* and *Yaudheyī* or *Pauravī* ; familiar N. for *deva-dattaka*; pl. N. of the *Śūdras* in *Krauñca-dvīpa* BhP. ;

10.2.3.（*ā*）f. fam. for *deva-dattikā*;

10.2.4.（*devikā*）f. N. of a class of goddesses of an inferior order（pl. the oblations made to them , viz. to *Anu-matī* , *Rākā* , *Sinīvalī* , *Kuhū* , and to *Dhātṛi* TS. ;）; of the wife of *Yudhishṭhira* and mother of *Yaudheya* MBh; of a river MBh.; of a country; the thorn-apple;

10.2.5.（*devakī*）f. see below.

10.3. 【梵漢辭典,p359】（形容詞）=deva，天堂的，天人的。

11. जिनेन jinena 名詞 勝者，佛陀

11.1. 【詞尾變化】jinena 是 jina 的單數工具格形，所以字典查 jina。
11.2. 資料前面已有說明。

12. मुक्ता muktā 動詞／過去被動分詞　放射；釋放
12.1. 【詞尾變化】Muktā 是√muc 的過去被動分詞形，所以字典查√muc。
12.2. 資料前面已有說明。

13. इयम् iyam 代名詞　此；這個
13.1.【詞尾變化】iyam 是 ayam 的陰性代名詞單數主格形，所以字典查 ayam。
13.2. 資料前面已有說明。

14. रश्मिः raśmiḥ 形容詞　光明
14.1. 【詞尾變化】raśmiḥ 是 raśmi 的陽性主格單數形，所以字典查 raśmi。
14.2. 資料前面已有說明。

【筆者試譯】：我和這些百千萬億無量眾生，
在這裡看見這一切。
天人國界的花開燦爛，
從佛陀這裡發出一道光明

【什公漢譯】：佛放一光，我及眾會，見此國界，種種殊妙。

【英 譯 本】：From this spot I behold all this; those numerous
kotis of creatures; both this world and
heaven covered with flowers, owing to the single
ray shot forth by the Gina.

【信譯研究】：信譯。

【第四十九頌】

अहो प्रभावः पुरुषर्षभस्य
अहोऽस्य ज्ञानं विपुलं अनास्रवम्।
यस्यैकरश्मिः प्रसृताद्य लोके
दर्शेति क्षेत्राण बहू सहस्रान्॥४९॥

【羅馬譯音】

aho prabhāvaḥ puruṣarṣabhasya
aho'sya jñānaṁ vipulaṁ anāsravam|
yasyaikaraśmiḥ prasṛtādya loke
darśeti kṣetrāṇa bahū sahasrān||49||

【句義解析】

aho prabhāvaḥ puruṣa-rṣabhasya
aho 'sya jñānaṁ vipulaṁ anāsravam|
Yasyaika-raśmiḥ prasṛtā dya loke
darśeti kṣetrāṇa bahū sahasrān||49||

【辭彙研究】

1. अहो aho 感歎詞　表示喜悅，讚賞

1.1 【詞尾變化】沒有詞尾變化。

1.2 【摩威梵英,p126】

1.2.1（instead of *ahā*〔= *ahar*〕 in comp. before the letter *r*）. often ifc. *aha* m. or n.; see also *ahna*.

1.2.2 ind. a particle（implying joyful or painful surprise）Ah!（of enjoyment or satisfaction）Oh!（of fatigue , discontent , compassion , sorrow , regret）*Alas*! *Ah*!（of praise）*Bravo*!（of reproach）*Fie*!（of calling *Kum.*）*Ho*! *Halo*!（of contempt）*Pshaw*! Often combined with other particles of similar signification , as *aho dhik* or *dhig aho* , *aho bata.*

1.3 【梵漢辭典,p50】

1.3.1（感歎詞）〔表示喜悅，悲痛，驚愕，生氣，讚賞，斥責等之感歎詞〕；（經文）嗚呼；大哉；奇哉，稀有，甚奇稀有；快哉。

2. प्रभाव: prabhāvaḥ 名詞　神力；神通

2.1 【詞尾變化】prabhāvaḥ 是 prabhāva 的陽性單數主格形，所以字典查 prabhāva。

2.2 【摩威梵英,p684】

2.2.1 m.（ifc. f. *ā*）might , power , majesty , dignity , strength , efficacy MBh.

（-*veṇa* , -*vāt* and -*vatas* ind. by means or in consequence of , through , by）; supernatural power; splendour , beauty MBh.; tranquillizing , conciliation （?）; N. of the chapters of the *Rasikapriyā*; N. of a son of Manu *Sva-rocis*;

2.2.2 -*ja* mfn. proceeding from conscious majesty or power;

2.2.3 -*tva* n. power , strength Ka1m. ;

2.2.4 -*vat* mfn. powerful , strong , mighty MBh.

2.3 【梵漢辭典,p900】（陽性名詞）力，威嚴；品位；超自然力；效能；統治（位格）的權力；壯麗，華美；（經文）威，威勢，威德，力，威力，威神力，威神之力，威神自在力，威光，神便威力，神力，勢力，自在力，功力，功能，勢用；通，神通，妙，殊妙，眞妙，妙莊嚴；光明。

3. र्षभस्य rṣabhasya 形容詞　屬於傑出的；超群的

3.1 【詞尾變化】rṣabhasya 是 rṣabha 的陽性單數屬格形，故字典查 rṣabha。

3.2 資料前面已有說明。

4. अहोऽस्य aho 'sya 代名詞　確實地這個

4.1 【詞尾變化】aho 'sya 根據連音規則是從 ahaḥ asya 變化過來。ahaḥ 就是 aha 的陽性單數主格形。asya 則是 idam 的單數陽性屬格形。這裡字典查 aha。

4.2 【摩威梵英,p124】

4.2.1 ind.（as a particle implying ascertainment , affirmation , certainty）surely , certainly RV.;（as explaining , defining）namely;（as admitting , limiting）it is true , I grant , granted , indeed , at least 〔For the rules of accentuation necessitated in a phrase by the particle *aha*.

4.2.2 n.（only Ved. ; nom. pl. *ahā* RV. AV. ; gen. pl. ahānām RV）= *aḥar* q.v. , a day ;

4.2.3 often ifc. aha m. or n. ; see also *ahna* s.v.

4.3 【梵漢辭典,p48】

4.3.1（質詞）確實地，當然，實在地，正好，亦即，至少；〔經常僅用來強調先行之語詞〕。

4.3.2（中性名詞）〔--° 大致爲（陽性）〕日，晝；（經文）日。

5. ज्ञानं jñānaṁ 名詞　智慧

5.1 【詞尾變化】jñānaṁ 根據連音規則是從 jñānam 變化過來，也就是 jñāna 的陽性單數主格形。所以字典查 jñāna。

5.2 資料前面已有說明。

6. विपुलं vipulaṁ 形容詞　廣大的

6.1 【詞尾變化】vipulaṁ 根據連音規則是從 vipulam 變化過來的，而 vipulam 則是 vipula 的陽性單數對格形。字典查 vipula。

6.2 【摩威梵英,p975】

6.2.1 mf(*ā*)n.(prob. fr. *pula* = *pura* ; cf. under √*pul*)large , extensive , wide , great , thick , long（also of time）, abundant , numerous , important , loud（as a noise）, noble（as a race）MBh.;

6.2.2 m. a respectable man; N. of a prince of the Sauviras MBh. ; of a pupil of *Deva-śarman*（who guarded the virtue of *Ruci* , his preceptor's wife , when tempted by Indra during her husband's absence）MBh. ; of a son of *Vasu-deva* BhP. ; of a mountain（either *Meru* or the *Himālaya*）;

6.2.3(*ā*)f. the earth; a form of the *Āryā* metre(in which the caesura is irregular ; divided into 3 species , *Ādi-* , *Aṇya-* , and *Ubhaya-vipulā*）;（in music）a kind of measure *Saṃgīt.* ;

6.2.4 n. a sort of building;

6.2.5 -*grīva* mfn. long-necked R. ;

6.2.6 -*cchāya* mfn. having ample shade , shady , umbrageous;

6.2.7 -*jaghanā* f. a woman with large hips ib. ;

6.2.8 -*tara* mfn. larger or very large;

6.2.9 –*tā* f., -*tva* n.（MBh.）largeness , greatness , extent , width , magnitude ;

6.2.10 dravya mfn. having great wealth , wealthy;

6.2.11 -*pārśva* m. N. of a mountain Buddh. ;

6.2.12 -*prajña*（MBh.）, -*buddhi* mfn. endowed with great understanding ;

6.2.13 -*mati* mfn. id. ;

6.2.14 m. N. of a Bodhi-sattva Buddh. ;

6.2.15 -*rasa* m. `having abundant juice' , the sugar-cane;

6.2.16 -*vrata* mfn. one who has undertaken great duties MBh. ;

6.2.17 -*śroni* mf（*ī*）n. having swelling hips;

6.2.18（-*ṇī-bhara* mf〔*ā*〕n. id. Amar.）;

6.2.19 -*skandha* m. `broad-shouldered' N. of Arjuna ;

6.2.20 -*sravā* f. = -*lāsravā* L. ;

6.2.21 -*hṛdaya* mfn. large-hearted , large-minded（v.l.）;

6.2.22 -*lāyatākṣa* mfn. having large and long eyes;

6.2.23 -*lārtha-bhoga-vat* mfn. having great wealth and many enjoyments;

6.2.24 -*lāśravā* f. Aloe Perfoliata ;

6.2.25 -*lekṣaṇa* mfn. large-eyed ;

6.2.26 -*loraska* mfn. broad-chested ib. ;

6.2.27 -*laūjas* mfn. having great strength , very strong.

6.3 【梵漢辭典,p1447】（形容詞）〔=vipura:起自 Pṛ 1.〕大的，廣大的，擴展的，廣闊的，後的，長的（或就時間而言），深的，許多的，眾多的，豐富的，多數的，高的（聲音）;（經文）大，多，廣，寬，柏，大大，廣博，最大，廣大，弘廣，寬博，彌曠，無量。

7. अनास्रवम् anāsravam 形容詞　無有煩惱的；無漏的

7.1 【詞尾變化】anāsravam 是 anāsrava 的陽性單數對格形，所以字典查 anāsrava。或是 an-āsrava 情況下，查 āsrava。

7.2 【摩威梵英,p162, āsrava】m. the foam on boiling rice; a door opening into water and allowing the stream to descend through it;（with Jainas）the action of the senses which impels the soul towards external objects（one of the seven Sattvas or substances ; it is two fold , as good or evil）; distress , affliction , pain.

7.3 所以 an—āsrava 就是 non—foam on boiling rice; non-distress。

7.4 【梵漢辭典,p90】（陽性形容詞）脫離有漏煩惱;（經文）淨，無漏，無流。

8. यस्यैक Yasyaika 代名詞　做爲這一個

8.1 【詞尾變化】根據連音規則，Yasyaika 可拆解成 Yasya eka，eka 爲一的意思。Yasya 爲 ya 的陽性單數屬格。字典查 ya。

8.2 資料前面已有說明。

9. प्रसृता द्य prasṛtā dya 片段語詞　今日遍滿

9.1 【詞尾變化】prasṛtā dya 根據連音規 則可拆解成 prasṛta adya 這兩個字。prasṛta 爲「遍滿」，而「今日」。兩者均無詞尾變化。

9.2 資料前面已有說明。

10. लोके loke 名詞　國界；國土

10.1 【詞尾變化】loke 是 loka 的陽性單數於格形，所以字典查 loka。

10.2 資料前面已有說明。

11. दर्शेति darśeti 動詞　使看見

11.1 【詞尾變化】darśeti 似以 Prakrit 規則爲√dṛś 的現在式第三人稱複數形變化，所以字典查√dṛś。

11.2 資料前面已有說明。

12. क्षेत्राण kṣetrāṇa 名詞　領地；地點

12.1 【詞尾變化】kṣetrāṇa 疑似 kṣetra 的中單數工具格（非梵文變化，其字根確定爲 kṣetra），字典查 kṣetra。

12.2 資料前面已有說明。

13. बहू bahū 形容詞　多量的

13.1 【詞尾變化】bahū 是 bahu 陽性主格複數形。（非梵文變化，其字根確定爲 bahu）字典查 bahu。

13.2 資料前面已有說明。

14. सहस्रान् sahasrān 形容詞　千；數千

14.1 【詞尾變化】sahasrān 是 sahasra 的複數對格形，字典查 sahasra。

14.2 資料前面已有說明。

【筆者試譯】：偉大啊！那佛陀勝者的威德啊！
確實這個智慧廣大，無有煩惱的（佛陀），
他此刻那一道光芒照亮了整個國土，
讓眾多無量的國土（眾生）都看見了。

【什公漢譯】：諸佛神力，智慧希有，放一淨光，照無量國。

【英 譯 本】：O how powerful is the Leader of men! how
extensive and bright is his knowledge ! that a single
beam darted by him over the world renders visible
so many thousands of fields!

【信譯研究】：信譯。這裡梵文偈頌裡出現了幾個非梵文的單字，可能是俗語（Prakrit）。

【第五十頌】

आश्चर्यप्राप्ताः स्म निमित्त दृष्ट्वा

इममीदृशं चाद्भुतमप्रमेयम्।

वदस्व मञ्जुस्वर एतमर्थं

कौतूहलं ह्यपनय बुद्धपुत्र॥५०॥

【羅馬譯音】

āścaryaprāptāḥ sma nimitta dṛṣṭvā

imamīdṛśaṁ cādbhutamaprameyam|

vadasva mañjusvara etamarthaṁ

kautūhalaṁ hyapanaya buddhaputra||50||

【句義解析】

Āścarya-prāptāḥ sma nimitta dṛṣṭvā

Imam īdṛśaṁ cādbhutam aprameyam|

vadasva Mañjusvara etam arthaṁ

kautūhalaṁ hy apanaya Buddha-putra||50||

【辭彙研究】

1. प्राप्ताः prāptāḥ 形容詞　到達；成就

1.1 【詞尾變化】prāptāḥ 是 prāpta 的陽性單數主格形，所以字典查 prāpta。

1.2 資料前面已有說明。

2. दृष्ट्वा dṛṣṭvā 動名詞　看見；注意到

2.1 【詞尾變化】dṛṣṭvā 是√dṛś 的動名詞，字典查√dṛś。

2.2 資料前面已有說明。

3. ईदृशं īdṛśaṁ 形容詞　如是；就是這樣

3.1 【詞尾變化】īdṛśaṁ 根據連音規則，是從 īdṛśam 變化過來，而 īdṛśam 是 īdṛśa 的陽性單數對格形，所以字典查 īdṛśa。

3.2 資料前面已有說明。

4. चाद्भुतम् cādbhutam 形容詞　稀有奇特的；不可思議的

4.1 【詞尾變化】cādbhutam 根據連音規則，是 ca 與 adbhutam 結合而成。Ca 爲「與」，而 adbhutam 是 adbhuta 的單數對格形，所以字典查 adbhuta。

4.2 資料前面已有說明。

5. अप्रमेयम् aprameyam 未來被動分詞／形容詞　不可測的；不可限量的

5.1 【詞尾變化】aprameyam 是 aprameya 的陽性單數對格形，所以字典查 aprameya。

5.2 【摩威梵英,p58】mfn. immeasurable , unlimited , unfathomable; not to be proved.

5.3 【梵漢辭典,p142】

5.3.1（未來被動分詞）無量，無限，無邊，不可分的，不可舉證的；（經文）無量，無限，無邊，不可量，無邊量，不可度量，莫能限量。（數詞）（經文）無邊。

5.3.2（未來被動分詞）（經文）無量，無邊，無量無邊。

6. वदस्व vadasva 動詞　你告訴；說

6.1 【詞尾變化】vadasva 是√vad 的祈使句第二人稱單數形，所以字典查√vad。

6.2 資料前面已有說明。

7. मञ्जुस्वर Mañjusvara 名詞　文殊師利菩薩

7.1 【詞尾變化】沒有詞尾變化。

7.2 【摩威梵英,p774】

7.2.1 mfn. id. MBh. ;

7.2.2 m.= -*śrī* Buddh.

7.3 【梵漢辭典,p706】（形容詞）和悅的聲音。（陽性）（經文）〔佛名〕妙音，（譯音）〔菩薩名=Mañju-śrī〕文殊師利菩薩。

8. अर्थं arthaṁ 名詞　動機

8.1 【詞尾變化】arthaṁ 根據連音規則是從 artham 變化過來，而 artham 是 artha 的陽性單數對格形，所以字典查 artha。

8.2 資料前面已有說明。

9. कौतूहलं kautūhalaṁ 名詞　好奇心；疑心

9.1 【詞尾變化】kautūhalaṁ 根據連音規則是從 kautūhalam 變化過來，而 kautūhalam 是 kautūhala 的中性單數對格形，所以字典查 kautūhala。

9.2 資料前面已有說明。

10. ह्य hy 不變格　由於～緣故

10.1 【詞尾變化】hy 因爲後面接 apanaya 的關係，是從 hi 變化過來。故字典查 hi。

10.2 資料前面已有說明。

11. अपनय apanaya 形容詞　除去；排解

11.1 【詞尾變化】沒有詞尾變化。

11.2 【摩威梵英,p49】m. leading away , taking away ; bad policy , bad or wicked conduct.

11.3 【梵漢辭典,p131】

11.3.1（陽性）（形容詞）除去；否決；排拒；（經文）除，除去，拔去，離，令離，遠離，永離；息，怯；破；開解。

11.3.2（陽性）（名詞）輕率，愚昧之舉動；壞主意，惡行。

【筆者試譯】：他們看見了如此不可思議成就的瑞相，
這般如此稀有而不可測的（神變）！
文殊師利菩薩！你說說這個因緣，
就爲了怯除佛子們的疑惑吧！

【什公漢譯】：我等見此，得未曾有，佛子文殊，願決眾疑。

【英譯本】：we are astonished at seeing this sign and
this wonder, so great, so incomprehensible.
Explain me the matter, O Mañgusvara! the sons of
Buddha are anxious to know it.

【信譯研究】：信譯。

【第五十一頌】

चत्वारिमा पर्ष उदग्रचित्ता-

स्त्वां चाभिवीक्षन्तिह मां च वीर।
जनेहि हर्षं व्यपनेहि काङ्क्षां
त्वं व्याकरोही सुगतस्य पुत्र॥५१॥

【羅馬譯音】

catvārimā parṣa udagracittā-
stvāṁ cābhivīkṣantiha māṁ ca vīra|
janehi harṣaṁ vyapanehi kāṅkṣāṁ
tvaṁ vyākarohī sugatasya putra||51||

【句義解析】

Catvār imā parṣa udagra-cittās
tvāṁ cābhivīkṣant iha māṁ ca vīra|
janehi harṣaṁ vyapanehi kāṅkṣāṁ
tvaṁ vyākarohī sugatasya putra||51||

【辭彙研究】

1. चत्वार् Catvār 形容詞，數詞　四

1.1 【詞尾變化】Catvār 是 catur 的（陽性／中性）〔強幹形〕。

1.2 資料前面已有說明。

2. पर्ष parṣa 形容詞　堆，群

2.1 【詞尾變化】沒有詞尾變化。

2.2 【摩威梵英,p609】

2.2.1 m.（√ parṣ , pṛṣ?）a bundle , sheaf RV.

2.2.2 mfn. = paruṣa , rough , violent（as wind）BhP.

2.3 【梵漢辭典,p869】（形容詞）=paruṣa;粗暴的，猛烈的（風）。

2.4 【譯筆研究】這裡明顯地，梵漢辭典的部份漏錄一筆，也就是【摩威梵英,p609】第一個意思：a bundle，一大堆人。這裡根據前後文，取其義。

3. उदग्र udagra 形容詞　興奮

3.1 【詞尾變化】沒有詞尾變化。

3.2 【摩威梵英,p184】mfn. having the top elevated or upwards , over-topping , towering or pointing upwards , projecting ; high , tall , long; increased , large , vast , fierce , intense; haughty Prasannar. ; advanced（in age）; excited , enraptured.

3.3 【梵漢辭典,p1315】（形容詞）（頂部朝上的），被舉起的，高的，長的，大的，高聳的，在高位的；由（--°）提高或增大的；老的（年齡）；因（--°）而激動的或暴怒的；（°--）非常地，極端地；（經文）明淨，歡喜踴躍。

4. चित्तास् cittās 形容詞／過去被動分詞　注意

4.1 【詞尾變化】cittās 根據連音規則是由於後面的 tvāṁ 關係，是從 cittāḥ 變化過來，也就是陽性複數主格形。字典查 citta。

4.2 資料前面已有說明。

5. त्वां tvāṁ 代名詞　你

5.1 【詞尾變化】tvāṁ 根據連音規則是從 tvām 變化過來，是 tvam 的陽性單數對格形。字典查 tvam。

5.2 資料前面已有說明。

6. चाभिवीक्षन्त cābhivīkṣant 動詞　看出

6.1 【詞尾變化】cābhivīkṣant 爲 ca 與 abhivīkṣant 的連接，而 abhivīkṣant 爲 abhi-vi-īkṣant 是從 abhi-vi-√īkṣ 變化過來的現在第三人稱複數形。所以字典查 abhi-vi-√īkṣ。

6.2 【摩威梵英,p61,abhi】ind.（a prefix to verbs and nouns , expressing）to , towards , into , over , upon.（As a prefix to verbs of motion）it expresses the notion or going towards , approaching ,（As a prefix to nouns not derived from verbs）it expresses superiority , intensity; e.g. abhi-tāmra, abhi-nava q.v.（As a separate adverb or preposition）it expresses（with acc.）to , towards , in the direction of , against ; into; for , for the sake of ; on account of ; on , upon , with regard to , by , before , in front of ; over. It may even express one after the other , severally e.g. vṛkṣaṃ vṛkṣam abhi , tree after tree.

6.3 【摩威梵英,p949,vi】2 n. an artificial word said to be = anna.

6.4 【摩威梵英,p170, √īkṣ】cl. 1. to see , look , view , behold , look at , gaze at ; to watch over（with acc. or rarely loc.）AV.; to see in one's mind , think , have a thought MBh.; to regard , consider Kum. ; to observe(the stars); to foretell for(dat. ; lit. to observe the stars for any one): Caus., to make one look at（with acc.）（This root is perhaps connected with.）

6.5 【梵漢辭典,p504, abhi-vi-√īkṣ】（動詞）觀看～，眺望；看出，認知；（經文）觀，瞻。

7. मां māṁ 代名詞　我

7.1 【詞尾變化】māṁ 根據連音規則是從 mām 變化過來，而 mām 則是 aham 的陽性對格單數形，所以字典查 aham。

7.2 資料前面已有說明。

8. वीर vīra 名詞　英雄；大丈夫

8.1 【詞尾變化】沒有詞尾變化。

8.2 【摩威梵英,p1005】

8.2.1 m. a man ,（esp.）a brave or eminent man , hero , chief（sometimes applied to gods , as to Indra , Vishṇu; pl. men , people , mankind , followers , retainers）RV.; a hero（as opp. to a god）; a husband MBh. ; a male child , son（collect. male progeny）RV. AV.;（collect. male progeny）RV. AV.; the male of an animal AV.;(with , *Tāntrikas*)an adept(who is between the *divya* and the *paśu*) Rudray. ; (in dram.) heroism (as one of the 8 Rasas〔q.v.〕; the *Vīra-carita*〔q.v.〕exhibits an example) ; an actor; a partic. Agni（son of Tapas）MBh. ; fire ,（esp.）sacred or sacrificial fire; N. of various plants（*Terminalia Arunja* ; Nerium Odorum ; Guilandina Bonduc , manioc-root）L. ; N. of an Asura MBh. ; of a son of *Dhṛita-rāśṭra* ib. ; of a son of *Bharad-vāja* ib. ; of a son of *Puruśa Vairāja* and father of *Priya-vrata* and *Uttāna-pāda*; of a son of *Gṛṇjima* ib. ; of two sons of *Kṛṣṇa* BhP. ; of a son of *Kṣupa* and father of *Viviṇśa* MārkP. ; of the father of *Līlāvatī* ib. ; of a teacher of Vinaya Buddh. ; of the last Arhat of the present *Avasarpiṇi*; of various authors;（pl.）of a class of gods under *Manu Tāmasa* BhP. ;

8.2.2（*ā*）f. a wife , matron（whose husband and sons are still alive）; an intoxicating beverage ib. ; N. of various plants and drugs（Flacourtia Cataphracta ; Convolvulus Paniculatus ; Gmelina Arborea ; the drug

Ela-vāluka &c.）；（in music）a partic. *Śruti Saṃgīt.* ; N. of the wife of *Bharad-vāja*; of the wife of Karaṃ-dhama MārkP. ; of a river MBh.;

8.2.3 n. a reed（Arundo Tibialis）; the root of ginger（?）; pepper ; rice-gruel ; the root of Costus Speciosus , of Andropogon Muricatus;

8.2.4 mf（*ā*）n. heroic , powerful , strong , excellent , eminent.

8.3 【梵漢辭典,p1447】（陽性）人，（尤指）有利的人，英雄；戰士，首長，領導者；〔單數及複數〕眾人，人民；部下，是從（複數）；英雄；〔諸神之名，尤指 Indra 神〕（吠陀）；丈夫（史詩）；男孩，兒子，（集合詞的）南的子孫（吠陀）；英雄氣概（rasa）（修辭）；〔人名〕；（經文）佛；勇，猛，勤，勇健，勇猛，雄猛；多利；耐苦，精勤不懈；能幹，不能退，無畏憚。

9. जनेहि janehi　名詞　由許多人

9.1 【詞尾變化】janehi 爲 jana 的 Prakrit 的工具格複數形變化，但這個字梵文、Prakrit 與巴利文都有，意思大致相同，但這個字是 Prakrit 的變化方法，是 jana 的陽性複數工具格形，是混合梵文的寫法。所以字典查 jana。〔註 63〕

9.2 【摩威梵英,p410】

9.2.1 mf（*ī*）n. \`generating' see puraṃ- ;

9.2.2 m.（g. *vṛṣādi*）creature ", living being , man , person , race, people , subjects（the sg. used collectively e.g. *daivya* or *divyā j-* " , divine race ' , the gods collectively RV. ; *mahat j-* , many people ; often ifc. denoting one person or a number of persons collectively , e.g. *preśya-* , *bandhu-* , *sakhī-*, qq. vv. ; with names of peoples; *ayaṃ janaḥ*, \`this person , these persons ' , I , we MBh; *eṣa j-*）RV.; the person nearest to the speaker（also with *ayam* or *asau* , this my lover "）; a common person , one of the

〔註 63〕有關佛教混合梵文文法變化，請見請見 Franklin Edgerton 編《Buddhist Hybrid Sanskrit Grammar And Dictionary》（I），published by Munshiram Manoharal Publishers Pvt. Ltd, Delhi, India,1993。P58。其餘有關 jana 的意思請見 Franklin Edgerton 編《Buddhist Hybrid Sanskrit Grammar And Dictionary》（II），published by Munshiram Manoharal Publishers Pvt. Ltd, Delhi, India,1993。p.237。T.W. Rhys Davids 與 William Stede 所編的《Pali-English Dictionary》,published by Motilal Banarsidass publishers Pvt. Ltd.,Delhi, India,2003, p.278.

people; the world beyond the *Mahar-loka*;

9.2.3（*-nā*）m.（g. *aśvādi*）N. of a man（with the patr.）;

9.2.4（*ā*）f. `birth', *a-jana* , the unborn.

9.3 【梵漢辭典,p521】（陽性名詞）生物，人，個人，民族，種族；人民，臣民；眾人〔常爲集合體之意--°〕（--°）之種或族，卑賤之人，此人；（經文）人，仁，男女，眾，眾生，有情；人民；者，眾生，諸人；世間。

10. हर्षं harṣaṁ 形容詞　歡喜；毛髮豎起的

10.1 【詞尾變化】harṣaṁ 根據連音規則是從 harṣam 變化過來，而 harṣam 是 harṣa 的陽性單數對格形，所以字典查 harṣa。

10.2 資料前面已有說明。

11. व्यपनेहि vyapanehi 形容詞　遍佈；充滿

11.1 【詞尾變化】vyapanehi 疑似爲 vyāpanehi 異寫，是 vyāpana 的陽性複數工具格形，其變化方式如同本偈頌內第九個單字混合梵文寫法相同。

11.2 【摩威梵英,p1037】n. spreading though , pervading , penetration , covering , filling.

11.3 【梵漢辭典,p1486】（中性形容詞）遍滿，充滿，瀰漫；（經文）遍滿。

12. काङ्क्षां kāṅkṣāṁ 名詞　願望；欲求

12.1 【詞尾變化】kāṅkṣāṁ 根據連音規則是從 kāṅkṣām 變化過來，而 kāṅkṣām 是 kāṅkṣā 的陰性單數對格形，所以字典查 kāṅkṣā。

12.2 【摩威梵英,p268】f.（ifc.）wish , desire , inclination.

12.3 【梵漢辭典,p563】（陰性名詞）願望，欲求，意向；（經文）求，悕求，愛，疑，疑惑，疑悔，狐疑，疑（網）；迷倒，顛倒；不決；惑。

13. व्याकरोही vyākarohī 動詞　解說

13.1 【詞尾變化】vyākarohī 根據學者研究是從 vyā-√kṛ 的強幹變化過來，故字典查 vyā-√kṛ）。

13.2 【摩威梵英,p1035】P. Ā. *-karoti* , *-kurute* , to undo , sever , divide , separate from（instr.）RV. AV.; to expound , explain , declare MBh. ;（with Buddhists）to predict（esp. future births）; to prophesy anything（acc.）about any one（acc.）; Pass. *-kriyate* , to be divided or separated.

13.3 【梵漢辭典,p606】（動詞）分開，區別；說明，解說，解答；就（對格）

作（對格）的決定性預言（佛教的術語）;（經文）示，說，解說，宣說，宣揚；答，作答，達嚴，能正答；記，記說，記別，計莂，授記，授其記，與授記，授與記別，授決。

【筆者試譯】：這裡有四種（階層）的人興奮注目著（世尊放大光明這件事情），
大家在這裡都看到了我，也看到了你這位大丈夫，
由於（這是）許多人心中共同的疑惑的緣故，
你向佛子們說明吧！

【什公漢譯】：四眾欣仰，瞻仁及我，世尊何故，放斯光明。

【英 譯 本】：The four classes of the congregation in joyful expectation gaze on thee, O hero, and on me; gladden（their hearts）; remove their doubts; grant a revelation, O son of Sugata!

【信譯研究】：信譯。

【第五十二頌】

किमर्थमेषः सुगतेन अद्य
प्रभास एतादृशको विमुक्तः।
अहो प्रभावः पुरुषर्षभस्य
अहोऽस्य ज्ञानं विपुलं विशुद्धम्॥५२॥

【羅馬譯音】

kimarthameṣaḥ sugatena adya
prabhāsa etādṛśako vimuktaḥ|
aho prabhāvaḥ puruṣarṣabhasya
aho'sya jñānaṁ vipulaṁ viśuddham||52||

【句義解析】

Kim artham eṣaḥ sugatena adya

prabhāsa etādṛśako vimuktaḥ|
aho prabhāvaḥ puruṣa-rṣabhasya
aho 'sya jñānaṁ vipulaṁ viśuddham||52||

【辭彙研究】

1. अर्थम् artham 名詞　原因，動機
 1.1 【詞尾變化】artham 是 artha 的陽性單數對格形，
 1.2 資料前面已有說明。
2. एषः eṣaḥ 代名詞　這個
 2.1 【詞尾變化】eṣaḥ 是 etad 的陽性單數主格形，所以字典查 etad。
 2.2 資料前面已有說明。
3. अद्य adya 副詞　今天
 3.1 【詞尾變化】沒有詞尾變化。
 3.2 【摩威梵英,p19】
  3.2.1 mfn. fit or proper to be eaten ;
  3.2.2（*am*）ifc.（cf. *annadya* , *havir adya*）n. food.
  3.2.3 2（Ved. *adyā*）ind.（fr. pronom. base *a* , this , with *dya* for *dyu* q.v. , Lat. *ho-dic*）, to-day ; now-a-days ; now.
 3.3 【梵漢辭典,p41】
  3.3.1（未來被動分詞）可吃的，可食的。
  3.3.2（吠陀，或 *ā*）（副詞）今日，今；（經文）今，今日。
4. प्रभास prabhāsa 名詞　耀眼；美麗
 4.1 【詞尾變化】沒有詞尾變化。
 4.2 【摩威梵英,p684】
  4.2.1 M. \`splendour' , \`beauty' N. of a Vasu MBh. ; of a being attendant on Skanda ib. ; of a deity under the 8th Manu;（with Jainas）of one of the 11 *Gaṇādhipas*; of a son of a minister of *Candraprabha* king of *Madra*;（pl.）N. of a race of *Ṛiśis* MBh. ;
  4.2.2 m. or n. N. of a celebrated place of pilgrimage on the west coast of the *Dekhan* near *Dvārakā* MBh.（also *-kṣetra* n. *-kṣetra-tīrtha* n. *-deśa* m.）;
 4.3 【梵漢辭典,p900】（陽性）（光輝）〔某 Vasu 之名〕;〔Candra-prabha 大

臣之子〕；（經文）光，光明，明，明照，普照，照明，光巍巍。

4.4 【譯筆研究】這裡值得我們注意的是，這個字在梵英字典的意思是以某種生物爲主（being attendant）的意思。沒有形容詞，但是佛典的譯語取其引申的形容詞，去除實質原義。

5. एतादृशको etādṛśako 形容詞 如此；此一

5.1 【詞尾變化】etādṛśako 根據連音規則，是從 etādṛśakaḥ 變化過來，而 etādṛśakaḥ 是 etādṛśaka 的陽性單數主格形，所以字典查 etādṛśaka。

5.2 【摩威梵英, etādṛśaka】無此字，應非梵文。

5.3 【艾格混梵,p155】adj.（=Skt. °śa，案：指 etādṛśa）, such: SP 15.13; 87.11（both vss, -ka may be m.c.）

5.4 【摩威梵英,p231, etādṛśa】mf(ī)n. such , such like , so formed , of this kind , similar to this RV.

5.5 【梵漢辭典,p436】（形容詞）（經文）斯。

6. विमुक्तः vimuktaḥ 形容詞 已經解脫的

6.1 【詞尾變化】vimuktaḥ 是 vimukta 的陽性單數主格形，所以字典查 vimukta。

6.2 【摩威梵英,p980】

6.2.1 see under I. vi-√muc.

6.2.2 mfn. unloosed , unharnessed &c. ; set free , liberated（esp. from mundane existence）, freed or delivered or escaped from MBh. ; deprived of（instr.）MBh. ; launched（as a ship）; given up , abandoned , relinquished , deserted ib. BhP. ; hurled , thrown MBh. ; emitted or discharged by , flowing from（comp.）; shed or bestowed on（loc.）;（a snake）which has recently cast its skin MBh.; dispassionate ;

6.2.3 -*kaṇṭha* mfn. having the throat or voice unloosed , raising a loud cry（*am* ind. aloud , at the top of one's voice）Amar. ;

6.2.4 -*keśa* mfn. having flowing or dishevelled hair BhP. ;

6.2.5 -*tā* f. loss of（gen.）;

6.2.6 -*pagraha* mfn. with slackened reins;

6.2.7 -*maunam* ind. breaking silence;

6.2.8 -*śāpa* mfn. released from the（consequences）of a curse;

6.2.9 -*sena* m. N. of a teacher Buddh. ;

6.2.10 -*tācārya* m. N. of an author.

6.3 【梵漢辭典,p1436】(過去被動分詞)->Muc;(經文)離,脫,卻,消滅,無解,解脫,遠離,得解脫,善解脫,已解脫,得度脫,已得解脫。

7. प्रभाव: prabhāvaḥ 名詞　威德之力;神通力

7.1 【詞尾變化】prabhāvaḥ 是 prabhāva 的陽性單數主格形,所以字典查 prabhāva。

7.2 資料前面已有說明。

8. षभस्य rṣabhasya 形容詞　超群,勝群的

8.1【詞尾變化】rṣabhasya 是 rṣabha 的陽性單數屬格形,所以字典查 rṣabha。

8.2 資料前面已有說明。

9. ज्ञानं jñānaṁ 名詞　知識;智慧

9.1 【詞尾變化】jñānaṁ 根據連音規則是從 jñānam 變化過來的,而 jñānam 則是 jñāna 的陽性單數對格形,所以字典查 jñāna。

9.2 資料前面已有說明。

10. विपुलं vipulaṁ 形容詞　廣大的,大的

10.1【詞尾變化】vipulaṁ 根據連音規則是從 vipulam 變化過來,也就是 vipula 的陽性單數對格形,所以字典查 vipula。

10.2 資料前面已有說明。

11. विशुद्धम् viśuddham 形容詞　完全清淨的;究竟清淨

11.1 【詞尾變化】viśuddham 是 viśuddha 的陽性單數對格形,所以字典查 viśuddha。

11.2 資料前面已有說明。

【筆者試譯】:今天從佛祖(這情況),這是什麼因緣啊?
如此耀眼的,已經解脫了的,
非常稀有啊!這威德神通的大丈夫啊!
這(他)確實是(有)廣大而完全清淨的智慧啊!

【什公漢譯】:佛子時答,決疑令喜,何所饒益,演斯光明?

【英 譯 本】: Why is it that the Sugata has now emitted
such a light? O how great is the power of the
Leader of men! O how extensive and holy is his knowledge!

【信譯研究】: 信譯。觀察第五十三頌之譯文（鳩譯闕文），可知鳩譯之第五十二頌譯文是爲合併梵本第五十二與五十三頌。

【第五十三頌】

यस्यैकरश्मी प्रसृताद्य लोके
दर्शेति क्षेत्राण बहून् सहस्रान्।
एतादृशो अर्थ अयं भविष्यति
येनैष रश्मी विपुला प्रमुक्ता॥५३॥

【羅馬譯音】

yasyaikaraśmī prasṛtādya loke
darśeti kṣetrāṇa bahūn sahasrān|
etādṛśo artha ayaṁ bhaviṣyati
yenaiṣa raśmī vipulā pramuktā||53||

【句義解析】

Yasyaika-raśmī prasṛtā dya loke
darśeti kṣetrāṇa bahūn sahasrān|
etādṛśo artha ayaṁ bhaviṣyati
yenaiṣa raśmī vipulā pramuktā||53||

【辭彙研究】

1. प्रसृताद्य prasṛtādya 片段語　今日所生
   1.1 【詞尾變化】prasṛtādya 是由兩個字所形成：prasṛta-adya，而 adya 前面已有說明，prasṛta 沒有詞尾變化，字典查 prasṛta。
   1.2 資料前面已有說明。
2. लोके loke 名詞　於國土

2.1 【詞尾變化】loke 是 loka 的陽性單數於格形，所以字典查 loka。

2.2 資料前面已有說明。

3. दर्शेति darśeti 動詞　看見，注意，注目

3.1 【詞尾變化】darśeti 是√dṛś 的第三人稱複數形，所以字典查√dṛś。

3.2 資料前面已有說明。

4. कषेत्राण kṣetrāṇa 名詞　領地；國土

4.1 【詞尾變化】kṣetrāṇa 是 kṣetra 的陽性複數屬格形，〔註 64〕所以字典查 kṣetra。

4.2 資料前面已有說明。

5. एतादृशो etādṛśo 形容詞　如此；此一

5.1 【詞尾變化】etādṛśo 根據連音規則是從 etādṛśaḥ 變化過來，而 etādṛśaḥ 是 etādṛśa 的單數主格形，所以字典查 etādṛśa。

5.2 資料前面已有說明。

6. अयं ayaṁ 代名詞　此一

6.1 【詞尾變化】ayaṁ 根據連音規則是 ayam 變化過來的，字典查 ayam。

6.2 資料前面已有說明。

7. भविष्यति bhaviṣyati 動詞　發生；產生；出現

7.1 【詞尾變化】bhaviṣyati 是√bhū 的第三人稱單數未來式形，所以字典查√bhū。

7.2 資料前面已有說名。

8. येनैष yenaiṣa 關係代名詞+代名詞　如此

8.1 【詞尾變化】yenaiṣa 是根據連音規則是從 yena 與 eṣa 的結合變化而來，eṣa 爲 etad 的陽性主格單數形；yena 則是 ya 的陽性單數具格形；字典查 ya 與 etad。

8.2 資料前面已有說明。

9. विपुला vipulā 形容詞　廣大；大的

〔註 64〕以 a 結尾的名詞，其屬格的複數形，是用-āṇa 結尾的，特別是在頌偈裡面常見，此一規則請見 Franklin Edgerton 編《Buddhist Hybrid Sanskrit Grammar And Dictionary》（I），published by Munshiram Manoharal Publishers Pvt. Ltd, Delhi, India,1993。p59。

9.1 【詞尾變化】vipulā 這裡是根據佛教混合梵文變化規則，知道是 vipula 的陽性單數主格形，字典查 vipula。〔註 65〕

9.2 資料前面已有說明。

10. प्रमुक्ता pramuktā 形容詞／過去被動分詞　放出，發出

10.1 【詞尾變化】pramuktā 的情況與上面相同，字典查 pramukta。

10.2 資料前面已有說明。

【筆者試譯】：今天在國土裡面所出現的這一道光，
使無量的國土看見了，
今天（現在）就會出現這樣情況：
讓廣大光明放射出來。

【什公漢譯】：缺譯。

【英 譯 本】：That one ray extending from him all over
the world makes visible many thousands of fields.
It must be for some purpose that this great ray has
been emitted.

【信譯研究】：非信譯。沒有譯出，因融入了上一頌的翻譯當中。這或許就是梵文的頌偈表現重複之故，所以翻譯者刪煩，將兩頌簡併爲一頌。

【第五十四頌】

ये अग्रधर्मा सुगतेन स्पृष्टा-
स्तद बोधिमण्डे पुरुषोत्तमेन।
किं तेह निर्देक्ष्यति लोकनाथो
अथ व्याकरिष्यत्ययु बोधिसत्त्वान्॥५४॥

〔註 65〕艾格頓說：有關-ā 結尾的部份，發生在主格單數，主要則是在詩歌而需要長音結尾的韻腳時，這也許會和主格複數形搞混，不過有時會發生在使用主格單數場合使用主格複數的情況。（-ā occurs as nom. sg., chiefly in verses where meter requires a long.　Perhaps confusion with the nom. pl. is concerned; it appears that nom. sg. Forms are used in the pl……）請見請見 Franklin Edgerton 編《Buddhist Hybrid Sanskrit Grammar And Dictionary》（I），published by Munshiram Manoharal Publishers Pvt. Ltd, Delhi, India,1993。P50。

【羅馬譯音】

ye agradharmā sugatena spṛṣṭā-
stada bodhimaṇḍe puruṣottamena|
kiṁ teha nirdekṣyati lokanātho
atha vyākariṣyatyayu bodhisattvān||54||

【句義解析】

ye agra-dharmā sugatena spṛṣṭās
tada bodhi-maṇḍe puruṣottamena|
kiṁ te ‘ha nirdekṣyati loka-nātho
atha vyākariṣyaty ayu bodhisattvān||54||

【辭彙研究】

1. स्पृष्टास् dharmā 名詞　法

1.1 【詞尾分析】dharmā 是以佛教混合梵文的變化方式，是 dharma 的陽性複數主格，所以字典查 dharma。

1.2 資料前面已有說明。

2. स्पृष्टास् spṛṣṭās 過去被動分詞／形容詞　獲得；證得

2.1 【詞尾分析】spṛṣṭās 根據連音規則，是從 spṛṣṭāḥ 變化過來的，而 spṛṣṭāḥ 是√spṛś 的過去被動分詞之陽性複數主格形，所以字典查√spṛś。

2.2 資料前面已有說明。

3. तद tada 副詞　在那時

3.1 【詞尾分析】tada 在字典中查不到，疑爲 tadā 的異寫，字典查 tadā。

3.2 【摩威梵英,p434】ind. at that time , then , in that case（often used redundantly , esp. after tatas or purā or before atha MBh. ; correlative of yad , yatra , yadā〔MBh.〕 , yadi , yarhi 〔BhP〕 , yatas , `since' , 〔MBh.〕 , ced）

3.3 【梵漢辭典,p1266】（副詞）在那時，其時〔在（史詩）中常與 tataḥ，purā 及 atha 連用成爲冗詞〕;〔常與 yataḥ, yatra, yad, yadā, yadi, yarhi, ced（關聯）〕;在當時;（經文）爾時，此時，彼時，于時，即於爾時。

4. मण्डे maṇḍe 名詞　煮熟穀物的浮沫；心

4.1 【詞尾分析】maṇḍe 爲 maṇḍa 的陽性於格單數形，故字典查 maṇḍa。

4.2 【摩威梵英,p775】

4.2.1 m. n.（ifc. f. *ā*）the scum of boiled rice（or any grain）; the thick part of milk , cream , MBh.（cf. *dadhi-m-*）; the spirituous part of wine（W. also `foam or froth ; pith , essence ; the head'）;

4.2.2 m.（only L.）Ricinus Communis ; a species of potherb ; a frog（cf. *maṇḍūka*）; ornament , decoration ; a measure of weight（= 5 *Māshas*）;

4.2.3（*ā*）f. the emblic myrobalan tree; spirituous or vinous liquor , brandy;

4.2.4 n. see *nau-maṇḍā*.

4.3 【梵漢辭典,p700】

4.3.1（陽性／中性）煮熟穀物的浮沫；奶油，乳脂；酒精成分高的部份，酒精；（經文）餅；汁，米汁；果，果汁；水，漿，醍醐，妙，清涼，上味；心，相合。

4.3.2（經文）座，場。

5. पुरुषोत्तमेन puruṣottamena 形容詞　最優秀的人

5.1 【詞尾分析】puruṣottamena 是 puruṣottama 的陽性單數工具格形，所以字典查 puruṣottama。

5.2 【摩威梵英,p673】m. the best of men , an excellent or superior man; the best of servants , a good attendant; the highest being , Supreme Spirit, N. of Viṣṇu or Kṛṣṇa MBh. ; = -kṣetra Cat. ;（with Jainas）an Arhat ; N. of the fourth black Vāsudeva ; a Jina（one of the generic terms for a deified teacher of the Jaina sect）; N. of sev. authors and various men.

5.3 【梵漢辭典,p993】（陽性）至高的人；最好的僕人；優等存在的，至高我；〔Viṣṇu 及 Kṛṣṇa 神號〕;〔諸人之名〕;（經文）大丈夫，士中尊。

6. तेऽह te ‘ha 代名詞與副詞　確實他

6.1 【詞尾分析】te ‘ha 是由 te 與 aha 所結合而成，te 是 ta 的陽性單數於格形，aha 則無詞尾變化。字典查 ta 與 aha。

6.2 資料前面已有說明。

7. निर्देक्षयति nirdekṣyati 動詞　預言；宣佈

7.1 【詞尾分析】nirdekṣyati 是 nir-√diś 的第三人稱單數未來式形，所以字典查 nir-√diś。

7.2 【摩威梵英,p555】P. -diśati（aor. -adikṣat. p. -diśya; inf. -deṣṭum MBh.）, to point to（acc.）, show; to assign anything to , destine for（dat. or gen.）; to indicate , state , name , define , specify MBh.; to take for , regard as（with double acc.）; to announce , proclaim , foretell , prophesy MBh.; to recommend , advise , suggest（with double acc.）: Desid. -didikṣati , to wish to point out or define more closely.

7.3 【梵漢辭典,p393】（動詞）指示（對）；分配給（對格／屬格）；指定，特定，命名；決定；宣佈（對格）爲（對格），預言，將（對格）看作（對格）；（經文）說，作說，能說，分別，解釋，敷演；讀，稱讚，稱歎，達。

8. नाथो nātho 名詞　皈依處；庇護者

8.1 【詞尾分析】nātho 根據連音規則是 nāthaḥ 變化過來，而 nāthaḥ 是 nātha 的陽性主格單數形，所以字典查 nātha。

8.2 【摩威梵英,p534】

8.2.1 n. refuge , help AV.;

8.2.2 m. a protector , patron , possessor , owner , lord（often ifc. , esp. in names of gods and men e.g. *govinda-* , *jagan-*; but also mf〔*ā*〕n. possessed of occupied by , furnished with cf. *sa-*）; a husband（esp. in voc.）MBh.; a rope passed through the nose of a draft ox; N. of sev. authors.

8.3 【梵漢辭典,p772】

8.3.1（中性名詞）庇護，援助；幫助；（經文）歸處。

8.3.2（陽性）（屬格）的保護者，擁護者，統治者，主人，擁有者，（在呼格尤其指）丈夫；（經文）尊，皈依處；諸佛如來。

8.3.3（形容詞）擁有，由～所佔有的，備有～；（經文）依，依怙，大依怙，所依怙，救護，大依護，主，佛，佛世尊，救世，如來，大師，尊。

9. व्याकरिस्यत्य् vyākariṣyaty 動詞　說明；對～做決定性的預言，授記

9.1 【詞尾分析】vyākariṣyaty 根據連音規則是從 vyākariṣyati 變化過來，而 vyākariṣyati 是 vyā-√kṛ 第三人稱單數未來式形，所以字典查 vyā-√kṛ。

9.2 資料前面已有說明。

10. अयु ayu 形容詞　無限多；許多

10.1 【詞尾分析】與漢譯相比對，ayu 爲 ayuta 的簡寫，故字典查 ayuta。

10.2 【摩威梵英,p86】

10.2.1 mfn.（√1. *yu*）, unimpeded AV.; N. of a son of Rādhika BhP.

10.2.2 n. 〔*as* m. only MBh.〕 , `unjoined , unbounded' , ten thousand , a myriad RV. AV.; in comp. a term of praise（see *ayutādhyāpaka*）,（g. *kāṣṭhādi* q.v.）

10.3 【梵漢辭典,p231】

10.3.1（形容詞）不受妨礙。

10.3.2（過去被動分詞）不受限制。

10.3.3（中性形容詞）一萬；（經文）萬，億，垓，阿由他。

11. बोधिसत्तवान् bodhisattvān 名詞　菩薩們

11.1 【詞尾分析】bodhisattvān 爲 bodhisattva 的陽性負數對格形，所以字典查 bodhisattva。

11.2 資料前面已有說明。

【筆者試譯】：最好，最上的法是由佛陀所傳，
此刻，（是）菩提之心，最上的尊者，
能夠認定誰將會是世界的庇護者，
授記給今天在場這麼多的菩薩們。

【什公漢譯】：佛坐道場，所得妙法，爲欲說此，爲當授記。

【英 譯 本】：Is the Lord of men to show the primordial
laws which he, the Highest of men, discovered on the
terrace of enlightenment? Or is he to prophesy
the Bodhisattvas their futre destiny?

【信譯研究】：信譯。但是這裡有一個單字值得討論，就是 bodhi-maṇḍe 的「maṇḍe」（maṇḍa）被翻譯成「道場」。但是這個字在梵文原來的意思，是指煮米汁的泡沫，或是牛奶裡面最薄的部份，有「最重要，最精要」的部份意思，是一個譬喻詞。古代是將「道場」視爲等同「最重要，最精要」的意思。

【第五十五頌】

अनल्पकं कारणमेत्त भेष्यति

यद्दर्शिताः क्षेत्रसहस्र नेके।
सुचित्रचित्रा रतनोपशोभिता
बुद्धाश्च दृश्यन्ति अनन्तचक्षुषः॥५५॥

【羅馬譯音】

analpakaṁ kāraṇametta bheṣyati
yaddarśitāḥ kṣetrasahasra neke|
sucitracitrā ratanopaśobhitā
buddhāśca dṛśyanti anantacakṣuṣaḥ||55||

【句義解析】

analpakaṁ kāraṇam etta bheṣyati
yad darśitāḥ kṣetra-sahasra neke|
Sucitra-citrā ratanopaśobhitā
Buddhāś ca dṛśyanti ananta-cakṣuṣaḥ||55||

【辭彙研究】

1. अनल्पकं analpakaṁ 名詞　眾人

1.1 【詞尾變化】analpakaṁ 根據連音規則是從 analpakam 變化過來，而 analpakam 是 analpaka 的陽性單數主格形，所以字典查 analpaka。

1.2 資料前面已有說明。

2. कारणम् kāraṇam 名詞　原因；因緣

2.1 【詞尾變化】kāraṇam 是 kāraṇa 的陽性單數對格形，所以字典查 kāraṇa。

2.2 資料前面已有說明。

3. एत्त etta 副詞　此處

3.1 【詞尾變化】etta 是 Prakrit 語，相當於梵文的 atra，所以字典查 atra。〔註 66〕

〔註 66〕在艾格頓《佛教混合梵文辭典》說到 etta 的時候，說到：「etta, adv.（in mg.=SKt. atra;=Pali etta, at least once for usual ettha, Pv i.5.6 repeated comm., to be sure with v.l. ettha, but the gloss 28.33 has etta without v.l.; cf. ettha）here, hither: Mv i.35.5 etta, etta, here, here!（so app. All mss., at least as far as tt, not tth, is concerned）; for SP 16.5（vs） WT read with their ms. K' kāraṇam etta（=atra）,

3.2 資料前面已有說明。

4. भेष्यति bheṣyati 動詞 畏懼；害怕

4.1【詞尾變化】bheṣyati 是√bhī 未來式第三人稱單數形，所以字典查√bhī。

4.2【摩威梵英,p758】cl. 3. also cl. 1. to fear , be afraid of（abl. or gen. , rarely instr , or acc.）RV. ; to fear for , be anxious about（abl.）, to terrify , put in a fright , intimidate RV.

4.3【梵漢辭典,p267】（動詞）第一類動詞；畏懼，害怕（從格，屬格）；擔心（從格）；（經文）畏，懼，怯，怖，恐怖，恐畏，憂怖，有憂懼，生驚怖，嫌棄。

5. दर्शिता: darśitāḥ 動詞 注目，注意

5.1【詞尾變化】darśitāḥ 是 darśita 的，即√dṛś 使役形被動分詞之陽性複數主格形，字典查√dṛś。

5.2 資料前面已有說明。

6. नेके neke 形容詞 不只一個；許多的

6.1【詞尾變化】neke 是 neka 的陽性單數於格形，故字典查 neka。但是 neka 是巴利文，相當於梵文 naika，即 na eka。〔註 67〕字典查 naika。

6.2【摩威梵英,p523】

6.2.1 mf（*ā*）n. not one , more than one , various , manifold , numerous , many（also pl.）;

6.2.2 -*cara* mf（*ī*）n. going in troops , gregarious（animal）BhP. ;

6.2.3 -dṛś m. `many-eyed' N. of a son of *Viśvāmitra* MBh. ;

6.2.4 -*dravyoccaya-vat* mfn. furnished with plenty of various goods ib. ;

---

for KN kāraṇeva（unmetr.） allegedly with all Nep. Mss.（Kshgar rec. quoted as kāraṇam eta）.」這說明 etta 就是梵文的 atra，也就是巴利文的 etta。請見 Franklin Edgerton 編《Buddhist Hybrid Sanskrit Grammar And Dictionary》（II），published by Munshiram Manoharal Publishers Pvt. Ltd, Delhi, India,1993。p155。

〔註 67〕在《巴利文辭典》說到 neka 的時候，說到：「（adj.）[Sk. Naika=na eka, cp. aneka]not one, several, many Sn 308;Vv 53.6 （°citta varicgated = nānāvidhacitta VvA 236）, 64.1 （id.=anekacitta VvA 275）;Tikp 366.」這說明 neka 就是梵文的 naika。法華經寫本原來是從民間語言轉化爲梵文，此處有巴利文者即爲明證。請見 T. W. Rhys Davids & William Stede 編《Pali-English Dictionary》，published by Motilal Banarsidass Publishers Pvt. Ltd, Delhi, India,2003。P377。

6.2.5 -*dhā* ind. manifoldly , in various ways or parts MBh. Hariv. &c. ;

6.2.6 -*puṭa* mfn. showing many rents or gaps , torn（cloud）;

6.2.7 -*pṛṣṭha* m. pl. `many-backed' N. of a people MBh.（v.l. -*ṣṭa*）;

6.2.8 -*bhāvāśraya* mfn. ` not abiding in one condition' , changeable , fickle , unsteady;

6.2.9 -*bheda* mfn. of many kinds , various , manifold;

6.2.10 -*māya* mfn. using many artifices or stratagems MBh. ;

6.2.11 -*rūpa* mf（*ā*）n. multiform , various;

6.2.12 -*rṣi*（for -*ṛṣi*）m. N. of a man ; pl. his family Pravar. ;

6.2.13 -*varṇa* mfn. many-coloured MBh. ;

6.2.14 -*vikāpa* mfn. manifold , various;

6.2.15 –*vidha* mfn. id. Var. ;

6.2.16 -śas ind. repeatedly , often;

6.2.17 -*śastramaya* mf（*ī*）n. consisting of various missiles（rain）;

6.2.18 -*kātman* mfn. of manifold nature.

6.3 【梵漢辭典,p758】（形容詞）比一多的，許多的；（複數）各種的，多數的。

6.4 【譯筆研究】此處即是明證。蓋因法華經等大乘經典原來是民間語言，後來轉寫成梵文，但偈頌部份保持原樣，裡頭不僅有 Prakrit，也有巴利文，這說明了大乘經典原來也是民間各方語言寫成的情況。

7. सुचित्रचित्रा Sucitra-citrā 形容詞+名詞　美麗燦爛的裝飾

7.1 【詞尾變化】Sucitra 沒有詞尾變化。Citrā 是 citra 的陽性主格複數形，但其變化是以 Prakrit 方式，而非梵文。該字前面已有資料說明，所以字典查 Sucitra。

7.2 【摩威梵英,p1223】

7.2.1 mf（*ā*）n. very distinguished AV. ; very manifold; very variegated;

7.2.2 m. N. of a serpentdemon MBh. ; of a king ib. ;

7.2.3（*ā*）f. a kind of gourd. ;

7.2.4（-*tra*）-*bījā* f. Embelia Ribes.

7.3 【梵漢辭典,p1220】（陽性名詞）〔某惡鬼之名〕；（經文）嚴飾。

8. रतनोपशोभिता ratanopaśobhitā 形容詞　用寶物裝飾

8.1 【詞尾變化】ratanopaśobhitā 是 ratanopaśobhita 的陽性主格複數形，但其變化是以 Prakrit 方式，而非梵文。Ratanopaśobhita 根據連音規則，是 ratana 與 upaśobhita 的結合，ratana 是中印度俗語寫法，即梵文的 ratna，〔註 68〕資料前面已有說明，字典查 upaśobhita。

8.2 【摩威梵英,p208, upaśobhita】mfn. adorned , ornamented , decorated MBh.

8.3 【梵漢辭典,p1020, ratanopaśobhita】(°-na-up°)(形容詞)(俗語)〔=ratnop°〕(經文)；眾寶嚴淨。

9. बुद्धाश्च Buddhāś ca 名詞　與佛陀們

9.1 【詞尾變化】根據連音規則，Buddhāś ca 即由 Buddhāḥ ca 變化過來。Buddhāḥ 即 Buddha 的陽性複數主格形。所以字典查 Buddha。

9.2 資料前面已有說明。

10. दृश्यन्ति dṛśyanti 動詞　注意到；看到

10.1 【詞尾變化】dṛśyanti 是從√dṛś 的第三人稱複數形，所以字典查√dṛś。

10.2 資料前面已有說明。

11. अनन्तचक्षुषः cakṣuṣaḥ 形容詞　光明的

11.1 【詞尾變化】cakṣuṣaḥ 是 cakṣus 的中性單數屬格形，所以字典查 cakṣus。

11.2 【摩威梵英,p382】

11.2.1 mfn. seeing RV.; AV;

11.2.2 m. N. of a *Marut* ; of a *Ṛiṣi*（with the patr. *Mānava* , author of RV.）*Ṛānukr.* ; of another *Ṛiṣi*（with the patr. *Saurya* , author of RV.）ib. ; of a son of Anu;

11.2.3 f. N. of a river BhP. ;

11.2.4 n. light , clearness RV. SV. ; the act of seeing（dat. inf. = -*kṣase*）AV. ; aspect RV. ; faculty of seeing , sight RV. AV.; a look RV. AV. ; the eye RV.（often ifc. cf. *a-* , *a-ghora-* , *a-dabdha-*）;

〔註 68〕在艾格頓《佛教混合梵文辭典》說到 ratna 的時候，說到：「(or MIndic ratana)（案：MIndic 即 Middle Indic，指中世印度）」這說明 ratana 就是梵文的 ratna 之中世印度寫法。請見 Franklin Edgerton 編《Buddhist Hybrid Sanskrit Grammar And Dictionary》(II)，published by Munshiram Manoharal Publishers Pvt. Ltd, Delhi, India,1993。P450。

11.3 【梵漢辭典,p307】（形容詞）觀看，（中性名詞）眼睛；視界；視力，瞥見；光，光明；（經文）視；眼，目，眼目。

【筆者試譯】：此處眾生將會驚懼的原因，
這樣被看到的國土何止上千個！
（用）許多寶物裝飾得光輝燦爛！
也看到了許多佛陀！

【什公漢譯】：示諸佛土，眾寶嚴淨，及見諸佛，此非小緣。

【英 譯 本】：There must be a weighty reason why so
many thousands of fields have been rendered visible,
variegated, splendid, and shining with gems, while
Buddhas of infinite sight are appearing.

【信譯研究】：信譯。這首頌偈特別能夠說明，《法華經》的經文有以印度民間俗語寫成的部份。這首頌偈當中有巴利文、Prakrit、中世紀印度的寫法，凡此都充分說明了這一點。

【第五十六頌】

पृच्छेति मैत्रेयु जिनस्य पुत्र
स्पृहेन्ति ते नरमरुयक्षराक्षसाः।
चत्वारिमा पर्ष उदीक्षमाणा
मञ्जुस्वरः किं न्विह व्याकरिष्यति॥५६॥

【羅馬譯音】

pṛccheti maitreyu jinasya putra
spṛhenti te naramaruyakṣarākṣasāḥ|
catvārimā parṣa udīkṣamāṇā
mañjusvaraḥ kiṁ nviha vyākariṣyati||56||

【句義解析】

pṛcche ti Maitreyu jinasya putra

spṛhenti te nara-maru-yakṣa-rākṣasāḥ|
Catvār imā parṣa udīkṣamāṇā
Mañjusvaraḥ kiṁ nviha vyākariṣyati||56||

【辭彙研究】

1. पृच्छेति pṛcche ti 動詞 如是，我請問

 1.1 【詞尾變化】pṛcche 是√prach（praś）的現在式第一人稱單數形，資料前面已有說明；ti 則無詞尾變化，但此字並非梵文。

 1.2 【艾格混梵,p253,ti】ti（=Pali, Pkt. Id.）, =Skt. iti;

2. मैत्रेयु Maitreyu 名詞 彌勒菩薩

 2.1 【詞尾變化】Maitreyu 根據學者研究，即爲 Maitreyo 的異寫，根據連音規則即知爲 Maitreyaḥ，即 Maitreya 的陽性單數主格形，字典查 Maitreya。〔註 69〕

 2.2 資料前面已有說明。

3. जिनस्य jinasya 名詞 勝者的；佛陀的

 3.1 【詞尾變化】jinasya 是 jina 的陽性單數屬格形，所以字典查 jina。

 3.2 資料前面已有說明。

4. स्पृहेन्ति spṛhenti 動詞 對～深生敬愛

 4.1 【詞尾變化】spṛhenti 是√spṛh 的現在式第三人稱複數形，所以字典查√spṛh。

 4.2 【摩威梵英,p1269】(connected with √spardh , spṛdh)cl. 10. P. , to be eager , desire eagerly , long for（dat. gen. , or acc.）RV.; to envy , be jealous of（dat. gen. , or acc.）MBh.

 4.3 【梵漢辭典,p1192】(動詞)對～迫切期望或渴望的；對～忌妒或羨慕的；(經文)深生愛樂。

5. राक्षसाः rākṣasāḥ 名詞 羅刹

 5.1 【詞尾變化】rākṣasāḥ 是 rākṣasa 的陽性複數主格形，所以字典查 rākṣasa。

 5.2 資料前面已有說明。

〔註 69〕請見荻原雲來，土田勝彌編《改訂梵文法華經》，東京：山喜房佛書林出版,1994。P14。

6. उदीक्षमाणा udīkṣamāṇā 動詞／現在被動分詞　仰望；眺望

6.1 【詞尾變化】udīkṣamāṇā 是 ud-√īkṣ 的現在被動分詞形，所以字典查 ud-√īkṣ。

6.2 【摩威梵英,p186】Ā. -īkṣate to look up to S3Br. R. ; to look at , regard , view , behold MBh. ; to wait , delay , hesitate ; to expect MBh.

6.3 【梵漢辭典,p504】(動詞) 仰視～，眺望；看守；等待；期待；(經文) 觀，願，欣樂，瞻察。

7. मञ्जुस्वरः Mañjusvaraḥ 名詞　文殊師利菩薩

7.1 【詞尾變化】Mañjusvaraḥ 是 Mañjusvara 的陽性單數主格形，所以字典查 Mañjusvara。

7.2 資料前面已有說明。

8. किं न्व kiṁ nv 句型 是否可以？

8.1 【詞尾變化】nv 與前面的 kim 連用，形成 kiṃ～na vā，形成「非～亦非～」「是～或不是」。

8.2 請參考【摩威梵英,p282】與【梵漢辭典,p1365】。

9. व्याकरिष्यति vyākariṣyati 動詞　解說

9.1 【詞尾變化】vyākariṣyati 是 vyā--kariṣyati，也就是 vyā-√kṛ 未來式第三人稱複數形。所以字典查 vyā-√kṛ。

9.2 資料前面已有說明。

【筆者試譯】：我彌勒菩薩請問這位佛子，
人，天人，夜叉，羅剎所敬愛的，
四種眾生（都在）熱烈仰望，等待著，
文殊師利菩薩，是否（請）在此解說原因為何？

【什公漢譯】：文殊當知，四眾龍神，瞻察仁者，為說何等？

【英 譯 本】：Maitreya asks the son of Gina; men, gods,
goblins, and Titans, the four classes of the congregation,
are eagerly awaiting what answer Mañgusvara
shall give in explanation.

【信譯研究】：信譯。

【小結】

1. 本段是本品內容最多，文句最長的部份，總共有五十六頌。但鳩摩羅什此段翻譯絕大多數都是信譯，都是忠於原文。

2. 值得注意的是，鳩摩羅什當中存有相當的不規則句數對譯現象，由於梵本內容的頌偈都是四句一頌，鳩摩羅什為了保持這個體裁，也希望用四句，來對譯，這可從譯作裡面大量使用四句對譯的情況看出。但是畢竟梵文表達方式與中文表達方式不同，所以詩頌對譯的情況，讓鳩摩羅什煞費苦心，在本品裡面，詩偈部分總共有兩群，到了第二群，鳩摩羅什便不使用四言詩來翻譯，改用五言詩。

【第十段】

अथ खलु मञ्जुश्रीः कुमारभूतो मैत्रेयं बोधिसत्त्वं महासत्त्वं तं च सर्वावन्तं बोधिसत्त्वगणमामन्त्रयते स्म-महाधर्मश्रवणसांकथ्यमिदं कुलपुत्रास्तथागतस्य कर्तुमभिप्रायः, महाधर्मवृष्ट्यभिप्रवर्षणं च महाधर्मदुन्दुभिसंप्रवादनं च महाधर्मध्वजसमुच्छ्रयणं च महाधर्मोल्कासंप्रज्वालनं च महाधर्मशङ्खाभिप्रपूरणं च महाधर्मभेरीप राहणनं च महाधर्मनिर्देशं च अद्य कुलपुत्रास्तथागतस्य कर्तुमभिप्रायः। यथा मम कुलपुत्राः प्रतिभाति, यथा च मया पूर्वकाणां तथागतानामर्हतां सम्यक्संबुद्धानामिदमेवंरूपं पूर्वनिमित्तं दृष्टमभूत्, तेषामपि पूर्वकाणां तथागतानामर्हतां सम्यक्संबुद्धानामेवं रश्मिप्रमोचनावभासोऽभुत्। तेनैवं प्रजानामि-महाधर्मश्रवणसांकथ्यं तथागतः कर्तुकामो महाधर्मश्रवणं श्रावयितुकामः, यथेदमेवंरूपं पूर्वनिमित्तं प्रादुष्कृतवान्। तत्कस्य हेतोः? सर्वलोकविप्रत्यनीयकधर्मपर्यायं श्रावयितुकामस्तथागतोऽर्हन् सम्यक्संबुद्धः, यथेदमेवंरूपं महाप्रातिहार्यं रश्मिप्रमोचनावभासं च पूर्वनिमित्तमुपदर्शयति॥

【羅馬譯音】

atha khalu mañjuśrīḥ kumārabhūto maitreyaṁ bodhisattvaṁ mahāsattvaṁ taṁ ca sarvāvantaṁ bodhisattvagaṇamāmantrayate sma-mahādharmaśravaṇasāṁkathyamidaṁ kulaputrāstathāgatasya kartumabhiprāyaḥ, mahādharmavṛṣṭhayabhipravarṣaṇaṁ ca mahādharmadundubhisaṁpravādanaṁ ca mahādharmadhvajasamucchrayaṇaṁ ca mahādharmolkāsaṁprajvālanaṁ ca mahādharmaśaṅkhābhiprapūraṇaṁ ca mahādharmabherīparāhaṇanaṁ ca mahādharmanirdeśaṁ ca adya kulaputrāstathāgatasya kartumabhiprāyaḥ| yathā mama kulaputrāḥ pratibhāti, yathā ca mayā pūrvakāṇāṁ tathāgatānāmarhatāṁ samyaksaṁbuddhānāmidamevaṁrūpaṁ pūrvanimittaṁ dṛṣṭamabhūt, teṣāmapi pūrvakāṇāṁ tathāgatānāmarhatāṁ samyaksaṁbuddhānāmevaṁ raśmipramocanāvabhāso'bhut| tenaivaṁ prajānāmi-mahādharmaśravaṇasāṁkathyaṁ tathāgataḥ kartukāmo mahādharmaśravaṇaṁ śrāvayitukāmaḥ, yathedamevaṁrūpaṁ pūrvanimittaṁ prāduṣkṛtavān| tatkasya hetoḥ? sarvalokavipratyanīyakadharmaparyāyaṁ śrāvayitukāmastathāgato'rhan samyaksaṁbuddhaḥ, yathedamevaṁrūpaṁ mahāprātihāryaṁ raśmipramocanāvabhāsaṁ ca pūrvanimittamupadarśayati||

【第一句】

atha khalu Mañjuśrīḥ kumāra-bhūto Maitreyaṁ bodhisattvaṁ mahāsattvaṁ taṁ ca sarvāvantaṁ bodhisattva-gaṇam āmantrayate sma-mahā-dharma-śravaṇa-sāṁkathyam idaṁ kula-putrās tathāgatasya kartum abhiprāyaḥ,
mahā-dharma-vṛṣṭhay-abhipravarṣaṇaṁ ca
mahā-dharma-dundubhi-saṁpravādanaṁ ca
mahā-dharma-dhvaja-samucchrayaṇaṁ ca
mahā-dharmolkā-saṁprajvālanaṁ ca
mahā-dharma-śaṅkhābhiprapūraṇaṁ ca
mahā-dharma-bherī-parāhaṇanaṁ ca mahā-dharma-nirdeśaṁ ca adya kula-putrās tathāgatasya kartum abhiprāyaḥ|

【辭彙研究】

1. कुमारभूतो kumāra-bhūto 名詞 法王子

1.1 【詞尾變化】kumāra-bhūto 根據連音規則，是從 kumāra-bhūtaḥ 變化過來的，而 kumāra-bhūtaḥ 是 kumāra-bhūta 的陽性主格單數形。所以字

典查 kumāra-bhūta。

1.2　資料前面已有說明。

2. तंच taṁ ca 代名詞+連接詞　他與

2.1 【詞尾變化】taṁ ca 根據連音規則，是從 tam ca 變化過來，tam 是 ta 的陽性單數對格形，所以字典查 ta ca。

2.2　資料前面已有說明

3. सर्वावन्तं sarvāvantaṁ 形容詞　一切；周遍

3.1 【詞尾變化】sarvāvantaṁ 根據連音規則是從 sarvāvantam 變化過來，而 sarvāvantam 是 sarvāvat 的陽性單數對格形，所以字典查 sarvāvat。

3.2 【摩威梵英,p1188】mfn. containing everything; entire , complete.

3.3 【梵漢辭典,p1145】（形容詞）（經文）普，一切，皆，周遍，一切悉，具種種，具諸種種。

4. गणम् gaṇam 形容詞　群眾

4.1 【詞尾變化】gaṇam 是 gaṇa 的陽性單數對格形，所以字典查 gaṇa。

4.2 【摩威梵英,p343】

4.2.1 m. a flock , troop , multitude , number , tribe , series , class（of animate or inanimate beings）, body of followers or attendants RV. AV. ; troops or classes of inferior deities（especially certain troops of demi-gods considered as *Śiva's* attendants and under the special superintendence of the god; cf. *-devatā*）; a single attendant of *Śiva*; N. of *Gaṇeśa*; a company , any assemblage or association of men formed for the attainment of the same aims; the 9 assemblies of *Ṛiśis* under the *Arhat Mahā-vīra Jain.* ; a sect in philosophy or religion ; a small body of troops（= 3 *Gulmas* or 27 chariots and as many elephants , 81 horses , and 135 foot）MBh.; a series or group of asterisms or lunar mansions classed under three heads（that of the gods , that of the men , and that of the Ra1kshasas）;（in arithm.）a number;（in metre）a foot or four instants（cf. *-cchandas*）;（in Gr.）a series of roots or words following the same rule and called after the first word of the series（e.g. ad-*ādi* , the g. *ad.* or the whole series of roots of the 2nd class ; *gargādi* , the g. *garga.* or the series of words commencing with *garga*）; a particular group of

Sāmans; a kind of perfume; = *vāc*（i.e. `a series of verses'）; N. of an author ;

4.2.2（*ā*）f. N. of one of the mothers in *Skanda's* retinue MBh.

4.3 【梵漢辭典,p444】（陽性）群眾，大眾；多數；階級；部隊，追隨者；軍隊（中低階的）神群〔尤指 Gaṇeśa 統治下的 Śiva 神的追隨者〕；Śiva 神的隨員之一；社會，聯合，集團；（韻律的）韻腳〔即四短音構成的單位〕；（符合文法規制的詞根或字的）一串；（經文）眾，聚，大眾，徒眾，憒眾，部眾，海會。

5. आमन्त्रयते āmantrayate 動詞　向～講話；演說

5.1 【詞尾變化】āmantrayate 為 ā-√mantr 的現在式第三人稱單數形，所以字典查 ā-√mantr。

5.2 【摩威梵英,p146】Ā. -mantrayate（pf. -mantrayām-āsa）to address , speak to ; to summon; to call , ask , invite MBh.; to salute , welcome MBh.; to bid farewell , take leave MBh.

5.3 【梵漢辭典】沒有收錄此字，估計是漏收。

6. सांकथयम् sāṁkathyam 名詞　談話；宣說

6.1 【詞尾變化】sāṁkathyam 是 sāṁkathya 的中性單數對格形，所以字典查 sāṁkathya。

6.2 資料前面已有說明。

7. कुलपुत्रास् kulaputrās 名詞　善男子；好人家青年

7.1 【詞尾變化】kulaputrās 根據連音規則是從 kulaputrāḥ 變化過來的，kulaputrāḥ 則是 kulaputra 的陽性複數主格形，所以字典查 kulaputra。

7.2 【摩威梵英,p295】

7.2.1 m. a son of a noble family , respectable youth MBh.; the plant Artemisia indica;

7.2.2（*ī*）f. the daughter of a good family , high-born or respectable girl（= *-duhitṛ*）;

7.2.3 *kulaputra-jana* m. a son of a noble family.

7.3 【梵漢辭典,p633】（陽性）良家男子；高貴良善的青年；（經文）善男子，族姓子，族姓。

8. तथागतस्य tathāgatasya 名詞　如來

8.1 【詞尾變化】tathāgatasya 是 tathāgata 的陽性單數屬格形，所以字典查 tathāgata。

8.2 資料前面已有說明。

9. कर्तुम् kartum 動名詞　表示；說明

9.1 【詞尾變化】kartum 是√kṛ 的不變格（動名詞）形，所以字典查√kṛ。

9.2 資料前面已有說明。

10. अभिप्रायः abhiprāyaḥ 名詞　目標；方向

10.1 【詞尾變化】abhiprāyaḥ 是 abhiprāya 的陽性單數主格形，所以字典查 abhiprāya。

10.2 【摩威梵英,p66】m. aim; purpose , intention , wish; opinion; meaning , sense（as of a word or of a passage）.

10.3 【梵漢辭典,p12】（陽性名詞）目的，志向，願妄，意見，意義，概念，觀察，理解，現象，幻象，想念，概念；（經文）願，所願，深心所願，意願，誓願，欲，欲求，所欲，願欲，樂，意樂，志樂，欲樂，心所樂，所求，希求，思惟悕求，意，故意，別意，密亦，意一，意趣；心，念，心念，思，想，志性，所趣。

11. वृस्थय् vṛṣṭhay 名詞　雨

11.1 【詞尾變化】vṛṣṭhay 根據學者研究，認爲與 vṛṣṭi 相當，故字典查 vṛṣṭi。〔註 70〕

11.2 【摩威梵英,p1013】

11.2.1 f.（sg. and pl.）rain RV.（ifc. often = a shower of cf. *puṣpa-*} , *śaravṛ-*）;（in *Sāṃkhya*）one of the four forms of internal , acquiescence（cf. *salila*）MW. ;

11.2.2 m. a partic. ; N. of a son of *Kukura*（cf. *vṛṣṭa*）VP.

11.3 【梵漢辭典,p1477】（陰性）（單數）（複數）雨；（經文）雨，甘雨。

12. अभिप्रवर्षणं abhipravarṣaṇaṁ 形容詞　降下的

〔註 70〕該字應爲巴利文形，照水野弘元考訂巴利文與梵文轉寫規則來看，這個字應該可以轉爲梵文 vṛṣṭi，請見江島惠教等編《梵藏漢法華經原典總索引》，日本東京：靈友會，1991 年出版。頁 954。並水野弘元《巴利文法》，台北：華宇出版社，民國 75 年出版。頁 67。

12.1 【詞尾變化】abhipravarṣaṇaṁ 根據連音規則從 abhipravarṣaṇam 變化過來，abhipravarṣaṇam 爲 abhi-pra-varṣaṇa 的陽性單數對格形，其餘前面均有資料說明，字典查 varṣaṇa。

12.2 【摩威梵英,p972】

12.2.1 mf（ī）n.（mostly ifc.）raining（with *astram* , a missile causing rain）BhP. ;

12.2.2 n. raining , causing to rain , pouring out , shedding out gifts upon（comp.）; sprinkling.

12.3 【梵漢辭典,p1393】（形容詞）下～之雨，（中性）下雨，如然下雨；豐富給予；（經文）雨，降雨。

13. संप्रवादनं saṁpravādanaṁ 名詞　交互演奏出

13.1 【詞尾變化】saṁpravādanaṁ 根據連音規則，爲 saṁpravādanam 變化過來，saṁpravādanam 爲 saṁ-pra-vādana 的陽性單數對格形，所以字典查 vādana。

13.2 【摩威梵英,p940】

13.2.1 m. a player on any musical instrument , musician. ;

13.2.2 n. = -*daṇḍa*;（ifc. f. *ā*）sound , sounding , playing a musical instrument , music MBh.

13.3 【梵漢辭典,p1367】（陽性）〔起自 Vad 的（使役形）〕樂器的演奏者，樂器的演奏；器樂。

14. समुच्छ्रयणं samucchrayaṇaṁ 形容詞　高舉的

14.1 【詞尾變化】samucchrayaṇaṁ 根據連音規則，是從 samucchrayaṇam 變化過來，而 samucchrayaṇam 則疑似是 sam-ucchraya 的複數屬格形，故字典查 sam-ucchraya。

14.2 【摩威梵英,p1165】

14.2.1 mfn. who or what rises or grows up;

14.2.2 m. raising aloft , erection , elevation MBh. SaddhP. ; height , length ; an eminence , hill , mountain MBh. ; rising , rise , exaltation , high position MBh.; increase , growth , high degree; stimulation; accumulation , multitude;（with Buddh.）birth（according to others , `" body "'）; opposition , enmity.

14.3 【梵漢辭典,p1115】（形容詞）成長的（生物）。（陽性）豎起，提高；高度，長度；高處，山；上升，高漲，高的地位，增大，刺激；（經文）高，身，量，高舉，崇高，化身，尊位，貢高，極尊貴位。

15. दर्मोल्का dharmolkā 形容詞　法炬；法燈

15.1 【詞尾變化】沒有詞尾變化。但 dharmolkā 是 dharma—ulkā 所組成，所以字典查 ulkā。

15.2 【摩威梵英,p218】f. , a fiery phenomenon in the sky , a meteor , fire falling from heaven RV.AV. MBh. ; a firebrand , dry grass. set on fire , a torch;（in astrol.）one of the eight principal *Daśās* or aspect of planets indicating the fate of men; N. of a grammar.

15.3 【梵漢辭典,p378, dharmolkā】（陰性名詞）法燈；（經文）法炬。

16. संप्रज्वालनं saṁprajvālanaṁ 形容詞　燃燒的

16.1 【詞尾變化】saṁprajvālanaṁ 根據連音規則是從 saṁprajvālanam 變化過來的，而 saṁprajvālanam 則是 saṁ--pra--jvālana 的陽性單數對格形，jvālana 疑爲 jvalana 的異寫，字典查 jvalana。

16.2 【摩威梵英,p428】

16.2.1 mfn. inflammable , combustible , flaming MBh. ; shining;

16.2.2 m. fire MBh.; the number 3.; corrosive alkali; Plumbago *śeylanica*;

16.2.3 n. blazing;

16.2.4（*ā*）f. N. of a daughter of Takshaka（wife of Ṛiceyu or Ṛikṣa）.

16.3 【梵漢辭典,p541】

16.3.1（形容詞）燃燒，照明；（經文）熾盛。

16.3.2（陽性）火；強鹼（腐蝕鉀）；（經文）火。

16.3.3（中性）燃燒的；（經文）光，熱，熾然，熾盛，光熾盛；照耀，顯著，放光。

17. शङ्खाभिप्रपूरणं śaṅkhābhiprapūraṇaṁ 形容詞　充滿海螺的（聲音）

17.1 【詞尾變化】śaṅkhābhiprapūraṇaṁ 根據連音規則是從 śaṅkhābhiprapūraṇam，也就是 śaṅkha-abhi-pra-pūraṇa 的中性單數對格形，śaṅkha，abhi，pra 前面均有資料說明，字典查 pūraṇa。

17.2 【摩威梵英,p642】

17.2.1 mf（ī）n. filling , completing , satisfying causing , effecting; drawing（a bow）MW.

17.2.2 m. `completer' , N. of the masculine ordinal numbers from dvitīya upwards;a dam , bridge; the sea; a medicinal oil or embrocation; N. of a man;N. of the author of RV;

17.2.3（ī）, f. an ordinal number in the feminine gender; Bonibax Heptaphyllum;（du.）the cross threads in weaving cloth , warp.;N. of Durg?MW. ;of one of the two wives of the popular deity;

17.2.4 n. the act or filling or filling up , puffing or swelling up AV.;fulfilling , satisfying.;furnishing , equipping. ; drawing or bending a bow to the full.;（in medic.）injection of fluids or supplying with food;（in astron.）the revolution of a heavenly body through its orbit.;（in arithm.）multiplication;rain;a sort of cake. ;Cyperus Rotundus. ;the cross threads in weiving cloth , warp.

17.3 【梵漢辭典,p12, abhiprapūraṇa】（中性）充滿；（經文）吹。

18. भेरी bherī 名詞　鼓

18.1 【詞尾變化】沒有詞尾變化。

18.2 【摩威梵英,p766】f.（rarely °ri）a kettle-drum MBh.

18.3 【梵漢辭典,p267】（陰性名詞）半月形的鼓；（經文）鼓，大鼓。

19. पराहणनं parāhaṇanaṁ 形容詞　搥打；打擊

19.1 【詞尾變化】parāhaṇanaṁ 根據連音規則是從 parāhaṇanam 變化過來，而 parāhaṇanam 是 parā-haṇana 的中性單數對格形，但根據學者研究，haṇana 是從字根√han 變化過來，所以字典查√han。）

19.2 【摩威梵英,p1287, √han】cl. 2. to strike , beat（also a drum）, pound , hammer（acc.）, strike &c. upon（loc.）RV. to smite , slay , hit , kill , mar , destroy ib. to smite , slay , hit , kill , mar , destroy ib. to strike off, to ward off , avert, to hurt , wound（the heart）, to hurl（a dart）upon（gen.）,（in astron.）to touch , come into contact, to obstruct , hinder, to repress , give up , abandon（anger , sorrow）, to go , move; Caus: to cause to be slain or killed , kill , slay , put to death , punish, to notify a person's death, to mar , destroy, to wish to kill or destroy RV, to strike = tread upon（loc. or acc.）RV. to slay , to dispel（darkness）, destroy（evil , harm）ib. to hurt , injure , wound.

19.3 【梵漢辭典,p841, parāhaṇana】（中性）（經文）擊。

20. निर्देशं nirdeśaṁ 形容詞　表明；敘述

20.1【詞尾變化】nirdeśaṁ 根據連音規則是從 nirdeśam 變化過來，而 nirdeśam 則是 nirdeśa 的中性單數對格形，所以字典查 nirdeśa。

20.2 資料前面已有說明。

21. कुल kula 形容詞　團體

21.1 【詞尾變化】沒有詞尾變化。

21.2 【摩威梵英,p294】

21.2.1 n.（ifc. f. ā）a herd , troop , flock , assemblage , multitude , number ,（of quadrupeds , birds , insects , or of inanimate objects e.g. *go-kula* , a herd of cows; *mahiṣīk-}* , a herd of female buffaloes; *ali-k-* , a swarm of bees;*alaka-k-* , a multitude of curls BhP.）; a race , family , community , tribe , caste , set , company;（ifc. with a gen. sg.）a lot , gang（e.g. *caurasya-k-* , a gang of thieves）; the residence of a family , seat of a community , inhabited country（as much ground as can be ploughed by two ploughs each drawn by six bulls Comm. on; a house , abode MBh. ; a noble or eminent family or race MBh.; high station（in comp. `chief , principal'）; the body L. ; the front , forepart; a blue stone ; N. of *Śakti* and of the rites observed in her worship; = *kula-nakṣatra* q.v.;

21.2.2 m. the chief of a corporation or guild ; = *kula-vāra* q.v.; N. of a man;

21.2.3（*ā*）f. `a principal day' N. of the 4th and 8th and 12th and 14th day in a *pakṣa* , or half-month;

21.2.4（*ī*）f. a wife's elder sister; the plant Solanum Jacquini or Solanum longum.

21.3 【梵漢辭典,p632】（中性）獸群，群；群集，集團，一群或一團；種性，種族；團體，工會；高貴的門第；住處，家，住宅；裁判官；（經文）族，宗族，家族，種，種族，種姓，姓種族，族姓，性，親，眷屬，善家，家，戶。

22. पुत्रास् putrās 名詞　兒子們

22.1 【詞尾變化】putrās 根據連音規則，就是從 putrāḥ 變化過來，而 putrāḥ 就是 putra 的陽性複數主格形，所以字典查 putra。

22.2 資料前面已有說明。

【筆者試譯】：於是文殊師利法王子向彌勒大菩薩他與（在場）一切菩薩眾們說道：「各位善男子們！（我）過去聽聞如來（所）說明（佛法）的目標方向，（當場）落起大『法雨』，奏起大（聲）『法鼓』與『法器樂』，高舉大『法旗』，燃起大『法炬』，充滿著『法螺』的聲音，擂擊大『法鼓』的聲音，演說『大法』，與今天佛子們（看見的）如來的說法（景況）相同。」

【什公漢譯】：爾時文殊師利語彌勒菩薩摩訶薩及諸大士：「善男子等，如我惟忖，今佛世尊，欲說大法，雨大法雨，吹大法螺，擊大法鼓，演大法義。諸善男子，我於過去諸佛曾見此瑞，放斯光已即說大法，是故當知，今佛現光亦復如是。」

【英 譯 本】：Whereupon Mañgusrî, the prince royal, addressed Maitreya, the Bodhisattva Mahâsattva, and the whole assembly of Bodhisattvas（in these words）: It is the intention of the Tathâgata, young men of good family, to begin a grand discourse for the teaching of the law, to pour the great rain of the law, to make resound the great drum of the law, to raise the great banner of the law, to kindle the great torch of the law, to blow the great conch trumpet of the law, and to strike the great tymbal of the law. Again, it is the intention of the Tathâgata, young men of good family, to make a grand exposition of the law this very day.

【信譯研究】：信譯。

【第二句】

yathā mama kula-putrāḥ pratibhāti, yathā ca mayā pūrvakāṇāṁ tathāgatānām arhatāṁ samyaksaṁbuddhānām idam evaṁ-rūpaṁ pūrva-nimittaṁ dṛṣṭam abhūt, teṣām api pūrvakāṇāṁ tathāgatānām arhatāṁ samyak-saṁbuddhānām evaṁ raśmi-pramocanāvabhāso 'bhut|

【辭彙研究】

1. मम mama 代名詞　我

1.1 【詞尾變化】mama 是 aham 的陽性單數屬格形，所以字典查 aham。

1.2 資料前面已有說明。

2. प्रतिभाति pratibhāti, 動詞　於～照射（光芒）

2.1 【詞尾變化】pratibhāti 是 prati-√bhā 的第三人稱單數形，所以字典查 prati-√bhā。

2.2 【摩威梵英,p668】

2.2.1 P. *-bhāti* , to shine upon（acc.）; to come in sight , present or offer one's self to（gen. or acc.）MBh.; to appear to the mind（also with *manasi*）, flash upon the thoughts , become clear or manifest , occur to（acc. or gen.）MBh.; to seem or appear to（gen. acc. with or without *prati*）as or like（nom. with or without *iva*, or *yathā* , or *-vat* ind.）MBh. ; to seem fit , appear good , please to（gen.or acc.）

2.2.2 f. an image; light , splendour（see *niṣ-pr-*）; appearance（*a-pr-*）; fitness , suitableness（*a-pr-*）; intelligence , understanding MBh.; presence of mind , genius , wit; audacity , boldness（*a-pr-*）; a thought , idea; a founded supposition; fancy , imagination MBh. ;

2.2.3 *-kṣaya* m. loss or absence of knowledge , want of sense;

2.2.4 *-tas* ind. by fancy or imagination;

2.2.5 --*nvita*（*-bhānv-*）mfn. intelligent , wise ; confident , hold ;

2.2.6 *-balāt* ind. by force of reason or intelligence , wisely;

2.2.7 *-mukha* mfn. at once hitting the right , quick-witted（confident , arrogant）;

2.2.8 *-vat* mfn. endowed with presence of mind , shrewd , intelligent. ; confident , bold. ;

2.2.9 m. the sun , the moon , fire ;

2.2.10 *-vaśāt* ind. = *-tas* ,;

2.2.11 *-vilāsa* m. N. of sev. wks. ;

2.2.12 *-hāni* f. privation of light , dulness , darkness ; = *-kṣay*} ib.

2.3 【梵漢辭典,p249】（動詞）在～之上發光，照射；於（人的～（對格或屬格））顯露自己，使～明白的；出現於（同上）之心，使～明白或理解的，浮想出～；（對格±prati 或屬格）（主格±iva, yathā 或-vat 副詞）以爲或看似～；（人的（對格），（屬格））看得清楚，對～有意的；（經文）說，樂說，能說，辯說，當說，能喜說，說法，樂辯，辯才，以辯才宣示；誦，辨了，惟忖。

3. मया mayā 代名詞　我

3.1 【詞尾變化】mayā 是 aham 的陽性單數工具格形，所以字典查 aham。

3.2 資料前面已有說明。

4. पूर्वकाणां pūrvakāṇāṁ 形容詞（很多個）以前的；很久以前的

4.1 【詞尾變化】pūrvakāṇāṁ 根據連音規則是從 pūrvakāṇām 變化過來的，而 pūrvakāṇām 是 pūrvaka 的陽性複數屬格形，所以字典查 pūrvaka。

5. तथागतानाम् tathāgatānām 名詞　如來們的

5.1 【詞尾變化】tathāgatānām 是 tathāgata 的陽性複數屬格形，所以字典查 tathāgata。

5.2 資料前面已有說明。

6. अर्हतां arhatāṁ 名詞　很多阿羅漢

6.1 【詞尾變化】arhatāṁ 根據連音規則，是從 arhatām 變化過來，而 arhatām 是 arhat 的陽性複數屬格形，所以字典查 arhat。

6.2 資料前面已有說明。

7. सम्यक्संबुद्धानाम् samyaksaṁbuddhānām 形容詞；過去被動分詞　正等正覺

7.1 【詞尾變化】samyaksaṁbuddhānām 是 samyaksaṁbuddha 的陽性複數屬格形，字典查 samyaksaṁbuddha。

7.2 資料前面已有說明。

8. पूर्वनिमित्तं pūrva-nimittaṁ 形容詞　在前面的（在東方的）原因；理由；象徵

8.1 【詞尾變化】pūrva-nimittaṁ 當中，pūrva 沒有詞尾變化，而 nimittaṁ 根據連音規則是從 nimittam 變化過來，而 nimittam 是 nimitta 的陽性單數對格形，所以字典查 nimitta。

8.2 資料前面已有說明。

9. दृष्टम् dṛṣṭam 形容詞／過去被動分詞　被看見

9.1 【詞尾變化】dṛṣṭam 是 dṛṣṭa 的陽性單數對格形，字典查 dṛṣṭa。

9.2　資料前面已有說明。

10. भूत् abhūt 動詞　發生；成爲

10.1 【詞尾變化】abhūt 是√bhū 第三人稱單數的不定過去式形，所以字典查√bhū。

10.2　資料前面已有說明。

11. तेषाम् teṣām 代名詞　這

11.1 【詞尾變化】teṣām 是 tad 的陽性複數屬格形，所以字典查 tad。

11.2　資料前面已有說明。

12. प्रमोचनावभासोऽभुत् pramocanāvabhāso 'bhut 結合詞　放散光芒

12.1 【詞尾變化】

12.1.1 pramocanāvabhāso 'bhut 根據連音規則，可拆成 pramocanāvabhāso abhut 二字，而後者前面已有資料說明。

12.1.2 前者 pramocanāvabhāso 根據連音規則，從 pramocanāvabhāsaḥ 變化過來。

12.1.3 pramocanāvabhāsaḥ 則爲 pramocana 與 avabhāsaḥ 的結合。

12.1.4 pramocana 沒有詞尾變化。

12.1.5 avabhāsaḥ 爲 avabhāsa 的陰性單數屬格形，資料前面已有說明。

12.1.6 abhut 疑爲 abhūt 的異寫，abhūt 部分資料前面已有說明。

12.1.7 所以資料查 pramocana。

12.2 【摩威梵英,p686】

12.2.1 mf（ī）n. liberating from（comp.）MBh.；

12.2.2（ī）f. a species of cucumber;

12.2.3 n. setting free , the act of liberating from（comp.）; discharging , emitting , shedding MBh.（Cf. *unmocana-pramocana.*）

12.3 【梵漢辭典,p921】

12.3.1（形容詞）自～解放的；（經文）能濟，普濟，救濟，度脫；

12.3.2（中性形容詞）流（淚）；自～獲得自由或解脫的。

【筆者試譯】:（照射在）我的善男子們身上的光明，就像是從我很久很久以前（經驗），許多如來，應供（阿羅漢），正等正覺們的，這個類似如此美麗耀眼的（景象），讓（大眾）看見。這在很久很久以前，許多的如來們，應供（阿羅漢），正等正覺們的，正是放過這樣的光明。

【什公漢譯】：欲令眾生咸得聞知一切世間難信之法，故現斯瑞。

【英 譯 本】：Thus it appears to me, young men of good family, as I have witnessed a similar sign of the former Tathâgatas, the Arhats, the perfectly enlightened. Those former Tathâgatas, &c., they, too, emitted a lustorous ray,

【信譯研究】：信譯。這部份梵文所表現的正是文殊菩薩將問題重複表明一次，然後再開啓答案以前的預備動作。這也正是本文前面曾經說明過梵典原文比較有繁複的表現，鳩摩羅什用簡潔的方式一筆帶過，用「刪煩」來作動態對等。

【第三句】

tenaivaṁ prajānāmi-mahā-dharma-śravaṇa-sāṁkathyaṁ tathāgataḥ kartu-kāmo mahā-dharma-śravaṇaṁ śrāvayitu-kāmaḥ, yathedam evaṁ-rūpaṁ pūrva-nimittaṁ prāduṣkṛtavān|

【辭彙研究】

1. तेनैवं tenaivaṁ 代名詞+副詞　正如這
   1.1 【詞尾變化】
      1.1.1 tenaivaṁ 根據連音規則是從 tena evaṁ 兩個字結合過來。
      1.1.2 tena 是 tad 的陽性單數工具格形，字典查 tad。
      1.1.3 evaṁ 是從 evam 變化過來，也就是 eva 的陽性單數對格形，故字典查 eva。
   1.2 資料前面已有說明。
2. प्रजानामि prajānāmi 動詞　自～而生
   2.1 【詞尾變化】prajānāmi 疑似 prajanāmi 的異寫，是 pra-√jan 的現在式第一人稱單數形。字典查 pra-√jan。
   2.2 資料前面已有說明。
3. सांकथ्यं sāṁkathyaṁ 名詞　說話；宣說
   3.1 【詞尾變化】sāṁkathyaṁ 根據連音規則是從 sāṁkathyam 變化過來，而 sāṁkathyam 則是 sāṁkathya 的陽性單數對格形，所以字典查

sāṁkathya。

3.2　資料前面已有說明。

4. तथागतः tathāgataḥ 名詞　如來

4.1【詞尾變化】tathāgataḥ 是 tathāgata 的陽性單數主格形，字典查 tathāgata。

4.2　資料前面已有說明。

5. कर्तुकामो kartukāmo 形容詞　想要做的或打算要做的

5.1【詞尾變化】kartukāmo 根據連音規則是從 kartukāmaḥ 變化過來，而 kartukāmaḥ 則是 kartukāma 的陽性單數主格形，所以字典查 kartukāma。

5.2【摩威梵英,p257】mfn. desirous or intending to do.

5.3【梵漢辭典,p575】（形容詞）想要或打算要做的；（經文）欲令，欲作恩。

6. श्रवणं śravaṇaṁ 名詞　聽聞

6.1【詞尾變化】śravaṇaṁ 根據連音規則是從 śravaṇam 變化過來，而 śravaṇam 是 śravaṇa 的陽性單數對格形，所以字典查 śravaṇa。

6.2　資料前面已有說明。

7. श्रावयितुकामः śrāvayitukāmaḥ 形容詞　想要讓～聽的

7.1【詞尾變化】śrāvayitukāmaḥ 是 śrāvayitukāma 的陽性單數主格形，而 śrāvayitukāma 根據學者研究可分析成 śrāvayitu-kāma，〔註 71〕也就是 √śru—kāma，（śrāvayitu 應爲√śru 的使役動詞命令型的第三人稱單數不規則形）所以字典查√śru 與 kāma。

7.2　資料前面已有說明。

8. यथेदम् yathedam 代名詞　如他

8.1【詞尾變化】yathedam 是 yatha 與 idam 的結合，所以字典查 yatha 與 idam。

8.2　資料前面已有說明。

9. प्रादुष्कृतवान् prāduṣkṛtavān 形容詞　顯現出來的

9.1【詞尾變化】prāduṣkṛtavān 可分析成兩個字，爲 prāduṣ 與 kṛtavān 兩個字，prāduṣ 沒有詞尾變化，而 kṛtavān 是 kṛtavat 的陽性單數主格形，字典查 kṛtavat。

9.2【摩威梵英,p707, prāduṣ】in comp. for prādur（cf. above）.

〔註 71〕請見江島惠教等編《梵藏漢法華經原典總索引》，日本東京：靈友會，1991 年出版。頁 996。

9.3 【摩威梵英,p707, prādur】ind.（prob. fr. prā = pra + dur , `out of doors' ; prā-dūs g. svar-ādi ; -duṣ before k and p;）forth , to view or light , in sight AV.（with as , or bhū , to become manifest , be visible or audible , appear , arise , exist ; with kṛ , to make visible or manifest , cause to appear , reveal , disclose）.

9.4 【摩威梵英,p302, prādur】（副詞）（在户外）〔與 As, BHū, Kṛ 或 BHū, Kṛ 的衍生形連用，但採用 °--之形〕向外，可見地，明白地，在目前；〔與 BHū, Kṛ 連用〕變清楚地，顯現，顯露自己，發起，鳴響；〔與 Kṛ 連用〕始明白，使明示；顯現，點燃（火）；（經文）應起。

9.5 【摩威梵英,p302, kṛtavat】

9.5.1 mfn. perf. p. P. $\sqrt{}$*kṛ*, one who has done or made anything ; one who holds the stake at a game（?）;

9.5.2（*tī*）f. N. of a river.

9.6 【梵漢辭典,p617, kṛtavat】（過去主動分詞）所爲；（經文）作，曾所作。

【筆者試譯】：這正是從聽聞大法的宣說而有的——如來想要做的（就是）想讓聽聞大法的人，就面前顯現這樣的徵兆來，讓他們看到。

【什公漢譯】：缺譯。

【英 譯 本】：and I am convinced that the Tathâgata is about to deliver a grand discourse for the teaching of the law and make his grand speech on the law everywhere heard,

【信譯研究】：非信譯。缺譯所致。

【第四句】

tat kasya hetoḥ? Sarva-loka-vipratyanīyaka-dharma-paryāyaṁ śrāvayitu-kāmas tathāgato'rhan samyak-saṁbuddhaḥ, yathedam evaṁ-rūpaṁ mahā-prātihāryaṁ raśmi-pramocanāvabhāsaṁ ca pūrva-nimittam upadarśayati||

【辭彙研究】

1. तत् tat 代名詞　它

1.1 【詞尾變化】tat 是 tad 的中性單數主格形，所以字典查 tad。

1.2 資料前面已有說明。

2. कस्य kasya 疑問代名詞 什麼

2.1 【詞尾變化】kasya 是 ka 的中性單數屬格形，所以字典查 ka。

2.2 資料前面已有說明。

3. हेतोः hetoḥ 名詞 ～的原因

3.1 【詞尾變化】hetoḥ 是 hetu 的中性單數屬格形，所以字典查 hetu。

3.2 資料前面已有說明。

4. विप्रत्यनीयक vipratyanīyaka 形容詞 難信的

4.1 【詞尾變化】沒有詞尾變化。

4.2 【摩威梵英,p951】mfn. id. Lalit.

4.3 【梵漢辭典,p1446】（形容詞）（經文）難信。

5. पर्यायं paryāyaṁ 名詞 課程；經典

5.1 【詞尾變化】paryāyaṁ 根據連音規則是從 paryāyam 變化過來，即 paryāya 的中性單數對格形，字典查 paryāya。

5.2 資料前面已有說明。

6. श्रावयितुकामस् śrāvayitu-kāmas 形容詞 想要讓～聽的

6.1 【詞尾變化】śrāvayitu-kāmas 根據連音規則，是 śrāvayitu-kāmaḥ 變化而來，而 śrāvayitu-kāmaḥ 則是 śrāvayitu-kāma 陽性單數主格形，所以字典查 śrāvayitu-kāma。

6.2 資料前面已有說明。

7. तथागतोऽर्हन् tathāgato'rhan 名詞 如來，阿羅漢

7.1 【詞尾變化】

7.1.1 根據連音規則，tathāgato'rhan 是由兩個字組成：tathāgato 與 arhan，

7.1.2 tathāgato 根據連音規則，是從 tathāgataḥ 變化過來，也就是 tathāgata 的陽性單數主格形，字典查 tathāgata。

7.1.3 arhan 是 arhat 的陽性單數主格形，所以字典查 arhat。

7.2 資料前面已有說明。

8. सम्यक्संबुद्धः samyaksaṁbuddhaḥ, 名詞 正等正覺

8.1 【詞尾變化】samyaksaṁbuddhaḥ 是 samyaksaṁbuddha 的陽性單數主格

形，所以字典查 samyaksaṁbuddha。

8.2 資料前面已有說明。

9. प्रातिहार्यं prātihāryaṁ 形容詞 神通變化的

9.1 【詞尾變化】prātihāryaṁ 根據連音規則，是從 prātihāryam 變化過來，而 prātihāryam 是 prātihārya 的陽性單數對格形，所以字典查 prātihārya。

9.2 資料前面已有說明。

10. प्रमोचनावभासं pramocanāvabhāsaṁ 形容詞 發散光芒

10.1【詞尾變化】pramocanāvabhāsaṁ 根據連音規則是從 pramocanāvabhāsam 變化過來，而 pramocanāvabhāsam 則是 pramocanāvabhāsa 的陽性單數對格形，所以字典查 pramocanāvabhāsa。

10.2 資料前面已有說明。

11. पूर्वनिमित्तम् pūrva-nimittam 形容詞+名詞 在前面的原因；徵兆；象徵

11.1 【詞尾變化】pūrva-nimittam 是 pūrva-nimitta 的陽性單數對格形，字典查 pūrva-nimitta。

11.2 資料前面已有說明。

12. उपदर्शयति upadarśayati 動詞 凝視，觀察

12.1 【詞尾變化】upadarśayati 爲 upa—darśayati，爲 upa--√dṛś 的使役動詞現在式第三人稱單數形，所以字典查 upa--√dṛś。

12.2 【摩威梵英,p199】

12.2.1P. to descry , perceive RV.; to look at or regard（with indifference）MBh.: Pass. to be perceived , be or become visible , appear RV.: Caus. to cause to see , show , exhibit MBh.; to cause to appear , present a false show , deceive , illude ; to explain , illustrate.

12.2.2 k f. aspect , look , appearance.

12.3 【梵漢辭典,p401】（動詞）（冷靜）凝視；觀察；表示，顯現，現出，裝扮，說明，解說；（經文）示，示見，顯示；現，發現，顯現，顯了，露，令他見，告言，宣說，增發。

【筆者試譯】：原因是什麼呢？一切世間難信的法（課程／經典）分別想要讓（眾生）聽，所有如來，阿羅漢，正等正覺者，正是爲了這樣的原因，讓人看見如此美麗景象的神通變化，發散光芒。

【什公漢譯】：缺譯。

【英 譯 本】：And because the Tathâgata, &c., wishes that this Dharmaparyâya meeting opposition in all the world be heard everywhere, therefore does he display so great a miracle and this fore-token consisting in the luster occasioned by the emission of a ray.

【譯筆研究】：非信譯。鳩摩羅什省略未譯。疑似刪煩。

【小結】

有兩句非信譯。鳩摩羅什在此段內充分展現了意譯的風格，疑似將比較繁複的梵本內文刪減成比較精鍊的漢文。

【第十一段】

अनुस्मराम्यहं कुलपुत्रा अतीतेऽध्वनि असंख्येयैः
कल्पैरसंख्येयतरैर्विपुलैरप्रमेयैरचिन्त्यैरपरिमितैरप्रमाणैस्ततःपरेण परतरं
यदासीत्-तेन कालेन तेन समयेन चन्द्रसूर्यप्रदीपो नाम तथागतोऽर्हन्
सम्यक्संबुद्धो लोक उदपादि विद्याचरणसंपन्नः सुगतो लोकविदनुत्तरः
पुरुषदम्यसारथिः शास्ता देवानां च मनुष्याणां च बुद्धो भगवान्। स धर्मं
देशयति स्म आदौ कल्याणं मध्ये कल्याणं पर्यवसाने कल्याणम्। स्वर्थं सुव्यञ्जनं
केवलं परिपूर्णं परिशुद्धं पर्यवदातं ब्रह्मचर्यं संप्रकाशयति स्म। यदुत श्रावकाणां
चतुरार्यसत्यसंप्रयुक्तं प्रतीत्यसमुत्पादप्रवृत्तं धर्मं देशयति स्म
जातिजराव्याधिमरणशोकपरिदेवदुःखदौर्मनस्योपायासानां समतिक्रमाय
निर्वाणपर्यवसानम्। बोधिसत्त्वानां च महासत्त्वानां च
षट्पारमिताप्रतिसंयुक्तमनुत्तरां सम्यक्संबोधिमारभ्य सर्वज्ञज्ञानपर्यवसानं धर्मं
देशयति स्म॥

【羅馬譯音】

anusmarāmyahaṁ kulaputrā atīte'dhvani asaṁkhyeyaiḥ
kalpairasaṁkhyeyatarairvipulairaprameyairacintyairaparimitairapramāṇaistataḥpar

eṇa parataraṁ yadāsīt-tena kālena tena samayena candrasūryapradīpo nāma tathāgato'rhan samyaksaṁbuddho loka udapādi vidyācaraṇasaṁpannaḥ sugato lokavidanuttaraḥ puruṣadamyasārathiḥ śāstā devānāṁ ca manuṣyāṇāṁ ca buddho bhagavān| sa dharmaṁ deśayati sma ādau kalyāṇaṁ madhye kalyāṇaṁ paryavasāne kalyāṇam| svarthaṁ suvyañjanaṁ kevalaṁ paripūrṇaṁ pariśuddhaṁ paryavadātaṁ brahmacaryaṁ saṁprakāśayati sma| yaduta śrāvakāṇāṁ caturāryasatyasaṁprayuktaṁ pratītyasamutpādapravṛttaṁ dharmaṁ deśayati sma jātijarāvyādhimaraṇaśokaparidevaduḥkhadaurmanasyopāyāsānāṁ samatikramāya nirvāṇaparyavasānam| bodhisattvānāṁ ca mahāsattvānāṁ ca ṣaṭpāramitāpratisaṁyuktamanuttarāṁ samyaksaṁbodhimārabhya sarvajñajñānaparyavasānaṁ dharmaṁ deśayati sma||

【第一句】

anusmarāmy ahaṁ kula-putrā atīte 'dhvani asaṁkhyeyaiḥ kalpair asaṁkhyeyatarair vipulair aprameyair acintyair aparimitair apramāṇais tataḥ pareṇa parataraṁ yadāsīt-tena kālena tena samayena Candrasūryapradīpo nāma tathāgato 'rhan samyak-saṁbuddho loka udapādi vidyā-caraṇa-saṁpannaḥ sugato loka-vid anuttaraḥ puruṣa-damya-sārathiḥ śāstā devānāṁ ca manuṣyāṇāṁ ca buddho bhagavān|

【辭彙研究】

1. अनुस्मराम्य् anusmarāmy 動詞　想起；回憶

   1.1 【詞尾變化】anusmarāmy 根據連音規則，是從 anusmarāmi 變化過來的，而 anusmarāmi 是 anu-√smṛ 的現在式第一人稱單數形，字典查 anu-√smṛ。

   1.2【摩威梵英,p41】to remember , recollect: Caus. P. -*smārayati* , or -*smarayati* , to remind（with acc.）.

   1.3 【梵漢辭典,p1184】（動詞）記憶，回憶（對格）；表白（自白）；（經文）念，思念，憶，隨念，思憶，憶時，憶念，追憶，隨憶念。

2. अतीते atīte 過去被動分詞　過去的

2.1 【詞尾變化】atīte 是 atīta 的陽性單數於格形，所以字典查 atīta。

2.2 【摩威梵英,p16】

2.2.1 mfn. gone by , past , passed away , dead ; one who has gone through or got over or beyond , one who has passed by or neglected ; negligent ; passed , left behind ; excessive ;

2.2.2 m. N. of a particular;

2.2.3（*am*）n. the past.

2.3 【梵漢辭典,p195】（過去被動分詞／形容詞）過去，過去的；（經文）過，去，過去，謝；滅，出。

3. ऽध्वनि 'dhvani 名詞　世；時間

3.1 【詞尾變化】根據連音規則，'dhvani 是從 adhvani 變化過來的，而 adhvani 是 adhvan 的陽性單數於格形，所以字典查 adhvan。

3.2【摩威梵英,p24】ā m. a road , way , orbit ; a journey , course ; distance ; time Buddh. and Jain. ; means , method , resource ; the zodiac（?）, sky , air ; a place ; a recension of the Vedas and the school upholding it ; assault（?）; ifc. adhva , as.

3.3 【梵漢辭典,p36】（陽性）路；旅行；徘徊，距離；時；（經文）路，道路，世路，行旅；世，時。

4. असंख्येयैः asaṁkhyeyaiḥ 未來被動分詞　無量數；未來還有很多要數的

4.1 【詞尾變化】asaṁkhyeyaiḥ 是 asaṁkhyeya 的陽性複數工具格形，字典查 asaṁkhyeya。

4.2 【摩威梵英,p118】

4.2.1 mfn. innumerable MBh. BhP.;

4.2.2 m. a N. of Śiva.;

4.2.3（*am*）n. an innumerable multitude; an exceedingly large number Buddh.

4.3 【梵漢辭典,p167】（未來被動分詞）〔=a-saṃkhya〕；（經文）〔數詞〕無數，無央數，不可屬，不可計，阿僧衹，僧衹。

5. कल्पैर् kalpair 形容詞　劫

5.1 【詞尾變化】kalpair 根據連音規則是從 kalpaiḥ 變化過來，是 kalpa 的陽性複數工具格形，所以字典查 kalpa。

5.2 【摩威梵英,p262】

5.2.1 mf（*ā*）n.（*klṛp*），practicable，feasible，possible; proper，fit，able，competent，equal to BhP.；

5.2.2 m. a sacred precept, law, rule, ordinance, manner of acting，proceeding，practice（esp. that prescribed by the Vedas）RV. MBh.；the most complete of the six Vedāṇgas（that which prescribes the ritual and gives rules for ceremonial or sacrificial acts）; one of two cases，one side of an argument，an alternative; investigation，research Comm. on *Sāṃkhyak.*；resolve，determination；（in medic.）treatment of the sick，manner of curing; the art of preparing medicine，pharmacy; the doctrine of poisons and antidotes；

5.2.3（ifc.）having the manner or form of anything，similar to，resembling，like but with a degree of inferiority，almost; a fabulous period of time（a day of *Brahmā* or one thousand *Yugas*，a period of four thousand，three hundred and twenty millions of years of mortals，measuring the duration of the world；a month of *Brahmā* is supposed to contain thirty such *Kalpas*；according to the MBh.，twelve months of *Brahmā* constitute his year，and one hundred such years his lifetime；fifty years of Brahma1's are supposed to have elapsed，and we are now in the *śvetavārāha-kalpa* of the fifty-first；at the end of a *Kalpa* the world is annihilated；hence *kalpa* is said to be equal to *kalpānta* below；with Buddhists the *Kalpas* are not of equal duration）BhP.；N. of Mantras which contain a form of *klṛp*；a kind of dance；N. of the first astrological mansion；N. of a son of *Dhruva* and *Bhrami* BhP.; of *Śiva* MBh.; the tree of paradise；= *-taru* below;（with *Jainas*）a particular abode of deities；

5.2.4（*am*）n. a kind of intoxicating liquor.

5.2.5 Nom. Ā -pāyate，to become a Kalpa，to appear as long as a Kalpa.

5.3 【梵漢辭典,p553】

5.3.1（形容詞）可實行的，可能的；能勝任或有能力做（屬格／於格）的，適合於～；幾乎等於～，幾乎；（經文）如，猶如，似；等，同；喻；作。

5.3.2（陽性）教誡，聖訓，法則，規則，習慣，風俗，（成爲 Veda 六支分之一）有關儀式規則的主文，（尤指 Veda 規定的）實行義務；宇宙論的時間（Brahman 神的一日=千 yuga）；二者之一；探求，調查；決心；疾病的治療，治療的方法；調製藥品的技術；〔星宿之一〕；〔Dhruva 與 Bhrami 的兒子之名〕；〔Śiva 神號〕；（經文）儀軌，細軌，細法事；方便，想，念，想念，妄想，覺，覺想；執，執著，分別，能分別，分別妄心，妄想分別，釋，解，分別時節，（譯音）劫；劫波，劫簸；可。

6. असंख्येयतरैर् asaṁkhyeyatarair 形容詞　比無量還更多

6.1 【詞尾變化】asaṁkhyeyatarair 根據連音規則爲 asaṁkhyeyataraiḥ 變化，而 asaṁkhyeyataraiḥ 爲 asaṁkhyeyatara 的陽性複數工具格，所以字典查 asaṁkhyeyatara。

6.2 【摩威梵英】資料同前面第四個單字。

6.3 【梵漢辭典,p168】（形容詞比較級）（經文）復過無數，過於算數。（譯音）無量阿僧祇。

7. विपुलैर् vipulair 形容詞　廣大的

7.1 【詞尾變化】vipulair 根據連音規則，爲 vipulaiḥ 所變化，而 vipulaiḥ 爲 vipula 的陽性複數工具格形，字典查 vipula。

7.2 資料前面已有說明。

8. अप्रमेयैर् aprameyair 形容詞　無量的

8.1 【詞尾變化】aprameyair 根據連音規則，爲 aprameyaiḥ 所變化，而 aprameyaiḥ 爲 aprameya 的陽性複數工具格形，字典查 aprameya。

8.2 資料前面已有說明。

9. अचिन्त्यैर् acintyair 形容詞　不可思議

9.1 【詞尾變化】acintyair 根據連音規則，爲 acintyaiḥ 所變化，而 acintyaiḥ 爲 acintya 的陽性複數工具格形，字典查 acintya。

9.2 【摩威梵英,p9】

9.2.1 mfn. inconceivable , surpassing thought;

9.2.2 m. N. of Śiva.

9.3 【梵漢辭典,p25】

9.3.1（未來被動分詞）不可想像；（經文）非心，難思，不思議，不可議，不可思議，不可思惟，不可思量，不應思議，難可思議，無所思惟。

9.3.2（陽性）〔Śiva 神名〕；（中性）（經文）〔數詞〕不可思，不可思議。

9.3.3（形容詞）（經文）難思，不思議，難思議；更不思，不可思議，不思議，脫思議，不能思議，非可思議，不可得思議，不可數思議。

10. अपरिमितैर् aparimitair 形容詞　無邊

10.1 【詞尾變化】aparimitair 根據連音規則，為 aparimitaiḥ 所變化，而 aparimitaiḥ 為 aparimita 的陽性複數工具格形，字典查 aparimita。

10.2 【摩威梵英,p51】mfn. unmeasured , either indefinite or unlimited AV.

10.3 【梵漢辭典,p134】（過去被動分詞）不可量，不可限；（經文）無量。

11. अप्रमाणैस् apramāṇais 形容詞　無可量；不知道怎麼量

11.1 【詞尾變化】apramāṇais 根據連音規則，為 apramāṇaiḥ 所變化，而 apramāṇaiḥ 為 apramāṇa 的陽性複數工具格形，字典查 apramāṇa。

11.2 【摩威梵英,p58】n. a rule which is no standard of action MBh. ;（in discussion）a statement of no importance or authority.

11.3 【梵漢辭典,p141】（中性）非行為的準則；無權威；無價值；（經文）廣，廣大；無量，難量，不可度量，無有限量，無量，無邊。

12. ततः tataḥ 副詞　在那時

12.1 【詞尾變化】tataḥ 是 tad 的陽性單數從格形，所以字典查 tad。

12.2 資料前面已有說明。

13. परेण pareṇa 副詞　越過

13.1 【詞尾變化】沒有詞尾變化。

13.2 【摩威梵英,p606】see under 1 para.

13.3 【摩威梵英,p586】

13.3.1 mf（ā）n. far , distant , remote（in space）, opposite , ulterior , farther than , beyond , on the other or farther side of , extreme ; previous（in time）, former ; ancient , past ; later , future , next ; following , succeeding , subsequent ; final , last ; exceeding（in number or degree）, more than ; better or worse than , superior or inferior to , best or worst , highest , supreme , chief RV.; strange , foreign , alien , adverse , hostile ib. ; other than , different from（abl.）; left , remaining; concerned or anxious for（loc.）;

13.3.2 m. another（different from one's self）, a foreigner , enemy , foe , adversary RV.; a following letter or sound of the palace of Mitravindā ib. ;

13.3.3 m. or n. the Supreme or Absolute Being , the Universal Soul ;

13.3.4（ā）f. a foreign country , abroad（?）; a species of plant L. ; N. of a sound in the first of its 4 stages; a partic. measure of time ; N. of a river MBh. ; of a goddess（cf. s.v.）n. remotest distance MBh. ; highest point or degree ib. ; final beatitude; the number 10 ,000 ,000 ,000（as the full age of Brahma1）; N. of partic.; any chief matter or paramount object; the wider or mare extended or remoter meaning of a word Jaim.;（in logic）genus ; existence（regarded as the common property of all things）;

13.3.5（*am*）ind. afterwards , later ;（with abl.）beyond , after MBh.; in a high degree , excessively , greatly , completely ib. ; rather , most willingly , by all means ib. ; I will , so be it. ; at the most , at the utmost , merely , no more than , nothing but ib. ; but , however , otherwise ;

13.3.6（*pareṇa*）ind. farther , beyond , past（with acc.）RV.; thereupon , afterwards , later than , after（with abl.or gen.）. MBh. ;

13.3.7（pare）ind. later , farther , in future , afterwards RV. MBh.

13.4 【梵漢辭典,p850】（副詞／介詞）在～（對格）的對面，越過～；經過～；在（從格／屬格）之後；其後，於後，後來；（經文）過。

14. परतरं parataraṁ 形容詞　又後面

14.1 【詞尾變化】parataraṁ 根據連音規則，爲 parataram 所變化，而 parataram 爲 paratara 的陽性單數對格形，paratara 爲 para 的比較級，所以字典查 para。

14.2 【摩威梵英】資料前面已有說明。

14.3 【梵漢辭典,p848】

14.3.1（形容詞）〔帶到外面：pṛ 2.〕：

14.3.1.1〔關於地點〕彼（從格）遙遠的；遠隔的，遠方的；對面的（岸）；來（世）；

14.3.1.2〔關於時間〕過去的，以前的；未來的，以後的；在（從格）之後，最後的，最遙遠的（年代），最高的（年歲，生存期間）；（經文）後，當來。

14.3.1.3〔關於數量〕超過，更多的；剩下的；（經文）餘。

14.3.1.4〔關於順序〕接續，繼～而來。

14.3.1.5〔關於程度〕（從格）更傑出的，更刀的，更好的，更壞的；最好的，卓越的，最善的；最上部的，最深的，最大的；（經文）勝，最勝，利。

14.3.1.6〔關於範圍〕超越（從格），即（從格）無法到達的；

14.3.1.7〔關於含義〕別的，外來的，未知的，敵對的；與～（從格）不同的；（經文）他，異。

14.3.2（陽性）後裔；他人；反對者，敵人，仇敵；宇宙精神，覺對者；（經文）他，他人，餘，餘物。

14.3.3（中性）最遠距離；高度，頂上，頂點；至福；（字詞）進一步或最高意義；主要目的，主要事物。

14.3.4（形容詞）以～爲主=以～爲目的；熱衷於～，對～深爲感動；主要由～構成的或以～爲主要目的，完全依據～；（經文）住，取，貪著。

15. यदासीत् yadāsīt 關係代名詞+動詞　在於那個時間點

15.1 【詞尾變化】yadāsīt 根據連音規則是從 yadā 與 āsīt 兩個字結合而成。而 yadā 根據連音規則是從 yadaḥ 變化過來，也就是 yad 的陽性複數對格形，資料前面已有說明。Āsīt 爲√as 的未完成過去式的第三人稱單數形，所以字典查√as。

15.2【摩威梵英,p117】cl.2. P. *asti* ; p. m. *sat* f. *satī*）to be , live , exist , be present ; to take place , happen ; to abide , dwell , stay ; to belong to（gen. or dat.）; to fall to the share of. happen to any one（gen.）; to be equal to（dat.）; to turn out , tend towards any result , prove（with dat.）; to become ; to be.

15.3 【梵漢辭典,p162】（動詞，II）在，存在，起，發起，住，存於，在於～，屬於～，歸於～；持有或擁有，存在於，在～特有的；在～做準備，可與～相比，使～變成可能；在～變成充足的；在～發生的；（經文）有，在，住在，轉。

16. कालेन kālena 名詞　從那（時）

16.1 【詞尾變化】kālena 爲 kāla 的陽性單數工具格形，所以字典查 kāla。

16.2 資料前面已有說明。

17. समयेन samayena 名詞　時

17.1 【詞尾變化】samayena 爲 samaya 的陽性單數工具格形，所以字典查 samaya。

17.2 【摩威梵英,p1164】m.（ifc. f. *ā*）coming together , meeting or a place of meeting AV.; intercourse with（instr.）; coming to a mutual understanding , agreement , compact , covenant , treaty , contract , arrangement , engagement , stipulation , conditions of agreement , terms ; convention , conventional rule or usage , established custom , law , rule , practice , observance MBh. BhP. ; order , direction , precept , doctrine MBh. ;（in rhet.）the conventional meaning or scope of a word ; appointed or proper time , right moment for doing anything, opportunity , occasion , time , season MBh. ; juncture , circumstances , case ; an ordeal; sign , hint , indication; demonstrated conclusion ib. ; limit , boundary ib. ; solemn address , harangue , speech , declaration ;（in gram.）a Vedic passage which is the repetition of another one;（in dram.）end of trouble or distress ; N. of a son of Dharma; N. of the author of a Mantra.

17.3 【梵漢辭典,p1084】（陽性）一起來的，集會的場所；一致，同意，合約，裁決，約定；條約；條件；與～交往的；爲～所指定的或適當的時間，場合，時間，季節，機會，好時機；情況或事情；習慣，一般的習俗，慣例，例行，規則；法令，教訓，戒律，教義；（語言的）一般意思或使用範圍；（經文）約，時，候，劫，宗，本文，三昧，三摩野。

18. चन्द्रसूर्यप्रदीपो Candrasūryapradīpo 名詞　日月燈明

18.1 【詞尾變化】Candrasūryapradīpo 根據連音規則是從 Candrasūryapradīpaḥ 變化過來，而 Candrasūryapradīpaḥ 是 Candrasūryapradīpa 的陽性單數主格形。Candrasūryapradīpa 可拆解成 Candra—sūrya—pradīpa 三個字，其中 Candra（名詞）月亮，sūrya（名詞）太陽，資料前面均已有說明，字典查 pradīpa。

18.2 【摩威梵英,p680】

18.2.1 m. a light , lamp , lantern MBh. ; N. of wk. ;

18.2.2 -*mañjarī* f. N. of Comm. on the Amara-koṣa ;

18.2.3 -*śaraṇa-dhvaja* m. N. of a Mahoraga-rāja ;

18.2.4 -*sāha* m. N. of a prince ;

18.2.5 -*siṁha* m. N. of an author.

18.3 【梵漢辭典,p906】(陽性)燈火;燈,注釋;(經文)光,明,現,燈,燈光,燈明,燈炬,燈焰,燈燭,燃燈,炬,火把。

19. तथागतोऽर्हन् tathāgato 'rhan 名詞　如來,應供(阿羅漢)

19.1 【詞尾變化】tathāgato 'rhan 根據連音規則爲 tathāgataḥ 與 arhan 二字,其中 tathāgataḥ 爲 tathāgata 的陽性單數主格形,arhan 爲 arhat 的陽性單數主格形,所以字典查 tathāgata 與 arhat。

19.2 資料前面已有說明。

20. सम्यक्संबुद्धो samyak-saṁbuddho 名詞　正等正覺

20.1 【詞尾變化】samyak-saṁbuddho 根據連音規則,是從 samyak-saṁbuddhaḥ 變化過來,也就是 samyak-saṁbuddha 的陽性單數主格形,所以字典查 samyak-saṁbuddha。

20.2 資料前面已有說明。

21. उदपादि udapādi 動詞　生起;生

21.1 【詞尾變化】udapādi 據學者研究,應該是從字根 ut-√pad 變化過來的,〔註 72〕所以字典查 ut-√pat。

21.2 【摩威梵英,p180】(ud-pad)ā -padyate , to arise , rise , originate , be born or produced ; to come forth , become visible , appear ; to be ready MBh. BhP. ; to take place , begin: Caus. P. -pādayati(rarely Ā. -te), to produce , beget , generate ; to cause , effect ; to cause to issue or come forth , bring forward MBh.; to mention , quote(see ut-panna).

21.3 【梵漢辭典,p823】(動詞)(經文)生,有,起,出生,生起,出興。

22. विद्या vidyā 名詞　知識

22.1 【詞尾變化】沒有詞尾變化。

22.2 【摩威梵英,p964】f. knowledge, science , learning , scholarship , philosophy RV.(according to some there are four Vidyās or sciences , 1. trayī , the triple Veda ; 2. ānvīkṣikī , logic and metaphysics ; 3. daṇḍa-nīti , the science of government ; 4. vārttā , practical arts , such as

〔註 72〕請見江島惠教等編《梵藏漢法華經原典總索引》,日本東京:靈友會 1985 年出版,頁 189。

agriculture , commerce , medicine; and Manu vii , 43 adds a fifth , viz. ātma-vidyā , knowledge of soul or of spiritual truth ; according to others , Vidyā has fourteen divisions , viz. the four Vedas , the six Vedāṇgas , the Purāṇas , the Mīmāṇsā. Nyāya , and Dharma or law; or with the four Upa-vedas , eighteen divisions ; others reckon 33 and even 64 sciences 〔=kalās or arts〕 ; Knowledge is also personified and identified with Durgā ; she is even said to have composed prayers and magical formulas）; any knowledge whether true or false（with Pa1s3upatas）; a spell , incantation MBh. ; magical skill; a kind of magical pill（which placed in the mouth is supposed to give the power of ascending to heaven）; Premna Spinosa; a mystical N. of the letter i. ; a small bell .

22.3 【梵漢辭典,p1420】（陰性）知事，學識，學術（尤其指三吠陀的知識）；咒法，咒術；咒語，（佛教術語）明咒；（經文）慧，解，識，明了，明，術，明處，五明處，明論；明咒，咒禁，咒術，明咒力。

23. चरण caraṇa 名詞　行動

23.1 【詞尾變化】沒有詞尾變化。

23.2 【摩威梵英,p389】

23.2.1 m. n.（g. *ardharcādi*）a foot;（ifc. pl.）`the feet of' , the venerable MBh.; a pillar , supor; the root（of a tree）; a Pāda or line of a stanza ; a dactyl ; a 4th part（*pāda*）; a section , subdivision; a school or branch of the Veda MBh. ;

23.2.2 n. going round or about , motion , course RV; acting , dealing , managing ,（liturgical）performance , observance AV.; behaviour , conduct of life; good or moral conduct MBh.; practising; grazing; consuming , eating; a particular high number.

23.3 【梵漢辭典,p314】

23.3.1（陽性／中性）足（腳）；Veda 的學派；柱，支持；部分，細別；（經文）足，腳，師，行，遊步。

23.3.2（中性）徬徨；進路；處置；（慶典的）舉行；（善良的）行爲；實行，遂行；（經文）行，道

24. संपन्नः saṁpannaḥ 形容詞　成就的

24.1 【詞尾變化】saṁpannaḥ 爲 saṁpanna 的陽性單數主格形，所以字典查 saṁpanna。又 saṁpanna 即 saṁ--panna，即 saṁ-√pad

24.2 【摩威梵英,p1172】Ā *-padyate*, to fall or happen well , turn out well , succeed , prosper , accrue to（dat. or gen.）AV.; to become full or complete（as a number）, amount to; to fall together , meet or unite with , obtain , get into , partake of（instr. or acc.）MBh.; to enter into , be absorbed in（acc. or loc.）; to be produced , be brought forth , be born , arise MBh.; to become , prove , turn into（nom.）MBh.; to be conducive to , produce（dat.）;（with adv. in *sāt*）to become thoroughly; to fall into a Person's , power;（with adv. in *tra*）to fall to a person's share; to produce a partic. sound（as that expressed by an onomatopoetic word in *ā*）: Caus. *-pādayati*（rarely*-te*）, to cause to succeed , cause to arise , bring about , produce , effect , accomplish（with *śuśrūṣām* and gen. , `to obey'）MBh.; to make full , complete; to transform , make or turn into（acc.）; to provide or furnish with（instr. ; with *kriyayā* , to charge or entrust a person with a business'）MBh. SaddhP. ; to afford to , procure for（dat. or gen.）MBh.; to attain , obtain , acquire AV.; to ponder on , deliberate MBh. ; to consent , agree: Desid. of Caus. *-pipādayiṣati*: Intens. *-panīpadyate* , to fit well.

24.3 【梵漢辭典,p1103】（過去被動分詞）（經文）具，足；獲；備，具足，成就，成立，圓滿；充滿；得圓滿，成就具足，茂盛，隆盛，有者；極鮮白。

25. सुगतो sugato 形容詞　佛陀

25.1 【詞尾變化】sugato 根據連音規則，即 sugataḥ 的變化，而 sugataḥ 是 sugata 的陽性單數主格形，所以字典查 sugata。

25.2 資料前面已有說明。

26. लोकविद् loka-vid 形容詞　對世間精通的

26.1 【詞尾變化】沒有詞尾變化。

26.2 資料前面已有說明。

27. अनुत्तरः anuttaraḥ 形容詞　無上的

27.1【詞尾變化】anuttaraḥ 是 anuttara 的陽性單數主格，所以字典查 anuttara。

27.2 資料前面已有說明。

28. दम्य damya 形容詞／未來被動分詞　馴服；調御

28.1 【詞尾變化】沒有詞尾變化。

28.2 【摩威梵英,p469】

28.2.1 mfn. tamable BhP.;

28.2.2 m. a young bullock that has to be tamed MBh.

28.2.3 mfn. being in a house , homely RV.

28.3 【梵漢辭典,p346】（未來被動分詞）可馴服的；（經文）調御。

29. सारथिः sārathiḥ 名詞　駕馭者

29.1 【詞尾變化】sārathiḥ 是 sārathi 的陽性單數主格形，所以字典查 sārathi。

29.2 【摩威梵英,p1208】m.（fr. *sa-ratha*）a charioteer , driver of a car , coachman（forming a mixed caste , commonly called Sārthī , and supposed to have sprung from a *Kṣatriya* father and *Brāhman* mother）RV.; any leader or guide（see *nau-* , *vākya-s-*）; a helper , assistant（see *karma-s-*）; the son of a *Saratha*（q.v.）; the ocean; N. of a town.

29.3 【梵漢辭典,p1135】（陽性）馭者；（經文）導，御者；調御者；馭者；調御之師，調御大師。

30. शास्ता śāstā 動詞　控制；教導

30.1 【詞尾變化】śāstā 是√śās 的迂迴未來式第三人稱單數形，所以字典查√śās。

30.2 【摩威梵英,p1060】

30.2.1（cf. śaṃs）cl. 2. , to chastise , correct , censure , punish RV.; to restrain , control , rule , govern MBh.; to administer the laws MBh. ; to direct , bid , order , command , enjoin , decree（with an inf. or a sentence followed by iti）ib. ; to teach , instruct , inform（with two acc. , or with acc. of pers. and dat. or loc. of thing）RV.; to confess（a crime）; to announce , proclaim; to predict , foretell; to blame , reject , disdain（?）RV. ; to praise , commend（=śaṃs）: Pass. to be chastised or corrected MBh.: Caus., to recommend.

30.2.2 f. command ; a commander , ruler RV.

30.2.3 strong form of 1. śas.

30.2.4 strong form for 3. Śas.

30.3 【梵漢辭典,p1146】(動詞)矯正,譴責,懲罰,控制,管制,執法;支配,統治,掌控,指示或命令做~,關於,教訓,告誡,稱讚,自白。(經文)教授,教誡,教訓,調御。

31. देवानां devānāṁ 名詞　天人

31.1 【詞尾變化】devānāṁ 根據連音規則是 devānām 變化過來,而 devānām 是 deva 的陽性複數屬格形,所以字典查 deva。

31.2 資料前面已有說明。

32. मनुष्याणां manuṣyāṇāṁ 形容詞　人的

32.1 【詞尾變化】manuṣyāṇāṁ 根據連音規則是從 manuṣyāṇām 變化過來,而 manuṣyāṇām 是 manuṣya 的陽性複數屬格形,所以字典查 manuṣya。

32.2 【摩威梵英,p784】

32.2.1 mf(ā)n. human , manly , useful or , friendly to man RV. ;

32.2.2 m. a man , human being RV.; a man(as opp. to woman); a husband; a class of deceased ancestors(those who receive the Piṇḍa offering).

32.3 【梵漢辭典,p711】

32.3.1(形容詞)人的;適合人們的;對人類有好,有益人類的。

32.3.2(陽性)人類;男子;丈夫;人類的祖先;(經文)人,丈夫,人身,人類,人民,世人,國人,土人。

33. बुद्धो buddho 名詞　佛陀

33.1 【詞尾變化】buddho 根據連音規則是從 buddhaḥ 變化過來,而 buddhaḥ 則是 buddha 的陽性單數主格形,所以字典查 buddha。

33.2 資料前面已有說明。

34. भगवान् bhagavān 名詞　世尊

34.1 【詞尾變化】bhagavān 是 bhagava 的陽性複數對格形,所以字典查 bhagava。

34.2 資料前面已有說明。

【筆者試譯】:我回想起過去世上的佛子在無法數許多世以前(無量劫),廣大無量無邊,不知道該怎麼數的時間,從那某個時間點算起,有一位名叫日月燈明的如來,應供(阿羅漢),成就世間正等正覺者(正遍知),知識與修行的成就者(明行足),得到涅槃者(善逝),明白世間知識者(世間解），無上者（無上士），駕馭馴服眾生者（調御丈夫），能當天界與人間的師範（天人師），覺悟者（佛），世人都敬重者（世尊）。

【什公漢譯】：諸善男子，如過去無量無邊不可思議阿僧祇劫，爾時有佛，號日月燈明如來、應供、正遍知、明行足、善逝、世間解、無上士、調御丈夫、天人師、佛、世尊。

【英 譯 本】：I remember, young men of good family, that in the days of yore, many immeasurable, inconceivable, immense, infinite, countless Æons, more than countless Æons ago, nay, long and very long before, there was born a Tathâgata called Kandrasûryapradîpa, an Arhat, &c., endowed with science and conduct, a Sugata, knower of the world, an incomparable tamer of men, a teacher（and ruler）of gods and men, a Buddha and Lord.

【信譯研究】：信譯。

【第二句】

sa dharmaṁ deśayati sma ādau kalyāṇaṁ madhye kalyāṇaṁ paryavasāne kalyāṇam|

【辭彙研究】

1. धर्मं dharmaṁ 形容詞　佛法
   1.1 【詞尾變化】dharmaṁ 根據連音規則，是從 dharmam 變化過來，而 dharmam 則是 dharma 的陽性單數對格形，所以字典查 dharma。
   1.2 資料前面已有說明。
2. देशयति deśayati 動詞　講授
   2.1 【詞尾變化】deśayati 是√diś 的使役動詞現在式第三人稱單數形，所以字典查√diś。
   2.2 資料前面已有說明。
3. आदौ ādau 形容詞　開始的
   3.1 【詞尾變化】ādau 爲 ādi 的陽性單數於格形，所以字典查 ādi。
   3.2 【摩威梵英,p136】
   3.2.1 m. beginning , commencement ; a firstling , first-fruits ; ifc. beginning

with , et caetera , and so on;

3.2.2 ādau ind. in the beginning , at first.

3.2.3 mfn. beginning with ā.

3.3 【梵漢辭典,p38】（陽性）始（經文）初，最初，始，前，先；元，本，本來。

4. कल्याणं kalyāṇaṁ 形容詞　良善的

4.1 【詞尾變化】kalyāṇaṁ 根據連音規則，是從 kalyāṇam 變化過來，而 kalyāṇam 則是 kalyāṇa 的陽性單數對格形，所以字典查 kalyāṇa。

4.2 【摩威梵英,p263】

4.2.1 mf（ī）n. beautiful , agreeable RV.; illustrious , noble , generous ; excellent , virtuous , good ; beneficial , salutary , auspicious ; happy , prosperous , fortunate , lucky , well , right RV. AV. MBh.;

4.2.2 m. a particular（sung at night）; N. of a *Gandharva* ; of a prince; of the author of the poem *Gītā-gaṅgā-dhara* ;

4.2.3（ī）f. a cow ; the plant Glycine Debilis ; red arsenic ; a particular *Rāgiṇī* ; N. of *Dākṣāyaṇī* in Malaya ; N. of one of the mothers attending on *Skanda* MBh.; N. of a city in the *Dekhan* and of one in Ceylon ; a river in Ceylon ;

4.2.4（am）n. good fortune , happiness , prosperity ; good conduct , virtue ; a festival; gold; heaven; N. of the eleventh of the fourteen *Pūrvas* or most ancient writings of the *Jainas* ; a form of salutation.

4.3 【梵漢辭典,p555】（形容詞）美麗的，可愛的；善良的，有道德的，傑出的，高尚的；受祝福的，吉祥的，幸運的，繁榮的，正直的；（經文）善，賢善，親善，眞善，善勝，正眞，眞實；淨，淨調柔，妙，妙善，微妙。

5. मध्ये madhye 形容詞　中間的

5.1 【詞尾變化】沒有詞尾變化。

5.2 【摩威梵英,p782】ind. in the middle , in the midst , within , between , among , in the presence of MBh.

5.3 【梵漢辭典,p673】

5.3.1（形容詞）中的；中央的，普通的，平凡的，居中的，中型的，適度的，中間的；中性的；（經文）中，間，中間，中央。

5.3.2（陽性／中性）身體的中部，腰部；（經文）腰，中間，中央，內側，內部；頂點。

6. पर्यवसाने paryavasāne 形容詞　後面；結束

6.1 【詞尾變化】paryavasāne 是 paryavasāna 的陽性單數於格形，所以字典查 paryavasāna。

6.2 【摩威梵英,p607】n. end , termination , conclusion , issue; comprehending , including , amounting to（loc.）.

6.3 【梵漢辭典,p872】（形容詞）完結，終了；到達（於格）；包含；（經文）終，後，最後；後際，究竟，盡，窮盡，窮，期。

【筆者試譯】：那麼，過去講授佛法，開始（講）的時候很好，中間（講）的時候也很好，結尾（講）的時候也很好。

【什公漢譯】：演說正法。初善，中善，後善。

【英 譯 本】：He showed the law; he revealed the duteous course which is holy at its commencement, holy in its middle, holy at the ends,

【信譯研究】：信譯。

【第三句】

svarthaṁ suvyañjanaṁ kevalaṁ paripūrṇaṁ pariśuddhaṁ paryavadātaṁ brahma-caryaṁ saṁprakāśayati sma|

【辭彙研究】

1. स्वर्थं svarthaṁ 形容詞　追求崇高的價值

1.1 【詞尾變化】svarthaṁ 根據連音規則，是從 svartham 變化過來，而 svartham 則是 svartha 的陽性單數對格形，所以字典查 svartha。

1.2 【摩威梵英,p1282】mf（ā）n. pursuing or serving worthy ends RV.

1.3 【梵漢辭典,p1258】（形容詞）追求崇高目標的，心向高身目標的；（經文）義善；妙義，義妙；其義深遠；義達微妙，其義微妙，文義殊勝。

2. सुव्यञ्जनं suvyañjanaṁ 形容詞　明顯的；清晰易解的

2.1 【詞尾變化】suvyañjanaṁ 根據連音規則，是從 suvyañjanam 變化過來，

而 suvyañjanam 則是 suvyañjana 的陽性單數對格形，suvyañjana 是 su—vyañjana 兩字組合，su 前面已有資料說明，所以字典查 vyañjana。

2.2 【摩威梵英,p1029】

2.2.1 mfn. manifesting , indicating ;

2.2.2 m.（once for n. ; cf. below）a consonant; *Pandanus Odoratissimus* ; = *vāditra-karman* ;

2.2.3（*ā*）f.（in rhet.）implied indication , allusion , suggestion; a figurative expression;

2.2.4 n. decoration , ornament RV.; manifestation , indication; allusion , suggestion; figurative expression , irony , sarcasm; specification; a mark , badge , spot , sign , token; insignia , paraphernalia ; symptom（of a disease）; mark of sex or gender（as the beard , breasts）, the private organs（male or female）MBh.; anything used in cooking or preparing food , seasoning , sauce , condiment MBh.; a consonant; a syllable; the letter; a limb , member , part; a day; purification of a sacrificial animal; a fan ;

2.2.5 -*kāra* m. the preparer of a sauce or condiment MBh. ;

2.2.6 -*guṇa*（?）m. N. of wk. on condiments in cookery ;

2.2.7 -*saṃgama* m. a collection or group of consonants;

2.2.8 -*saṃdhi* m.（in gram.）the junction of consonants ib. , ;

2.2.9 -*saṃnipāta* m. a falling together or conjunction of consonants ib. ;

2.2.10 -*sthāne* ind. in the place of sauce or seasoning ib. ;

2.2.11 -*hārīkā* f. N. of a female demon supposed to remove the hair of a woman's pudenda;

2.2.12 -*nodaya* mfn. followed by a consonant;

2.2.13 -*nopadha* mfn. preceded by a consonant ib.

2.3 【梵漢辭典,p1249, suvyañjana】（經文）語善，言巧妙，語巧妙，妙言辭，字言妙。

3. परिपूर्णं paripūrṇaṁ 過去被動分詞　圓滿

3.1 【詞尾變化】paripūrṇaṁ 根據連音規則，是從 paripūrṇam 變化過來，而 paripūrṇam 則是 paripūrṇa 的陽性單數對格形，所以字典查 paripūrṇa。

3.2 【摩威梵英,p597】

3.2.1 mfn. quite full; completely filled or covered with , occupied by（comp.）MBh.; accomplished , perfect , whole , complete ib. ; fully satisfied , content R. ;

3.2.2 *-candra-vimala-prabha* m. N. of a Sama1dhi ;

3.2.3 *-tā* f. *-tva* n. completion , fulness , satiety , satisfaction ;

3.2.4 *-bhāṣin* mfn. speaking perfectly i.e. very wisely ;

3.2.5 *-mānasa* mfn. satisfied in mind ;

3.2.6 *-mukha* mf（ī）n. having the face entirely covered or smeared or painted with（comp.）Caurap. ;

3.2.7 *-sahasra-candra-vatī* f. `possessing a thousand full moons' , N. of Indra's wife;

3.2.8 *-vyañjanatā* f. having the sexual organs complete（one of the 80 secondary marks of a Buddha）;

3.2.9 *-ṇārtha* mfn. having attained one's aim; full of meaning , wise（as a speech）MBh. ;

3.2.10 *-ṇendu* m. the full moon.

3.3 【梵漢辭典,p862】（過去被動分詞）被～充滿或填滿的；（經文）滿，圓滿，善圓滿，已滿，盈滿，遍滿，充滿，普滿，彌滿，滿足，已滿足，已具足，備，圓，圓融。

4. परिशुद्धं pariśuddhaṁ 形容詞　具備完整的；圓滿的

4.1 【詞尾變化】dharmaṁ 根據連音規則，是從 dharmam 變化過來，而 dharmam 則是 dharma 的陽性單數對格形，所以字典查 dharma。

4.2 資料前面已有說明。

5. पर्यवदातं paryavadātaṁ 形容詞　非常有成就；單純而完美的

5.1 【詞尾變化】paryavadātaṁ 根據連音規則，是從 paryavadātam 變化過來，而 paryavadātam 則是 paryavadāta 的陽性單數對格形，所以字典查 paryavadāta。

5.2 【摩威梵英,p607】mfn.（√dai）perfectly clean or pure; very accomplished; well acquainted or conversant with（loc.）.（*-tva* n.）; well known , very familiar ib.

5.3 【梵漢辭典,p872】（過去被動分詞）（經文）淨，悉淨，皎潔，白，清白，鮮白，潔白；皆消除。

6. बह्मचर्यं brahma-caryaṁ 形容詞　清淨梵行

6.1 【詞尾變化】brahma-caryaṁ 根據連音規則，是從 brahma-caryam 變化過來，而 brahma-caryam 則是 brahma-carya 的陽性單數對格形，所以字典查 brahma-carya。

6.2 資料前面已有說明。

7. संप्रकाशयति saṁprakāśayati 動詞　開示；宣說

7.1 【詞尾變化】saṁprakāśayati 爲 saṁ--pra—kāśayati 所結合，也就是 saṁ--pra—√kāś 的使役動詞現在式第三人稱單數。所以字典查 saṁ--pra—√kāś。

7.2 【摩威梵英】個別部份資料前面已有說明，但結合的無。

7.3 【梵漢辭典,p577, saṁ--pra—√kāś】(使役動詞)照耀，除障，發表；(經文)照，顯，開示，顯示，眞實開示，開顯；宣說，廣說，解說；使～明識。

【筆者試譯】：其講授內容是追求崇高價值，清晰易解，圓滿而完備精純的梵行。

【什公漢譯】：其義深遠，其語巧妙，純一無雜，具足清白梵行之相。

【英 譯 本】：good in substance and form, complete and perfect, correct and pure.

【信譯研究】：信譯。

【第四句】

yad uta śrāvakāṇāṁ catur-ārya-satya-saṁprayuktaṁ
pratītya-samutpāda-pravṛttaṁ dharmaṁ deśayati sma
jāti-jarā-vyādhi-maraṇa-śoka-parideva-duḥkha-daurmanasyopāyāsān
āṁ samatikramāya nirvāṇa-paryavasānam|

【辭彙研究】

1. श्रावकाणां śrāvakāṇāṁ 名詞　聲聞，阿羅漢

1.1 【詞尾變化】śrāvakāṇāṁ 根據連音規則，是從 śrāvakāṇām 變化過來，而 śrāvakāṇām 則是 śrāvaka 的陽性單數對格形，所以字典查 śrāvaka。

1.2　資料前面已有說明。

2. सत्य satya 形容詞　眞諦；眞理

2.1　【詞尾變化】沒有詞尾變化。

2.2　【摩威梵英,p1135】

2.2.1 mf(ā)n. true , real , actual , genuine , sincere , honest , truthful , faithful , pure , virtuous , good. successful , effectual , valid RV;

2.2.2 m. the uppermost of the seven Lokas or worlds（the abode of Brahma1 and heaven of truth ; see loka）L. ; N. of the ninth Kalpa（q.v.）; the Aśvattha tree ; N. of Viṣṇu ; of Rāma-candra ; of a supernatural being; of a deity presiding over the *Nāndī-mukha Śrāddha* ; of one of the *Viśve Devāh* ; of a *Vyāsa*; of a son of *Havir-dhāna* BhP. ; of a son of *Vitatya* MBh. ; of one of the 7 *Ṛiśis* in various *Manvantaras*;

2.2.3（with *ācārya*）N. of an astronomer（author of the *Horā-śāstra*）;

2.2.4 pl. N. of a class of gods in various *Manvantaras* ;

2.2.5（ā）f. speaking the truth , sincerity , veracity ; a partic. ; N. of Durgā; of *Śita1* ; of *Satyavatī*（mother of *Vyāsa*）; = *satya-bhāmā* MBh.; of the family deity of the *Kutsas* and *Atharvans*; of a daughter of Dharma（and wife of *Śaṃ-yu*）MBh. ; of the mother of *Satya*（=*tuṣita*）; of the wife of *Manthu*（and mother of *Bhauvana*）BhP. ; of a daughter of *Nagna-jit*（and wife of *Kṛiṣṇa*）ib. ;

2.2.6（*am*）n. truth , reality RV.; speaking the truth , sincerity , veracity ; a solemn asseveration , vow , promise , oath AV.; demonstrated conclusion , dogma; the quality of goodness or purity or knowledge ; the first of the four Yugas or ages; a partic. mythical weapon ; the uppermost of the 7 Lokas（see under m.）BhP. ; one of the 7 *Vyāhṛitis* ; partic. Satya-formula; = *udaka* , water; N. of *Sāmans*;

2.2.7（*am*）ind. truly , indeed , certainly , verily , necessarily , yes , very well RV.

2.3　【梵漢辭典,p1158】（形容詞）實際的，現實的，純正的，眞實；順利的，有靈驗的（祈禱），被實現的（願望）；足以信賴的，忠實的，誠實的；有確鑿證據的（一致）。（中性）現實，眞實，誠實；說眞實語，約定，發誓，宣誓；（經文）眞，實，諦，眞實，眞諦，眞諦理，實諦，誠，誠諦，聖諦，賢善，有義利，誓願事，誓言，至誠。

3. संप्रयुक्तं saṁprayuktaṁ 形容詞　相應；應，套住

3.1 【詞尾變化】saṁprayuktaṁ 根據連音規則，是從 saṁprayuktam 變化過來，而 saṁprayuktam 則是 saṁprayukta 的陽性單數對格形，字典查 saṁprayukta。

3.2 資料前面已有說明。

4. प्रतीत्य pratītya 動名詞　因緣

4.1 【詞尾變化】沒有詞尾變化。

4.2 【摩威梵英,p673】

4.2.1 n. confirmation , experiment RV.; comfort , consolation ;

4.2.2 -*samutpāda* m.（Buddh.）the chain of causation.（twelvefold ; cf. Dharmas.）.

4.3 【梵漢辭典,p955】（動名詞）緣於～，依～之理，由於～，～之故，（經文）因，依因，託，緣，緣起，緣生，因緣，藉。

5. समुत्पाद samutpāda 名詞　生

5.1 【詞尾變化】沒有詞尾變化。

5.2 【摩威梵英,p1166】m. rise , origin , production.

5.3 【梵漢辭典,p1118】（陽性）出生；（經文）生，起，發，生起，發心。

6. प्रवृत्तं pravṛttaṁ 過去被動分詞　轉變；生滅

6.1 【詞尾變化】pravṛttaṁ 根據連音規則，是從 pravṛttam 變化過來，而 pravṛttam 則是 pravṛtta 的陽性單數對格形，字典查 pravṛtta。

6.2 資料前面已有說明。

7. व्याधि vyādhi 形容詞　病的（痲瘋病）

7.1 【詞尾變化】沒有詞尾變化。

7.2 【摩威梵英,p1037】m. disorder , disease , ailment , sickness , plague（esp. leprosy）MBh.; Disease personified（as a Child of *Mṛtyu* or Death）VP. ; any tormenting or vexatious person or thing ; Costus Speciosus or Arabicus.

7.3 【梵漢辭典,p1482】（陽性）患病，即並，病痛，災厄；（經文）病，疾

病，痼疾，疾疫，病痰，患苦，苦患，著諸病，病名目，消渴病，膏肓，證，病過證。

8. मरण maraṇa 形容詞　死亡的

8.1 【詞尾變化】沒有詞尾變化。

8.2 【摩威梵英,p789】n. the act of dying , death ,（ifc. dying by ; -*ṇaṁ* 1. kṛ *Ā. kurute* , to die）MBh. ; passing away , cessation（as of lightning or rain）;（in astrol.）the 8th mansion ; a kind of poison（prob. w.r. for *māraṇa*）; a refuge , asylum BhP.

8.3 【梵漢辭典,p712】（中性）垂死；死亡；死滅；停止；（經文）死，滅，滅度，生滅，終，命終，壽終，喪亡，衰亡。

9. शोक śoka 名詞　痛苦，煩惱

9.1 【詞尾變化】沒有詞尾變化。

9.2 【摩威梵英,p1091】

9.2.1 mfn. burning , hot AV. ;

9.2.2（śoka）m.（ifc. f. *ā*）flame , glow , heat RV. AV.; sorrow , affliction , anguish , pain , trouble , grief for（gen. or comp.）RV.; Sorrow personified（as a son of Death or of Dron2a and Abhimati）Pur. ;

9.2.3（*ī*）f. see below.

9.3 【梵漢辭典,p1188】（陽性）火焰，白熱；對～的苦惱，悲傷，悲哀，痛苦；（經文）憂，愁，愁悲，憂愁，憂悲，憂慼，憂慘，憂苦，愁憂，愁惱，愁歎，苦哀，苦衰，眾苦。

10. परिदेव parideva 形容詞　悲歎

10.1 【詞尾變化】沒有詞尾變化。

10.2 【摩威梵英,p595】m. lamentation MBh.

10.3 【梵漢辭典,p852】（陽性）牢騷或怨言，悲嘆；（經文）悲，歎，悲嘆，憂，痛哭，不安。

11. दौर्मनस्योपायासानां daurmanasyopāyāsānāṁ 形容詞　沮喪疲累

11.1 【詞尾變化】daurmanasyopāyāsānāṁ 根據連音規則，是從 daurmanasyopāyāsānām 變化過來，而 daurmanasyopāyāsānām 則是 daurmanasyopāyāsa 的陽性複數對格形，daurmanasyopāyāsa=

daurmanasya-upāyāsa，前者無詞尾變化，後者字典查 daurmanasya-upa--āyāsa。

11.2 【摩威梵英,p499, daurmanasya】n. dejectedness , melancholy , despair

11.3 【摩威梵英,p148, upa】資料前面已有說明。

11.4 【摩威梵英,p148, āyāsa】m. effort , exertion（of bodily or mental power）, trouble , labour MBh. ; fatigue , weariness MBh.

11.5 【梵漢辭典,p355, daurmanasya】（中性）沮喪，悲哀；（經文）擾，憂，憂惑，憂苦，憂患，愁，憂愁，愁憂，愁惱，惱，憂惱，苦惱，悲，心不安，意不樂。

11.6 【梵漢辭典,p1348,upāyāsa】（陽性）煩惱，困難，迷惑；不安，混亂，不平靜；（經文）惱，苦惱，憂惱，擾惱，熱惱，患，勞倦，迷亂。

12. समतिक्रमाय samatikramāya 形容詞　超越；遠離

12.1 【詞尾變化】samatikramāya 是 samatikrama 的陽性單數從格形，所以字典查 samatikrama。

12.2 【摩威梵英,p1154】m. going entirely over or beyond; deviating from , transgressing , omission.

12.3 【梵漢辭典,p1082】（陽性）（屬格）的省略或忽視；（經文）超，離，度，渡，過，捨，犯，息，能越，超過，遠哩，永超。

13. निर्वाण nirvāṇa 形容詞　涅槃

13.1 【詞尾變化】沒有詞尾變化。

13.2 【摩威梵英,p557】

13.2.1 mfn. blown or put out , extinguished（as a lamp or fire）, set（as the sun）, calmed , quieted , tamed, dead , deceased（lit. having the fire of life extinguished）, lost , disappeared MBh. ; immersed , plunged ; immovable ;

13.2.2 *-bhūyiṣṭha* mfn. nearly extinguished）, or vanished ;

13.2.3 n. blowing out , extinction , cessation , setting , vanishing , disappearance ; extinction of the flame of life , dissolution , death or final emancipation from matter and re-union with the Supreme Spirit MBh. ;

13.2.4（with Buddhists and Jainas）absolute extinction or annihilation（=*śūnya*）of individual existence or of all desires and passions. ; perfect calm or repose or happiness , highest bliss or beatitude MBh.; N. of an

Upanishad ; instructing in sciences ; bathing of an elephant ; the post to which an elephant is tied; offering oblations;

13.2.5 -*kara* m. `causing extinction of all sense of individuality' , a partic.;

13.2.6 -*kāṇḍa* m. or n. N. of wk. ;

13.2.7 -*tantra* see *bṛhan-nirvāṇat-* and *mahā-n-* ; -*da* mfn. bestowing final beatitude MBh. ;

13.2.8 -*daśaka* n. N. of wk. ;

13.2.9 -*dīkṣita* m. N. of a grammarian;

13.2.10 -*dhātu* m. the region of *Nirvāṇa Vajracch.*;

13.2.11 -*purāṇa* n. offering oblations to the dead;

13.2.12 -*prakaraṇa* n. N. of wk. ;

13.2.13 -*priyā* f. N. of a Gandharvī Kāraṇḍ. ;

13.2.14 -*maṇḍapa* m. N. of a temple , *Skandap.* ;

13.2.15 -*mantra* n. N. of a mystical formula;

13.2.16 -*maya* mf（*ī*）n. full of bliss VP. ;

13.2.17 -*mastaka* m. liberation , deliverance ;

13.2.18 -*yoga-paṭala-stotr*a and -*yogottara* n. N. of wks. ;

13.2.19 -*ruci* m. pl. `" delighting in final beatitude "'N. of a class of deities under the 11th Manu BhP. ;

13.2.20 -*lakṣaṇa* mfn. having complete bliss as its characteristic mark. ;

13.2.21 -*ṣaṭka* n. N. of a Stotra ;

13.2.22 -*saṃcodana* m. a partic. *Samādhi* ;

13.2.23 -*sūtra* n. N. of partic. Buddh. Sūtras ;

13.2.24 -*Nopaniṣad* f. N. of an *Upanishad.*

13.3 【梵漢辭典,p800】（過去被動分詞）消滅；生命火焰的熄滅，解除，究竟的解放，與絕對一致的；專注於～完全解脫；完全滿足，最大的幸福（佛教術語）；（經文）滅，滅度，寂靜，寂滅，安穩，涅槃。

14. पर्यवसानम् paryavasānam 形容詞　到達，最後

14.1 【詞尾變化】paryavasānam 是 paryavasāna 的陽性單數對格形，所以字典查 paryavasāna。

14.2 資料前面已有說明。

【筆者試譯】：曾經有的與聲聞行者因緣相應者，講授四聖諦，因緣生滅法。（讓他）遠離生，老，病，死，悲傷，沮喪，苦難，疲累，到達涅槃境地。

【什公漢譯】：為求聲聞者，說應四諦法。度生老病死，究竟涅槃。為求辟支佛者，說應十二因緣法。

【英 譯 本】：That is to say, to the disciples he preached the law containing the four Noble Truths, and starting from the chain of causes and effects, tending to overcome birth, decrepitude, sickness, death, sorrow, lamentation, woe, grief, despondency, and finally leading to Nirvâna;

【信譯研究】：非信譯。鳩譯裡面有「十二因緣」、「辟支佛」，原文都沒有。

【第五句】

bodhisattvānāṁ ca mahāsattvānāṁ ca ṣaṭ-pāramitā-pratisaṁyuktam anuttarāṁ samyak-saṁbodhim ārabhya sarvajña-jñāna-paryavasānaṁ dharmaṁ deśayati sma||

【辭彙研究】

1. बोधिसत्त्वानां bodhisattvānāṁ 名詞 菩薩
   1.1 【詞尾變化】bodhisattvānāṁ 根據連因規則是從 bodhisattvānām 變化過來，而 bodhisattvānām 是 bodhisattva 的陽性複數對格形，所以字典查 bodhisattva。
   1.2 資料前面已有說明。
2. महासत्त्वानां mahāsattvānāṁ 形容詞 摩訶薩；大菩薩
   2.1 【詞尾變化】mahāsattvānāṁ 根據連因規則是從 mahāsattvānām 變化過來，而 mahāsattvānām 是 mahāsattva 的陽性複數對格形，所以字典查 mahāsattva。
   2.2 資料前面已有說明。
3. प्रतिसंयुक्तम् pratisaṁyuktam 形容詞 與～相應
   3.1 【詞尾變化】pratisaṁyuktam 是 pratisaṁyukta 的陽性單數對格形，所以字典查 pratisaṁyukta。
   3.2 【摩威梵英,p671】mfn.（$\sqrt{}$yuj）bound or attached to something else MBh.

3.3 【梵漢辭典,p953】（過去被動分詞）與～有關係；（經文）相應，繫，所繫，具足。

4. अनुत्तरां anuttarāṁ 形容詞　無上的

4.1 【詞尾變化】anuttarāṁ 根據連因規則是從 anuttarām 變化過來，而 anuttarām 是 anuttara 的陽性複數對格形，所以字典查 anuttara。

4.2 資料前面已有說明。

5. सम्यक्संबोधिम् samyak-saṁbodhim 形容詞　正覺

5.1 【詞尾變化】samyak-saṁbodhim 是 samyak-saṁbodhi 的陰性單數對格形，所以字典查 samyak-saṁbodhi。

5.2 【摩威梵英,p1181, samyak】in comp. for samyañc.

5.3 【摩威梵英, saṁbodhi】無此字。應爲 Prakrit。

5.4 【梵漢辭典,p1122】（陰性）（經文）正覺，正等正覺，正眞之道，正眞道，三藐三菩提。

6. आरभ्य ārabhya 動名詞　從～開始；最初

6.1 【詞尾變化】沒有詞尾變化。

6.2 【摩威梵英,p150】

6.2.1 mfn. ifc. =*ā-rabdhavya* q.v.

6.2.2 ind. p. having begun ; beginning with.

6.3 【梵漢辭典,p148】（動名詞）從～開始；最初；（經文）以，依，依～故～。

7. सर्वज्ञ sarvajña 形容詞　一切智慧

7.1 【詞尾變化】沒有詞尾變化。

7.2 【摩威梵英,p1185】

7.2.1 mf（*ā*）n. all-knowing , omniscient（said of gods and men , esp. of ministers and philosophers）; a Buddha; an Arhat（with Jainas）; N. of Śiva ; of various men Buddh. ;

7.2.2（*ā*）f. N. of Durgā; of a Yoginī;

7.2.3 -*jñānin* mfn. thinking one's self omniscient;

7.2.4 -*tā* f.（MBh.）or -*tva* n.（MBh.）omniscience ;

7.2.5 -*deva*（Buddh.）, -*nārāyaṇa* m. N. of scholars ;

7.2.6 -*putra* m. N. of Siddha-sena;

7.2.7 -*bhaṭṭa* m. N. of a man ib. ;

7.2.8 -*mānin* mfn.（=-*jñānin*）;

7.2.9 -*mitra* m. N. of various persons; Bundh. ;

7.2.10 -*m-manya* mfn.（-*jñānin* ; -*ya-tā* f.）Rājat. ;

7.2.11 -*rāmeśvara-bhaṭṭāraka* m. N. of an author;

7.2.12 -*vāsudeva* m. N. of a poet ib. ;

7.2.13 -*viṣṇu* m. N. of a philosopher;

7.2.14 –*vyavasthāpaka* N. of wk. ;

7.2.15 -*śrī-nārāyaṇa* m. N. of an author;

7.2.16 -*sūnu* m. patr. of Skanda;

7.2.17 -*jñātma-giri* or -*mamuni* m. N. of an author ;

7.2.18 -*jñārdha-śarīriṇī* f. N. of *Umā*.

7.3 【梵漢辭典,p1140】（形容詞）了解一切的，全知的；（經文）一切智；一切種智。

8. पर्यवसानं paryavasānaṁ 形容詞　完成；到達

8.1 【詞尾變化】paryavasānaṁ 根據連因規則是從 paryavasānam 變化過來，而 paryavasānam 是 paryavasāna 的陽性複數對格形，所以字典查 paryavasāna。

8.2 資料前面已有說明。

【筆者試譯】：菩薩與大菩薩們，開始就講與六度波羅蜜相應的（佛法），無上正等正覺，證得一切的智慧，這樣的佛法。

【什公漢譯】：爲諸菩薩，說應六波羅蜜，令得阿耨多羅三藐三菩提，成一切種智。

【英 譯 本】：and to the Bodhisattvas he preached the law connected with the six Perfections, and terminating in the knowledge of the Omniscient, after the attainment of supreme, perfect enlightenment.

【信譯研究】：信譯。

【小結】

本段有一句非信譯，絕大部分羅什所譯皆忠實原文。